PAX INDICA

An elected Member of Parliament, former minister of state for external affairs and former under-secretary-general of the United Nations, Shashi Tharoor is the prize-winning author of twelve previous books, both fiction and non-fiction. A widely published critic, commentator and columnist, he served the United Nations during a twenty-nine-year career in refugee work and peacekeeping, at the Secretary-General's office and heading communications and public information. In 2006 he was India's candidate to succeed Kofi Annan as UN Secretary-General, and emerged a strong second out of seven contenders. He has won India's highest honour for overseas Indians, the Pravasi Bharatiya Samman, and numerous literary awards, including a Commonwealth Writers' Prize.

For more on Shashi Tharoor, please see www.tharoor.in.

Praise for the Book

'*Pax Indica* is a great introduction for those interested in reading about India's foreign policy and its evolution since independence'—*DNA*

'[Tharoor's] view of the world and India's role in it is hearteningly sane; he has a diplomat's faith in dialogue and cooperation effecting incremental benefits'—*Tehelka*

'A remarkable survey of India's international interests, covering enormous ground . . . Whatever your own views, *Pax Indica* will enlarge your understanding, and encourage more attention to our still hesitant and unsure engagement with the world'—K.S. Bajpai

'A comprehensive dissertation on the diverse fields of India's endeavours since Independence . . . a timely book, very well written, a must-read for students and professionals alike'—Jaswant Singh

'This exceptionally lively and well-written survey of India's international relations challenges preconceptions that foreign policy must be dull'—David Malone

SHASHI THAROOR

PAX INDICA

India and the World of the 21st Century

PENGUIN BOOKS

PENGUIN BOOKS

Published by the Penguin Group

Penguin Books India Pvt. Ltd, 11 Community Centre, Panchsheel Park, New Delhi 110 017, India

Penguin Group (USA) Inc., 375 Hudson Street, New York, New York 10014, USA

Penguin Group (Canada), 90 Eglinton Avenue East, Suite 700, Toronto, Ontario, M4P 2Y3, Canada (a division of Pearson Penguin Canada Inc.)

Penguin Books Ltd, 80 Strand, London WC2R 0RL, England

Penguin Ireland, 25 St Stephen's Green, Dublin 2, Ireland (a division of Penguin Books Ltd)

Penguin Group (Australia), 707 Collins Street, Melbourne, Victoria 3008, Australia (a division of Pearson Australia Group Pty Ltd)

Penguin Group (NZ), 67 Apollo Drive, Rosedale, Auckland 0632, New Zealand (a division of Pearson New Zealand Ltd)

Penguin Books (South Africa) (Pty) Ltd, Block D, Rosebank Office Park, 181 Jan Smuts Avenue, Parktown North, Johannesburg 2193, South Africa

Penguin Books Ltd, Registered Offices: 80 Strand, London WC2R 0RL, England

First published in Allen Lane by Penguin Books India 2012
Published in Penguin Books 2013

Copyright © Shashi Tharoor 2012

ISBN 9780143420187

Not for sale in the US and UK

Typeset in Minion by R. Ajith Kumar, Delhi
Printed at Thomson Press India Ltd, New Delhi

ALWAYS LEARNING **PEARSON**

'Those dreams are for India, but they are also for the world'—Jawaharlal Nehru, 'Tryst with destiny' speech, 15 August 1947

As a major power India can and must play a role in helping shape the global order. The international system of the twenty-first century, with its networked partnerships, will need to renegotiate its rules of the road; India is well qualified to help write those rules and define the norms that will guide tomorrow's world. That is what I have called Pax Indica: not global or regional domination along the lines of a Pax Romana or a Pax Britannica but a 'Pax' for the twenty-first century, a peace system which will help promote and maintain a period of cooperative coexistence in its region and across the world.

Contents

Contents

Chapter One

Revisiting the Tryst with Destiny

At midnight on 15 August 1947, independent India was born as its first prime minister, Jawaharlal Nehru, proclaimed 'a tryst with destiny—a moment which comes but rarely in history, when we pass from the old to the new, when an age ends and when the soul of a nation, long suppressed, finds utterance'. It was an hour of darkness, too, with the flames of Partition blazing across the land, hundreds of thousands being butchered in sectarian savagery and millions seeking refuge across the arbitrary lines that had vivisected their homelands. Yet in the midst of these horrors, mingled with the joy of that sublime moment when, in Nehru's memorable words, India awoke to life and freedom, our prime minister remained conscious of his country's international obligations. In his historic speech about India's 'tryst with destiny', Nehru, speaking of his country's dreams, said: 'Those dreams are for India, but they are also for the world, for all the nations and peoples are too closely knit together today for any one of them to imagine that it can live apart. Peace has been said to be indivisible; so is freedom, so is prosperity now, and so also is disaster in this One World that can no longer be split into isolated fragments.' It was typical of that great nationalist that, at a time when the fires of Partition were blazing across the land, he thought not only of India, but of the world.

In a sense, this was not entirely surprising, because India had, for millennia, been engaged with the rest of the world. The north of India had witnessed a series of visitations and invasions, ranging from armed hordes of Macedonians, Scythians, Persians and Central Asians marching in through the north-west in quest of pillage and plunder to learned Chinese scholars crossing the Himalayas in the north and north-east in quest of

1

learning and wisdom. The South, with its long coastlines, had enjoyed trade relations with the Roman Empire, the Arab lands to the west and the east coast of Africa, while extending its religious and cultural influence to the Asian countries to the east. Historical records and archaeological excavations demonstrate that India's connections with the rest of the world go at least as far back as the Harappan civilization of 2500–1500 BC, which maintained extensive links with Mesopotamia. Europe's history of trading relations with India is borne out in the writings of the ancient historians Herodotus, Pliny, Petronius and Ptolemy, and long precedes the colonial experience. The naval expansionism of the southern Chola and Pallava empires took Indian influences directly to Thailand, Malaya, Indonesia and Cambodia. Later, the Mughal Empire served as the centre of an Indo-Persian world that straddled both the Bay of Bengal and the Arabian Sea, and whose influence stretched east as well as west—so that Thai kings named themselves after Deccani sultans and the first epic poet of Aceh (in Sumatra) was born in Surat (in Gujarat). It could indeed be argued that the India of today is the direct product of millennia of contact, trade, immigration and interaction with the rest of the world. Nehru was thus speaking as heir to this history.

Yet for two centuries before that moment, India had been unable to express its voice or exercise its place in the world. The British had usurped that right from it; when India, under colonial rule, was made a founding member of the League of Nations after the First World War, its delegation included a former England cricket captain, C.B. Fry. Those who spoke for India in the world did so with Britain's interests uppermost in their minds. India's authentic voice had only been heard in those international conferences of subaltern groups where nationalists like Jawaharlal Nehru spoke for his oppressed and excluded people, or in the resolutions passed annually by the Indian National Congress on the international situation—resolutions which had no discernible effect on the decision-makers in London who determined where India would stand in world affairs.

So when Nehru spoke at that midnight moment, he was speaking for a nation that had found its own voice in the world again, and was determined to use it to express a worldview radically different from that which had been articulated by India's British rulers in previous decades.

And he was doing so as a convinced internationalist himself, one who had seen much of the world in his extensive travels and was resolved to apply his own understanding of it to his newly independent nation's stance in world affairs.

In the six decades since Nehru's India constituted itself into a sovereign republic, the world has become even more closely knit together than he so presciently foresaw. Indeed, as the twenty-first century enters its second decade, even those countries that once felt insulated from external dangers—by wealth or strength or distance—now fully realize that the world is truly 'knit together' as never before, and that the safety of people everywhere depends not only on local security forces, but also on guarding against terrorism; warding off the global spread of pollution, of diseases, of illegal drugs and of weapons of mass destruction; and on promoting human rights, democracy and development.

Jobs everywhere, too, depend not only on local firms and factories, but on faraway markets for products and services, on licences and access from foreign governments, on an international environment that allows the free movement of goods and persons, and on international institutions that ensure stability—in short, on the international system that sustains our globalized world.

Today, whether you are a resident of Delhi or Dili, Durban or Darwin, whether you are from Noida or New York, it is simply not realistic to think only in terms of your own country. Global forces press in from every conceivable direction. People, goods and ideas cross borders and cover vast distances with ever greater frequency, speed and ease. We are increasingly connected through travel, trade, the Internet; through what we watch, what we eat and even the games we play. The ancient Indian notion encapsulated in the Sanksrit dictum 'vasudhaiva kutumbakam' (the world is a family) has never been truer.

These benign forces are matched by more malign ones that are equally global. In my time as a career official at the United Nations, I learned that the world is full of 'problems without passports'—problems that cross all frontiers uninvited, problems of terrorism, of the proliferation of weapons of mass destruction, of the degradation of our common environment, of contagious disease and chronic starvation, of human rights and human wrongs, of mass illiteracy and massive displacement.

Such problems also require solutions that cross all frontiers, since no one country or group of countries can solve them alone.

One simply cannot forget that 9/11 made clear the old cliché about our global village—for it showed that a fire that starts in a remote thatched hut or dusty cave in one corner of that village can melt the steel girders of the tallest skyscrapers at the other end of our global village.

In such a world, issues that once seemed very far away are very much in your backyard. What happens in North America or North Africa—from protectionist politics to civil society uprisings to deforestation and desertification to the fight against AIDS—can affect your lives wherever you live, even in North India. And your choices here—what you buy, how you vote—can resound far away. As someone once said about water pollution, we all live downstream. We are all interconnected, and we can no longer afford the luxury of not thinking about the rest of the planet in anything we do.

It has taken us some time to internalize this conviction in India. After all, self-reliance and economic self-sufficiency were a mantra for more than four decades after independence, and there were real doubts as to whether the country should open itself up further to the world economy. Whereas in most of the West most people axiomatically associated capitalism with freedom, India's nationalists associated capitalism with slavery—for, after all, the British East India Company had come to trade and stayed on to rule. So India's nationalist leaders were suspicious of every foreigner with a briefcase, seeing him as the thin edge of a neo-imperial wedge. Instead of integrating India into the global capitalist system, as only a handful of post-colonial countries like Singapore chose to do, India's leaders (and those of most former colonies) were convinced that the political independence they had fought for so hard and long could only be guaranteed through economic independence. So self-reliance became the mantra, the protectionist barriers went up and India spent forty-five years increasingly divorced from global trade and investment. (Which only goes to show that one of the lessons you can learn from history is that history can sometimes teach you the wrong lessons.)

It was only after a world-class balance of payments crisis in 1991, when our government had to physically ship its reserves of gold to London to stand collateral for an International Monetary Fund (IMF) loan, failing which we might have defaulted on our debt, that India liberalized its economy under our then finance minister Manmohan Singh. The amount of gold possessed by the women of the household has often been seen, in Indian culture, as a guarantee of the family's honour; surrendering the nation's gold to foreigners betokened a national humiliation that the old protectionism could not survive. Since then, India has become a poster child for globalization. It is now widely accepted across the political spectrum that our growth and prosperity would be impossible without the rest of the world.

Young Indians today are likely to spend a lot of their adult lives interacting with people who don't look, sound, dress or eat like them. Unlike their parents, they might well work for an internationally oriented company with clients, colleagues or investors from around the globe; and increasingly, they are likely to take their holidays in far-flung destinations. The world into which they will grow will be full of such opportunities. But along with such opportunities, today's young Indians may also find themselves vulnerable to threats from beyond India's borders: terrorism, of course, but also transnational crime syndicates, counterfeiters of currency, drug smugglers, child traffickers, pirates and—almost as disruptive—Internet hackers and spammers, credit-card crooks and even imported illnesses like swine flu.

Yet many Indians have not yet fully realized the importance of their government devising policies to deal with such challenges that would affect their, and one day their children's, lives. Should such policies, in an ever more interdependent world, even be called foreign? One of the reasons that foreign policy matters today is that foreign policy is no longer merely foreign: it affects people right where they live. Each of us should want our government to seize the opportunities that the twenty-first-century world provides, while managing the risks and protecting us from the threats that this world has also opened us up to.

Indians therefore have a growing stake in international developments. To put it another way, the food we grow and we eat, the air we breathe and our health, security, prosperity and quality of life are increasingly affected by what happens beyond our borders. And that means we can simply no longer afford to be indifferent about our neighbours, however distant they may appear. Ignorance is not a shield; it is not even, any longer, an excuse.

Much of my own life has been conducted on the global stage. Born in London but brought up in India, I left the country at nineteen, studied abroad and joined the United Nations, serving it in Europe, in Southeast Asia and in the United States while helping douse humanitarian and peacekeeping fires around the world. I returned to India, more than three decades after leaving it, to play a part in its public life and contribute to developing, whether in or out of office, its vision of the world in the twenty-first century.

And yet it is not as an unreconstructed internationalist myself that I write this volume. It is true that I have had the privilege of acquiring extensive international experience, especially during those nearly three decades of service at the UN, and I value the perspective this has given me on the world. But my own focus, in the relatively short period that I have been in public life, has inevitably been on the domestic realities of our country. When I think of the world today, I am conscious of the need to think of it not as a former UN official, but from the perspective of a member of Parliament from Thiruvananthapuram, which despite being the capital of Kerala is still two-thirds a rural constituency. Though the city has long had connections to the outside world—one of its shipping harbours, Poovar, was the legendary Ophir of 'King Solomon's Mines', and it was one of the first Indian cities to enjoy air services in the 1930s, at the same time as Karachi and Mumbai—the concerns of most of its residents are largely domestic. I am obliged to remember that the bulk of my time in recent months has been spent in listening, and giving political expression, to the voices of the poor, the marginalized and the downtrodden in my district, a place emblematic in many ways of our ancient land now roaring into life in the twenty-first century.

What does looking at India's foreign policy mean from that perspective? For me, frankly, the basic task for India in international affairs is to wield a foreign policy that enables and facilitates the domestic transformation of India. By this I mean that we must make possible the transformation of India's economy and society through our engagement with the world, while promoting our own national values (of pluralism, democracy, social justice and secularism) within our society. What I expect from my national leaders is that they work for a global environment that is supportive of these internal priorities, an environment that would permit us to concentrate on our domestic tasks. Ensuring the country's security, and its freedom to make its own decisions in its own interests, is the first and most obvious of those priorities; but then comes the need to maintain good relations with those nations that are essential suppliers of the investment and trade, energy and mineral resources, food supplies and water flows without which growth, development and the elimination of poverty would not be possible. India is engaged in the great adventure of bringing progress and prosperity to a billion people through a major economic transformation. At the broadest level, the objective of India's foreign policy must be to protect that process of domestic social and economic transformation, by working for a benign environment that will ensure India's security and bring in global support for our efforts to build and change our country for the better.

So a fisherwoman in Thiruvananthapuram may not have the slightest idea who the foreign minister of India is or care about the American withdrawal from Afghanistan, but she will know if the price of diesel for her husband's boat or kerosene for her kitchen stove has become unaffordable; she understands international economics when a foreign trawler catches fish in waters her husband and his ancestors have fished in for generations; her livelihood is affected when fear of terrorism imposes restrictions on the movement of her community's boats, or when fear of piracy leads a foreign vessel to shoot at one carrying her brothers. Foreign policy might seem an abstraction to people like her, but it is relevant to her life just as much as to the diplomat in the pin-striped suit who speaks for India in global forums.

In one of his short stories, Franz Kakfa, writing of the idea of 'empire', observed:

One of the most obscure of our institutions is that of the empire itself. ... [T]he teachers of political law and history in the schools of higher learning claim to be exactly informed on these matters, and to be capable of passing on their knowledge to their students. The further one descends among the lower schools the more, naturally enough, does one find teachers' and pupils' doubts of their own knowledge vanishing, and superficial culture mounting sky-high around a few precepts that have been drilled into people's minds for centuries, precepts which, though they have lost nothing of their eternal truth, remain eternally invisible in this fog of confusion. But it is precisely this question of the empire which in my opinion the common people should be asked to answer, since after all they are the empire's final support.

Substitute the words 'foreign policy' for 'empire', and one has a distillation of the problem this book attempts, however partially, to address.

But that is clearly not the whole story. Because as India changes domestically, its changes will have an inevitable impact on the outside world. So if Indians like me contemplate the shape of the world over, say, the next twenty or twenty-five years, we would also have to ask ourselves what sort of role the transformation of India in that time span would enable our country to play on the global stage, how we engage with it and what sort of responsibilities we are prepared to assume. To the extent that we can project an Indian vision on the world, what would a 'Pax Indica' look like?

————

Indians can never afford to forget the condition in which we found our country at the onset of independence. From a nation that had once been among the world's richest, and which as late as 1820 accounted (in the estimate of the late British economic historian Angus Maddison) for 23 per cent of global GDP, we had been reduced by 1947 into one of the poorest, most backward, most illiterate and diseased societies on earth. From 1900 to 1947 the rate of growth of the Indian economy was not even 1 per cent, while population grew steadily at well over 3.5 per cent. Imperial rule left a society with 16 per cent literacy, practically no domestic industry and over 90 per cent living below what today we would call the poverty line. The impoverishment of India was the starkest reality that India's nationalist leaders had to face. It was therefore natural that our domestic transformation should be the overriding priority even in the making of foreign policy.

This is where non-alignment came in. It is understandably fashionable to scoff at the concept when there is no longer a pair of superpowers to be non-aligned between, but its origins were unexceptionable. At a time of great pressure to join one of the two Cold War alliances, as so many countries had done around us, our first prime minister, Jawaharlal Nehru, chose to stay free of such entanglements in the pursuit of our enlightened self-interest. We had spent too long with foreigners deciding what was good for us internationally; we were not going to mortgage our freedom of action or decision to any alliance when we had just begun to appreciate the value of our own independence. So we stayed out of other countries' fights, and sought to judge each issue on its merits, rather than taking sides automatically or based on alliance politics.

This was not a policy of neutrality, as some, like Dwight Eisenhower's secretary of state, John Foster Dulles, wrongly called it. (Dulles went on to add, infuriatingly, that 'neutrality between good and evil is itself evil'.) We were not neutral; we did not cut ourselves off from the world or abdicate our international responsibilities. But our leaders were determined that the independence we had fought so hard for should not be compromised, that our sovereignty should be safeguarded and our right to take our own decisions should be unquestioned. Underlying India's approach from the start was a firm belief in the importance of preserving our own strategic autonomy, which we have always seen as essential if we are to have a chance to develop India as we wish to. Indeed, one of my favourite—though undoubtedly apocryphal—stories is of Dulles saying to Nehru (in words that have become more famous in recent years on the lips of a later American leader): 'Are you with us or against us?' Nehru answered, 'Yes.' In other words, we were with the United States when we agreed with it, against it when we didn't. It's a good story, if an implausible one, because it goes to the heart of the Indian approach.

In practice, this assertive non-alignment meant that we tried, with varying degrees of success, to have good relations with all the major powers irrespective of ideology, including both the United States and the Soviet Union, and indeed both China and the Soviet Union. We built economic links wherever we could to serve our development. So we constructed the public-sector Bhilai and Bokaro steel plants with the Soviet Union when the West refused to help, but we also received

PL-480 wheat and Green Revolution technology from the United States. We engaged in an active peace diplomacy on disarmament to minimize the risks of conflict as a result of the Cold War bipolar world, and on decolonization for the same reason but also in pursuit of our anti-imperial ideals. In the emerging world of free and independent (and overwhelmingly non-aligned) states, we played an active role in the institutions of global governance, notably the United Nations and the Bretton Woods institutions, to promote those very ends. Arguably all of this gave India a standing in the world out of all proportion to its true strength and unrelated to its modest economic and military power.

Taken together, these actions also sought to build the material basis for our strategic autonomy. This was when modern industry and scientific and technical higher education truly began on an effective scale in India, as did our atomic energy and space programmes, and our defence research and production, all aimed at building autonomous national capabilities. The avoidance of external entanglements was intended both to give us the space to pursue our own development and to avoid the restraints on our freedom of action that alliance commitments might have engendered.

It is easy to forget the constraints within which this policy operated. The bipolar world of those days was one of uncompromising superpowers. The means available to us in our foreign policy were extremely limited. And we lacked the traditional sources of international power in terms of military capability, raw materials or geostrategic leverage. But we marched to the tune of our own drummer, even if it meant marching alone.

The results of these policies were quite remarkable and helped lay the foundations of our diversified industrial base, our platform of excellence in higher education, our independent strategic capabilities, and ultimately of the over 6 per cent a year GDP growth that we have enjoyed for nearly three decades, since Rajiv Gandhi became prime minister of India, and the nearly 8 per cent growth of the last ten years. But we rarely portrayed it as such in the first five decades of our independence. For even if our foreign policy had been motivated by the challenge of development, its articulation was driven by the nation's historical experience. The struggle for freedom against British imperialism dictated some of our political sympathies in favour of other anti-colonial struggles elsewhere in the world. Our reaction to the experience of two world wars added to our determination not to get entangled in other countries' conflicts, and to work to end those wherever we could. This bias in favour of peace was underscored by the non-violent nature of our own independence movement, which predisposed us to a certain moral conviction that our ways were preferable to those that resorted to violence. We therefore expressed, and acted in accordance with, what former foreign secretary J.N. Dixit called a 'commitment to co-operation rather than confrontation'. This, allied to a newly independent land's pride in its own civilization, led to India pronouncing itself on world affairs as if from a moral high ground, not a posture guaranteed to win friends and influence other (supposedly morally inferior) nations. In a phrase typical of this attitude, Dixit (a fine and highly respected diplomat) wrote of India's 'catalytic role . . . in establishing a moral and just world order ensuring peace and co-operation all over the world'. Such claims for a moral underpinning to India's foreign policy did not always resonate well with other countries, which assumed that New Delhi was engaged in the exercise of promoting and defending its national interests, just as they were. It led to criticisms of Indian hypocrisy and sanctimoniousness that our diplomats never entirely lived down. When defeat in the war with China in 1962 seemed to expose the hollowness of India's claims to global leadership, the country's standing went down in the eyes of the world— this time also disproportionately, given India's real worth and potential.

Ironically we might have won much more praise for honestly justifying our foreign policy in more realistic terms. Non-alignment was both a way of safeguarding a sovereignty long fought for and recently won and a way of avoiding compromising it through the compulsions of bloc politics. Nonetheless India was much more open to the West in the early years than hindsight suggests; in many ways, though, it was driven away by Western condescension towards what the United States and the United Kingdom largely saw as Indian pretensions to an equality in world affairs that it did not deserve, and the West's leanings towards Islamic Pakistan, seen as a doughty ally against godless communism. India's domestic economic preference for a 'socialist pattern of society' with bureaucrats, rather than businessmen, on the 'commanding heights' of the Indian economy understandably found little favour in the West; the US Congress once passed a resolution refusing to help India construct a public-sector steel plant since it was 'not the United States' business to help build socialism in India'. The West was noticeably sympathetic to Pakistan over Kashmir, an issue on which India was supported by the Soviet Union, which frequently vetoed anti-Indian resolutions on the subject at the UN Security Council. This, coupled with Moscow's eager bear hug, gave Indian non-alignment a distinctly pro-Soviet coloration over time, exemplified by the 1971 treaty of peace, friendship and cooperation that seemed to signal the death knell of India's equidistance from the superpowers. That treaty was occasioned by the Bangladesh crisis, the largest refugee movement in human history (10 million Bengalis) flooding into India, and a sense in New Delhi of the inevitability of war to resolve it; the fear was of a possible two-front war with both China and Pakistan, which the treaty sought to dispel. India was thus using the USSR to forestall China, not the West. All this suggests a degree of compulsion about India's basic choices; in a very fundamental sense, it was non-aligned because, in the global circumstances, it could be nothing else.

There are, of course, those who disagree with this view, and who suggest that alliance with the West from the very beginning might well have been a better choice, permitting India greater opportunities for higher-trajectory economic growth (à la South Korea or Thailand, which made such a choice) and global political influence. It would also have accorded with India's position as a democracy, and placed New Delhi on the 'winning side' at the end of the Cold War. As a teenage supporter of the Swatantra Party, I was inclined towards this view myself, but found I was in a minuscule minority; there is no doubt that many of today's advocates who critique Nehru for not taking the 'winning side' speak with the benefit of 20/20 hindsight. Barring very few (essentially the supporters of the Swatantra Party and some members of the Bharatiya Jana Sangh), pro-Western leanings found few adherents in postcolonial India: the overwhelming intellectual climate of the 1950s and 1960s was in favour of a Nehruvian vision of prudent equidistance. Of course, India's contrasting stands in 1956 on the Suez crisis and the USSR's invasion of Hungary exposed our non-alignment to be somewhat partisan, reflecting a leftward leaning that was a consequence of both our historical legacy and our need to put strategic daylight between ourselves and our former rulers. But non-alignment reflected a broad national consensus, and it is difficult to deny that the alternative of alignment with the West could have stunted India's influence on the world stage, and its decades of leadership of the developing world, which gave it a stature that no mere subordinate ally of a superpower would have enjoyed.

There were concrete benefits too. On the basis of what was achieved in the first forty years after independence, it was possible for Indian foreign policy to use the favourable international situation after 1991 to take major steps in furthering our basic objectives. The reform and opening up of our economy that year coincided with the end of the bipolar Cold War world. In the following decade and a half, the world economy and world trade grew at a pace that was unprecedented in human history, creating favourable external conditions for India's growth. And India was well placed to take advantage of the situation, thanks in no small part to a foreign policy which enabled us to work with all the major powers without exception—and to get help (if I may be allowed to mangle Marx) from each according to their capacity, to us according to our need.

This prompted an astute student of Indian foreign policy, the Canadian diplomat and scholar David Malone, whose 2011 book *Does the Elephant Dance? Contemporary Indian Foreign Policy* is perhaps the most impressive and substantial recent volume on the subject, to observe:

In stark contrast to the Nehruvian years during which India achieved considerable status in the international sphere with barely any achievements on the domestic front, chiefly by taking the moral high ground in foreign affairs, post-1990 India was no longer as convinced of its moral uniqueness and began to think of itself as a nation like several others in the quest of greater power. This favoured the normalization of traditionally antagonistic relationships with neighbouring countries, a greater commitment to international institutions that might legitimize its emerging power status, a positive approach to relations with the world's remaining superpower, and, importantly, greater focus on national defence, including in the nuclear sphere.

The India of the second decade of the twenty-first century has made significant strides from the overestimated India of the 1950s and the underestimated India of the 1960s. Since 1947 it has raised literacy from 16 per cent to 74 per cent, reduced child mortality and increased life expectancy (from 31 to 72), and raised the rate of growth of the Indian economy from below 1 per cent to over 8 per cent, while reducing the percentage of the population living below the poverty line from some 90 per cent to just over 30 per cent. Foreign direct investment (FDI) into India is illustrative of our changing orientation to the world: from a cumulative total of $15.4 billion in the entire decade of the 1990s to $37.7 billion in 2009–10 alone (though this has since dropped). India's share of global gross domestic product (GDP) in PPP terms has doubled from 2.5 per cent in 1980 to 5.5 per cent in 2010; its share in world merchandise exports increased from 0.4 per cent in 1980 to 1.5 per cent in 2010 and in world service exports from 0.7 per cent to 3.3 per cent. While figures do not always tell the complete story, the India that punched above its weight in the 1950s and below its undoubted potential in the 1960s is now poised to become the world's third largest economy in purchasing power parity (PPP) terms in 2012, according to the IMF. It is a country whose real and visible weight counts in the world.

Our foreign policy today has also outgrown much of its earlier post-colonial rhetoric. In the past, India's policy pronouncements on the world were often justified on the grounds that our position was right in principle rather than in practice, that they were correct more than they were useful. Foreign policy was seen by its practitioners, starting with Nehru, as an end in itself, unrelated to the more mundane economic needs of the nation. Today, India's foreign policy is much more overtly focused on the task of facilitating India's economic growth in order to bring our billion-strong masses into the twenty-first century. We are open about our need to cultivate good relations with countries that can assist us in that process—trading partners and investors in our economy; suppliers of energy resources and assurers of food security; and partners in our fundamental objective of keeping our people safe, secure and free to develop their human and economic potential without external interference or threats. We need to ensure reliable and multiple sources of these resources, predicated upon good relations with the countries that can provide them and a peaceful environment in which our development and growth can flourish. These are all pragmatic underpinnings of our foreign policy—one aiming to shore up the key domestic objective of transforming our own society and economy.

Since foreign policy is developed and conducted by the institutions of the state, its conception and articulation reflects the conditions that the state finds itself in, mediated through the state's orchestration of the aspirations of the people it seeks to represent. This means that India's geography, its political culture and environment, its domestic institutions and federal structure, all play a vital role in the making of its foreign policy. Not surprisingly, different constituents of India pursue their different interests, impacting foreign policy sometimes directly and sometimes indirectly, as we discuss in a later chapter on the influence of domestic policies. As the state evolves and the people's attitudes change, foreign policy shifts. This has already become apparent since 1991, when India, in the commentator C. Raja Mohan's formulation, 'crossed the Rubicon' from its traditional foreign policy to its present one.

Malone, for one, saw this as a fundamental change in Indian foreign policy making: 'Indian foreign policy in the twenty-first century is characterized by a marked shift towards pragmatism and a willingness to do business with all,' he observed, 'resembling in none of its important specifics that of Indira Gandhi in the mid-1970s, and even less that of her father in the 1950s and 1960s.'

Yet it is not merely a self-centred, economic-determinist approach to the world that dominates Indian thinking. Nehru's old globalist orientation is still hard-wired into the consciousness of policy-makers. The main difference is that the post-colonial chip has fallen off our shoulder; New Delhi can now afford to look at the globe from a position of authority. Today we can take our sovereignty for granted; we know no one would dare threaten it. Our strategic autonomy is a fact of life and no longer something that has to be fought for. We are now in a position to graduate from a focus on our own sovereign autonomy to exercising a vision of responsibility on the world stage, from a post-colonial concern with self-protection to a new role participating in the making of global rules and even playing a role in imposing them.

India has a self-evident interest in helping to create an enabling international environment for our own national objectives. International trade has an increasingly direct bearing on our national well-being; over 30 per cent of our GDP is now accounted for by our imports and exports, and our growth and prosperity depend on continued imports of fertilizer, energy, metals and capital, as well as continued receptivity to Indian migrants (in 2010 India was the second largest emigrant nation of the world with 11.4 million migrants and the top remittance receiving nation in the world with $55 billion in inward remittances). It obviously serves our national purposes to expend our energies and resources in working to ensure a peaceful and equitable global order, to preserve the freedom of the seas and open sea lanes of communication, to explore outer space and cyberspace in ways that help all of humanity—all the 'global public goods' that international theorists theorize about, but which have a tangible impact on our everyday lives.

One tangible example of India's new-found willingness to engage the outside world—specifically, the foreign private sector—in our domestic development lies in the way we have developed our telecommunications sector, perhaps the single most remarkable example of India's recent transformation through liberalization. Foreign companies, technology and expertise helped build India's initial wireless networks between 1995 and 2002. The initial networks were built by Indian companies in joint ventures with global multinational corporations such as BT, AT&T, Telstra, US West, Swiss PTT and Bell Canada; a large part of the technology was sourced from the European firms Nokia, Siemens, Alcatel-Lucent and Ericsson, while US companies like Cisco, HP and IBM remain prominent providers of the telecom technology which powers India's networks. Realizing that the interests of India's citizens in large-scale and widespread availability of telecommunications needed an international approach, the government has encouraged foreign technology, and the size of the Indian market has helped lower costs both for handsets and infrastructure, with some of the lowest tariffs for mobile services anywhere in the world. The result is that today we have nearly 900 million SIM cards in circulation and are poised to overtake China in 2012 to become the world's largest telecom market—something that the old, protected and inward-focused Indian telecom system could never have aspired to. International engagement has empowered the ordinary Indian and changed his daily life.

Internationalism, as Nehru demonstrated in his speech at that first moment of independence, has always been a vital part of our national DNA. It was also typical of Nehru's internationalist vision that his words, uttered sixty-four years ago, were not only profoundly right, but could be spoken today without the change of a comma. And yet we pursue our internationalism today in a world where all the unifying forces of interdependence—satellite communications, easy jet travel, the Internet, the ability to move capital with the click of a mouse in an increasingly globalized world—are challenged by the destructive forces of division that are equally global. The terrorists of 26/11 used the instruments of globalization and convergence—the ease of communication, GPS and mobile telephone technology, five-star hotels frequented by the transnational business elite, and so on—as instruments for their fanatical agenda. Similarly, on 9/11 in New York, rather than as forces to bring the world closer together, the terrorists also used similar tools—crashing the jet aircraft into those towers emblematic of global capitalism, while the doomed victims of the planes made frantic mobile phone calls to their loved ones.

In other words, the very forces that, through globalization, are pulling us together seem at the same time, through international terrorism, to be driving us apart. The terrible notion of a 'clash of civilizations' has entered our discourse, as the often benign forces of religion, culture and society have become causes of conflict, rather than of succour, in many places.

Both 9/11 and 26/11 were grotesque reflections of this paradoxical phenomenon of convergence and disruption, unity and division, in today's world. For an India striding confidently into the twenty-first century, it is not enough to navigate our way cautiously between these forces. We must work to build a world which accentuates convergence and prevents the forces of disruption from succeeding. This is in our national interest; it is also an essential aspect of the responsibility we must exercise if we are to live up to being worthy of the kind of nation we are becoming.

India has been directly affected by both global trends, of convergence and disruption. On the one hand, we are a far more globalized economy than most, and more so than we ever were in the days when we raised the protectionist barriers to shield us while we developed our autonomous national capabilities. We are today more connected through trade and travel—much more than ever before—with the international system, and trade and foreign investment account for a steadily increasing share of our GDP. Indian firms have become multinationals, investing abroad to a level that in some recent years has exceeded the FDI coming into India. Indians work everywhere, and have acquired a reputation for mathematical, computing and engineering skills that are prized by international employers. Foreign companies are hiring Indians in India to do research and development for their globally branded products; GE and Phillips, for instance, employ more researchers in India than in their worldwide headquarters. Our relationship with each of the major powers has grown rapidly, and China is now our single largest trading partner. India's soft power stretches across the globe, with our popular cinema in the vanguard, influencing the hearts and minds of foreigners almost everywhere. Our political relationships have also been strengthened. With the United States, it was possible for us to undertake the civil nuclear initiative, removing the limitations that had been placed on us after the 1974 and 1998 nuclear tests. Today we can admit—indeed, we can boast—that our links with the world are one reason for the highest-ever growth rates that we enjoyed between 2003 and 2008.

But the external situation has been changing considerably. Politically, the world is entering a period of transition from dominance by a single power to a more balanced distribution of power in the international system, though this still falls short of true multi-polarity. India had barely adjusted to the reality of a unipolar world when the United States' seemingly unchallengeable dominance of the world order began to fade in the first decade of the twenty-first century. New powers are rising, new alliances are forming, and we are witnessing the rise of a new global power in China, the only visible contender for the superpower status now enjoyed singularly by the United States. Challenges in India's immediate neighbourhood, particularly in Pakistan and Afghanistan, but also in Bangladesh, Sri Lanka and Nepal, have made us conscious that our development is vulnerable to the impact of forces and events beyond our borders.

As the world transitions to something closer to real multi-polarity, we should realize that the existing power holders can hardly be expected to easily cede power to others. Even if academic seminarians take the notion of new 'rising powers' for granted, no formerly risen power is prepared to fall. Many will seek to stay in place, even if it means continuing the existing inequities in the international order. In some cases new and old powers are busy cultivating the very states whose influence they are simultaneously trying to check. In turn, this will mean an opportunity for other countries to build new coalitions with each other in their efforts to find a better place in the sun. This could lead to clashes, unless the entire international architecture is reshaped cooperatively—an objective India can, and should, work towards, and to which we shall return later in this volume.

India today disposes of far greater leverage in its extended neighbourhood than before, but arguably bears greater responsibility as well. Our impact on regional issues such as peace and security prospects in South Asia, or even on issues broader afield such as Southeast and East Asian economic integration, is already considerable and will grow in ways that could not have been imagined two decades ago. Our role is also of determining importance on such global issues as the management of climate change, the provision of energy security and the global macro-economic discussions in the G20 about coordinating ways to pull the world out of recession.

The world economic crisis, which started as a financial crisis at the heart of the Western capitalist system, has not yet ended. Fortunately, while India has been affected, it has been one of the few economies that continue to show growth, attaining 6.9 per cent in the 2011–12 fiscal year. Nor is it clear that the world economy will return to an expansionary phase any time soon. Our search for markets, technology and resources to fuel our growth will be more complicated than it has been in the recent past. International developments will inevitably affect us. Inflation, for instance, a hot-button political issue in India, is only very partially the result of policies pursued by the elected Indian government. Among the significant causes of rising prices in India is the massive injection of liquidity by the developed Western countries into the world economy to promote their own recovery from the global economic crisis. This has been magnified by a rise in oil and commodity prices, itself partly caused by the availability of more capital but also compounded by the uncertain political climate in a Middle East torn by 'jasmine revolutions' and mounting civil strife. To suggest that domestic economics can be pursued without reference to foreign policy is no longer a serious proposition.

So while India's strategic goals must remain the same—to enable the domestic transformation of India by accelerating our growth, preserving our strategic autonomy, protecting our people and responsibly helping shape the world—achieving these goals in the present economic climate will be a challenge to our skill and ingenuity. As protectionism grows and closes markets, and as credit is sucked back into developed economies for their own stimulus and recovery, we will have to rely much more on growing our own domestic market. The world of today is not going to provide as propitious an environment for India's growth and prosperity as the world of two decades ago did, when we first liberalized. This brings me right back to the underlying theme of this book: the importance of using our international policies to serve our fundamental objective of pulling poor people in India out of poverty and into the twenty-first-century globalized economic system.

What shape should our foreign policy take to enable us to cope with such a world? Decades ago, the scholar Richard A. Falk summarized six broad criteria for evaluating foreign policy in a democracy, which seem broadly relevant to our challenge even today. A country's foreign policy should, first of all, be a desirable one—approved means (means approved by the general public) must be used in pursuit of approved ends (goals approved by national institutions like Parliament), with the bases of approval made explicitly. It should be effective—those approved means should be successful in accomplishing the ends sought. It should be popular, since in a democracy it is important that an elected government's foreign policy positions enjoy high levels of public support. It should be legitimate—both the means and the ends of foreign policy should be in accord with the Constitution, and with India's solemn international obligations and treaty commitments, including respecting the constraints embodied in international law. Falk's final two criteria are perhaps both idealistic and contestable: he suggests that foreign policy should be populist (the means and ends of foreign policy should reflect public participation, with influence on policy-making filtering upwards to the decision-makers as well as downwards from them) and equitable (the domestic costs, burdens and sacrifices resulting from a country's foreign policy should be distributed fairly within society).

India's foreign policy has arguably done a good job in reflecting most of these criteria, though it is clear that we still have a way to go before we can express satisfaction with our performance on all counts. But Falk's list is worth bearing in mind as a yardstick when we examine India's international standing in the rest of this volume.

So what does all this mean for the reshaped world that we hope will emerge in the next couple of decades? What can we project for the world of the next twenty years?

I have little doubt that the international system—as constructed following the Second World War—will be almost unrecognizable by 2030 owing to the rise of emerging powers, a transformed global economy, a real transfer of relative wealth and economic power from the West, or the North, to other countries in the global South, and the growing influence of non-state actors, including terrorists, multinational corporations and criminal networks. In the next two decades, this new international system will be coping with the issues of ageing populations in the developed world; increasing energy, food and water constraints; and worries about climate change and migration. India's transformation will mean that resource issues—including energy, food and water, on all of which demand is projected to outstrip easily available supplies over the next decade or so—will gain prominence on the international agenda.

We must be determined to pursue our domestic transformation, and to do so responsibly. The energy demands this process will make on the world will be huge, and we must seek to fulfil our energy requirements through a mix of efficient and environmentally friendly means (hydro, solar, wind and nuclear, in addition to the still-unavoidable thermal- and petroleum- or gas-driven forms of energy). Our foreign policy must serve this objective too: the India–US nuclear agreement was a step in this direction. So too will be an Indian policy on climate change that respects the world's anxieties about global warming while preserving the capacity to do what it takes to connect the deprived and excluded among our people to the opportunities the twenty-first century offers.

The global environment, in both senses of that phrase, could undermine many of the aspirations of Indian foreign policy.

Our demand for food will inevitably rise as well, perhaps by 50 per cent in the next two decades, as a result of our growing population, their rising affluence and the improved dietary possibilities available to a larger middle class. We will need to multiply our sources of food, including developing agricultural land abroad, in Africa and even Latin America. Lack of access to stable supplies of water, particularly for agricultural purposes, is reaching critical proportions and the problem will worsen because of rapid urbanization over the next twenty years. We will need skilful and creative diplomacy to ensure that interruptions in the flow of water across our borders do not bedevil relations with our neighbours.

All this underscores my initial point, that foreign policy is basically about fulfilling domestic objectives. Let us never forget that if we succeed—*when* we succeed—in our national transformation, we will be including more and more of our people in the great narrative of hope that has been the narrative of social and economic development in the West over the last two hundred years. We will be connecting 500 million Indians to their own country and to the rest of the world. Half a billion Indian villagers will join the global village. That is an exciting prospect and I am sure, for some, an alarming one.

This underscores the need for increased, more democratic and more equitable global governance. Let us look even further than the next two decades. Growth projections for Brazil, Russia, India and China (the BRIC countries) indicate they will collectively match the original G7's share of global GDP by 2040–50. All four probably, and certainly India, will continue to enjoy relatively rapid economic growth and will strive for a multipolar world in which their capitals are among the poles. New Delhi is already a magnet for visiting potentates and tributaries; it will certainly be among the half-dozen places from which the twenty-first century world will be run.

The experts tell us that historically, emerging multipolar systems have been more unstable than bipolar or unipolar ones. The rise of China is one of the great and visible events of our geopolitics, and it appears to be matched by a comparable decline in the political will and economic self-confidence of the Western powers, at a time when several 'emerging' nations are acquiring strength and confidence on the global stage. In a world in which some great powers are no longer quite as great as some formerly minor states, and where a powerful China is scrutinized carefully for signs of incipient hegemonic tendencies, there are serious questions about the future of the world order. Might China seek to challenge the existing global system, as a rising Germany did at the beginning of the twentieth century, or to reorder the structures of international organization, as a triumphant United States did after the Second World War? Should a country like India work actively in these circumstances to reform and strengthen the world order in order to create a pattern of several powerful states cooperating with each other in an inclusive multipolar world system?

The recent, indeed ongoing, global financial crisis underlines that the next twenty years of transition to a new system are fraught with risks. Global policy-makers will have to cope with a growing demand for multilateral cooperation when the international system will be stressed by the incomplete transition from the old to the new order. And the new players will not want to cooperate under the old rules.

The multiplicity of actors on the international scene could, if properly accommodated, add strength to our ageing post–Second World War institutions, or they could fragment the international system and reduce international cooperation. Our era is characterized by common vulnerabilities among potential rivals—the United States and China, for instance, with one a vital market for the other and the latter a major debtor of the former—as well as growing interdependencies among former enemies, such as the Russian supply of oil and gas to West Europe. Countries like India have no desire to challenge the international system as did other rising powers like Germany and Japan in the nineteenth and twentieth centuries, but wish to be given a place at the global high table. Without that, they would be unlikely to volunteer to share the primary burden for dealing with such issues as terrorism, climate change, proliferation and energy security, which concern all of us.

These issues will remain key concerns even as resource issues move up on the international agenda. The old divides between East and West, North and South, capitalist and communist, developed and developing are becoming largely irrelevant; the twenty-first-century world is not one of simple binaries. Failing states, terrorist groups, transnational Islamist movements, non-governmental organizations (NGOs) and civil society have also all begun to impact the choices of governments. Ours is an era where 'non-state actors' can nearly bring two armies to war. Terrorism is the tragic blight of our times, but far too much ink has been expended on it to merit extensive treatment in this book. But its appeal could diminish if economic opportunities for youth are increased and greater political pluralism is offered in many societies.

Yet in saying this, I am conscious that India's story could be seriously affected by the failure of other countries in our neighbourhood to do either. To take our most pressing immediate challenge, a democratic Pakistan determined to focus on its own people's economic development would be good news for India. On the other hand, a flailing Pakistan, with a burgeoning population of uneducated, unemployable and frustrated youth prey to the blandishments of radical religious fanatics, and ruled by a military-dominated system that sees its security in destabilizing others, could be a major threat to India. Inevitably this will remain a major preoccupation of Indian foreign policy for the foreseeable future, and we will address it in detail in the next chapter.

The risk of nuclear weapon use over the next twenty years is greater now with the potential emergence of new nuclear weapon states and the increased risk of the acquisition of nuclear materials by terrorist groups. Pakistan's willingness to allow its territory to be used for attacks against India like the assault on Mumbai on 26/11 inevitably carries the risk of sparking off a larger conflagration. Pakistan's refusal to agree to a 'no first-use of nuclear weapons' pact with India is grave, and its brinkmanship in such matters as the attacks on our embassy in Kabul raises the spectre of continued hostility between our two nuclear powers. This is why our prime minister has made such an extraordinary effort to sustain dialogue with Pakistan. There are also genuine questions regarding the ability of a state like Pakistan to control and secure its nuclear arsenals in the event of internal disruption.

This is one more reason why India will remain a strong proponent of universal nuclear disarmament. India's approach to nuclear disarmament, nuclear non-proliferation and, by extension, to arms control is essentially based on the belief that there exists close synergy between all three. Non-proliferation cannot be an end in itself, and has to be linked to effective nuclear disarmament. Nuclear disarmament and non-proliferation should be seen as mutually reinforcing processes. Effective disarmament must enhance the security of all states and not merely that of a few.

India had set out goals regarding nuclear disarmament as far back as June 1988, when the then prime minister of India, Rajiv Gandhi, presented to the United Nations an Action Plan for ushering in a nuclear weapons–free world. He argued that the 'alternative to co-existence is co-destruction'. Even today, India is perhaps the only nuclear weapons state to express its readiness to negotiate a Nuclear Weapons Convention leading to global, non-discriminatory and verifiable elimination of nuclear weapons.

Such global aspirations have long been part of India's basic foreign policy posture. But while global institutions continue to adapt to the new world, regional ones could emerge into prominence. The world economic crisis should give us an opportunity to promote economic integration with our neighbours in the subcontinent who look to the growing Indian market to sell their goods and maintain their own growth. Yet as long as South Asia remains divided by futile rivalries and some continue to believe that terrorism can be a useful instrument of their strategic doctrines, that is bound to remain a distant prospect. That is why our neighbourhood will also be examined in a later chapter.

As a result the structure of this book is rather like an onion; it begins with Pakistan and peels outwards, from South Asia and the neighbourhood to the broader world beyond. This method permits us to see starkly what overwhelmingly occupies our short-term thinking before engaging with the broader concerns that must occupy a more prominent place in our international reflection. In the process of peeling this onion, I hope (without too many tears!) to offer my readers, in particular the younger generation of Indians, a worldview that helps orient them to their national and global inheritance. The book deals much less with the history of India's foreign policy than with contemporary trends and future prospects, partly because history has not always been a reliable guide to the present (who could have imagined in 1998 the signing of the Indo-US nuclear deal in 2008?), and partly because my concern is principally with tomorrow, not yesterday. While much of the book's detail is anchored in 2012, its broad thrust is intended to be relevant for some time to come.

I believe strongly that we must work to create a world in which Indians can prosper in safety and security, a world in which a transformed India can play a worthy part. This is a time in our national evolution when we must rethink the assumptions of our political philosophy, and rise to the need to refurbish our institutions with new ideas. An India led by rational, humane and open-minded ideas of itself must develop a view of the world that is also broad-minded, accommodative and responsible. That would be in keeping with the aspiration that Nehru launched us on when he spoke of our tryst with destiny. As we embark on the second decade of the twenty-first century, the time has indeed come for us to redeem his pledge.

Chapter Two

Brother Enemy

Nearly six and a half decades after independence and Partition, Pakistan remains India's biggest foreign policy challenge.

Pakistan was hacked off the stooped shoulders of India by the departing British in 1947 as a homeland for India's Muslims, but (at least until very recently, if one can extrapolate from the two countries' population growth trends) more Muslims have remained in India than live in Pakistan. Pakistan's relations with India have ever since been bedevilled by a festering dispute over the divided territory of Kashmir, India's only Muslim-majority state. Decades of open conflict and simmering hostility, punctuated by spasms of bonhomie that always seem to sputter out into recrimination, have characterized a relationship that has circumscribed India's options and affected its strategic choices. The knowledge that our nearest neighbour, populated as it is by a people of a broadly similar ethnic mix and cultural heritage, defines itself in opposition to India and exercises its diplomatic and military energies principally to thwart and undermine us has inevitably coloured India's actions and calculations on the regional and global stage. The resort by Pakistan to the sponsorship of militancy and terrorism within India as an instrument of state policy since the 1980s has made relations nearly as bad as in the immediate aftermath of independence.

When Pakistan was created in the Partition of 1947, the 544 'princely states' (nominally ruled by assorted potentates but owing allegiance to the British Raj) were required to accede to either of the two new states. The maharaja of Jammu and Kashmir—a Muslim-majority state with a Hindu ruler—dithered over which of the two to join, and flirted optimistically with the idea of remaining independent. Pakistan, determined to wrest the territory, sent in a band of irregulars, who made considerable inroads before being distracted by the attractions of rapine and pillage. The panicked maharaja, fearing his state would fall to the marauders, acceded to India, which promptly paradropped troops who stopped the invaders (by now augmented by the Pakistani Army) in their tracks. India took Pakistan's aggression to the UN as an international issue and declared a ceasefire that left it in possession of roughly two-thirds of the state.

To ascertain the wishes of the Kashmiri people, the UN mandated a plebiscite, to be conducted after the Pakistani troops had withdrawn from the territory they had captured. India had insisted on a popular vote, since the Kashmiri democratic movement, led by the fiery and hugely popular Sheikh Abdullah, was a pluralist movement associated with India's Congress party (Abdullah was president of the Indian States' Peoples' Congress, a body set up by the Congress party to represent independence-minded people in the princely states) rather than with the Muslim League that had demanded the creation of Pakistan, and New Delhi had no doubt that India would win a plebiscite. For the same reason, conscious of Abdullah's popularity, Pakistan refused to withdraw, and the plebiscite was never conducted. The dispute has festered ever since.

Four wars (in 1947–48, 1965, 1971 and 1999), all initiated by Pakistan, have been fought across the ceasefire line, now dubbed the Line of Control (LoC), without materially altering the situation. In the late 1980s, a Pakistan-backed insurrection by some Kashmiri Muslims, augmented by militants infiltrated across the LoC and supplied with arms and money by Pakistan, began. Both the militancy and the response to it by Indian security forces have caused great loss of life, damaged property and all but wrecked a Kashmiri economy dependent largely on tourism and the sale of handicrafts. In the process, both countries have suffered grievously: India, whose citizens have been killed in large numbers and which has had to deploy over half a million men under arms to keep the peace, and Pakistan, whose strategy of 'bleeding India to death' through insurgency and terrorism, in Kashmir and beyond, has accomplished little of value, while making its military enormously powerful within Pakistan and disproportionately well-resourced (largely thanks to Kashmir, the Pakistani Army controls a larger share of its national budget than any army in the world does).

If Kashmir is, to Pakistanis, the main casus belli, the horrors that were inflicted on Mumbai by terrorists from Pakistan at the end of November 2008 remain the starting point for any Indian's discussion of Pakistan. They have left an abiding impact on all Indians. India picked itself up after the assault, but it counted the cost in lives lost, property destroyed and, most of all, in the scarred psyche of a ravaged nation. Deep and sustained anger across the country—at its demonstrated vulnerability to terror and at the multiple institutional failures that allowed such loss of life—prompted the immediate resignations of the home minister in Delhi and the chief minister and his deputy in Maharashtra. But '26/11' in Mumbai represented a qualitative change in Pakistan's long-running attempts to pursue 'war by other means'. The assault, and the possibility of its recurrence, implied that there could be other consequences, yet to be measured, that the world will have to come to terms with in the future—consequences whose impact could extend well beyond India's borders, with implications for the peace and security of the region, and the world.

I had grown up in Bombay, as it was then called, and so watched the unfolding horror there in November 2008 with profound empathy. There is a savage irony to the fact that the attacks in Mumbai began with terrorists docking near the Gateway of India. The magnificent arch, built in 1911, has ever since stood as a symbol of the openness of the city. Crowds flock around it, made up of foreign tourists and local yokels; touts hawk their wares; boats bob in the waters, offering cruises out to the open sea. The teeming throngs around it daily reflect India's diversity, with Parsi gentlemen out for their evening constitutionals, Muslim women in burqas taking the sea air, Goan Catholic waiters enjoying a break from their duties at the stately Taj Mahal Hotel, Indians from every corner of the country chatting in a multitude of tongues. On 26 November, barred and empty, ringed by police barricades, as it was seen on TV, the Gateway of India—the gateway *to* India, and to India's soul—stood as mute testimony to the most serious assault on the country's pluralist democracy.

The terrorists who heaved their bags laden with weapons up the steps of the wharf to begin their assault on the Taj, like their cohorts at a dozen other locations around the city, knew exactly what they were doing. Theirs was an attack on India's financial nerve centre and commercial capital, a city emblematic of the country's energetic thrust into the twenty-first century. They struck at symbols of the prosperity that was making the Indian model so attractive to the globalizing world—luxury hotels, a café favoured by foreigners, the city's Jewish centre. The terrorists also sought to polarize Indian society by claiming to be acting to redress the grievances, real and imagined, of India's Muslims. And by singling out Americans and Israelis for special attention, they demonstrated that their brand of Islamist fanaticism is anchored less in the absolutism of pure faith than in the geopolitics of hatred.

The attack on the Jewish Chabad-Lubavitch centre and the killing of its residents was particularly sad, since India is justifiably proud of the fact that it is the only country in the world with a Jewish diaspora going back 2500 years where there has never been a single instance of anti-Semitism (except when the Portuguese came to inflict it in the sixteenth century). This is the first time that it has been unsafe to be Jewish in India—one more proof that the terrorists were not Indian, since Indian Muslims have never had any conflict with Indian Jews, but that they were pursuing a foreign agenda. Indeed, this was clearly not just an attack on India; the terrorists were also taking on the 'Jews and crusaders' of Al Qaeda lore. With this tragedy, India became the theatre of action for a global battle.

After the killings, the platitudes flowed like blood. Terrorism is unacceptable; the terrorists are cowards; the world stands united in unreserved condemnation of this latest atrocity, and so mind-numbingly on. Commentators in America tripped over themselves to pronounce the night and day of carnage India's 9/11. But India has endured many attempted 9/11s, notably a ferocious assault on its Parliament in December 2001 that nearly led to all-out war against the assailants' sponsors, Pakistan. In 2008 alone, terrorist bombs had taken lives in Jaipur, in Ahmedabad, in Delhi and (in an eerie dress rehearsal for the effectiveness of synchronicity) several different places on one searing day in Assam. Jaipur is the lodestar of Indian tourism to Rajasthan; Ahmedabad is the primary city of Gujarat, the state that is projected by many as a poster child for India's development, with a local

GDP growth rate of 14 per cent; Delhi is the nation's political capital and India's window to the world; Assam was logistically convenient for terrorists from across a porous border. Mumbai combined all the four elements of its precursors: by attacking it, the terrorists hit India's economy, its tourism and its internationalism, and they took advantage of the city's openness to the world.

So the terrorists hit multiple targets in Mumbai, both literally and figuratively. They caused death and destruction to our country, searing India's psyche, showing up the limitations of its security apparatus and humiliating its government. They dented the worldwide image of India as an emerging economic giant, a success story of the era of globalization and an increasing magnet for investors and tourists. Instead the world was made to see an insecure and vulnerable India, a 'soft state' besieged by enemies who could strike it at will.

Indians have learned to endure the unspeakable horrors of terrorist violence ever since malign men in Pakistan concluded that it was cheaper and more effective to bleed India to death than to attempt to defeat it in conventional war. There had, after all, been four unsuccessful wars—the failed attempts by Pakistan in 1947–48 and 1965 to wrest control over Kashmir, the 1971 war that resulted in the birth of Bangladesh from the ruins of the former East Pakistan and the undeclared Kargil war of 1999, in which Pakistani soldiers were dressed in mufti to conceal their identities when they surreptitiously seized the heights above Kargil in Kashmir, until being repelled in a heroic but costly action by the Indian Army. Attack after attack on Indian soil since then has been proven to have been financed, equipped and guided from across the border, including two suicide bombings of the Indian embassy in Kabul, the first of which was publicly traced by American intelligence to Islamabad's dreaded military special-ops agency, the Inter-Services Intelligence (ISI), and its 'Directorate S' that collaborates with and directs terrorists and militants. The risible attempt by anonymous sources to claim 'credit' for the Mumbai killings in the name of the 'Deccan Mujahideen' merely confirmed that the killers are not from the Deccan. The Deccan lies inland from Mumbai; one does not need to sail the waters of the Arabian Sea to the Gateway of India to get to the city from there. In its meticulous planning, sophisticated coordination and military precision, including the use of reconnaissance missions and GPS equipment, as well as its choice of targets, the assault on Mumbai bore no trace of what its promoters tried to suggest it was—a spontaneous eruption by angry young Indian Muslims. This horror, despite Pakistan's initial (and subsequently discredited) denials, was not home-grown.

The geopolitical reverberations of the carnage placed Islamabad firmly in the dock. The interrogation of the one surviving terrorist, Ajmal Kasab, and evidence from satellite telephone intercepts and other intelligence, led to an international consensus that the attacks were masterminded by the Wahhabi-inspired Lashkar-e-Taiba, a terrorist group patronized, protected and trained by the ISI as a useful instrument in Islamabad's proxy war against India in Kashmir.

While Pakistan chafes at its inability to wrest the Kashmir valley from India, and resorts to all conceivable means to win that territory, it has understandably accepted its inability to do so through conventional warfare. That is why, for more than two decades now, a succession of Pakistani military rulers has made it a point to support, finance, equip and train Islamist militants to conduct terrorist operations in India, to bleed India from within and to inflict upon it what a Pakistani strategist called 'death by a thousand cuts'.

India's response has been defensive, not belligerent. India is a status quo power that seeks nothing more than to be allowed to grow and develop in peace, free from the destructive attentions of the Pakistani military and the militants and terrorists it sponsors. Pakistan has sought to obscure this reality by seeking to convince the West and China that its militarism is in response to an 'Indian threat', a notion assiduously peddled in Washington and London by highly paid lobbyists for Islamabad. The rationale for this argument goes back to 1971, when India, in their version of the narrative, attacked and dismembered Pakistan. This action, it is suggested, reveals India's intentions: it is simply waiting for the opportunity to do to what remains of Pakistan what it did to the country's old political geography.

The facts, of course, are quite different. Pakistan's genocidal military crackdown on its own eastern half sent 10 million Bengali refugees flocking into India, the largest refugee movement in human history. India could not care for these people indefinitely, and sought a permanent solution—which, given the intransigence of Islamabad's military rulers, could only lie in the independence of East Pakistan (which became Bangladesh). India accordingly supported the secessionist guerrillas operating against the Pakistani occupation there. It was in fact the Pakistani military that gave India an excuse to launch all-out war by attempting a pre-emptive air strike on Indian air force bases and then declaring war on India, which New Delhi happily accepted as a cue to sweep into the east and liberate Bangladesh. That done, India called a ceasefire in the west, instead of continuing to march in to subjugate Pakistan (entirely feasible in those pre-nuclear days) or even to free its own territory in Kashmir from Pakistani rule. These are not the actions of a nation that has any additional designs on Pakistan. In fact 1971 offered a unique set of historical circumstances that are no longer replicable. And they require brutality and short-sightedness on a colossal scale from Pakistan itself, which presumably is also not going to be repeated.

For these reasons, the notion of any Indian 'threat' is preposterous; bluntly, there is not and cannot be an 'Indian threat' to Pakistan, simply because there is absolutely nothing Pakistan possesses that India wants. If proof had to be adduced for this no-doubt-unflattering assessment, it lies in India's decision at Tashkent in 1966 to give 'back' to Pakistan every square inch of territory captured by our brave soldiers in Pakistan-Occupied Kashmir, including the strategic Haji Pir Pass, all of which is land we claim to be ours. If we do not even insist on retaining what we see as our own territory, held by Pakistan since 1948 but captured fair and square in battle, why on earth would we want anything else from Pakistan?

No, the 'Indian threat' is merely a useful device cynically exploited by the Pakistani military to justify their power (and their grossly disproportionate share of Pakistan's national assets, as brilliantly spelled out in Ayesha Siddiqa's book *Military Inc.*). The central problem bedevilling the relationship between the two subcontinental neighbours is not, as Pakistani propagandists like to suggest, Kashmir, but rather the nature of the Pakistani state itself—specifically, the stranglehold over Pakistan of the world's most lavishly funded military (in terms of percentage of national resources and GDP consumed by any army on the planet). To paraphrase Voltaire on Prussia, in India, the state has an army; in Pakistan, the army has a state. Unlike in India, one does not join the army in Pakistan to defend the country; one joins the army to run the country. The military has ruled Pakistan directly for a majority of the years of its existence, and indirectly for most of the rest. No elected civilian government has been allowed to complete its full term, with the exception of Zulfikar Ali Bhutto, initially appointed to power by the outgoing military junta, later elected in his own right and overthrown by his generals at his first attempt at re-election. The army lays down the 'red lines' no civilian leader—and not even the 'free' media—dare cross. In return, the military establishment enjoys privileges unthinkable in India. In addition, serving and retired military officials run army-controlled shopping malls, petrol stations, real-estate ventures, import–export enterprises, and even universities and think tanks. Since the only way to justify this disproportionate dominance of Pakistani state and society is to preserve the myth of an 'Indian threat', the Pakistani military will, many in India believe, continue to want to keep the pot boiling, even if Kashmir were to be handed over to them on a silver salver with a white ribbon tied around it. In the analysis of the Pakistani commentator Cyril Almeida, the army is not strategically interested in peace; it may not want war (which general relishes dying?) but it does not want peace either.

In 2008, just before the terrorist assault, the newly elected civilian government in Islamabad had shown every sign of wanting to move away from this narrative of hatred and hostility. But Pakistan is a deeply divided nation. As the Kabul bombing showed, the disconnect between the statements of the government and the actions of the ISI suggested that the government is too weak to control its own security apparatus. An attempt to place the ISI under the interior ministry in the summer of 2008 had to be rescinded when the army refused to accept the order (even after it had been officially announced on the eve of the Pakistani prime minister's first visit to Washington). When, in the wake of the Mumbai attacks, Pakistani President Zardari acceded to the request of Indian Prime Minister Manmohan Singh to send the head of the ISI to India to assist Indian authorities in their investigation, the Pakistani military again forced the civilian government into a humiliating climbdown, saying a lower-level official might be sent instead. (He wasn't.)

As the former Indian diplomat Satyabrata Pal trenchantly noted, 'The ISI may well be Pakistan's answer to the Holy Roman Empire, which was neither holy, Roman nor an empire: it has no intelligence, it does Pakistan no service and will in time inter it.' The Islamist extremism nurtured by a succession of military rulers of Pakistan has now come to haunt its well-intentioned but lamentably weak elected civilian government. Attacks against the Pakistani state over the last few years have proved that terrorism, created, nurtured and equipped by Pakistan's military, is now well and truly out of its government's control. The militancy once sponsored by its predecessors now threatens to abort Pakistan's sputtering democracy and seeks to engulf India in its flames. President Zardari, Benazir Bhutto's widower, surely realizes that India's enemies in Pakistan are also his own: the very forces of Islamist extremism responsible for his wife's assassination in December 2007 were also behind the bombing of Islamabad's Marriott Hotel in the summer of 2008. There has never been a stronger case for firm and united action by the governments of both India and Pakistan to cauterize the cancer in their midst. This is not as implausible as it sounds. There is a rational argument on both sides that things have gone too far in the wrong direction, and that cooperation is the only way forward. The problem is that each terrorist attack undermines the case for such an approach and discredits the dwindling minority on both sides who believe it to be both true and necessary.

Rarely had a Pakistani civilian government been more inclined to pursue peace with India than Zardari's in 2008. Whereas his predecessor, General Pervez Musharraf, had mastered the art of saying one thing and doing another, Zardari had been pushing for greatly expanded trade and commercial links with India and the liberalization of the restrictive visa regime between the two countries. Indeed his foreign minister was in Delhi for talks on these issues when the terrorist assault occurred. Zardari had also begun winding down his government's official support for Kashmiri militancy against the government in New Delhi, and had announced the disbanding of the ISI's political wing. When he went so far as to propose a 'no first-strike' nuclear policy, matching India's stance but violating his own military's stated nuclear doctrine, Indians had begun to believe that at long last they had found a Pakistani ruler who understood that normalizing relations with India would be of great practical benefit to Pakistan itself.

The terrorists and their patrons clearly wish to thwart any moves in the direction of a rapprochement between the two countries, which would thwart their destructive Islamist agenda. But the Mumbai terror assault only seemed to confirm that—though President Zardari is adept at going on Indian television and saying what his viewers across the border wish to hear—the peacemakers in Islamabad are not the ones who call the shots in that country.

Pakistan at first predictably denied any connection to the events, but each passing revelation rendered its denials less and less plausible. President Zardari even claimed that the captured terrorist was not Pakistani. It took an intrepid British journalist of Pakistani descent to track down Ajmal Kasab's native village of Faridkot in Punjab, report his parents' identities and confirm his background. The parents were promptly spirited away by the Pakistani authorities, the villagers silenced and the next journalist who tried to follow the story, an American, was beaten up for his pains.

Those first weeks of Pakistani denial after 26/11 rankled, because many in India had thought—having paid too much attention to the earlier positive noises from President Zardari—that when 26/11 happened, it would be a golden opportunity for the civilian government of Pakistan to stand up and say, 'We're in this fight together. The people who did this to you are going to do the same thing to us, and we want to work alongside with you. Our intelligence agencies will join you in the investigation.' Instead of which, we got denial, obfuscation, delay and deceptive sanctimony.

When Zardari initially agreed to India's request for the ISI chief to visit New Delhi, he stated that Pakistan 'will cooperate with India in exposing and apprehending the culprits and masterminds' behind the attacks. It soon became clear that this was not an objective unanimously shared in Islamabad. The ISI is not exactly keen on cooperating with an investigation into the massacre's Pakistani links. The Mumbai attacks bore many of the trademarks of the extremist 'fedayeen' groups based in Pakistan, notably the Lashkar-e-Taiba, which in the past has benefited from the patronage of the ISI. Whether the Pakistani military is orchestrating the violence or merely shielding its perpetrators, it clearly has no interest in seeing its protégés destroyed. It soon became apparent that for all of President Zardari's soothing words, the Pakistani government cannot ensure that different elements of the state fall in line with the government's vision. And the country's civilian government—India's official interlocutors—dare not cross the red lines drawn by the military, for fear of being toppled. If India is to take Islamabad's professions of peaceful intent seriously, credible action with visible results is required. It has not been much in evidence in recent years.

Despite its denials and its disingenuous calls for more proof—all of which had the effect, whether by accident or design, of buying time for the perpetrators to cover their tracks, to husband their resources and to reinvent their identities—Pakistan has never been more isolated in the international community. It is now universally accepted that the massacre in Mumbai was planned in and directed from Pakistani territory, and the inability of the Pakistani government to prevent its soil from being used to mount attacks on another state make a mockery of its pretensions to sovereignty. No one wishes to undermine President Zardari's civilian government, which remains the one hope for something approaching a moderate, secularist regime in that country. But it is an understatement to point out that Zardari does not enjoy the unstinting support of his own security establishment. And his weakness makes it less and less useful for outsiders to shore him up.

Before the attacks on Mumbai, the United States had been promoting a reduction of India–Pakistan tensions, in the hope—openly voiced by then president-elect Barack Obama (and repeated by him in office)—that this would free Pakistan to conduct more effective counterinsurgency operations against the Taliban and Al Qaeda in its north-western tribal areas. Pakistan has six times the number of troops deployed against India than it has deployed on its western border to fight the Taliban and Al Qaeda. Obama therefore called for promoting a rapprochement between India and Pakistan as a key objective of US foreign policy in the region. Peaceful relations with India would have permitted more resources to be shifted from east to west. Instead the perennial danger is of the Pakistani military, despite India's restraint, moving in the other direction. Washington fears that India–Pakistan tension will make its own task in

Afghanistan more difficult. But for a long time, Washington found few takers in India for continuing a peace process with a government that did not appear to control significant elements of its own military. Now that India and Pakistan are talking, the Pakistani military has been able to move some of its military resources westward, with no discernible impact on the country's security.

Ironically, Zardari had proven to be a useful ally of the United States before 26/11; in addition to overtly lowering the temperature with India, he was cooperating tacitly with American Predator strikes against the Islamic extremists in the Afghan borderlands, much to the resentment of pro-Islamist elements in his own military. This cooperation would be jeopardized if the seething anger throughout India at the Pakistani sponsors of terror boiled over; the hardliners in Islamabad's army headquarters will then have the justification they need to jettison a policy they dislike and turn their weapons back towards their preferred enemy, the Indians. Obama had pointed out during the 2008 US presidential election campaign that American military assistance to Pakistan was being diverted to the purchase of jet aircraft and battle tanks aimed at India, rather than on the tools needed to combat the militants in its lawless tribal belt. After Mumbai, Washington's biggest fear became that the Pakistani military might seek to move its forces away from the western border with Afghanistan, where the United States wants them to aid NATO's fight against the Taliban and Al Qaeda, and reinforce the eastern border with India instead. This is why it is important for India not to give them any excuse to do so.

With Pakistan initially denying all responsibility for the murderous rampage that was planned on its soil, India seemed to have no good options. It was a typically Pakistani conundrum: the military wasn't willing, and the civilian government wasn't able. And the fear remained that expecting Zardari to fulfil even India's minimal demands might be tantamount to asking him to sign his own death warrant. What we needed done had to be done in a way that did not undermine the civilian government.

At the same time, India had to act: we all knew that anything that smacked of temporizing and appeasement would further inflame the public just a few months before national elections were due. But New

Delhi also knew that though some hotheads in India were calling for military action, including strikes on terrorist facilities in Pakistani territory, this would certainly lead to a war that neither side could win. If anything, such an Indian reaction would play into the hands of the terrorists, by strengthening anti-Indian nationalism in Pakistan and easing the pressure on the Islamists. And since both India and Pakistan have nuclear weapons, the risk of military action spiralling out of control is always too grave for any responsible government to contemplate.

Some loud Indian voices on the country's ubiquitously shrill 24/7 news channels pointed enviously to Israel's decisive action against neighbouring territories that have provided sanctuary for those conducting terrorist attacks upon it. They clamorously asked why India could not do the same.

As Israeli planes and tanks exacted a heavy toll on Gaza barely a month after 26/11, these opinion leaders in India watched with an unusual degree of interest—and some empathy. New Delhi joined the rest of the world in calling for an end to the military action, but its criticism of Israel was muted. For as Israel demonstrated anew its determination to put an end to attacks upon its civilians by militants based in Hamas-controlled Gaza, many in India, still smarting from the horrors of the Mumbai attacks, asked: couldn't we do it too?

For many Indian commentators, the temptation to identify with Israel was strengthened by the seizing of Mumbai's Jewish centre (the Chabad-Lubavitch house) by the terrorists on 26/11 and the painful awareness that India and Israel share many of the same enemies. India, with its 150-million-strong Muslim population, has long been a strong supporter of the Palestinian cause and remains staunchly committed to an independent Palestinian state. But 26/11 confirmed what had become apparent in recent years—that the forces of global Islamist terror had added Indians to their reviled target-list of 'Jews and crusaders'. If Israel was frequently attacked by rockets raining upon it from across its border, India had suffered repeated assaults by killers trained, equipped, financed and directed by elements based next door in Pakistan. When White House Press Secretary Dana Perino equated members of Hamas to the Mumbai killers, her comments were widely circulated in India.

Yet there the parallels end. Israel is a small country living in a permanent state of siege, highly security-conscious and surrounded by forces hostile to it; India is a giant country whose borders are notoriously permeable, an open society known for its lax and easy-going ways. Whereas Israel's toughness is seen by many as its principal characteristic, India is seen even by its own citizens as a soft state, its underbelly penetrated easily enough by determined terrorists. Where Israel notoriously exacts grim retribution for every attack on its soil, India has endured with numbing stoicism an endless series of bomb blasts, including at least six other major assaults in different locations in 2008 alone. Terrorism has taken more lives in India than in any country in the world after Iraq, and yet India, unlike Israel, has seemed to be unable to do anything about it.

If Israel has Hamas as its current principal adversary, India has a slew of terrorist organizations to contend with—Lashkar-e-Taiba and its transmogrified cousins, Jaish-e-Mohammad, Jamaat-ud-Dawa and more. But whereas Hamas operates without international recognition from the territory of Gaza, where its legitimacy is questioned even by the Palestinian Authority, India's murderous enemies function from the soil of a sovereign member state of the United Nations, Pakistan. And that makes all the difference.

Hamas is in no condition to resist Israel's air and ground attacks in kind, whereas an Indian attack on Pakistani territory, even one targeting terrorist bases and training camps, would invite swift retaliation from the Pakistani Army. Israel can dictate the terms of its military incursion and end it when it judges appropriate, whereas an Indian military action would immediately spark a war with a well-armed neighbour that neither side could win. And at the end of the day, one chilling fact would prevent India from thinking it can take a leaf out of the Israeli playbook: the country that foments, and at the very least condones, the terror attacks on India is a nuclear power.

So India went to the international community with evidence to prove that the Mumbai attacks were planned in Pakistan and conducted by Pakistani citizens who were in contact throughout with handlers in Pakistan. New Delhi had briefly hoped that the proof might enable Islamabad's weak civilian government to rein in the violent elements in its society. But Islamabad's reaction has been one of denial. Yet no one doubts that Pakistan's all-powerful military intelligence apparatus has, over the last two decades, created and supported terror organizations as instruments of Pakistani policy in Afghanistan and India. When the Indian embassy in Kabul was hit by a suicide bomber in July 2008, American intelligence sources told the *New York Times* that not only was Pakistan's ISI behind the attack, but the ISI had made little effort to cover its tracks. It knew perfectly well that India would not go to war with Pakistan to avenge the killing of its diplomatic personnel.

And indeed it did not. The fact is that India knows that war will accomplish nothing. Indeed, it is just what the terrorists want—a cause that will rally all Pakistanis to the flag, making common cause with the Islamists against the hated Indian enemy, and providing the army an excuse to abandon the unpopular fight against the Taliban and Al Qaeda in the West for the far more familiar terrain of the Indian border in the East. There is no reason to play into the hands of those who seek that outcome.

And yet—when Indians watched Israel take the fight to the enemy, killing those who launched rockets against it and dismantling many of the sites from which the rockets flew, some could not resist wishing they could do something similar in Pakistan. India understands, though, that the collateral damage would be too high, the price in civilian lives unacceptable and the risks of the conflict spiralling out of control too acute for them to contemplate such an option. So they place their trust in international diplomacy—and so Israel was doing what India could never permit itself to do.

At the same time, for any Indian government, inaction is not an option. By showing restraint, ignoring the calls of hotheads for air strikes and missile attacks and by pressuring the United States to work on its near-bankrupt clients in Islamabad—who have received some $11 billion in military assistance since 9/11, ostensibly to fight Islamist terror but much of it spent on those who have fomented such terror—India has achieved appreciable results. Under US pressure, the Pakistani leadership arrested some twenty militants, including Zakiur Rahman Lakhvi, the reputed operational mastermind of the Mumbai horror, and in February 2009 released a report finally admitting that five of the attackers were Pakistani. This was an important first step, but it did not go far enough:

there are still too many evasions and denials, including the suggestion that the attacks were masterminded elsewhere than Pakistan. Also, house arrests and nominal bannings are not enough for Indians: we have seen this movie before. The Lashkar was banned in 2001—by General Musharraf under duress after 9/11—only to re-emerge as the ostensibly humanitarian group Jamaat-ud-Dawa, and in that guise is even more powerful than before. Its head, Hafiz Muhammad Saeed, remained free to preach vitriolic hatred against India in his Friday sermons and to serve, at the very least, as a catalyst for murder and mayhem in our country. New Delhi is rightly insisting that Islamabad crack down completely on these militant groups, dismantle their training camps, freeze their bank accounts (not, as Musharraf did, with enough notice for them to be emptied and transferred to other accounts operated by the same people) and arrest and prosecute their leaders.

Though there is little appetite in Pakistan for such action, the UN Sanctions Committee under resolution 1267 has made it easier for Islamabad by proscribing the Jamaat-ud-Dawa and imposing travel bans and asset freezes of specific named individuals, including Saeed. China, which had opposed such a move when the United States and the United Kingdom had proposed it in 2006, supported it in 2008—a clear indication that in the wake of the Mumbai horrors it judged that such pro-Pakistani obstruction would no longer be compatible with its role as a responsible leader of the international system. What is essential is to sustain the pressure: the American decision in April 2012 to announce a bounty of $10 million on Hafiz Saeed's head is a welcome indication that the world has not given up its quest for justice. I had hoped that if our tragedy gave the semi-secular moderates in Pakistan the opportunity to crack down upon the extremists and murderers in their midst *in their own interest*, the suffering of a few hundred families in India on 26/11 might not be replicated in the lives of other Indians at the hands of these evil men in the years to come. But if the Pakistanis don't do so, the rest of us must.

The Indian state is no stranger to political violence within its territory, and it has evolved a very effective technique of dealing with it—combining ruthless law and order tactics with completely open co-optation into the democratic space. The former gives those using violence a disincentive to continue doing so; the latter gives them a positive reason to give up the gun in order to seek their objectives by other means. This has worked in places as far apart as Punjab and Mizoram, so that yesterday's terrorists become today's political candidates, tomorrow's chief ministers, and the day after tomorrow's leaders of the opposition, those being the vagaries of democracy.

But when you are talking about terror coming from across the border, those options are not available. The terrorists are not people who are seeking a ventilation of political grievances. These are not people who are coming to Mumbai because they want to have their space in making decisions about the country, the community, the future, whatever. These are people coming, unfortunately, with no objective other than destruction. Their objective is to sow terror and fear. And that is very different from the other kinds of terrorism India has dealt with domestically.

When these twenty young men set sail from Pakistan to wreak the havoc they did in Mumbai, I do not know how many of them realistically thought they would ever get back. But clearly, they had no political objectives beyond the undermining of India. They were not asking for the release of imprisoned terrorists. They were not asking for a change of government. They were not seeking anything other than to cause as much damage and death and destruction as possible, perhaps in order to provoke a war between India and Pakistan that would take the heat off Al Qaeda in Pakistan. For them to pretend to be standing up for the cause of Islam, when they killed forty-nine innocent Muslim civilians in the city of Mumbai, would be a travesty of anything that Islam stands for.

It is difficult to escape the conclusion that this kind of terrorism— terrorism as an end in itself, not as a means to something larger—can only be confronted implacably. There is no co-optation formula available. It just has to be nipped in the bud, ideally before it starts, and if that is not possible in its home base, deal with it firmly if and when it actually occurs.

It is fair to ask why 26/11 is the singular event that overwhelms the debate. Why does it overshadow the four wars, and even the preceding twenty years of terrorist support? The answer lies partly in its proximity: just over three years have passed since 26/11 as these words are written, and it looms large still, whereas the formal wars seem to belong to the history books, and the earlier terrorist blasts have been relegated to the footnotes. There is, of course, the continuing danger that 26/11 implies: this mutant species of political violence now offers a copybook template to any future terrorist group. More vital, though, is its intimate immediacy in a psychological sense. As the American novelist Don Delillo has written about terror attacks after 9/11: 'This catastrophic event changes the way we think and act, moment to moment, week to week, for unknown weeks and months to come, and steely years. Our world, parts of our world, have crumbled into theirs, which means we are living in a place of danger and rage.' The 'livestreaming' of the violence has brought about a new auditory and visual experience, as terrorism has been brought into the homes and living rooms of ordinary citizens by the ubiquity of contemporary mass media. Our policy-making machinery must learn to channel this sense of danger, this rage that seethes within, without letting our foreign policy be held hostage to 26/11.

It is fair to point out that since then Pakistan's own internal security has been racked by bouts of large-scale suicide attacks, bomb blasts and commando-style operations attacking army and naval bases. The ISI's response to these has revealed the ambivalence at the heart of its sadomasochistic relationship to terrorism: it suffers the whiplash of the very pain it seeks to inflict on others. Many close observers see in the ISI's actions a curious inward-looking organizational culture, characterized by small-minded hubris, tactical cleverness, bureaucratic self-preservation and wilful ignorance about genuine long-term security needs, all inflated by pretensions of historical grandeur. The entire enterprise is sustained in an establishment rhetoric couched in military and religious vocabulary, with grandiose strategic ambitions advocated largely by ex-military men who should know better, given Pakistan's multiple defeats at the hands of India. New Delhi can shake its head at this phenomenon, but it cannot afford either righteous rage or weary resignation in the face of such fundamental (and fundamentalist) hostility. It must remain vigilant even as it seeks to pursue an honourable peace.

Before concluding this section of our analysis, let me return to where I began, at the Gateway of India. Inevitably, after 26/11, the questions began to be asked abroad: 'Is it all over for India? Can the country ever recover from this?'

Of course, the answers are no and yes, but outsiders cannot be blamed for asking existential questions about a nation that so recently had been seen as poised for take-off. In the wake of the attacks, foreign tourists cancelled reservations in Indian hotels hundreds of miles from Mumbai, and some potential investors in the Indian economy delayed their investment-related plans and visits after seeing attacks upon hotels frequented by international businessmen. While these overreactions, given time, did subside, India has not fully returned to being the economic lodestar it once was in the eyes of international business, at least partly because of the ever-present threat of random violence. Two subsequent bomb blasts in Mumbai and one each in Pune and Delhi, though on a much smaller scale than 26/11, have served as reminders of that possibility.

India can recover from the physical assaults against it. It is striking that both the assaulted hotels, the Taj Mahal and the Trident, reopened their doors within a month of the terrorist attack. We are a land of great resilience that has learned, over arduous millennia, to cope with tragedy. Within twenty-four hours of an earlier Islamist assault on Mumbai, the Stock Exchange bombing in 1993, Mumbai's traders were back on the floor, their burned-out computers forgotten, doing what they used to before technology had changed their trading styles. Bombs and bullets alone cannot destroy India, because Indians will pick their way through the rubble and carry on as they have done throughout history.

But what *can* destroy India is a change in the spirit of its people, away from the pluralism and coexistence that has been our greatest strength. The prime minister's call for calm and restraint in the face of this murderous rampage was heeded; the masses mobilized in candlelight processions, not as murderous mobs. My big fear was that political opportunism in a charged election season could have led to some practising the politics of hatred and division. Indeed, I wrote while the attacks were still going on that 'if these tragic events lead to the demonization of the Muslims of India, the terrorists will have won'. I am heartened that instead Indians stayed united in the face of this tragedy. The victims included Indians of every faith, including forty-nine Muslims out of the 188 killed. There is anger, some of it directed inward, against our security and governance failures, but none of it against any specific community. That is as it should be. For India to be India, its gateway—to the multiple Indias within, and the heaving seas without—must always remain open.

———

Clearly, the international community would want to see that Pakistan implements its stated commitment to deal with terrorist groups within its territory, including the members of Al Qaeda, the Taliban's Quetta Shura, the Hezb-e-Islami, Lashkar-e-Taiba, and so many other like-minded terrorist groups that have been proliferating on Pakistani soil. Without this, the gains made in the last few years of international intervention in Afghanistan will be compromised, and it will become difficult to forestall the resumption of violence and terror in Afghanistan. The world has come to realize, at considerable cost, that terrorism cannot be compartmentalized—that any facile attempt to strike Faustian bargains with terrorists often result in such forces turning on the very powers that sustained them in the past. This implies exacting cooperation from Pakistan.

Some in Washington, notably the late Richard Holbrooke, tried to put the burden of this on India, suggesting that settling the Kashmir dispute on Islamabad's terms would remove the incentive for Pakistan to continue to seek 'strategic depth' (in other words, control of a puppet Islamist government) in Kabul. Such an approach would boil down to surrendering to blackmail. It is difficult to believe that any responsible policy-maker in Washington seriously expects India to compromise on its own vital national interests in order to persuade Pakistan to stop threatening the peace. India has taken upon itself the enormous burden of talking peace with a government of Pakistan that in the very recent past has proved to be, at best, ineffective and, at worst, duplicitous about the real threats emanating from its territory and institutions to the rest of South Asia.

In pursuing peace with Pakistan, the Government of India is indeed rolling the dice: every conciliatory gambit is a gamble that peace will not be derailed by the insincerity of the other side. There are not many takers in the Indian political space right now for pursuing a peace process with a government that does not appear to control significant elements of its own military. Few in India are prepared to accept the notion that the world in general, and India in particular, is obliged to live with a state of affairs in Pakistan that incubates terror while the country's institutions remain either unable or unwilling to push back against the so-called non-state actors that are said to be out of the government's control. Events in Pakistan, including attacks on its own military headquarters and a naval base, may, we hope, have stiffened Pakistani resolve to confront these 'non-state actors'. But it remains to be seen whether some in Islamabad are still seduced by the dangerous idea that terrorists who attack the Pakistani military are bad, but those who attack India are to be tacitly encouraged.

Our government is committed to peaceful relations with Pakistan. Indeed, our prime minister personally—and therefore the highest levels of our government—has a vision of a subcontinent living in peace and prosperity, focusing on development, not distracted by hostility and violence. But we need to see evidence of good faith action from Islamabad before our prime minister, who is accountable to Parliament and a public opinion outraged by repeated acts of terror, can reciprocate in full measure.

For the past three years, under sustained American pressure, the Pakistani Army has begun, however selectively, to take on the challenge of fighting some terrorist groups—not the ones lovingly nurtured by the ISI to assault India, but the ones who have escaped the ISI leadership's control and turned on Pakistan's own military institutions. Indians, for the most part, feel a great deal of solidarity with the Pakistani people. It is striking that no one in any official position in India has, in any way, given vent to Schadenfreude, or implied that the violence assailing Pakistan itself is a case of Pakistani chickens coming home to roost.

But the unpalatable fact remains that what Pakistan is suffering from today is the direct result of a deliberate policy of inciting, financing, training and equipping militants and jihadis over twenty years as an instrument of state policy. As Dr Frankenstein discovered when he built his monster, it is impossible to control the monster once it's built.

Attempts by glibly sophisticated Pakistani spokesmen to portray themselves as fellow victims of terror—indeed, to go so far as to compare the number of deaths suffered by Pakistan in its war against terrorism on its own soil with those inflicted upon India—seek to obscure the fundamental difference between the two situations. Pakistanis are not suffering death and destruction from terrorists trained in India. No one travelled from India to attack the Marriott Hotel in Islamabad or the naval base at Mehran. Indians, however, have suffered death and destruction from terrorists trained in and dispatched from Pakistan with the complicity—and some might argue, more—of elements of the Pakistani security forces and establishment. Pakistan has to cauterize a cancer in its own midst, but a cancer that was implanted by itself and its own institutions. And this will only happen if they eliminate the warped thinking, among powerful elements in Islamabad, that a terrorist who sets off a bomb at the Marriott in Islamabad is a bad terrorist whereas one who sets off a bomb at the Taj in Mumbai is a good terrorist. The moment the Pakistani establishment genuinely disavows the nurturing and deployment of terror as an instrument of state policy, and concludes that it faces the same enemy as India and should make common cause with it to stamp out the scourge, is the moment that a genuine prospect of peace will dawn on the subcontinent. Such a sentiment is, alas, far from even glimmering on the horizon.

And yet India has doggedly pursued peace. Within six months of 26/11 the prime minister travelled to Sharm el Sheikh in Egypt to meet with the Pakistani prime minister, where his conciliatory language in the joint statement that followed got him into a huge amount of political hot water back home, because he was perceived as offering the hand of peace at a time when Pakistan had done nothing to merit it. In any democracy, there are always limits as to how far a government can go in advance of its own public opinion. Subsequent moves have been undertaken a little more gingerly, but 'cricket diplomacy' (the invitation to Pakistani Prime Minister Gilani to watch the World Cup semi-final between the two countries in Mohali, India), 'designer diplomacy' (the visit of the elegantly and expensively accoutred Pakistani Foreign Minister Hina Rabbani Khar to New Delhi, both in 2011) and 'dargah diplomacy' (a lunch invitation to President Zardari from Prime Minister Singh when the former sought to make a 'spiritual visit' to a Sufi shrine in Ajmer in April 2012) have all been attempted to take the process of dialogue, however haltingly, forward. The resultant thaw, while involving no substantive policy decisions, has demonstrated Prime Minister Manmohan Singh's determination to change the narrative of Indo-Pak relations, and seize control of a process mired in stalemate.

Some Indian critics are less than enthused. New Delhi had justifiably suspended talks with Islamabad after the horrific Mumbai attacks of 26/11. By talking again at such a high level, even though there has been no significant progress in Pakistan bringing the perpetrators to book, India, they feel, has in effect surrendered to Pakistani intransigence. The new wide-ranging and comprehensive talks agreed to by the two sides, the critics point out, are the old 'composite dialogue' under another label, the very dialogue New Delhi had righteously called off since there was no point talking to people whose territory and institutions were being used to attack and kill Indians.

The fear in India remains that the government has run out of ideas in dealing with Pakistan—or at least that New Delhi has no good options, between a counterproductive military attack on the sources of terrorism and a stagnant silence. Our position, first articulated by our prime minister in Parliament in 2009, is that we can have a meaningful dialogue with Pakistan only if they fulfil their commitment, in letter and spirit, not to allow their territory to be used in any manner for terrorist activities against India. And yet it is also clear that 'not talking' is not much of a policy. Pakistan can deny our shared history but India cannot change its geography. Pakistan is next door and can no more be ignored than a thorn pierced into India's side.

India's refusal to talk worked for a while as a source of pressure on Pakistan. It contributed, together with Western (especially American) diplomatic efforts, to some of Islamabad's initial cooperation, including the arrest of Lashkar-e-Taiba operative Zakiur Rahman Lakhvi and six of his co-conspirators. But it has long passed its use-by date. The refusal to resume dialogue has stopped producing any fresh results; the only argument that justifies it—that it is a source of leverage—gives some in India the illusion of influence over events that New Delhi does not in fact possess.

Instead, it was ironically India—the victims of 26/11—who had come to seem intransigent and unaccommodative, rather than Pakistan, from whose soil the terrorist attacks were dispatched, financed and directed.

The transcendent reality of life on the subcontinent is that it has always been India that wishes to live in peace. India is, at bottom, a status quo power that would like to be left alone to concentrate on its economic development; Indians see Pakistan as the troublesome rebel, needling and bleeding its neighbour in an effort to change the power balance and wrest control of a part of Indian territory (Kashmir). Refusing to talk doesn't change any of that, but it brought India no rewards and in fact imposed a cost. When Pakistan was allowed to sound reasonable and conciliatory while India seemed truculent and unreasonable, New Delhi's international image as a constructive force for peace took a beating.

The thaw engendered by the two prime ministers at the cricket World Cup in March 2011—meeting at a major sporting event, devoid of rancour, which Pakistan lost fair and square to the eventual world champions—recognized that talking can achieve constructive results. It can identify and narrow the differences between the two countries on those issues between them that can be addressed. As Prime Minister Singh has realized, just talking about them can make clear what India's bottom lines are and the minimal standards of civilized conduct India expects from its neighbour. And should it prove necessary, dialogue can also be used to send a few tough signals.

'Cricket diplomacy' is not new on the subcontinent. It was tried twice before, each time with Pakistani military rulers travelling to watch cricket in India. General Zia-ul-Haq's visit to a match in Jaipur in 1986 was an exercise in cynicism, since it was aimed at defusing tensions stoked by his own policy of fomenting and aiding Sikh militant secessionism in India. General Pervez Musharraf's visit to a cricket stadium in Delhi in 2005 came at a better time in the two countries' relations, but foreshadowed a decline in the progress the two nations were making up to that point. Watching cricket does not necessarily lead to improved dialogue (especially when the other side's wickets are falling). But when two countries are genuinely prepared to engage, a grand sporting occasion can be a useful instrument to signal the change. That is what the 'spirit of Mohali' has brought about. Talks have since resumed; but a year later, it is still too early to pronounce oneself definitively on whether and how that spirit is translating into genuine progress on the ground.

The argument against dialogue with Pakistan is strongly held and passionately argued by many I respect. And yet I believe these critics are wrong. Not just because, as I have explained above, it is clear that we *are* doing the right thing, but also because it is time the critics too understood that we *do* have other options.

We are doing the right thing, because to say that we will not talk as long as there is terror is essentially to give the terrorists a veto over our own diplomatic choices. For talking can achieve constructive results. It can identify and narrow the differences between our two countries on those issues that can be dealt with, while keeping the spirit of dialogue (and implicitly of compromise) alive. At the same time, what is needed is sustained pressure—especially through US military and intelligence sources upon their Pakistani counterparts—to rein in the merchants of terror.

And yet, the extent of possible US pressure remains constrained by Afghanistan. For a while after 26/11 I had hoped that this time the terrorists had gone too far. The murderers of Mumbai had, after all, made powerful enemies by killing American, French and Israeli citizens as well as Indian ones. While previous bomb blasts took only Indian lives, it was easier for the rest of the world to regard terrorism in India as an Indian problem. Mumbai, I reasoned, had internationalized the issue. As they dominated the world's media for three gruesome days, the killers achieved a startling success for their cause, one that must have shaken anti-terrorist experts around the world, who now realize how easy it would be for ten men unafraid of death to hold any city in the world hostage. After all, how many hotels, schools, airports, markets or cinema theatres can you turn into fortifications everywhere in the world? But they also ensured that India will no longer be alone in its efforts to stamp out this scourge.

Or so I thought. But it became clear soon enough that as long as the war in Afghanistan continued, the world needed Pakistan more than Pakistan needed the world—and Pakistan knew it.

Afghanistan is where the tyranny of geography gives Pakistan an indispensable role in fulfilling the logistics needs for tens of thousands of US soldiers, who must be supplied, rationed and redeployed through Pak territory. (In my UN peacekeeping days I was told, by a grizzled American officer, the adage that amateurs discuss strategy, rank amateurs focus on tactics and true professionals concentrate on logistics.) It is no accident that at one point in 2009 reports began to surface that the United States was developing an alternative route through Central Asia to supply its forces in Afghanistan; but the mere fact that we were reading about it in the newspapers suggested that it was still more an idea than a reality, and the news was meant to serve as an unsubtle warning to the Pakistani military that if they thought that logistics had given them a stranglehold on the United States' options, other options could still be developed. Bluntly, they haven't been; the Central Asian route is much more expensive and, though the overwhelming dependence on Pakistan has been reduced with a smaller percentage of NATO supplies coming through that country than before, Islamabad remains logistically indispensable.

There is little doubt that the increase in terrorist actions in Afghanistan is directly linked to the support and sanctuaries available in the contiguous areas of Pakistan. This is why the United States unveiled an 'Af-Pak' strategy in March 2009: there was no viable way of dealing with Afghanistan without taking into account the role and responsibilities of Pakistan in sustaining the conflict there.

Islamabad's objectives in Afghanistan have had nothing to do with the well-being of that war-torn land. It has ruthlessly undermined its neighbour's security and stability in an effort to establish that Afghanistan is little more than Pakistan's backyard, a place whose only importance lies in providing Pakistani GHQ with 'strategic depth' against India. This objective was impossible to realize for the first five decades after independence, when successive governments in Kabul enjoyed better relations with New Delhi than with their Pakistani neighbours. It was only the creation (by Benazir Bhutto's government in the mid-1990s) of the Taliban and its ascent to power in Afghanistan that finally gave Pakistan a Kabul regime that functioned as a wholly owned subsidiary of the Rawalpindi military establishment. It didn't last long enough for Pakistan: 9/11, and the obligation to choose between a powerful and wealthy patron in the United States and an irresponsible and reviled client in Kabul, obliged Islamabad reluctantly to jettison its Afghan asset.

But Islamabad does not give up easily. Even while ostensibly allied to the United States in its Afghan war effort, Pakistan preserved its links with several of the extremist elements it had nurtured in Afghanistan, provided refuge to Mullah Omar and his ilk in Quetta, and—as we learned belatedly in 2011—shielded Osama bin Laden and his inner circle in the Pakistani garrison town of Abbottabad. (More recently we have learned that the prolific bin Laden lived, procreated and raised children in Peshawar, Swat and Haripur as well.) The strategy made sense to the devious minds in Rawalpindi: the Americans were bound to tire of their Afghan engagement one day, and when they left Pakistan would need to have the resources and assets in place to reassert the primacy they had enjoyed in Afghanistan before 9/11. The appearance of cooperation in fighting terror was essential to continue receiving generous American military aid, most of which could be used to shore up the Pakistani Army's overall strengths against India, but the fight had to be carefully waged only against select enemies, while shielding those terrorists who could be counted upon to serve Pakistan's interests in the longer term. (As the Pakistani journalist Ahmed Rashid puts it, the Pakistani Army 'seeks to ensure that a balance of terror and power is maintained with respect to India, and the jihadis are seen as part of this strategy'.) The Pakistani military also understood the importance of seeming to look for bin Laden but never finding him, and appearing to fight the 'war on terror' but never actually winning it, in order to maintain the continuing flow of American money for the very purposes its beneficiaries were seeking to subvert.

But while US pressure on Pakistan to end this duplicity is vital, it is not enough. International pressure will require serious attention to China's and Saudi Arabia's roles as allies of Pakistan, both bilaterally (as munificent donors of aid) and in multilateral institutions (notably the UN Security Council and the Organization of the Islamic Conference, respectively). China and Saudi Arabia have the capacity to reinforce the pressure on Pakistan or to provide Islamabad an escape valve from it; on the whole, it is not clear at this stage which way they will incline. China's importance to Pakistan is increasing with the gradual American disengagement from Pakistan, and what Beijing calls its 'all-weather friendship' shields Pakistan against the negative global fallout from its anti-Indian actions. Nonetheless China is concerned about encouragement given to Islamic militancy in its own western provinces by elements on Pakistani soil, which offers India a point of mutual interest. Engaging China thus becomes indispensable, even if its direct benefits might be minor, given China's own strategic interest in supporting Pakistan to balance India.

Saudi Arabia's indispensability to Pakistan comes from its financial assistance as well as its role as the custodian of global Islamic legitimacy. The Saudis have shown in recent years a desire to engage with India, not at the expense of Pakistan, but as a recognition of our country's international value in its own right. Giving the Saudi–Indian dialogue a security dimension is necessary for both sides, but particularly for an India that needs to sensitize its Saudi interlocutors to the threats and opportunities emerging from Pakistan. Going beyond Saudi Arabia, the role of international aid for development should not be underestimated, since Pakistan's economy is virtually bankrupt. This could mean that the influence of the United States in the IMF, and the European Union in providing development assistance, could prove considerable, should it be exercised in the direction of promoting more responsible conduct by the Pakistani state. This is more than a pious hope: as David Malone puts it, 'Pakistan's weapons suppliers and financiers are hard to sideline, their intelligence findings hard to duck, and the incentives—positive and negative—that they can offer [could prove] impossible for Pakistan to ignore.'

In other words, the world is not bereft of options; we do not have to reconcile ourselves to slipping back to business as usual in Pakistan. For the fact is that, on Pakistan's reluctance to take decisive action against the terrorism operating on its soil, we do have some credible options. The most significant of these lies in the United Nations, whose Security Council resolutions against terror were adopted under Chapter VII of the UN Charter and are binding on all member states, including Pakistan. The UN has established thirteen international conventions against terror, but years of negotiations on a draft pushed by India and the United States to adopt a comprehensive convention on terrorism have foundered on the objections of Islamic states, which have wanted to include strictures against 'state terrorism' and exemptions for 'national liberation movements'.

However, legal instruments are of limited utility against those who have contempt for international law. More effective could be two mechanisms created by the Security Council. One, the Sanctions Committee established under resolution 1267, has already been pressed into service in December 2008 to proscribe Jamaat-ud-Dawa, with scant impact on Pakistan. The other is resolution 1373, adopted immediately after 9/11, which imposes, under Chapter VII of the UN Charter (which governs enforcement measures), binding requirements on all member states to take a whole range of actions against suspected terror organizations. These include freezing financial transfers and interdicting arms supplies, reporting on the movements of suspected terrorists and upgrading national legislation to bring it into conformity with international requirements. In the event of continued inaction by Islamabad, the possibility of moving the Security Council to hold Pakistan in breach of resolution 1373, and threatening sanctions against the Pakistani state if compliance does not follow, is well worth pursuing. (It might even prompt someone in Pakistan to encash the $10 million reward the US is offering for the arrest of Hafeez Saeed.)

These resolutions require compliance from all states on controlling the activities of terrorists. Member states are required under resolution 1373 to report regularly to the Counter-Terrorism Committee about their actions to bring their national legislation into conformity with international requirements, to monitor the movements of suspected terrorists, arms transfers and financial flows to terrorist organizations. Resolution 1624 obliges states to pass laws forbidding incitement to commit acts of terror and to report such incitement to the committee. As it happens, since 1 January 2011, it is India that chairs the Counter-Terrorism Committee, for two years. The possibilities of using more fully the mechanisms afforded by the United Nations remain to be explored.

New Delhi could make it plain to Islamabad that, unless there is genuine and sustained cooperation on bringing the 26/11 plotters to book, we will not hesitate to use the international mechanisms available to us to ask Pakistan awkward questions, and to bring the weight of the international community to bear on the issue of Pakistan's failure to meet its international obligations. There are fair questions to be asked about the prosecution of suspected terrorists under custody and the lack of efforts to apprehend their remaining comrades; the failure to take any steps whatsoever to trace the handlers of the 26/11 killers, especially the chilling voice recorded on tape that exhorted the terrorists to kill their hostages; the open incitement to terror preached by the likes of Hafiz Saeed in open defiance of resolution 1624; and the survival, indeed flourishing, on Pakistani soil of proscribed organizations like the Jamaat-ud-Dawa, with burgeoning bank accounts receiving and disbursing funds. Should the answers not prove satisfactory, the next step to consider would be whether to hold Pakistan in non-compliance with the relevant Security Council resolutions, which in turn would lay the ground for selective sanctions—for example on the foreign travel of specific military leaders—in a bid to exact compliance.

Many fear that, if after a few token moves Pakistan lets things return to normal, the world may be forced to admit its own impotence. But we should not be too quick to surrender in the face of the continued intransigence of the killers of innocent civilians. The threat of sanctions could specifically target the Pakistani military, including a ban on the sale of weapons and the provision of any further military assistance to it. The UN could also be required to exclude the Pakistani Army from future peacekeeping operations, a vital source of both prestige and lucre for Islamabad's military. The world is far from running out of ideas to bring Pakistan's errant generals to heel.

Of course, such an approach should only be pursued when India judges that there is no prospect of voluntary compliance by Pakistan with the minimum desiderata for peaceful relations on the subcontinent. As these words are written, in early 2012, the atmosphere between the two countries is warming, and there is hope that resort to the drastic measures suggested above may not be necessary.

But if the pressure is not maintained, and if Pakistan is allowed to believe that, with the passage of time, Mumbai will have been forgotten and Islamabad will be off the hook, the consequences would be calamitous, not just for India but also for the world. It would have a chilling result: as long as a military-dominated Pakistan continues, willingly or helplessly, to harbour the perpetrators of Islamist terror, what happened in Mumbai could happen again. Next time, it could be somewhere else.

Of course, exercising the UN option will not be easy. It will require the cooperation of other countries, many of which have shown a propensity to look the other way as Pakistan has misbehaved on terrorism, and it will require us to expend a great deal of diplomatic energy to assemble the necessary majority on the Counter-Terrorism Committee. But the option exists; and if we do not wish to allow Pakistan to believe it can get away with whatever it wishes, and to act as if it can shrug off its complicity in the 26/11 attacks with impunity, we need to remind them that the option exists. A truly comprehensive dialogue is one place where we can make that message clear.

So yes, by all means, let us talk to Pakistan. It is what we say when we talk that will make all the difference.

———

Pursuing Pakistan at the United Nations may seem a drastic step to propose. But what is dismaying is that all India has asked for from Pakistan is two very simple things: to take action to bring the perpetrators of 26/11 to justice and to take steps to dismantle the infrastructure of terror built up over the last twenty years, from which so many attacks have been launched on our country. This would involve closing down the training camps, genuinely banning these organizations (and not just letting them reinvent themselves under other labels, of which the Arabic language seems to offer an inexhaustible profusion), really closing their bank accounts (again, instead of letting them be reopened under other names) and arresting known inciters of hatred and violence like Hafiz Muhammad Saeed. If these things are done, as Prime Minister Singh said in Parliament—which, in a political system like India's, is tantamount to a sacred oath—we will meet them more than halfway. But that first step has not been forthcoming.

The irony is that, as long as Manmohan Singh remains in office, Pakistan has in New Delhi the most peace-minded Indian prime minister that Islamabad could ever hope for. And yet they have failed to give him enough for him to be able to move forward, and march, as he manifestly wishes to, in the direction of amity. Instead, India has been faced with the extraordinary acquittal of Hafiz Muhammad Saeed, the result of a very feeble case mounted by the reluctant government in Islamabad, with the judge concluding that the UN Security Council's banning of

Jamaat-ud-Dawa has no validity in Pakistan, and that therefore its leader is free, because the organization is not banned. For a high court in a United Nations member state to cock a snook when the Security Council proscribes an organization that is guilty of terrorist actions, and for the Pakistani legal system, apparently with no particular countervailing pressure from the civilian government, to say, in effect, that Pakistan doesn't really take this requirement very seriously, is mind-boggling.

The two countries even had a bilateral agreement before 26/11, which established a joint working group on terrorism, meant to be a mechanism for information sharing. Not one useful piece of information came India's way on that joint working group. The terrorists came from the other side of the border, but not the information. India's experience merely confirmed that such mechanisms will only work where there is genuine goodwill, where there is no mistrust, where there is a basic understanding and cooperation. Where those ingredients are missing, it becomes impossible for Indians of good faith to rely on a duplicitous Pakistan.

This is why I fear there is as yet no substitute for exacting compliance with the existing international requirements. Security Council resolution 1373 is a very good example. It has very specific requirements—freezing financial transfers, intercepting arms flows, reporting on the movements of suspected terrorists. India has been very proud of the fact that it has been in full compliance with the resolution's requirements, and it has submitted complete reports to the Counter-Terrorism Committee. How can the world say that one country, Pakistan, will get a free pass on these obligations, and then be taken seriously?

Pakistan's defiance is partially based on the confidence engendered by its nuclear deterrent capability. This confidence could prove negative in its effects, prompting its military brass to launch a Kargil infiltration, dispatch terrorists to conduct strikes in India, or cock a snook at the international community, all of which it has indeed done already. But the same confidence could easily be used to more constructive ends: by telling themselves that as a nuclear power they have much less to fear from other nations, Pakistan could be emboldened to take positive steps towards peace, secure in the knowledge that they could not be coerced into conceding any vital national interest.

There is no doubt that a climate of peace can only be built on a foundation of trust, unimpeded by the use or the threat to use terror as a means to achieving narrow ends. British Prime Minister David Cameron recently reminded Pakistan that it could not win the respect of the world so long as it condoned the export of terror to India. To acknowledge that trust does not exist right now, however, is not to suggest that trust can never be built.

The differences that bedevil our relations with Pakistan can be surmounted if we can arrive at mutually acceptable parameters that can define our relationship in the future. Terrorism is certainly not one of those parameters. The Mumbai terrorist attack in November 2008 was a great setback on the path of normalization. Only credible action by Islamabad will instil a modicum of confidence in the people of India that dialogue is worthwhile and that our neighbours are as determined as us to give peace a chance. If such action is taken—for instance, against individuals and organizations known to be fomenting violence against India—the basis for building trust again can be laid. Until that is done, though, projects like the proposed Iran–Pakistan–India gas pipeline will never materialize, not so much because of US pressure on India to reject Iran's involvement as the understandable reluctance of Indians to place any significant element of their energy security in the hands of Pakistan, through whose tender mercies the pipeline would have to run.

The composite dialogue process between the two countries was launched in January 2004, following the commitment made by Pakistan at that time that it would not permit territory under its control to be used to support terrorism against India in any manner. The dialogue covered eight subjects: peace and security, including confidence-building measures; Jammu and Kashmir; terrorism and drug trafficking; friendly exchanges; economic and commercial cooperation; the Wullar barrage/Tulbul navigation project; Sir Creek; and Siachen. That six-year-old commitment by Pakistan lay in shreds after the overwhelming evidence of the involvement of elements in Pakistan in executing the Mumbai terror attack of November 2008, and in the conspiracy that planned, funded and launched it, coupled with an increase in ceasefire violations, continued infiltration across the LoC and the attacks on the Indian embassy in Kabul in July 2008 and October 2009, as well as the murderous assault in early

2010 on a residence housing Indian aid workers. Given the immense strain all this has placed on India–Pakistan relations in general and on the dialogue process in particular, it took a great deal of courage and statesmanship for the Indian leadership to resume the dialogue process. Though progress has been slow, the fact that it is happening at all is of momentous significance—but the incidents enumerated above point to the very fragility of the peace process, since so much is stacked against it.

It is worth recalling that the two countries have in fact come to agreement since the late 1980s on a number of issues. These have included such difficult and sensitive challenges as the protection of nuclear facilities, the inauguration of bus services between Indian and Pakistani cities, illegal immigration and the exchange of prisoners, and the establishment of trading routes and entry points to each other's territories. There have also been extensive discussions, both formal and through a 'back channel', as well as in the form of Track-II discussions featuring prominent parliamentarians, scholars, retired officials and commentators, between the two countries. However, the lack of trust between the governments and an aversion to taking political risk on both sides have meant that these have not culminated in agreements, even though the sensitive Kashmir issue has been discussed threadbare in all these processes.

Pakistan's evasive responses and denials in response to India's requests for cooperation in exposing the conspiracy behind the Mumbai terror attack and bringing all its perpetrators to justice had led to a sadly evident deterioration in bilateral relations. While India has gingerly resumed contact at various levels with Pakistan, a sustained and intense peace process requires a demonstration by Pakistan of a change of heart—and, more important, of a political will for peace. Of this there has been little evidence in recent years—quite the contrary. The inability or unwillingness of the Pakistani government to prevent its soil from being used to mount attacks on another state seriously undermines its own sovereignty, not just its credibility. The result is the slightly absurd phenomenon of the victims' government wanting to talk to the perpetrators' government, while the latter consistently fails to give the former anything to enable it politically to explain to its own voters why we are doing the talking.

———

The lack of political will within the Pakistani establishment to take firm action against terrorists is not hard to explain. One possible explanation is the sinister one, that those in power are happy to allow the terrorists to run free and wild, as long as they are only threatening India. Unleashing terrorism on India has long been seen by elements in Islamabad as a strategy that combines the merits of being inexpensive, low risk and effective, while doing enough damage to throw the adversary repeatedly off-balance. And should India be tempted to respond in kind to the repeated bleeding of its citizenry by Pakistani groups and their proxies, there is always the threat of a nuclear conflagration to bring the rest of the world's pressure on India to absorb the pain rather than retaliate militarily.

The more charitable explanation is that the rulers of Pakistan do not feel able to challenge militant groups and their leaders because they have become too popular with a radicalized and pro-Islamist populace, and so they fear that the political price to be paid domestically for opposing the terrorists would be too high. While India would love to see a Pakistani government that is determined to translate into concrete action the friendly sentiments repeatedly expressed by leaders like President Zardari, New Delhi has seen far too much evidence of a gap between profession and practice—and also of the vast gulf between what Pakistanis say to Indians in private and what they consider politically expedient to utter in Pakistan in public.

The media on both sides has also contributed to the atmosphere of confrontation between the two states. Television is a particular culprit. Though Indians tend to blame the Pakistani channels for consistently spewing venom against India and providing a platform to those who do, the standards may first have been lowered in India. A Pakistani television executive, Fahad Hussain, who has launched more than one channel in his country and studied India's media operations before doing so, put it bluntly to me: 'The reason we are hawkishly anti-India,' he said, 'is that we know it sells, and guess who taught us that.' He added, 'I launched channels that love to bash India because Indian media has taught us that being popular is more important than being responsible.' He went on to suggest that Pakistani politicians who are inclined to promote peace with India are circumvented by the hostility of the media, which restricts their options. This may be a somewhat cynical view, but it has a strong kernel of candour that obliges us to take it seriously.

The hardening of public opinion on both sides is undoubtedly a factor in the dismal state of the relations between India and Pakistan. In Pakistan, at least, the media has gone from reflecting attitudes to shaping them in a manner that has made it a significant obstacle to peace. The print media, especially in Urdu, is not much better. Despite the 'Aman ki Asha' (Wish for Peace) campaign conducted by two newspaper chains (one in each country) the very same publications carry far more negative articles about the other country than they do the positive ones under the 'Aman ki Asha' rubric. Textbooks in Pakistan, which since the days of Zulfikar Ali Bhutto speak of a '5000 year war with India', also contribute to the general attitude of hostility in the country to the neighbour to which it was once conjoined. Ordinary members of the Pakistani public may be prepared to live in peace with Indians, but the hatred being instilled in them from a variety of public platforms will need to be overcome if peace is to have a chance.

———

The contradiction between private attitudes and public posturing was readily apparent in the life and career of Benazir Bhutto of the Pakistan People's Party, whose assassination in late 2007 saw the international press posthumously conferring sainthood on the telegenic politician. But the widely expressed view that Benazir epitomized Pakistan's hopes for democracy and peace with India seriously overstates both what she represented and the implications of her demise.

The principal consequence of Benazir Bhutto's death was the setback it has dealt to the US-inspired plan to anoint her as the acceptable civilian face of continuing Musharraf rule. The calculations were clear: Musharraf was a valuable ally of the West against the Islamist threat in the region, but his continuing indefinitely to rule Pakistan as a military dictator was becoming an embarrassment. The former Chief Martial Law Administrator had to doff his uniform—long overdue, since he was three years past the retirement age for any general—and find a credible civilian partner to help make a plausible case for democratization. Benazir—well spoken, well networked in Washington and London, and passionate in her avowals of secular moderation, however self-serving—was the chosen one.

The other exiled civilian ex-prime minister, Nawaz Sharif, was none of these things and, having been the victim of General Musharraf's coup, was considerably less inclined to cooperate with his defenestrator. So Nawaz was returned to exile in Saudi Arabia when he attempted to come home and, when that ploy did not work (the Saudis having no particular desire to take Benazir's side over his), was disqualified from running for office on the risible grounds that his attempts as an elected prime minister to prevent a coup against himself amounted to hijacking and terrorism. This left the field free for Benazir to do sufficiently well in the elections to become prime minister of Pakistan for a third time.

Her first two stints had, however, been inglorious. From 1988 to 1990 she had been overawed by the military, whose appointed president duly dismissed her from office on plausible charges of corruption, mainly involving her husband, Asif Ali Zardari, who had acquired the nickname 'Mr Ten Percent'. Her second innings (1993–96) was, if anything, worse: charges of rampant peculation (and administrative adhockery) mounted, even as her avowedly moderate government orchestrated the creation of the Taliban in neighbouring Afghanistan. This time it was a president of Pakistan from her own party who felt obliged to dismiss her. To assume that a third stint would have been any different requires a leap of faith explicable only by the mounting international anxiety over Musharraf's fraying rule.

But Benazir's true merit lay in the absence of plausible alternatives. She was no great democrat—as her will, appointing her husband and nineteen-year-old son to inherit her party, confirms. The Bhuttoist ethos is a uniquely Pakistani combination of aristocratic feudalism and secular populism. To her, democracy was a means to power, not a philosophy of politics. But the same was true of the other contenders in Pakistan's political space—the conservative Punjabi bourgeoisie represented by Nawaz Sharif, the moderate pro-militarists grouped around Musharraf, the deeply intolerant Islamists and the assorted regionalist and sectarian parties whose appeal is limited to specific provinces. Musharraf knew that all that elections would ensure was a temporary rearrangement of the balance of forces among these diverse elements. But it would enable him to remain in charge as a 'civilian' president while portraying his Pakistan—more credibly than heretofore—as the last bastion of democratic moderation in the face of the Islamist menace. When this hope collapsed and Musharraf went into exile, the ascent of Benazir's widower, Asif Ali Zardari, to the presidency meant that a civilian of dubious repute—and one with very little ability to resist the entrenched power of the military behind the scenes—had now to assume this mantle.

Democrats in India may well believe that the Pakistani people deserve better, but it is difficult to imagine a viable alternative to military rule, cloaked to a greater or lesser degree in civilian raiment. As explained earlier, the central fact of Pakistani politics has always been the power of the military, which has ruled the country directly for thirty-two of its sixty-four years of existence and indirectly the other half of the time. The military can be found not only in all the key offices of government, but running real-estate and import–export ventures, petrol pumps and factories; retired generals head most of the country's universities and think tanks. The proportion of national resources devoted to the military is by far the highest in the world. Every once in a while a great surge of disillusionment with the generals pours out into the streets and a 'democratic' leader is voted into office, but the civilian experiment always ends badly, and the military returns to power, to general relief. The British political scientist W.H. Morris-Jones once famously observed that the only political institutions in Pakistan are the coup and the mob. Neither offers propitious grounds for believing that an enduring democracy is around the corner.

The elections that created Pakistan's current civilian government saw Benazir's party benefiting from a sympathy vote after her killing, but in the absence of a charismatic leader, it was inevitably obliged to come to an accommodation with the generals. Despite widespread anger at Musharraf's failure to protect Benazir, his successor, General Kayani, determines how far the civilian government can go on all the issues that matter to the country, and his personal authority has been confirmed by a three-year extension of his tenure beyond the scheduled retirement age. Kayani, a former head of the ISI, knows how useful the Islamist militants are to his military goals, but he is also conscious that his men have lost control of many of the more wild-eyed elements they had previously encouraged and funded. The result is a particularly delicate version of running with the hare and hunting with the hounds. The Islamists, who have never won more than 10 per cent of the popular vote nationally, fared even worse electorally in the aftermath of Benazir's killing; most people assume her killers were religious fundamentalists. The Islamist sympathizers in the Pakistani military, of whom there are many in key positions (notably in the ISI), are also on the defensive in the face of popular fury at Benazir's murder and the assaults on Pakistani military installations (IGHQ Rawalpindi and the naval base in Mehran, near Karachi) by Islamist fundamentalists. The great danger in Pakistan has always lain in the risk of a mullah–military coalition. The death of Benazir and the events in its aftermath have made that less likely for now, and that may remain her most significant legacy.

———

International affairs all too often seems a weighty subject, full of complexity and nuance, laden with portents of tension and conflict. No wonder it lends itself to overly solemn treatment, full of abstract analyses and obscure allusions: the relations between countries, it is usually assumed, cannot be understood through the recitation of trivial anecdotes.

True enough. And yet sometimes a minor incident, a tempest in a teacup, can illuminate broader foreign policy challenges. Something of this nature happened in the hot summer of 2011, when Aatish Taseer, the estranged son (by an Indian mother) of the assassinated Governor of Pakistani Punjab Salman Taseer, wrote a searing column in the *Wall Street Journal*, with the provocative title 'Why My Father Hated India', on the pathologies of hatred that in his view animated Pakistan's attitude to our country.

'To understand the Pakistani obsession with India, to get a sense of its special edge—its hysteria—it is necessary to understand the rejection of India, its culture and past, that lies at the heart of the idea of Pakistan,' Aatish Taseer averred. 'This is not merely an academic question. Pakistan's animus toward India is the cause of both its unwillingness to fight Islamic extremism and its active complicity in undermining the aims of its ostensible ally, the United States.'

He went on to make his point in language that was sharp and, at least to this reader, heartfelt and accurate. I do not know Aatish Taseer, nor had I met his colourful father, but I have admired the young man's writing, particularly his poignant ruminations on Salman Taseer's murder by his Islamist bodyguard earlier this year. So I was surprised to see the outraged reactions his article provoked from Pakistani liberal journalists. A number of them whose ideas I have appreciated and whom I 'follow' on the social networking site Twitter—the likes of Marvi Sirmed and Mosharraf Zaidi, widely respected progressive thinkers both—reacted with rage and derision. One of them, the estimable Ejaz Haider, who has penned some courageous pieces in the Pakistani press criticizing his own country and some morally deplorable ones defending Hafiz Saeed, went so far as to author an entire column to disparage and deconstruct Aatish Taseer's.

Young Taseer had, in his piece, put the onus on the Pakistani Army for that country's problems, and particularly for diverting the vast amounts of American aid it has received (he underestimated it at '$11 billion since 9/11') to arming itself against India. He added, powerfully, words I would have gladly put my own name to: 'In Afghanistan, it has sought neither security nor stability but rather a backyard, which—once the Americans leave—might provide Pakistan with "strategic depth" against India. In order to realize these objectives, the Pakistani army has led the U.S. in a dance, in which it had to be seen to be fighting the war on terror, but never so much as to actually win it, for its extension meant the continuing flow of American money. All this time the army kept alive a double game, in which some terror was fought and some—such as Laskhar-e-Tayyba's 2008 attack on Mumbai—actively supported.

'The army's duplicity was exposed decisively this May,' he went on, 'with the killing of Osama bin Laden in the garrison town of Abbottabad. It was only the last and most incriminating charge against an institution whose activities over the years have included the creation of the Taliban, the financing of international terrorism and the running of a lucrative trade in nuclear secrets. This army, whose might has always been justified by the imaginary threat from India, has been more harmful to Pakistan than to anybody else. It has consumed annually a quarter of the country's wealth, undermined one civilian government after another and enriched itself through a range of economic interests, from bakeries and shopping malls to huge property holdings.'

It is hard to imagine anyone in India, however sympathetic they might be to Pakistan, dissenting from this view of the malign role of the Pakistani military. In our naivety, we also tend to assume that Pakistani liberals would agree with us, seeing the salvation of their land lying in greater democracy and development, free of the stranglehold of the world's most lopsidedly funded military. Alas, judging by their reactions to Taseer's article, this seemed not to be the case.

In his rebuttal, Ejaz Haider went into great detail about the strength and deployment patterns of the Indian Army, as if to justify the Pakistani military's behaviour. But there was no recognition whatsoever that India's defence preparedness is prompted entirely by the fact that Pakistan has launched four incursions into our territory, in 1947, 1965, 1971 and 1999; that India is a status quo power that manifestly seeks nothing more than to be allowed to grow and develop in peace, free from the attentions of the Pakistani military and the militants and terrorists its sponsors; and, bluntly, that there is not and cannot be an 'Indian threat' to Pakistan, simply because India wants nothing from Pakistan except peace.

No, as I have already argued, the 'Indian threat' is merely a useful device cynically exploited by the Pakistani military to justify their power and pelf. But Pakistani liberals are particularly prone to the desire to prove themselves true nationalists; it is the best way to ensure that their otherwise heretical opinions are not completely discredited by the men in uniform who hold the reins of power in the state.

In a newspaper column, therefore, I wrote that this otherwise minor editorial spat had demonstrated to me that Indians needed to put aside our illusions that there are many liberal partners for us on the other side of the border who echo our diagnosis of their plight and share our desire to defenestrate their military. Nor, I added, should we be surprised: a Pakistani liberal is, after all, a Pakistani before he is a liberal.

This column provoked howls of even greater outrage across the border than young Taseer's original effort had. (It didn't help that an Indian headline writer had chosen to title it 'Delusional Liberals', which raised additional hackles among those in Pakistan who felt the noun, but not the adjective, applied to them.) The reactions, both in print and even more angrily in social media forums, were sharp. Inevitably, I was subjected to the usual bouts of invective and abuse that have so cheapened discourse in the age of the Internet, where the refuge provided by anonymity has encouraged a level of vileness that few would permit themselves to express face-to-face. But those need not detain us here. Far more interesting and worthy of attention were three columns in the mainstream Pakistani media responding to mine. By broadening and deepening the terms of the debate beyond the Taseer piece, they made my original column worth writing.

The tenor of the three articles (none of whose authors I had met by then or known personally) varied. The most liberal of the trio, Marvi Sirmed, in her column in the *Daily Times*, began by clarifying that she had actually no disagreement with the central thesis of Aatish Taseer's article (on the various misdeeds of the Pakistani military establishment), but had rejected the author's assertion that his father, Salman Taseer, the late Governor of Pakistani Punjab, 'hated' India. She also objected to Aatish's claim that Pakistan was the 'dream of a poet' (Muhammad Iqbal, who first wrote of a Muslim homeland within India), though this was not an issue I had dwelt on in my own piece. And she ended with two impressive points I had no difficulty acknowledging: that I should be more conscious of the diversity of the Pakistani liberal community, and that Ms Sirmed saw herself as a proud Pakistani whose love of her country did not oblige her to hate India. Marvi Sirmed is the kind of intelligent, broad-minded Pakistani most Indians would have no difficulty engaging with, and I tipped my (metaphorical) Gandhi cap to her.

Ejaz Haider, whose riposte to Aatish Taseer had sparked my initial piece, was less accommodating of my core argument, seeing it as an exercise in 'considered perception-formation and reinforcement'. By this he seemed to imply that my article was part of a devious Indian conspiracy to affect perceptions of his country negatively; in fact he titled his column 'It's Not Just Mr. Tharoor!' My fellow conspirators (on the basis of recent articles we had each written) apparently included young Taseer, the Mumbai-born American strategist Ashley Tellis and the Indian analyst Nitin Pai, who has suggested (as I have done separately) that the United States should end its overgenerous aid to Pakistan's military–jihadi complex. Ejaz Haider then proceeds to put words in our collective mouths to the tune that we seek 'India's supremacy in the region' and the resolution of disputes only 'on India's terms'. None of us has made so fatuous a suggestion, but the exaggeration was, alas, necessary to demolish our case.

Then Ejaz Haider (who, it must be said, is one of Pakistan's finest columnists, and whom I have enjoyed reading for years) got on to firmer ground. He admitted that there is a military–civilian divide in Pakistan, but argued that most of his country's conflicts with India have originated under, or at the instigation of, civilian politicians, not military rulers. In any case, this is 'Pakistan's internal matter' and acknowledging it should not imply any neglect of national security or abdication of Pakistani self-interest. And the clincher: 'we don't need advice from across the border' (especially, he adds gratuitously, from pundits who 'crawled on their bellies' during the Emergency, a charge from which all those he was responding to are in fact exempt).

Ejaz Haider was joined in the pages of Pakistan's *Express Tribune* by Feisal Naqvi, who found my arguments 'cretinous in the extreme' and 'gratuitously smug about India's lack of strategic ambitions'. Invective aside, Naqvi's argument was that while Pakistanis were obsessed with India, 'the opposite of India-obsessed is not India-submissive' (which, again putting words into my mouth, I allegedly want them to be). Mr Naqvi also finds, somewhere between the lines of my column, something I never wrote—a rejection of the very legitimacy of Pakistan's existence. Pakistani liberals, he asserts, are happy being Pakistani, value their military and have no desire to dismantle it. My article instead 'delegitimizes' them in the eyes of the Pakistani establishment. (Sigh.)

What was particularly interesting about these well-written responses is that they relied principally on refuting arguments I haven't made. I am totally reconciled to Pakistan's existence as an independent state, and have no desire to reintegrate it into a pre-Partition 'Akhand Bharat'—indeed, the demographic, social and political evolution of Pakistan since 1947 makes it quite unsuitable for any such reabsorption. I do understand that Pakistan has to survive in a tough neighbourhood and it needs a capable military. And I do not expect any Pakistani government, military or civilian, to act in anything but Pakistan's own best interest.

But—and alas, there is a but—I don't believe it is in Pakistan's best interest to be the country whose armed forces consume the largest percentage of national income of any military in the world. I don't believe it is in Pakistan's best interest to adopt a policy of seeking 'strategic depth' by destabilizing its neighbours. I don't believe it is in Pakistan's best interest to try to wrest Kashmir from India by fair means or foul. I don't believe it is in Pakistan's best interest to be the cradle and crucible of militant Islamist terrorism. I don't believe it is in Pakistan's best interest to be a country where no elected civilian government has ever served a full term. And I do believe that any Pakistani liberal worth the name (take a bow, Marvi Sirmed) should have no difficulty in agreeing with any of these propositions.

Even if they come from an Indian. Ay, there's the rub . . .

The same problem surfaced, in different guise, a few weeks later, when New Delhi played host to a visiting delegation of Pakistani parliamentarians, brought to India by an enterprising Islamabad NGO called PILDAT (Pakistan Institute of Legislative Development and Transparency). Few things in international affairs are more agreeable, all round, than the non-official dialogues diplomats refer to as 'Track-II'. But for all its non-official character, this was a high-powered delegation, including a vice-chairman of the Pakistani Senate, a deputy speaker, former ministers and a serving information secretary of the ruling party. On India's side of the parliamentary border, the meeting was co-chaired, in a commendably bipartisan spirit, by a former Congress party minister, Mani Shankar Aiyar, and the Bharatiya Janata Party's last foreign minister, Yashwant Sinha. I was, without quite intending to be it, the only dissident.

Don't get me wrong: I'm all in favour of Indo-Pak peace and bonhomie. I've seen a lot of it in my decades abroad—many is the time a Pakistani cab driver in New York has attempted to decline my money for the fare, saying that I was a brother (this of course always won him a bigger tip, but the spirit was genuine). Indians and Pakistanis overseas are almost always the best of friends, since being in foreign lands enhances their consciousness of what they have in common, which vastly exceeds what divides them. I would love to see a time when Pakistanis and Indians can cross each other's borders with the insouciance of Americans and Canadians, work in each other's countries, trade freely with each other and contribute equally to each other's films, music, clothing and creative lives, just as they did before 1947. I would be happy if that time came sooner rather than later. But, sadly, I am only too aware that it's not now.

The problem with Indo-Pak Track-II dialogues of the kind I witnessed in the capital is that they are essentially built on denial. They focus on making the visitors feel welcome, emphasize the feel-good aspects of their presence in our midst, celebrate the many things we have in common and try to brush the real problems under a carpet (not a Kashmiri carpet, since that might provoke disagreeable thoughts). In other words, they are a self-fulfilling exercise in self-vindication. Their success depends on denying the very disagreements that makes such dialogues necessary in the first place.

The event began with a somewhat odd opening panel discussion, where members of the audience rounded on the moderator, News X's Jehangir Pocha, for moderately raising some real questions, when his job had apparently been intended to be to orchestrate a paean of pious homilies to peace and brotherhood. So when I took the floor late in the next morning's session, I had been fairly warned. But after listening to several bromides from parliamentarians of both nationalities, I felt a dose of candour was necessary. So I pointed out that there were some genuine obstacles to be overcome if the peace and love we were all affirming was in fact to take root, rather than briefly blossom in the illusory sunshine of Track II. And those obstacles all lay in Pakistan.

First, India has long been in favour of placing the Kashmir dispute on the back burner and promoting trade, travel and the rest; it is Pakistan that has taken the view that there cannot be normal relations with India until Kashmir is settled, on terms acceptable to Islamabad. So inasmuch as there is hostility that such dialogues attempt to overcome, the hostility starts with Pakistan, which wants a change in the territorial status quo, and not with India, which is perfectly content to leave things as they are. Unless the Pakistani MPs present were willing to advocate a policy of across-the-board engagement with India despite the lack of a solution to the Kashmir dispute, our words would be just so much hot air.

One example of this asymmetry is that India had given Pakistan most favoured nation (MFN) trading status as far back as 1995, and Pakistan has still not reciprocated. It remains the only example on the entire planet of a one-sided MFN; no other country has ever refused to reciprocate an offer of MFN trading status from a neighbour. (In 2011, Pakistan announced it would finally extend MFN status to India, but the enabling legislation and the necessary regulations were yet to be written twelve months after the announcement.) India continues to show its good faith time after time, persisting in the peace talks even after the Kabul embassy bombing, offering aid after natural disasters in Pakistan (in one egregious instance, aid of $25 million offered by India in the wake of severe floods in Pakistan was initially rejected by Islamabad, which finally, grudgingly said it would be glad to have the money if given through the United Nations rather than directly). In the summer of 2009, when the country was still in a boil over the prime minister's visit to Sharm el Sheikh, the Indian team played the Pakistani team at a charity cricket match in England, with the proceeds going to the relief of displaced people from Swat in Pakistan—every penny being sent to the very country from which terrorists had attacked India just a few months previously. So the goodwill and the heart of India should not and cannot be doubted. It is unfortunately not being matched from the other side. There is no equivalent example that Pakistan can cite.

Then the Pakistani side's tendency to equate the two countries' experience of terrorism—'We are bigger victims of terrorism than you are,' one visitor said; 'If you can cite Mumbai, we can point at Samjhauta,' added another—omitted the basic difference that no one from India has crossed the border to inflict mayhem on Pakistan. Indians can and should sympathize with Pakistani victims of terrorism, but their tragedy is home-grown, an evil force turning on its creator; whereas Indians have died because killers from Pakistan, trained, equipped and directed by Pakistanis, have travelled to our country to kill, maim and destroy. There is no moral equivalence, and to pretend there is builds the dialogue on a platform of falsehood.

Finally, friendship has to be built on a shared perception of the danger—of a sincere acceptance by the Pakistani military establishment that those who attacked the Taj in Mumbai are just as much their enemies as those bombing the Marriott in Islamabad. This would require more than fuzzy words from parliamentarians—it needs genuine cooperation from Pakistan, including useful information-sharing and real action to arrest, prosecute and punish the perpetrators. The Samjhauta plotters are in jail in India, while Hafiz Saeed is still at large in Pakistan, preaching hatred.

If Islamabad genuinely shared the Manmohan Singh vision that the highest strategic interest of both countries lies in development and the eradication of poverty rather than in military one-upmanship, we could cooperate across the board, most obviously in trade—which would be of immense benefit to both countries, including certainly to a Pakistan that currently pays a premium for Indian goods imported via Dubai, and which also needs to gain export access to the gigantic Indian market for everything from its surplus cement to sporting goods. (It is hard to remember, today, that six decades ago the majority of Pakistan's trade was with India.) Normal trade relations could also be a precursor to the easing of geopolitical tensions. Until then, Track-II initiatives will feel good, but will remain on the wrong track.

———

What, then, is the way forward for India? It is clear that we want peace more than Pakistan does, because we have more at stake when peace is violated. To those who suggest that we should simply ignore our dysfunctional neighbours, accept the occasional terrorist blast (and prevent the ones we can), tell ourselves there is nothing we need from Pakistan and try to get on with our development free of the incubus of that benighted land, there is only one answer: we cannot grow and prosper without peace, and that is the one thing Pakistan can give us that we cannot do without. We cannot choose to be uninterested in Pakistan, because Pakistan is dangerously interested in us. By denying us the peace we crave, Pakistan can undermine our vital national interests, above all that of our own development. Investors shun war zones; traders are wary of markets that might explode at any time; tourists do not travel to hotels that might be commandeered by crazed terrorists. These are all serious hazards for a country seeking to grow and flourish in a globalizing world economy. Even if Pakistan cannot do us much good, it can do us immense harm, and we must recognize this in formulating our policy approaches to it. Foreign policy cannot be built on a sense of betrayal any more than it can be on illusions of love. Pragmatism dictates that we work for peace with Pakistan precisely so that we can serve our own people's needs better.

But we must do this without illusions, without deceiving ourselves about the existence of genuine partners for peace across the border, and without being taken in by the insincere press releases of the civilian rulers who are occasionally allowed to don the masks of power in Pakistan. We must accept that the very nature of the Pakistani state condemns us to facing an implacable enemy in the self-perpetuating military elite next door, for lasting peace would leave them without a raison d'être for their power and their privileges. We must not be deluded into making concessions, whether on Kashmir or any other issue, in the naive expectation that these would end the hostility of the ISI and its cohorts. We must understand that Pakistan's fragile sense of self-worth rests on its claim to be superior to India, stronger and more valiant than India, richer and more capable than India. This is why the killers of 26/11 struck the places they did, because their objective was not only to kill and destroy, but also to pull down India's growth, tarnish its success story and darken its lustre in the world. The more we grow and flourish in the world, the more difficult we make it for the Pakistani military to sustain its myth of superiority or even parity. There are malignant forces in Islamabad who see their future resting upon India's failure. These are not motives we can easily overcome.

This means that talking to plausible civilians has severe limitations. A smooth president, a bluff prime minister or a glamorous foreign minister makes for good television, but behind their affability they are each aware that a step too far could make them the targets of their own military establishment. We should be aware of this too, and we should ensure they are aware that we are aware. And yet we must engage Pakistan because we cannot afford not to. For even if we are talking to people who do not have the ultimate power to call off the killers, we know that their military overlords are listening, and that in the complicated arabesque that is Islamabad's civilian–military relationship, some of our messaging will get through to those who need to hear it.

As these words are written in March of 2012, it does seem that a subtle shift may be occurring in the atmospherics surrounding one of the most intractable problems of recent years, the dispute between India and Pakistan over Kashmir. The Pakistani military may have once thought that the fomenting of militancy and terrorism in India was an effective strategy of hurting the enemy on the cheap, but civilians in Islamabad have increasingly begun to realize (and to express the view) that Pakistan may have become the biggest victim of its own Kashmir policy. Its legacy has left the country with a distorted polity where the military has conducted four coups and is used to calling the shots behind the scenes; a collapsing economy, high unemployment and raging inflation; and a large number of unemployed and undereducated young men radicalized by years of Islamist propaganda against the Indian infidel. The result is a combustible mixture that threatens to consume the Pakistani state, with terrorists once sponsored by Islamabad now turning on their erstwhile patrons.

Leading members of the Pakistani establishment now say they are beginning to see this too. On a recent visit to Islamabad and Lahore, I sensed a widespread desire to put the dispute on the back burner and explore avenues of mutually beneficial cooperation with India. This impression emerged from private conversations, but Pakistanis are saying it openly too. In a recent interview, the Pakistani politician and religious leader Maulana Fazlur Rehman spoke frankly about Kashmir: 'Obviously, we are in favour of a political solution . . . Things have changed so much. *Now the concept of winning Kashmir has taken a back seat to the urgency of saving Pakistan*' (emphasis added).

Younger Pakistanis are going even further. The columnist Yaqoob Khan Bangash, for instance, openly derided the hallowed Pakistani argument that, as Muslims, Indian Kashmiris would want to join Pakistan: 'despite being practically a war zone since 1989, Indian Kashmir has managed a higher literacy, economic growth and per capita income rate than most of Pakistan,' he wrote. 'Why would the Kashmiris want to join Pakistan now? What do we have to offer them?'

Beyond that, many argue, the costs of the prolonged obsession with Kashmir have become unsustainable for a Pakistan mired in severe internal problems. Kashmiris, Bangash declared, 'should certainly not come at the cost of our own survival and not when all that we will be able to offer them is a failed state'. This is still a heretical position in Pakistan's public discourse. But it's a view that is gaining ground. When Indian Prime Minister Dr Manmohan Singh, a consistent advocate of peace with his nuclear-armed neighbour, suggested last summer that Pakistan should 'leave the Kashmir issue alone' and focus on its own internal problems, the comment did not elicit the customary howls of outrage in the Pakistani media. Instead, it was met with a grudging acknowledgement in Pakistan that perhaps, this time, the Indian leader was right.

It's a new national mood in Pakistan, and it may well be the time for India to seize the moment to build a lasting peace.

And yet—the problem will not be solved overnight. Even if, by some miracle, the Pakistani civilian and military establishment suddenly saw the light, concluded that terrorism was bad for them and decided to make common cause with India in its eradication, the task will not be accomplished with a snap of the fingers. Extremism is not a tap that can be turned off once it is open; the evil genie cannot be forced back into the bottle. The proliferation of militant organizations, training camps and extremist ideologies has acquired a momentum of its own. A population as young, as uneducated, as unemployed and as radicalized as Pakistan's will remain a menace to their own society as well as to ours. As a former Indian high commissioner in Pakistan, Satyabrata Pal, noted: 'These jihadi groups recruit from the millions of young Pakistanis who emerge from vernacular schools and madrassas, imbued with a hatred for the modern world, in which they do not have the skills to work. So while young Indians go to Silicon Valley and make a bomb for themselves, young Pakistanis go to the Swat Valley and make a bomb of themselves, the meanness of their lives justifying the end. Pakistan has betrayed its youth, which is its tragedy.'

This is not a counsel of despair. It is, instead, an argument to offer a helping hand. A neighbour full of desperate young men without hope or prospects, led by a malicious and self-aggrandizing military, is a permanent threat to twenty-first-century India. If India can help Pakistan transcend these circumstances and help it develop a stake in mutually beneficial progress, it will be helping itself as well. In such an approach lies the slender hope of persuading Pakistan that India's success can benefit it too, that, rather than trying to undercut India and thwarting its growth, Pakistan should look to the advantages that might accrue to it as a neighbour and partner of an upwardly mobile and increasingly prosperous India.

Such an India can build on the generosity it has often shown—as witness the unilateral MFN status it gave Pakistan—by extending itself to its neighbour, offering a market for Pakistani traders and industrialists, a creative umbrella to its artists and singers, and a home away from home for those seeking a refuge from the realities of Pakistani life. Many Pakistanis now realize that perpetual conflict with India is hampering Pakistan's own aspirations for economic growth and development. Multiplying our channels of contact—with 'back-channel diplomacy' conducted by 'special envoys' of the two leaderships (a formula used effectively by Musharraf and Manmohan Singh), direct contact between the two militaries (of which there is very little) and extensive people-to-people contact—is indispensable to the peace effort. NGOs and civil society—particularly those that channel the energy of young people, who are impatient with decades of hostility—can also play a useful role in developing relations that go beyond the prescriptions and the proscriptions of governments.

Sadly, India has reacted to 26/11 and other Pakistani provocations by tightening its visa restrictions and restraining other possibilities of cultural and social contact. This may be an area in which risks are worth taking, since the advantages of openly issuing visas and enhancing opportunities for Pakistanis in India outweigh the dangers; after all, the terrorists of 26/11 did not apply for Indian visas before coming onshore with their deadly baggage. I am strongly in favour of a liberal visa regime, which would require India to remove its current restrictions on which points of entry and exit the Pakistani visa holder can use, the number of places that may be visited and the onerous police reporting requirements. To begin with, a list can be drawn up of prominent Pakistanis in such fields as business, entertainment and media, who would be eligible for more rapid processing and for multiple-entry visas. It will be argued that Pakistan will not reciprocate such one-sided generosity, but India should not care. Insisting on parity with Pakistan is to bring ourselves down to their level. Let us show a magnanimity and generosity of spirit that in itself stands an outside chance of persuading Pakistanis to rethink their attitude to us.

More difficult politically but well worth doing might be to make concessions on issues where vital national interests are not involved. Not all the issues that divide India and Pakistan can be resolved across a table, but specific problems like trade, the military standoff on the Siachen glacier, the territorial boundary between the two nations at Sir Creek or contention over water flows through the Wullar Barrage and many other points of detail are certainly amenable to resolution through dialogue. It seems silly that public passions in Pakistan are being stirred over false claims that India is diverting Indus river water; much of this could be dispelled by candid and open talk to the Pakistani public by Indian officials. The new-found Pakistani willingness to reciprocate India's offer of MFN status in trade relations should be seized upon by India taking concrete steps to reduce the non-tariff barriers relating to security inspections, lab checks and clearances that have limited the extent of Pakistani exports to our country. India's financial services industry and its software professionals could also offer themselves to Pakistani clients, giving themselves a next-door market and providing services that Pakistan could use to develop its own economy. The education sector offers obvious opportunities, especially in these days of videoconferencing, which could allow students from one country to listen to lectures delivered in another. The prospects for cooperation in such areas as agriculture or the development of wind energy are bright. These are all 'easy wins' waiting to be pursued at the first opportunity.

The big questions—the Kashmir dispute and Pakistan's use of terrorism as an instrument of policy—will require a great deal more groundwork and constructive, step-by-step action for progress to be made. Afghanistan is an area of contention that, given a new climate of peace, could become an area for cooperation rather than a site of proxy conflict. By showing accommodativeness, sensitivity, foresight and pragmatic generosity in all the ways suggested above, India might be able to turn the bilateral narrative away from the logic of intractable hostility in which both countries have been mired for too long. Once that happens, it may even be possible to look beyond each other to economic cooperation with third countries: the Iran–Pakistan–India pipeline, for instance, or overland access for Indian goods through Pakistan and Afghanistan to Central Asia, neither of which looks feasible as long as Pakistan remains hostile territory.

The elephant in the room remains the Pakistani Army. Until the military men are convinced that peace with India is in their self-interest, they will remain the biggest obstacles to it. One hope may lie in the extensive reach of the Pakistani military apparatus and its multiple business and commercial interests. Perhaps India could encourage its firms to trade with enterprises owned by the Pakistani Army, in the hope of giving the military establishment a direct stake in peace. More military-to-military exchanges, even starting with such basic ideas as sporting contests between the two armies, would also help. The idea of joint exercises between the two militaries seems preposterous today, but it is entirely feasible in a UN peacekeeping context: just a few years ago, Indian aircraft strafed Congolese rebel positions in support of besieged Pakistani ground troops as part of a UN peacekeeping operation, MONUC.

In my UN days I personally witnessed the extraordinary degree of comradeship between Indian and Pakistani officers serving in the Peacekeeping Department headquarters in New York; perhaps being among foreigners served as a constant reminder of how much more they had in common with each other, so that they were frequently lunching together, visiting each other's homes and seeing the local sights together. Such contacts can and should be built upon to develop the right atmospherics for peaceful relations, which unavoidably require engagement with the Pakistani military. Indians are, understandably, among the strongest supporters of Pakistani democracy, at least in theory, but we have to live with the realities next door, and that requires us to see the Pakistani military not just as the problem, but as a vital element of the solution.

As good neighbours, Indians should be saddened by the continuing incidents of terrorist violence in Pakistan; we must wish Islamabad well in its efforts to repel militancy and fanaticism within its own borders. We would welcome indications that Islamabad shares our view that the forces of terrorism emanating from Pakistani soil are indivisible and that those plotting attacks on India from Pakistani territory are as much the enemies of Pakistan as they are of India. From such a diagnosis, the only possible prescription is that of cooperation, to build peace and security together. We hope that those who rule that country will make that diagnosis, and share the same prescription.

A former Indian high commissioner to Pakistan, G. Parthasarathy, once famously remarked that promoting peace between India and Pakistan is like trying to treat two patients whose only disease is an allergy to each other. This allergy has to be overcome. India does not covet any Pakistani territory. Because we wish to focus on our own people's development and prosperity in conditions of security, we remain committed to long-term peace with Pakistan. If the civilian government in Islamabad sees that the need is for concerted action against terrorists wherever they operate, whether in Pakistan, in India or in Afghanistan, we can find common ground. Our willingness to talk will best be vindicated by their willingness to act. Trust can be earned, which is why peace must be pursued. But we must pursue peace with our eyes wide open. To do so is, in the words of the veteran Indian diplomat K. Shankar Bajpai, the 'right, rational choice for a mature power'.

Too much of Indian public opinion is divided into sharply polarized camps of hawks and doves—the former insisting on nothing less than implacable hostility towards Islamabad, and hoping for the eventual destruction of Pakistan as we know it, the latter offering peace at any price, through a process 'uninterruptible' even if new terrorist strikes emanating from Pakistan were to occur. Neither position, in my view, is tenable, for all the reasons explicated above. Hostility is not a policy, and hostility in perpetuity is neither viable nor desirable between neighbours. And while the doves may be right that New Delhi's visceral reaction to the terror attacks is tantamount to giving the terrorists a veto over our foreign policy choices, no democratic government can allow its citizens to be killed and maimed by forces from across the border, without reacting in some tangible way that conveys to Pakistan that there is a price to be paid for allowing such things to happen.

At the same time, insisting that Pakistan must change fundamentally before India can make peace with it is not particularly realistic. A creative Indian government must seize on whatever straws in the wind float its way from Pakistan to explore the prospects of peace. New Delhi must do its best to ensure that the Islamabad establishment abandons the conviction that terrorism is the only effective instrument that obliges India to sit up and pay attention to Pakistan and engage with its interests. Accepting Pakistan the way it is but pushing for peace nonetheless is, in my view, the only way forward. It will mean isolating those elements and those issues that both sides consider intractable, and placing them on the back burner for now, in order to proceed with those that can be solved. Trust and understanding can be built on the basis of small agreements on seemingly marginal issues, thereby improving the atmosphere within which the more difficult problems can be tackled.

It is widely known that, during the latter stages of the Musharraf regime, the two countries came extremely close to a definitive conclusion on a number of pending issues, including Kashmir, until Musharraf's mounting domestic political difficulties made it impossible for him to clinch a deal. (Musharraf himself has implied that an agreement was also close with the previous Indian prime minister, Atal Bihari Vajpayee, until the BJP called an election that it lost; the process had then to start all over again.) It is surely not impossible to pick up the threads, but it is very difficult to pick up the threads in an atmosphere of violence, intimidation and mayhem. This is where Pakistan, too, bears a share of the responsibility for making progress towards peace. No democratic government worth its salt, and certainly no Indian government, will negotiate with a gun pointed at its head. A New Delhi that is prepared to make concessions will not want to make them if there is the slightest suggestion that it is doing so because it is intimidated by terrorist action. If Pakistan can make serious efforts to curb its extremists sufficiently to create a more propitious climate for a peace process, India would more readily seize the opportunity.

And yet, if there is another Mumbai—another horror perpetrated on a scale comparable to 26/11, with similar proof of Pakistani complicity—comparable restraint may be impossible, and all bets will be off. No democratic government can be seen to be sitting impotently while a neighbour assaults its society with impunity. This remains the greatest danger facing the subcontinent—of a feckless Pakistan either condoning or conniving in another major attack, and a beleaguered Indian government feeling the snapping of the last straw and launching retaliation. It is the duty of responsible people on both sides of the border to work to prevent this. There is hope for peace, and a determination in New Delhi to pursue it. But the primary onus for confining, if not destroying, the deadly virus that it has long incubated must rest on the Pakistani state. If it seizes that responsibility, it will not find India lacking.

Former prime minister Atal Bihari Vajpayee had once declared that you can change history but not geography. He was wrong: history, once it has occurred, cannot be changed. The time has come, instead, for the victims of geography to *make* history.

Chapter Three

A Tough Neighbourhood

In 1410, near the Sri Lankan coastal town of Galle, the Chinese admiral Zheng He erected a stone tablet with a message to the world. His inscription was in three languages—Chinese, Persian and Tamil—and his message was even more remarkable: according to Robert Kaplan's 2010 book *Monsoon*, it 'invoked the blessings of the Hindu deities for a peaceful world built on trade'. Six hundred years ago, a Chinese sailor-statesman called upon Indian gods as he set out to develop commercial links with the Middle East and East Africa through the Indian subcontinent.

The subcontinent has long been at the centre of Asia's most vital trade routes, and India's commanding position at the heart of South Asia places it in both an enviable and a much-resented position. As an editorialist in the Indian magazine *Seminar* observed: 'The overwhelming presence of India creates an asymmetry that pushes other, smaller countries, into suspecting hegemony in every proposal for greater cooperation, in turn feeding into an incipient irritation within India that its neighbours are united only in their anti-India sentiment.'

No one loves a huge neighbour: one need only ask the Mexicans what they think about the United States, or the Ukrainians their views on Russia. India cannot help the fact that, whether it wants to or not, it accounts for 70 per cent of the population of the eight countries that make up the subcontinent's premier regional organization, the South Asian Association for Regional Co-operation (SAARC). Worse, it accounts for 80 per cent of the region's collective GDP, and is by far its most militarily powerful member. Whenever India gets together with its neighbours, it occupies more space, and displaces more weight, than the rest of them combined. Even the most adroit diplomacy would not be able to skirt the implications of this inescapable reality: India is the proverbial 298-pound gorilla on the beach, whose slightest step will immediately be seen by the skinny 98-pounders as proof of insensitivity, bullying or worse.

Nonetheless, there is a widespread perception, which New Delhi would be unwise to ignore, that India's relations with the countries neighbouring it have been poorly managed. While its recent rise, unlike China's, is largely seen around the world as benign, India's neighbours hardly constitute an echo-chamber for global applause. Of the eight nations with which it shares a land or maritime border—Pakistan, China, Nepal, Bhutan, Bangladesh, Myanmar, Sri Lanka and the Maldives—there has been a history of problems, of varying degrees of difficulty, with six. (Two of these, Pakistan and China, are discussed in separate chapters and will only be tangentially referred to here.) Adding Afghanistan to the list (though technically it does not belong, after Pakistan's capture in 1948 of the strip of land in north-western Kashmir that made Afghanistan a territorial neighbour of India's), India has nine countries in its direct neighbourhood which are all, in varying degrees, vital to its national security. As Prime Minister Manmohan Singh remarked during his October 2011 visit to Bangladesh, 'India will not be able to realize its own destiny without the partnership of its South Asian neighbours.'

The charge that relations with most of them have been generally unsatisfactory is not untrue. Yet it is partly because of circumstances beyond India's own control. First, most of these nations share borders only with India, so what Professor S.D. Muni, in the title of one of his books, called 'the pangs of proximity' afflict each of them only in relation to India. Many have had to define their identity in relation to India; the sustaining historical narrative underpinning their nationalisms has often been derived from their anxiety to differentiate themselves from the Indian meganarrative. If India is a civilizational construct embracing unity amid vast diversity, each of its neighbours has to accentuate its own particularisms; for if separateness is not established, what distinguishes each of these countries from any Indian state? This anxiety to demonstrate 'not-Indianness' and resistance to any seeming cultural assimilation is often at the root of their concerns about Indian hegemony. In many cases, India became a factor in some countries' domestic politics, with

India-bashing often an easy route to cheap popularity in the hothouse politics of Pakistan, Bangladesh, Nepal or Sri Lanka.

More tangibly, each of these neighbouring nations has had to cope with internal crises whose effects spilled over into their relations with India. Just a few years ago, the picture across South Asia was bleak: Afghanistan battling the forces of a resurgent Taliban; Pakistan in turmoil, with the assassination of Benazir Bhutto and chaos in the streets; Nepal in the throes of a Maoist insurgency that toppled its monarchy; Bhutan managing a delicate transition from absolute monarchy to constitutional democracy; Bangladesh under military rule; Myanmar continuing to imprison Aung San Suu Kyi and her fellow democrats, while keeping the country an isolated tyranny; Sri Lanka convulsed by a bloody and brutal civil war that was well into its third decade; and even the Maldives facing mass disturbances in the lead-up to elections in which a formerly imprisoned dissident, Mohammed Nasheed, was seeking to defeat the long-time ruler Abdul Gayoom. The cliché that India lives in a tough and tumultuous neighbourhood could not have seemed truer.

And yet, in the last couple of years, there has been progress almost everywhere. Nepal's civil war is over and a coalition government holds the reins. Bhutan's political experiment, of a managed transition to multi-party democracy under a constitutional monarch, is going remarkably well. Bangladesh has held a free election and restored civilian democratic government. In Sri Lanka the military victory over the murderous forces of the Liberation Tigers of Tamil Eelam (LTTE) was followed by elections and notably conciliatory language by the triumphant, but not overly triumphalist, government. The Maldives elected the former dissident as president, the autocrat gamely made way, and the new democratic leader was bravely facing his country's many challenges until being forced to resign in a bloodless transfer of power to his vice-president in 2012. Even Myanmar held a relatively free election, albeit with severe restrictions, and freed its principal dissidents. Only in Afghanistan and Pakistan do fundamental difficulties persist. The prospects for peace, security and development look promising everywhere else on the subcontinent.

Listing the problems endemic to these countries is not to imply that India has been blameless in its own conduct. In Nepal, India's not-always-positive reputation for interference in that country's domestic affairs has generally not been undeserved. The border with Bangladesh has witnessed more shooting incidents in recent years than is explicable or reasonable, and despite the overwhelming imbalance between the two countries' forces, Indian border guards did not hesitate to shoot to kill Bangladeshi infiltrators, including migrant workers and petty smugglers, caught crossing the long and poorly demarcated border between the two countries. In Myanmar, India has abandoned its earlier policy of overt support for the democratic forces, extending support to the country's dictatorial junta to the disappointment of many of New Delhi's oldest friends. Relations with Sri Lanka remain complicated both by the history of India's prior involvement—support for the Tamil militancy, then a disastrous military intervention that engaged Indian troops in battles with the LTTE and resulted in their ignominious withdrawal—and by India's legitimate desire, made more urgent by its own domestic political imperatives, to see a political accommodation on the island that respects the aspirations of the Tamils. In all cases, India's prioritization of relations with global powers like the United States and China and its disproportionate focus in the neighbourhood on Pakistan have come at the cost of due attention to its other neighbours.

Of course it would be wrong to cite these examples as a reason to place the entire onus for any subcontinental dysfunctionalities on India alone. Large parts of South Asia have made great progress—economically, socially and politically—over the last few decades. Yet, there are a number of challenges that continue to beset the region and that hold back the true potential of our countries, individually as well as collectively. These include terrorism and extremism, and the use of these as instruments of state policy; and the daily terror of hunger, unemployment, illiteracy, disease and the effects of climate change. And less obvious but equally potent, restrictions on regional trade and transit that belong to an older, more mercantilist century. That many Indian states, in India's federal polity, have serious issues with their neighbours (concerns in Bengal and Bihar about movement of goods and people from Bangladesh and Nepal, for instance, or the treatment of Tamils in Sri Lanka, and at one time Pakistani support for separatist Khalistani militancy in Punjab) injects domestic political compulsions into New Delhi's thinking, particularly in an era of coalition governance, where the views of political allies must be imperatively taken into account. A political tendency in some of the neighbouring countries to adopt 'blame India' as a default internal political strategy has in turn bedevilled perceptions. These are among the factors that drag the people of the subcontinent back from the path of sustained peace, development and prosperity.

As I have already argued, the principal thrust of India's foreign policy ought to be to promote the country's domestic transformation, development and growth. The neighbourhood remains vital in this regard. Whereas more distant areas of the globe—the investment-generating countries of the Americas and Europe, and the energy-supplying countries in the Gulf, Africa and Central Asia—offer obvious opportunities for India, problems in the immediate neighbourhood generate both threats and opportunities—and the threats risk undermining India's efforts fundamentally. Weak and failing states, as scholars have noted, are able to subvert the larger ambitions of the more dominant countries neighbouring them. The Indian analyst Nitin Pai has gone so far as to argue that 'India's neighbours know that their own weakness is a source of implicit and explicit bargaining power'. Be that as it may, a rising India has an obvious interest in the success of its neighbours, since a stable neighbourhood contributes to an enabling environment for India's own domestic objectives, while disturbances on India's borders can act as a constraint on India's continued rise.

India's geopolitical strategists, both inside and outside government, have tended to see India's interests globally (witness the attention paid to relations with the United States, or India's role at the UN and the Non-Aligned Movement); in the neighbourhood, they have focused mainly on the threats to the nation's rise from the Pakistani military and its terrorist proxies, and to a somewhat lesser degree from the emergence of China and its impact on India's stature in the region. The result has been that the rest of the neighbourhood has sometimes been treated with neglect rather than close attention, and occasionally with a condescension that some have seen as arrogance. Whereas China is generally viewed as having managed its relationship with its neighbours well—though this image is fraying now with reports of Beijing's increasing belligerence in the South China Sea—India is widely considered not to have done enough to transform its neighbourhood from a liability into an asset.

Seventeen Indian states share land or maritime borders with foreign countries. The need to work for a peaceful periphery, devoid of the threat of extremism, is self-evident; less obvious but even more necessary is the need to embrace the neighbouring countries in a narrative of shared opportunity and mutually beneficial development.

This has worldwide implications for India. As the authors of a March 2012 report on India's external relations, 'Nonalignment 2.0', point out: 'India's ability to command respect is considerably diminished by the resistance it meets in the region. South Asia also places fetters on India's global ambitions. Our approaches to international law [and] international norms are overly inhibited by anxieties about the potential implications that our commitment to certain global norms may have for our options in the neighbourhood.'

For the Indian foreign policy maker, there is no getting away from the fundamental verities underpinning our relationships on the subcontinent. The question that all of us who belong to this ancient land need to ask ourselves is whether we desire peaceful coexistence and cooperation or are reconciled to being irretrievably mired in conflict and confrontation. A subcontinent at peace benefits all who live in it; one troubled by hostility, destructive rivalry, conflict and terror pulls us all down.

India must refuse to be dragged down by such forces. We need to look to the future, to an interrelated South Asian future where geography becomes an instrument of opportunity in our mutual growth story, where history binds rather than divides, where trade and cross-border links flourish and bring prosperity to all our peoples. Some will say these are merely dreams; yet there are few worthwhile achievements in the world that have not been preceded by ambitious aspirations. But dreams will only turn into reality if we take action to accomplish this brighter future together. Only work on the ground will help us overcome prejudiced mindsets, dogmatic doctrines and self-perpetuating myths. One thing is, however, clear. Our destinies are inextricably linked and we have to work together to lift our lives out of underdevelopment and conflict to peace and prosperity.

Our region has been blessed with an abundance of natural and human resources, a rich spiritual and civilizational heritage, a demography where youth is preponderant and a creative zeal manifest in all spheres of human endeavour. Our collective identity may be rooted in a turbulent history but the challenge is to translate the many factors that bind us into a self-sustaining, mutually beneficial and cooperative partnership that transcends the vicissitudes of the recent past. Indian officials like to argue that the people of South Asia have already made their choice and that the spirit—if not yet the reality—of an organization like SAARC embodies the aspirations of people from Herat to Yangon. It is imperative that all nations of SAARC work collectively to realize their vision. Yet, as Prime Minister Manmohan Singh noted at the April 2010 SAARC summit: 'We have created institutions for regional cooperation but we have not yet empowered them adequately to enable them to be more proactive.'

The Government of India, from the prime minister down, has a strategic vision of a peaceful subcontinent. The Indian foreign policy establishment genuinely believes that the peace, prosperity and security of our neighbours is in our interest. Many efforts have been made by India in recent years to ensure a marked improvement in its relations with most of its immediate neighbours, particularly following (and building upon) the articulation of the 'Gujral Doctrine' in 1996, which declared the accelerated development of every country in the subcontinent to be a key goal for India. Unlike some, India has never believed in undermining or destabilizing other countries; we believe that each of us deserves an equal chance to attend to the needs of our people without being distracted by hostility from any of our neighbours. When I was briefly a minister in the Government of India, I proudly declared that 'where we have disagreements, we will never abandon the path of dialogue and reconciliation. We are as resolute in our commitment to peace as we are firm in defending our country.' These are sentiments anchored in a long tradition, one that official India still gladly stands by.

A significant number of official initiatives have been taken in recent years to strengthen relations with the neighbours: regular contacts, including meetings of the top leaderships and of senior officials; an urgent emphasis on resolving major bilateral issues in order to build an atmosphere of trust; and a conscious stress on the economic dimension of these relations. India has repeatedly made it clear that it desires friendly, good-neighbourly and cooperative relations with all its neighbours. As by far the biggest country in the subcontinent (in size, population and GDP terms), we are often (in New Delhi's view, wrongly) perceived as throwing our weight around and (in my view, rightly) expected to show magnanimity in our dealings with our smaller neighbours. This we have done often in the past and must continue to do more often in the future. However, while it is not New Delhi's expectation that our neighbours display an equal measure of reciprocity, we certainly expect that they remain sensitive to our concerns regarding our sovereignty, our territorial integrity and our security. We do not think this is an unreasonable expectation. Within this framework a great deal can be achieved to our mutual benefit. People-to-people contacts, intra- and inter-regional connectivity, cultural exchanges, trade, investment flows and integrated approaches to vital issues like water, food, health, education and climate change will have to define any future architecture for the region.

It is also true that a cooperative future is not guaranteed unless we all work together on this unique project of a South Asia looking confidently to the future, each country secure in its own identity and putting development and the interests of its people above perceived fears and antagonistic posturing. No one country can do this alone. It must be a shared project.

The scourge of terrorism has cast its malevolent influence across the region and remains a major threat to all of us. It is a global menace, the epicentre of which is unfortunately located in our region, and whose malign influence has sometimes spread to other countries with which India shares borders. The ISI has been particularly active in Nepal and Bangladesh, which many strategists in Islamabad see as part of the 'soft underbelly' of the Indian state. This threat needs to be addressed purposively and with grim determination. Terrorism must be repudiated, and terrorists and those who provide them succour and sustenance must be tackled resolutely. It is imperative that all of India's neighbours understand that there are no 'good terrorists' and that those who strike Faustian bargains with such elements are often left to rue the consequences for their own countries. Part of India's uncompromising message to its neighbours must be that countries and organizations need to eschew the temptation to use terrorism as an instrument of state policy and stop selectively targeting only those terrorist entities that are at present perceived to be a threat to them. This is a short-sighted and self-destructive strategy, as Pakistan has already learned: it is one of the truisms of the subcontinental experience that those elements that profess an ideology of hatred, intolerance and terror often bite the hand that feeds them. The need is for concerted action against terrorists wherever they operate, whether in Pakistan, in India or in Afghanistan, and wherever they seek sanctuary or transit, whether in Bangladesh, in Nepal or in Myanmar.

It is, however, important for Indians to look beyond terrorism to the motivations of those who would give terrorists succour. This is often simply a manifestation of deeper issues at play—income inequality, environmental issues, social upheaval and displacement, the search for migrant work, and lack of access to education, all mounting to a paroxysm of frustration that can sometimes lash out blindly at the seemingly complacent strength of the Indian state. A Pakistani farmer who is repeatedly told about India's intransigence on Kashmir or its alleged diversion of Indus water; a devout Bangladeshi incessantly lectured about the sins of the Indian infidel; a Sri Lankan Buddhist taught that India gives aid and comfort to Tamil secessionist guerrillas—all these people could well become complicit in assaults on India, the Indian state and the Indian people. The need to correct such misguided views and to forge a common vision for all the peoples of the subcontinent are vital parts of the challenge facing India in South Asia.

———

Afghanistan, the newest member of the South Asian Association for Regional Cooperation, but geographically very much a part of our region, provides an example of how much we can achieve if we work together. Afghanistan is closer to India than the absence of a direct border between them might suggest. As David Malone pungently observes, 'psychologically, India and Afghanistan think of each other as neighbours and friends (their positive relationship deriving added saliency from the difficulties each has experienced with Pakistan)'. Afghanistan represents, for the countries of South Asia, the gateway to Central Asia and beyond, and to West Asia. Historically, it has formed the natural frontier in the north-west of the South Asian landmass. Given its geographic location,

Afghanistan has an immense potential to develop as a hub of trade, energy and transport corridors, which would help the long-term sustainability of development efforts in the region. This is something India would like to see happening, and that is why New Delhi was very happy to support the admission of Afghanistan to SAARC.

The other South Asian countries offer markets for Afghan produce, both agricultural and manufactured goods, which can help in the rapid development of the Afghan economy and the stabilization of that country. With its rapidly growing economy and outward-looking entrepreneurs, India has also emerged as a source of investment and capacity building expertise. As a significant bilateral donor, India has already spent $1.5 billion undertaking projects virtually in all parts of that country, in a wide range of sectors, including hydroelectricity, power transmission lines, road construction, agriculture and industry, telecommunications, information and broadcasting, education and health, fields which have been identified by the Afghan government as priority areas for reconstruction and development. India has supported maternal and child health hospitals (the Indira Gandhi Hospital in Kabul, connected through a telemedicine link with two superspeciality medical centres in India, is the country's largest and best), rebuilt and helped run girls' schools and carved a road across south-western Afghanistan, from Zaranj to Delaram, opening up a trade route towards the west to supplement the existing routes through Pakistan. We have lit up Kabul; the first time Kabul has 24 hours of electricity a day since 1982 is because of the courage and enterprise of Indian engineers in stringing up electrical cables at a height of 3000 metres from Pul-e-Khumri to bring power across the mountains to the capital.

Our education and training programmes for Afghans are the largest such programmes that India has for any country in the world, and India's is the largest skill and capacity development programme offered to Afghanistan by any country in the world. We have welcomed students and civil servants from Afghanistan to our educational and training institutions as part of our contribution towards helping stabilize the country and the region, increase capacity and human resource development and build upon the solid foundation of our historical and civilizational ties. India offers 675 scholarships a year to Afghan students.

We are digging tube wells in six provinces, running sanitation projects and medical missions, and working on lighting up a hundred villages using solar energy. India has also given at least three Airbus planes to Afghanistan's fledgling national airline, Ariana. Several thousand Indians are engaged in development work. We are currently engaged in the construction of the Salma Dam across the Hari Rud river in Herat, and we are finishing the Afghan Parliament building, a visible and evocative symbol of democracy and of India's desire to see the Afghan people determine their own political destiny. During his May 2011 visit to Afghanistan, Prime Minister Manmohan Singh announced additional assistance of $500 million, over and above India's existing commitments, which are now expected to cross the $2 billion mark.

In all this, our endeavour is to help Afghanistan stand on its own feet. We have no other agenda there, other than an acknowledgement that stability and pluralism in Afghanistan and its integration into the regional ecosystem are also fundamentally in our national interest. As an Indian I have no difficulty with the proposition that Afghanistan should not be seen as a battleground for competing spheres of influence. India and Afghanistan, of course, share a strategic and development partnership, based on millennia-old historical, cultural and economic ties. We have an abiding interest in the stability of Afghanistan, in ensuring social and economic progress for its people, and getting them on the track of self-sustaining growth, and enabling them to take their own decisions without outside interference. And we have paid a serious price for our efforts, in lives lost to terrorist action, including in two assaults on the Indian embassy in Kabul and on a residence occupied by Indian development workers, as well as the kidnapping and killing of road-building crews and construction personnel. But we have persisted.

The myriad problems that confront the country can only be resolved in a peaceful environment, devoid of violence and terror. The international community needs to come together to overcome this grave challenge. A sense of defeatism has been pervading some sections of international opinion. New Delhi feels that needs to be guarded against, because it runs the risk of encouraging insurgent groups into thinking they might actually triumph. India has argued, therefore, that Afghanistan needs a long-term commitment, even while remaining mindful of the challenges.

The Afghan people have displayed great courage and resilience, and a survival instinct even against the greatest odds. The international community must do its utmost to support them.

Given the turbulence of the past eight years and the recent dramatic decline in security, there is need for an intensified focus on security, governance and development by the Afghan government, and here the international community should do what it can to assist. Failure in Afghanistan's stabilization will entail a heavy cost for both the Afghan people and the region at large, including for Pakistan whose active current engagement in destabilizing the country could turn out to prove highly counterproductive.

While the Afghan government should spell out its priorities, the international community should come forward to provide the resources for fulfilling them. The Afghan leadership has itself stressed the need for a strong and genuine effort to improve governance, remove corruption and focus on development, especially in agriculture, rural development and infrastructure, with a shift in focus from the central to the provincial and district levels. All stakeholders now agree on the need for greater 'Afghanisation' of the development process.

The Afghan National Security Forces (ANSF) should be enlarged and developed in a professional manner, at a much faster pace. The ANSF should be provided appropriate resources, combat equipment and training. India is prepared to play its part, while mindful that any involvement in military matters in Afghanistan might be a neuralgic issue for Islamabad—a major reason for India's self-restraint in confining its efforts in Afghanistan to development, while other countries handle security. India is not a member of the US-led International Security Assistance Force (ISAF), a largely NATO operation to which New Delhi was not invited to contribute, given Pakistani sensitivities about any possible Indian military presence in Afghanistan. (I joked at the time that we were less interested in ISAF than in 'INSAF' or justice, which we wanted to prevail in Kabul.)

President Obama's announcement of a significant drawdown of American forces in Afghanistan, and an increasing emphasis on reconciliation with the Taliban, has obviously been studied attentively in New Delhi. It is hardly a secret that New Delhi sees the foreign military presence as indispensable in promoting political stability and economic reconstruction in Afghanistan. Without the security provided by a serious troop presence, the kind of developmental activities in which India is engaged would become impossible.

But no one in New Delhi really expects American forces to disappear overnight from Afghanistan, despite bin Laden's elimination. The withdrawal plan began with the departure of only 10,000 troops by the end of 2011. Later, when winter set in (traditionally the season when military activity declines), Washington withdrew another 5000, and when the snows melt and the US election season starts hotting up, Obama says he intends to bring an additional 22,000 of the 'surge' troops home by this September. Even if he does that—a decision that will surely have to take into account the ground realities at that time—it will still leave 68,000 US troops in Afghanistan, or twice the number deployed there when he became president. The plan is for NATO forces to shift to a less proactive role next year, acting principally in support of Afghan forces, with combat operations winding down in the course of 2014. That would mark the official 'withdrawal date'.

After that point, a residual American counterterrorism force would still remain in Afghanistan. Bases are being fortified to house US forces beyond 2014. Several NATO allies hope to be home by then, but a residual ISAF is very much on the cards. After all, the reason for the original US intervention was that Afghanistan should not again become a safe haven for the next bin Laden. Indications are that the United States will retain some 20,000 troops in Afghanistan, even in the most modest scenario.

Indians have every reason to be relieved. India realizes that an Afghanistan without ISAF is a land that will be prey to the machinations of Pakistan's notorious Inter-Services Intelligence, which had created, financed, officered and directed the Afghan Taliban in the 1990s. This would be a proven security threat to India: the Taliban regime of the day, functioning as a wholly owned subsidiary of the ISI, had been complicit in the hijacking of an Indian airliner in 1999, resulting in the release (in Kandahar) of three diehard terrorists from Indian custody, one of whom went on to kidnap and kill the American reporter Daniel Pearl.

In this context, America's interest in reconciliation with the Taliban has been studied in New Delhi with some concern. After rejecting this for some time (on the not-unreasonable grounds that there can be no such thing as a good terrorist), New Delhi has come around to accepting dialogue with those Taliban elements who are prepared to renounce violence. President Obama speaks of dealing with those who agree to break with Al Qaeda, abandon violence and abide by the Afghan Constitution, categories India would have no difficulty with. But New Delhi is wary of those who, under Pakistani tutelage, might pretend to be reborn constitutionalists, but seize the first opportunity after an American withdrawal to devour the regime that compromises with them.

This is why New Delhi stresses the importance of improving the capacity of the Afghan government to fight and overcome terrorism; if Kabul's sinews are not strengthened, it will again be vulnerable to an extremist takeover. The role of Pakistan—which has made no secret of its desire to control the government in Kabul in order to enjoy 'strategic depth' for its overambitious military—remains of particular concern. India shares the United States' commitment to what Obama, in December 2011, had described as the 'long-term security and development of the Afghan people'. But for New Delhi, any process of reconciliation should be Afghan led, as well as inclusive and transparent. India fully supports the 'red lines' laid down by the Afghan government in its London and Kabul communiqués, which it feels Kabul should not be forced to cross.

The bottom line for New Delhi remains the right of the Afghan people to decide their own destiny. It sees the role of the international community as helping Afghanistan to do just that. And it doesn't believe Kabul is ready for the world to give up on it yet.

There really are only two choices confronting the international community unless one counts 'cut and run'—to invest and endure or to improve conditions to a point that we can exit. India has already made up its mind—invest and endure is the way forward, because we believe in the cause of peace, democracy and development in Afghanistan. India trusts that the friends of Afghanistan will do likewise.

———

I will deal more briefly with some of India's other relationships in our neighbourhood, starting with India's northern neighbours, Nepal, Bhutan and Bangladesh.

India and Nepal share a unique relationship of friendship and cooperation underpinned by linguistic, cultural and civilizational links, wide-ranging commercial and economic ties, and extensive people-to-people contacts. It is said that when the princely states in British India were being integrated into the Indian Union, the maharaja of Nepal sent an emissary to find out where he had to sign up, but India demurred, recognizing the value of a buffer state on its northern border. So Nepal remained independent, but as the only country whose nationals required no passports to cross into India. The border is notoriously porous, and at times of trouble Nepalis swarm across it, transforming entire Indian neighbourhoods into Nepali colonies.

Few countries have a relationship as wide-ranging and multifaceted as that between India and Nepal. There is an open border between the two countries, extensive marital, kinship and cultural links, and nationals of one are treated as nationals by the other, adding up to a relationship as intense and intimate as it is possible to find between two sovereign states. Indian economic, political, educational, religious, spiritual and cultural influence on—some critics would say dominance of—Nepal is pervasive. The close connections between the armed forces of the two nations have in a sense made India the ultimate guarantor of law and order in Nepal (though this can create complications, as occurred in 2009 when India was accused of supporting the Nepali armed forces chief when he resisted demands from Maoist Prime Minister Prachanda to resign).

At the same time it has not always been seen as a wholly positive relationship. The former Indian diplomat Rajiv Sikri wrote that 'Indians have taken Nepal too much for granted. India's approach towards Nepal has been dismissive and neglectful. The Indian government and public have never shown adequate sensitivity to Nepali pride and uniqueness.' India has an evident stake in Nepalese stability, and our bilateral relations have to be based on common economic prosperity. To build interdependencies that integrate our two countries and create the necessary conditions for economic integration, it is imperative to ensure greater connectivity of goods, people and ideas. New Delhi does not seem to have appreciated sufficiently the importance of investing in rail and road links and using infrastructure development to promote greater integration with Nepal. The two countries are working on an economic package for developing a skill base for industrial development and an ambitious programme to upgrade the infrastructure along their borders. India clearly needs to go beyond its currently reactive approach to events on the ground in Nepal to evolve a positive agenda that would be more proactive, support economic growth and progress and serve to strengthen its democracy and civil society.

Increased bilateral trade with and investments in Nepal would contribute to economic development and prosperity for both countries. The 1996 trade treaty marked a turning point in trade relations between the two countries. It resulted in phenomenal growth of bilateral trade, which witnessed a sevenfold increase in a decade (Nepal's exports to India increased eleven times and Indian exports to Nepal increased six times). In addition, Indian investments in Nepal increased by seven times. The 2009 revised trade treaty has retained the positive features of the previous treaty and built on it to further enhance and expand bilateral trade between the two countries.

The problems that have arisen recently in the India–Nepal relationship, in the analysis of India's foremost scholar of Nepal, Professor S.D. Muni, resulted from a number of factors:

principal among them the Maoists' deviations from assurances sought by India and given by them on a number of bilateral issues; their propensity to use the China card beyond the 'red lines' drawn by India; [and] their unwillingness or incapacity to give up strong arm methods in dealing with their political opponents. Relevant as well were abrasive diplomatic behaviour of Kathmandu based Indian diplomacy; India's fears that the Maoists were inclined to and capable of changing Nepal's domestic power equations; and finally Delhi's fears that a Constitution drafted under assertive Maoist leadership may not be compatible with the democratic profile of Nepal.

These are all core issues that cannot be wished away. In addition, China's quickening activity in Nepal has not gone unnoticed in New Delhi. In recent years, China has been meeting with and courting Nepali political parties, and investing heavily in Nepali business and economic activities. A number of high-level (and high-profile) visits have taken place, and

Beijing has been commenting publicly on Nepali developments with a frequency and freedom that would not have previously been associated with that country.

Nepal is going through a historic transition and India has consistently maintained that the political process—the peace process, the drafting of the new constitution by a duly elected Constituent Assembly, and its implementation with the cooperation of all political tendencies in a democratically elected Parliament—has to be both Nepali owned and Nepali driven. There is some legitimate anxiety about the anti-Indian sentiments expressed by the Nepali Maoists, currently in government, though it is understood that reassurances have been conveyed to New Delhi that a Maoist-run Nepal would not allow itself to be used against Indian interests. Most Indians are with the people of Nepal in this period of historic transition and in their quest for a multiparty democracy.

The developments in our neighbourhood with respect to Bhutan, Sri Lanka, Bangladesh and the Maldives (at least until the recent change of regime) have been remarkably positive. They have pointed towards greater understanding, cooperation and partnership rather than towards disagreement, let alone conflict.

India's relations with Bhutan are an excellent example of good-neighbourly relations and—unlike some of the other relationships in the subcontinent—have been characterized by mutual understanding, trust and cooperation. The year 2009 was a momentous year in India–Bhutan relations. It marked the celebrations of the golden jubilee of the visit of Pandit Jawaharlal Nehru to Bhutan in 1958, the coronation of the fifth king of Bhutan and the 100th anniversary of the Wangchuck dynasty. India shared its experience of democracy and constitutional processes with Bhutanese officials working on the transition from monarchy to democracy. New Delhi welcomed Bhutan joining the ranks of democratic countries and the development has only helped strengthen relations. The previous client–state relationship reflected in the India–Bhutan friendship treaty of 1950 was altered when the treaty was updated in 2007; it now not only reflects the contemporary nature of the two countries' bilateral relationship but also lays the foundation for their future development in the twenty-first century.

India is the largest development partner of Bhutan. It has been providing assistance to Bhutan ever since the latter initiated planned development efforts in the early 1960s. Hydropower exports from Bhutan to India—aiming at a target of 10,000 MW of hydropower by 2020—have already overtaken tourism as the single largest contributor to the impressive recent growth in Bhutan's GDP. India has constructed three substantial hydroelectric projects—Chukha, Kurichhu and Tala—which are a major source of revenue generation for Bhutan, and the country is developing additional hydroelectric projects, for which India would remain the main customer. From 2006, Bhutan's exports to India have exceeded its imports from India, due to its growing exports of hydropower to its energy-starved southern neighbour.

Bhutan has other significant benefits from its relationship with India. It enjoys preferential trade and transit facilities that India does not accord to other states (bar Nepal). India finances nearly three-fifths of Bhutan's budget, holds 61 per cent of Bhutan's debt stock and has built crucial border roads and other major infrastructural facilities. India remains Bhutan's most important trade partner, its products constituting over 70 per cent of Bhutan's total imports, while Bhutan's exports to India are close to 99 per cent of its total exports. India is also committed to the construction of the first rail link between our countries and to assisting Bhutan in information technology development and dissemination.

It is a relationship that has comfortably weathered Bhutan's internal transition and its opening up to the wider world. In the words of a neutral and not-uncritical observer, the Canadian diplomat David Malone: 'In spite of clear Indian dominance of its small Himalayan neighbour, the relationship has been a genuinely friendly, positive, and mutually respectful one, with India working hard to keep its own profile in Bhutan as low as possible and the Bhutanese mostly expressing appreciation for India's contributions.'

The end of martial law in Bangladesh with the 2009 elections and the ushering in of a democratic government led by the Awami League opened up a window of opportunity for both sides to address issues of genuine mutual concern in a purposeful and focused manner that builds on our commonalities. It may be a cliché to speak of the multifaceted nature of relations between the two countries and the historical and traditional bonds of friendship the two countries share, but there is no doubt that the cliché is a cliché because it is true. It helps that Bangladesh, once again since 2009 under the leadership of Sheikh Hasina Wajed, daughter of Bangladesh's pro-India founding father, Sheikh Mujibur Rahman, seems to understand that its own prospects for prosperity are closely tied to India's.

Soon after coming to power, the government of Sheikh Hasina arrested and handed over a pair of wanted terrorists who had previously enjoyed sanctuary on Bangladeshi soil. The hostility of Bangladesh's few, but vociferous, anti-Indian Islamist politicians has been curbed by firm governmental action. Discussions on sharing of river waters, dam construction and similar issues have taken place in the framework of a mutual determination not to harm each other's interests. India's decision to permit duty-free access to the exports of the least developed countries has benefited Bangladeshi trade with India, which has burgeoned dramatically, with Bangladesh's exports to India crossing the $1-billion mark in a twelve-month period for the first time in 2012. Issues of road and rail connectivity are on the table, trade is being given a new impetus and both nations are cooperating on combating terrorism.

Most strikingly, a seemingly intractable territorial irritant—the existence of small enclaves of each country within the other's borders—was settled during Prime Minister Manmohan Singh's visit to Dhaka in September 2011 on terms that even Bangladeshis found generous on India's part. It is a pity that parliamentary ratification of the land transfer (which requires a two-thirds majority in both Houses that the United Progressive Alliance government does not have) has not yet happened. It will require an effort to persuade the opposition parties to cooperate, but the effort is well worth making; otherwise the perception that 'India does not deliver on its promises' will gain ground. While one much-anticipated agreement on the sensitive issue of sharing the waters of the river Teesta fell through at the last minute (on which more later), other accords ranged from trade, transit and transportation to electricity and an end to shootings on the border.

Of even greater long-term significance is a $10-billion project to provide transit through Bangladesh to India's north-eastern states, the so-called seven sisters, long the stepchildren of Indian development because of their geographical remoteness from India's booming economy, to which they are connected only through a thin sliver of Indian territory north of Bangladesh. In 1947 the North-East had a higher per capita income than most of the rest of India, but it has languished since independence because Partition cut it off from the Indian heartland. Greater integration with India will be a huge asset to Bangladesh as well, helping to develop roads, railways and trade and lifting the country's economic growth by an estimated 2 per cent additionally. While transit through Bangladesh would also have security benefits for India (it would simplify the military's task of bringing supplies and reinforcements to combat insurgencies in the North-East and to shore up our border defences against China), the economic benefits have clearly been uppermost in both countries' minds.

Both countries speak of their relations as (in the words of one Bangladeshi spokesman) 'time-tested and based on shared history, culture, language, religion, traditions and values'. The two countries' closer engagement has embraced areas as diverse as joint water resources management, land boundary demarcation, trade, power, connectivity, infrastructure development, cultural and educational exchange and poverty alleviation. While it may have been true that, for some years, Bangladesh was reluctant to sell natural gas to India for fear of being seen domestically as submitting to Indian 'exploitation', public opinion has shifted significantly. Polls conducted by both Bangladeshi and foreign researchers have confirmed that hostility towards India is now expressed only by a tiny minority and that regard for India, as well as support for its rise as a significant power, is a widespread sentiment. This is a welcome change, and augurs well for the future.

This is not to suggest that all is merely sweetness and light between the two countries. Bangladesh has, in the not-so-distant past, served as a haven for Islamist fanatic groups and even terrorists, and has provided a sanctuary for Indian insurgents in the North-East. It has also been a source of illegal migration into India—some 20 million Bangladeshis are reliably estimated to have slipped into the country over the last two decades and disappeared into the Indian woodwork—and of counterfeit currency, which is regularly infiltrated into India by ISI operatives through the porous borders with Bangladesh and Nepal in an attempt to undermine the Indian economy. There are also lingering issues of border management and transit-related questions as well as controversies over water-sharing. This last erupted in the headlines when the chief minister of the Indian state of Paschimbanga (West Bengal), Mamata Banerjee, an important coalition partner of the Manmohan Singh government, vetoed a proposed agreement in 2011 to share the waters of the river Teesta, claiming it would deprive her farmers of adequate water. This was widely seen as a setback for a relationship that was once again beginning to blossom after a long freeze. It is clear that cooperation on sharing the Teesta waters is indispensable for Sheikh Hasina to be able to claim that Bangladesh has gained from her friendship with India; and we must all help persuade the Paschimbanga leadership that these waters are not 'ours' to 'give', but a shared natural resource (as we accepted in the Indus waters treaty with Pakistan) which we should use responsibly and equitably.

One project that could unite all four countries discussed in this section—in the sort of shared endeavour that could yet define a better future for the subcontinent—is a subregional joint water resources management project involving Bangladesh, Bhutan, Nepal and India, intended primarily for flood control but that could go beyond it. The project, which has now begun to take off from the proverbial drawing board, envisages achieving both the mitigation and the augmentation of the dry season flows of the rivers that flow through the four countries. An added objective will be to harness the same rivers to generate hydroelectricity in a region where power shortages are perhaps the biggest obstacle to economic growth. If it happens, such a mutually beneficial project could offer a template for the rest of South Asia, helping change a narrative of hostility and stagnation into one of cooperation and dynamism.

———

At one level, nothing could be easier than speaking about India–Sri Lanka relations. After all, India is Sri Lanka's closest neighbour. The relationship between the two countries is more than 2500 years old and both sides have built, and built upon, a long legacy of intellectual, cultural, religious and linguistic exchange. Lanka features centrally in the sacred ancient epic the

Ramayana and, for that reason, is probably the one foreign country most non-political Indians are aware of. A significant Tamil minority on the island enjoys ties of kinship and cultural affiliation with India's southern state of Tamil Nadu. In recent years, the relationship between India and Sri Lanka has been marked by frequent and close contact at the highest political level, growing trade and investment, cooperation in the fields of education, culture and defence, as well as a broad understanding on major issues of international interest. As the Sri Lankan scholar and diplomat Dayan Jayatilleka eloquently put it: 'India inheres in the very fabric of the island. Sri Lanka is an inverted and miniaturized mirror of India. Even if the Tamil factor did not exist, Sri Lanka's relationship with India would be its most vital external relationship.'

Sri Lanka is also economically South Asia's most successful state in GDP terms, with a per capita income that is nearly double India's. The end of the conflict with the LTTE has brought about a greater possibility for peace and stability in Sri Lanka and its neighbourhood. India has historically done its best to oppose and prevent the internal and external destabilization of its friendly smaller neighbours. The end of the conflict has presented Sri Lanka with an opportunity to heal the wounds created by decades of protracted conflict, to make a new beginning and to build a better future for its people. It has also opened up greater options for India and Sri Lanka to cooperate bilaterally and enlarge our areas of engagement.

India had strongly supported the right of the Government of Sri Lanka to act against terrorist forces. At the same time, it conveyed at the highest level its deep concern at the plight of the mostly Tamil civilian population, emphasizing that their rights and welfare should not get enmeshed in hostilities against the LTTE. The conclusion of the armed conflict saw the emergence of a major humanitarian challenge, with nearly 300,000 Tamil civilians housed in camps for internally displaced persons (IDPs). India has emphasized to the Sri Lankan government the importance of focusing on issues of relief, rehabilitation, resettlement and reconciliation. India is now working actively in assisting in these 'four Rs' in Northern and Eastern Sri Lanka. We have provided humanitarian relief for the displaced people, medicines worth 225 million Sri Lankan rupees (about $1.8 million) and the services of a field hospital which treated more than 50,000 patients in 2009 before it was withdrawn.

India has also consistently advocated the need for IDPs to be resettled into their original habitations as early as possible. In order to help with this, India has provided shelter assistance for constructing temporary housing for IDPs, and starter packs of agricultural implements have been supplied to help resettling families begin livelihood-generating activities. Since Colombo argued that the requirement of demining is a major constraint on the speed of resettlement, the Government of India has fully financed seven Indian demining teams to help expedite resettlement. In other words, the Government of India has remained engaged with the task of helping the Government of Sri Lanka to return displaced people to their homes to resume their lives which had so cruelly been interrupted by conflict.

India openly expressed the hope that the largely incident-free first post-war elections, which returned President Rajapaksa to power and also gave him a strong parliamentary majority, would accelerate the process and reinforce a political consensus behind giving the Tamil people of Sri Lanka an honoured place in their own country, within the framework of a united Sri Lanka. The need for national reconciliation through a political settlement of ethnic issues has been reiterated by India at the highest levels and in a controversial vote in support of a US-sponsored resolution at the UN Human Rights Council in 2012. India's consistent position is in favour of a negotiated political settlement, which is acceptable to all communities and is compatible with democracy, pluralism and respect for human rights.

This is not a case of New Delhi interfering gratuitously in the internal affairs of its southern neighbour. India cannot help but be involved, both because it is Sri Lanka's closest neighbour geographically and because its own Tamil population—some 70 million people in the politically important southern state of Tamil Nadu—remains greatly concerned about the well-being of their ethnic cousins across the Palk Straits. India is staying engaged with Sri Lanka in the fraternal spirit that characterizes our friendship, and though visits between the two capitals are publicized enough to reassure public opinion in Tamil Nadu that the interests of their fellow Tamils are not being sold out, India has been careful to keep the details of its démarches quiet to avoid embarrassing the government in Colombo.

It is also relevant to note that Sri Lanka is one of the major recipients of development assistance, both grants and low-cost credit, given by the Government of India for an assortment of infrastructure-related projects. Plans for developing the interconnectivity of the Indian and Sri Lankan electricity grids, setting up e-learning centres and supplying buses for transportation in hilly and remote locations reflect Indian strengths that respond to Sri Lankan needs. There has been one major setback, however. Many analysts have deplored India's failure to accede to Sri Lanka's request to develop the port of Hambantota in President Rajapaksa's own constituency—and then watched in chagrin as China took on the task with its usual efficiency and speed. India's inability to be able to respond to such requests for large-scale infrastructural assistance remains a significant failing.

Cultural cooperation, on the other hand, is a very important aspect of the Indo-Lankan bilateral relationship. The Indian Cultural Centre in Colombo actively promotes awareness of Indian culture by offering classes in Indian music, dance, Hindi and yoga. Every year, cultural troupes from both countries exchange visits. India is also committed to the restoration of important icons of the cultural heritage of Sri Lanka. Accordingly, it is participating in the setting up of an International Buddhist Museum in Kandy and the restoration of the Thirukeeteswaram Temple in Mannar. A visa-issuing consulate and an Indian cultural centre opened in Jaffna recently to promote people-to-people contact and visits between the two countries and especially their Tamil areas.

Commercial relations are in better shape and are set to expand rapidly in the post-war environment. Trade between India and Sri Lanka has grown fast after the coming into force of the India–Sri Lanka free trade agreement (FTA) in March 2000, making Sri Lanka India's largest trade partner in SAARC. India in turn is Sri Lanka's largest trade partner globally, and the share of Sri Lanka in Indian imports has increased consistently each year. In July 2008, the two countries completed negotiations on a Comprehensive Economic Partnership Agreement, but political hesitations in Colombo have delayed its finalization and signature. With many prominent Indian brand names having obtained FDI approvals of nearly $500 million, India is the fourth largest investor in Sri Lanka.

It is striking that the India–Sri Lanka FTA has had a mutually beneficial positive trade creation effect. It is one of the few South–South agreements that are working credibly; in fact some researchers say that it could be an example for other South–South agreements to emulate. The success of the India–Sri Lanka FTA has proved that if the concerns of the smaller economy in the relationship are taken into account with more favourable treatment, then the size differential in the economies of the FTA partners do not matter. Being the first of its kind in the South Asian region, it has invited lot of interest among the exporters of the region. The building of a land bridge between the two nations, which has been talked of desultorily for years, will go an even longer way to integrating the Indian and Sri Lankan economies.

It would be facile to pretend that there are no irritants at all in the relationship between our countries. The condition of the Tamil people of Sri Lanka remains both an emotional and a political issue in India, erupting periodically in the hothouse politics of Tamil Nadu. Another issue, given the proximity of the territorial waters of both countries, especially in the Palk Straits and the Gulf of Mannar, relates to incidents of the straying of fishermen across territorial waters and some cases of poaching, often resulting in their interception by the other country's coast guard and subsequent incarceration, to a chorus of protests by agitated families and their political representatives. Both countries have agreed on practical arrangements to deal with the issue of bona fide fishermen of either side crossing the International Maritime Boundary Line. Through these arrangements, it has been largely possible to deal with the detention of fishermen in a humanitarian manner, though the occasional incident still occurs.

The way forward for the two countries clearly lies in India and Sri Lanka developing an even more intimate economic relationship—the rapid growth of the Indian economy undoubtedly benefits its southern neighbour—even while New Delhi, egged on by Tamil Nadu politicians, pushes Colombo towards making more visible progress in promoting reconciliation with Sri Lanka's own Tamil community, which remains still marginalized politically. The end of the war witnessed much widely reported brutality on the part of the Sri Lankan military, and the need for accountability, for the rehabilitation of the Tamils displaced from their homes by the conflict and for serious steps towards reconciliation and national integration is acute.

On the whole, however, the picture one can paint of India–Sri Lanka relations is a highly positive one. I witnessed at first hand the welcoming atmosphere in Colombo when the International Indian Film Awards (IIFA) took place there in July 2010, shortly after the end of the civil war. As I observed on that occasion, India and Sri Lanka need to look to the future, to a future in which our geographical proximity becomes a reason for closeness rather than controversy, where the past reminds us not of recent pain but of ancient commonalities, where religion and culture bring us together in a celebration of our common heritage. In our shared epic, the Ramayana, Lord Rama came to Lanka to reclaim Sita and left; the Indian emperor Ashoka's envoys brought Buddhism to Lanka and stayed. These ancient links unify us in spirit, in the spirit of the timeless tides that wash our shores and that have tied us together for millennia. The IIFA saw the film world taking its turn to build a new bridge to Lanka, a Rama Setu of the imagination. The way forward is clear, and well lit.

One should not leave India's southern waters without a reference to the Maldives, where India enjoys relations that are comparable to those with Bhutan—intimate and trouble-free. For years, New Delhi had the only foreign embassy located in the country; other ambassadors were accredited to the capital, Male, from elsewhere. While the Indian ambassador now has a few Asian brethren for company in the capital, his status in the island state epitomizes a 'special relationship' that was repeatedly affirmed to me personally by the then president Nasheed and his senior aides during a recent visit. When Nasheed was overthrown in 2012, one striking feature of the motley coalition that replaced him was that every one of its members reaffirmed the importance of continued strong relations with India.

Despite having been a close ally of President Gayoom (and having dispatched its paratroopers to overturn a coup attempt against him by Sri Lanka–based mercenaries in 1996), New Delhi had welcomed the results of the first multiparty democratic presidential and parliamentary elections in the Maldives that brought Nasheed to power and has taken a similar attitude to the new regime, remaining determined to work with whoever comes to power in that country. India was visibly active in the diplomatic activity that followed the change of government in 2012, and we have continued enhancing our cooperation in a range of areas, including maritime and coastal security, where we share common concerns. While there is legitimate ground for suggesting that India could have taken a more active stand in defence of the democratically elected president, its close involvement in ensuring a peaceful aftermath of the transfer of power cannot be faulted. The India–Maldives relationship has been nurtured over decades through regular high-level exchanges and by developing mutually identified infrastructure facilities in the Maldives using economic and technical assistance provided by India. At the people-to-people level, as the MP from Thiruvananthapuram, I am conscious of the close bonds we have with the people of the Maldives, many of whom can be seen in the Kerala capital on any given day. We are committed to strengthening and enhancing our bonds of friendship with these close cousins.

As elections in 2011 (and a by-election in 2012) both ratified and subtly altered the consequences of three decades of military rule in Myanmar, formerly (and to many nationalists, still) called Burma, the perspective from India may help explain much about the international survival and continued acceptability of the junta in that country.

Burma was ruled as part of Britain's Indian Empire until 1935, and the links between the two countries remained strong. An Indian business community thrived in the major Burmese cities, and cultural and political affinities between the two countries were well established. India's nationalist leader and first prime minister, Jawaharlal Nehru, was a friend of the Burmese nationalist hero Bogyoke (General) Aung San, whose daughter Suu Kyi studied in New Delhi.

When the generals in Rangoon (now Yangon) suppressed the popular uprising of 1988, overturned the results of a free election overwhelmingly won by Aung San Suu Kyi's National League for Democracy (NLD), shot students and arrested the new democratically elected leaders, leaving NLD leaders and party workers a choice of incarceration or exile, the

Government of India initially reacted as most Indians would have wanted it to. India gave asylum to fleeing students, allowed them to operate their resistance movement on the Indian side of the border (with some financial help from New Delhi) and supported a newspaper and a radio station that propagated the democratic voice. For many years, India was unambiguously on the side of democracy, freedom and human rights in Myanmar—and in ways more tangible than the rhetoric of the regime's Western critics. In 1995 Aung San Suu Kyi was awarded the Jawaharlal Nehru Award for International Understanding, India's highest honour given to a foreigner.

But then reality intruded. India's strategic rivals, China and Pakistan, began to cultivate the Burmese generals. Major economic and geopolitical concessions were offered to both suitors. The Chinese even began developing a port on the Burmese coast, far closer to Kolkata than to Canton. And the generals of the SLORC junta, well aware of the utility of what comes out of the barrel of a gun, began providing safe havens and arms to a motley assortment of anti–New Delhi rebel movements that would wreak havoc in the north-eastern states of India and retreat to sanctuaries in the newly renamed Myanmar.

This was troubling enough to policy-makers in New Delhi, who were being painfully reminded of their own vulnerabilities to a determined neighbour. The two countries share a 1600-kilometre land border and a longer maritime boundary with overlapping economic zones in the strategically crucial Bay of Bengal. Four of India's politically sensitive north-eastern states have international borders with Myanmar. These borders are porous and impossible to patrol closely; people, traders, smugglers and militants all cross easily in both directions. The potential threat to India from its own periphery is therefore considerable.

But the clincher came when large deposits of natural gas were found in Myanmar, which it was clear would not be available to an India deemed hostile to the junta. India realized that its rivals were gaining ground in its own backyard while New Delhi was losing out on new economic opportunities. The price of pursuing a moral foreign policy simply became too high.

So New Delhi turned 180 degrees. When Pakistan's President Musharraf travelled to Myanmar in 1999 to celebrate his country's new relationship with his fellow generals, India's then foreign minister Jaswant Singh soon followed. The increasingly forlorn resistance operations from Indian soil were shut down in the hope of reciprocation from the Burmese side. And New Delhi sweetened the Burmese generals' tea for them by providing both military assistance and intelligence support to their regime in their never-ending battles against their own rebels.

India's journey was complete: from standing up for democracy, New Delhi had gone on to aiding and enabling the objectives of the military regime. When monks were being mowed down on the streets of Yangon in 2006, the Indian government called for negotiations, muttered banalities about national reconciliation and opposed sanctions. New Delhi also sent its oil minister to negotiate an energy deal, making it clear the country's real priorities lay with its own national economic interests, ahead of its solidarity with Burmese democrats. (At the same time, Indian diplomats intervened discreetly from time to time on behalf of Suu Kyi, though their effectiveness was limited by New Delhi's unwillingness to alienate Rangoon.)

All this was in fact perfectly understandable. Officials in New Delhi were justified in reacting with asperity to Western critics of its policy: India needed no ethical lessons from a Washington or London that has long coddled military dictators in our neighbourhood, notably in Islamabad. Any Indian government's primary obligation is to its own people, and there is little doubt that the economic opportunities provided by Burmese oil and gas are of real benefit to Indians. India does not have the luxury of distance from Myanmar; there is also the strategic imperative of not ceding ground to India's enemies on its own borders. One inescapable fact of geopolitics remains: you can put your ideals on hold, but you cannot change who your neighbours are.

The member states of the Association of Southeast Asian Nations (ASEAN), on Myanmar's eastern flank, have made similar calculations. India's government therefore cannot be blamed for deciding that its national interests in Myanmar are more important than standing up for democracy there. As I wrote at the time, India's policy was being made with its head rather than its heart, but in the process we had lost a little bit of our soul.

And yet, paradoxically, the gradual opening up of Myanmar following the 2011 elections and the installation of a general-turned-civilian, Thien Sein, as president, may offer New Delhi some measure of vindication. As the new regime released political prisoners, permitted freedom of movement to the detained Aung San Suu Kyi, allowing her to contest and win a by-election, and even questioned the environmental and economic impact of a big Chinese dam project in the country's north, India's Western critics began grudgingly to acknowledge that genuine change might well be on the way. Countries like India that had maintained links with the junta and gently prised open its clenched fist may well have achieved more than those whose threats, bluster and sanctions had merely hardened the junta's heart.

After two decades of ruthless military rule under a remarkably opaque regime, Myanmar has witnessed an opening up of its political space amid evidence of self-assertion by the nominally civilian government. Aung San Suu Kyi's victory in a by-election to the Myanmarese Parliament offers a glimmer of hope that the fledgling political process in that country could yet be used by its democrats to create something resembling a genuine democracy. There is no doubt that the country's military rulers are cynically hoping to use her participation in the parliamentary process to bolster the illusion of freedom while continuing to exert real control over what goes on in their country. But such exercises in 'managed democratization' have often surprised their would-be manipulators in places as far apart as Iran and Indonesia. It is clearly in the interests of both India and the United States to work with this possibility. While China has always been much more comfortable dealing with an uncompromising military regime which could be guaranteed to uphold its interests, India's embrace of the junta has always been a more reluctant one, based on the compulsions of a common geography rather than the affinities of shared ideals.

Former foreign secretary Nirupama Rao told Indian reporters after visiting US President Barack Obama publicly chastised New Delhi in November 2010 for its indulgence of the Burmese junta in Naypyidaw (the new Burmese capital created by the military): 'Myanmar is not a country on the dark side of the moon but a country on our borders with which we have to deal.' It is telling that India's tri-services command on the Andaman Islands abuts Myanmar's maritime boundaries and is just about 20 kilometres away from Myanmar's Coco Islands, where China is believed to be building naval infrastructure. These are not considerations a responsible government overlooks.

In turn, by cancelling a $3.6-billion hydroelectric project (90 per cent of its electricity would have been exported to China), the Burmese government surprised most observers, even though Chinese analysts were quick to express understanding of Naypyidaw's desire not to be seen as wholly subservient to a much more powerful neighbour. But the signal is clear: Myanmar is not a vassal state of China, and is willing to diversify its foreign relations.

It is in Myanmar's interests to have more than one suitor wooing it; offsetting one neighbour against another is a time-honoured practice. Though China's engagement dwarfs India's, Myanmar–India bilateral trade reached $1.071 billion in 2010–11, including India's purchase of 70 per cent of Myanmar's exported agricultural produce, and India is now Myanmar's fourth largest trading partner after Thailand, Singapore and China. (India's privileged relationship with the junta in Naypyidaw also allowed it quicker humanitarian access than the United Nations and other international relief agencies enjoyed following the devastation caused by Cyclone Nargis in May 2008.)

Economics can always open the door to politics. 'That Myanmar could defy the Chinese [by cancelling the hydroelectric project],' wrote the Indian scholar Sreeram Chaulia, 'is being seen as a sign that political space exists for the United States to work as a facilitator of the democratisation process in Myanmar.' The November 2011 visit of US Secretary of State Hillary Clinton to Myanmar and Prime Minister Manmohan Singh's visit in May 2012 brought confirmation that India has been playing a quiet but effective role in promoting greater engagement with Naypyidaw.

India cannot and should not seek to outdo China in appeasing the military junta. Its natural instincts lie with the Burmese democrats, Aung San Suu Kyi and the former students for whom it has, over the years, shown its support. With Washington signalling a willingness to take Naypyidaw's political openness at face value, the stage is set for the region's democracies, especially India, to open Myanmar's windows to the world. China will be watching closely.

On the whole, therefore, India's engagement with its neighbours is, as it emerges from the foregoing narrative, both multi-pronged and less negative than many, even within India, assume. It is an engagement that is at the same time conducted bilaterally, regionally under the ambit of SAARC, and through what one might call subregional or even trans-regional mechanisms such as the Bay of Bengal Initiative for Multi-Sectoral Technical and Economic Cooperation (BIMSTEC), which includes some SAARC members and some ASEAN ones, or the Indian Ocean Rim Association for Regional Co-operation (IOR-ARC), which pulls together eighteen countries whose shores are washed by the Indian Ocean, including some South Asian nations and several on other continents. Since I have focused so far on the bilateral relationships, I will briefly discuss SAARC, leaving our cooperation within each of the other two multilateral frameworks to Chapter Five.

SAARC is an organization which has been quietly working to touch the lives of the people in South Asia without many Indians knowing much about it. Its most significant attribute is arguably what is increasingly being accepted as the asymmetric participation by India, as SAARC's largest member. New Delhi's increasing willingness to give far more than it takes from SAARC has also been the most important factor in strengthening intra-regional cooperation. SAARC's most significant shortcoming, on the other hand, is Pakistan's continuing hostility to India, which has often held progress on South Asian cooperation hostage to the bitter resentment of Islamabad. While this did, for several years, severely limit SAARC's potential, the other members have grown progressively impatient with Pakistani intransigence on some issues, and there is increasing talk of certain initiatives (such as a possible South Asian Free Trade Area, which Pakistan has resolutely opposed) proceeding with the involvement of just those members who are keen, rather than awaiting a consensus of all.

In this, Indian generosity is key, and in recent years New Delhi has not been found wanting. Not only has India's manner of discharging our commitment to this grouping inspired other SAARC member states to take initiatives on regional projects, but it has helped transform SAARC from a declaratory phase to an implementation drive that is at last gathering momentum. India has contributed nearly $200 million for the SAARC Development Fund (several multiples of all other countries' contributions put together) and enabled its operationalization. It is not yet widely known that India has also devoted considerable resources and political effort to setting up a world-class university as a direct SAARC project—the South Asia University in South Delhi, open to students from the eight SAARC members at an affordable (i.e., subsidized) cost. India is the largest contributor to the development of this university, chipping in over $230 million out of a total cost of some $300 million. The university has already started classes in temporary buildings pending the construction of its greenfield campus.

With increasing regional engagement on core areas of development, especially health, education, energy, agriculture and infrastructure, awareness about the effectiveness of SAARC in delivering the fruits of development to South Asians at the grass roots has begun to increase. These regional activities have enabled a large constituency of South Asians to be connected and benefit from basic infrastructure in health, education, food and infrastructure, hitherto unavailable to them. Consequently, there has been an exponential increase in intra-regional tourism and people-to-people exchanges, though there remains scope for very much more growth in these areas.

SAARC's transformation from declarations to actions has also generated interest among non-SAARC states, with nine observers— including, intriguingly, China—formally expressing their intent to engage with SAARC. Intra-regional cooperation has strengthened physical connectivity, helped overcome the challenges of the global economic crisis and the food crisis, and is encouraging greater cooperation in articulating a common SAARC position at many international forums.

I would like to believe that SAARC's evolutionary path towards economic prosperity in South Asia, though slow, is irreversible. Of course, we are all conscious that political setbacks can derail, or slow down, economic progress. But with increasing economic interdependence among member states, heading in the future towards a SAARC Customs Union, a South Asian free trade area or even, one day, a single SAARC currency no longer appears to be completely unrealistic.

As this broad-brush survey of opportunities in India's immediate neighbourhood suggests, it is time for New Delhi's dealings with its neighbours to be driven by both self-interest and magnanimity. The cliché of 'win-win' solutions can easily apply in the situations I have described, particularly if India extends its economic dynamism beyond its own borders and shares its burgeoning prosperity with the lands around it.

As India has benefited enormously from its own ability to participate in the global economy, so too will its neighbours benefit from access to and participation in India's economy. It is shocking—no milder word will do—that just 5 per cent of South Asia's trade is within the SAARC region, and that a region with 22 per cent of the world's population produces barely 6 per cent of its GDP. (The World Bank has even declared South Asia to be the world's least economically integrated region, with countries spending far more than they need to on goods they could have imported from within South Asia. A recent report titled 'Cost of Economic Non-Cooperation to Consumers in South Asia' contends that further trade integration among South Asian economies could yield $2 billion to consumers.) Changing this must be a priority; promoting regional prosperity will go a long way towards persuading India's neighbours that they have a stake in its success. This will require giving India's neighbourhood the same priority that Indian foreign policy has traditionally accorded to major powers like the United States and China, and balancing its understandable interest in global strategic issues with a regional focus on matters of trade, water resources, disaster management and cross-border movements of populations. The integration of India's border states with their foreign neighbours' economies would offer a win-win for both.

Indeed part of the challenge is that what is involved is not just integration, but the reintegration of economies torn asunder by history and politics. It would be of historic and sentimental value, as well as practical, if increasing South Asian integration served to reverse the severe economic damage inflicted by Partition in 1947. At that time, the stroke of a British pen severed road, rail and river links that had flourished in united India under the British Raj. Natural ports were cut off from their hinterlands, as Kolkata was from East Pakistan (later Bangladesh) and as Bangladesh's own Chittagong has been from India's north-eastern states. Mumbai and Karachi were once siblings, twin commercial cities that mirrored each other; today they are estranged neighbours. Political developments on the subcontinent since 1947 and the eruption of conflict have made the new barriers all but impenetrable. Their gradual easing, initially through economic cooperation, could produce significant benefits, including eventually in the area of security. But it is far from easy to put Humpty Dumpty back together again.

India's rise is no threat to any of its neighbours, but that is not enough; it must also afford them opportunities for their own growth and advancement. If it fails to do so, weak and unstable neighbours will constitute a threat to India itself, as our experience with terrorism, extremism and cross-border insurgency has demonstrated. For India to help promote development and strengthen the states in its own neighbourhood is a 'no-brainer', even if this is more difficult than making speeches at the UN about global risks emanating from distant lands. We have a shared history to build upon, and cultural affinities with every one of our neighbours that should be a source of commonality rather than of division. SAARC deserves more attention today than the Non-Aligned Movement; a water treaty with Bangladesh, Nepal and Bhutan deserves as much political energy to be expended on it as the Indo-US nuclear deal received.

India has a vital national responsibility to build its own infrastructure and extend it to our neighbourhood. Building more and better roads in the border areas and enhancing air, rail, river and sea connectivity with our neighbours must become more of a priority than they already are. This means devoting both resources and greater political attention to this objective. Pursuing economic integration with our neighbours is nothing less than a strategic goal, since the alternative is resentment at best and conflict at worst. The Chinese have made significant progress in building up their infrastructure up to their borders; there is a case for India to do the same and to connect the two together, to take advantage of the synergies that would result. (However, the atavistic fear remains, in some quarters, that this would facilitate a Chinese invasion, both metaphorically and literally.) Equally, India's broader engagement with the region and the globe could benefit all countries in an integrated South Asia: they should be invited to share the opportunities that their association with India makes possible, while understanding that distancing themselves from India would also deprive them of wider possibilities.

By the same logic, we must also cease insisting on bilateral solutions to our issues with our neighbours where they prefer regional ones. It is understandable that smaller countries sometimes feel that a purely bilateral negotiation with such a huge neighbour would place them at a disadvantage. Doing things with three or four neighbours at a time, or in the SAARC framework, would help even out the perception of Indian dominance, and should be welcomed by New Delhi for precisely that reason. Indian diplomacy in South Asia must evolve a new paradigm that suggests no hint of hegemonism but that is still capable of exercising leverage, no easy task but one well worth pursuing.

Several specific ideas have been mentioned in the present chapter; many more exist or can easily be developed. In a March 2012 speech, India's National Security Adviser Shivshankar Menon urged the region to 'move forward much more rapidly on connectivity, including energy and grid connectivity, tourism, people-to-people, trade and economic links that can make such a major contribution to improving our future'. A regionwide energy market could be created, building upon the example already mentioned of cooperation with Bangladesh, Bhutan and Nepal on hydropower. (The politician Mani Shankar Aiyar has even called for an Asian Oil and Gas Union, going beyond South Asia to embrace West Asian suppliers and East Asian consumers.) The process given a fresh thrust by Prime Minister Manmohan Singh's visit to Dhaka in September 2011 could result in reuniting Kolkata with its vast natural hinterland in Bangladesh, from which it has been cut off for decades. More trade and tourism among SAARC countries could help dispel misunderstandings which have led to major problems in the past. Easier availability of Indian visas, rather than insisting initially upon strict reciprocity, would facilitate people-to-people contact that could help dispel tensions. India's 'soft power'—Bollywood cinema, books and music, educational opportunities, health care (offering specialized treatment for South Asian nationals at discounted rates in Indian hospitals), sporting exchanges, tourism and cultural schemes built on shared history and heritage (like the joint celebration of the 1857 Revolt, which turned out to be a damp squib, or the more successful combined commemoration with Bangladesh of Tagore's 150th birthday)—must be consciously leveraged in the subcontinent as a source of goodwill. And adding substance to 'Look East' will transform India's own North-East as it drives its reach into the heartland of ASEAN, with which it has already signed a free trade agreement.

Shared management of the region's ecological resources is another possibility. Our environment is shared blessing and its future our shared destiny. The South Asian countries partake of a common geography, and the subcontinent's glaciers, mountains, river systems, rainfall patterns and even forests recognize no man-made boundaries. Managing these cooperatively could bring benefits vastly exceeding the costs of the diplomatic efforts required.

One of the most important challenges for Indian diplomacy in the subcontinent is to persuade its neighbours that India is an opportunity, not a threat. Far from feeling in any way besieged by India, they should be able to see it as offering access to a vast market and to a dynamic, growing economy which would provide their own economies with far greater opportunities than more distant partners (or even their own domestic markets) could provide. This would go beyond economic benefits: as David Malone argues, 'Economic cooperation represents the easiest "sell" to various constituencies within the countries of the region. Were this to prove successful, cooperation on more divisive and sensitive issues, such as terrorism, separatism, insurgency, religious fundamentalism, and ethnic strife, could be attempted with greater chances of success.' For these reasons, Delhi clearly should do more to make greater economic integration politically attractive and administratively feasible. Imaginative and major new projects to integrate India's north-eastern region with neighbouring countries—such as building efficient rail and road connectivity with Nepal, with and through Bangladesh, into Myanmar and on to Southeast Asia—will help create the physical integration from which economic integration will flow. (We will return to this in Chapter Five.) Winds of change are blowing in South Asia. There is a definite consolidation of democracy in all the countries of the region, every one of which has held elections within the last three years. Some of our neighbours have made significant strides in surmounting internal conflict and others are in the process of doing so. A subcontinent no longer bedevilled by mutual suspicion and distrust, and committed to democracy, economic cooperation and improved regional integration, is no longer a pipe-dream. If India has to fulfil its potential in the world, we have no choice but to live in peace with our neighbours, in mutual security, harmony and cooperation. Our stellar economic growth has added to the confidence with which we can approach our neighbours; the insecure are always less magnanimous. We have entered an era in which India can see borders not as barriers but as portals, and border areas not as buffer zones but as gateways of opportunity.

As Malone puts it: 'Indian policy in South Asia has improved in tone and quality in recent years. But it is not yet such as to induce either awe or affection amongst those neighbours who matter. India cannot aspire to be a truly convincing "great power" until it achieves a better handle on its region without the support and active involvement of outsiders. Indeed, India faces a circular challenge: unless its region becomes more cooperative (and prosperous), India is unlikely to develop into more than a regional power, but it is true as well that it cannot be a global power unless it reaches beyond its neighbourhood.'

It is a truth that we in India hold to be self-evident that it is in India's interest to be generous to its neighbours on the subcontinent (just as, as I have argued in the previous chapter, it is in India's interest, as the stronger country, to offer generous gestures to Pakistan in order to improve the atmosphere within which peace and progress are to be sought). Perhaps the best metaphor for India's most appropriate attitude to the countries on its periphery in this regard comes not from the soaring vision of Jawaharlal Nehru, whom I have often quoted, but from the more down-to-earth perspective of his successor as prime minister, the modest Lal Bahadur Shastri. Just as Nehru left Robert Frost's immortal lines—'Miles to go before I sleep'—on his bedside table when he died, Shastri kept some lines of the founder of the Sikh faith, Guru Nanak, on his desk. When translated into English they read: 'O Nanak! Be tiny like the grass, for other plants will wither away, but grass will remain ever green.' Shastri was seen by many Indians of exalted ambition as a tiny man, but he had the mind and heart of a giant. His vision of peaceful coexistence with our neighbours, through adopting the demeanour, the modesty and the freshness of grass, may well be the best way for India to ensure that its dreams remain evergreen in its own backyard. In this era of competing global powers seeking to influence South Asia in their own interests, India will do well if, like Shastri, it heeds Guru Nanak's wisdom.

Chapter Four

China and India: Competition, Cooperation or Conflict?

The rise of China and India in the world has become a cliché of contemporary political analysis. It is widely accepted that these are the two countries whose development is having and will have a significant impact on the global system, and on the world's sense of where international economic and political power will shift in the decades to come. The question we must consider is whether the two countries will compete, cooperate or even enter into conflict.

Of course, both China and India are extraordinary success stories of recent years. Both have multiplied their per capita income levels many times over since 1950, and have done so far faster in recent years than Britain or the United States did during and after the Industrial Revolution. The idea that both China and India could triple their current economies in the next fifteen years is not implausible to most economists, not even to the World Bank, if their annual assessment of Global Economic Prospects is any guide. I am not an economist, but I have always been profoundly sceptical of those who issue forecasts of any sort; to me, the future is never quite what it used to be. But few will disagree that China and India are going to be richer than they are now, both in absolute terms and in relative ones. That is why it is meaningful to speak of an increasing shift of economic and, as a result, political power—and to ask how the two countries, which fought a short but brutal war just fifty years ago, will deal with each other in the process.

China and India are the two most populous countries in the world, with India set to overtake China's population around 2025. They account for nearly a tenth of global GDP, a fifth of world exports and a sixth of all international capital flows. China and India are the world's second and eleventh largest economies in dollar terms, though both rank higher in PPP terms. China holds by far the largest foreign currency reserves in the world, at some $3 trillion; half of that is held in US paper, and if it pulled its money out of the US Treasury it could in one stroke destroy the US economy (at some considerable cost to itself, of course, which is why this won't happen, but it reflects how much the United States is dependent on it).

We can say with some confidence that India and China will continue to prosper and pull more millions out of poverty than they have ever done, that they will compete effectively with Western corporations for business, purchase foreign companies and assets, expand their trade and overseas investments, invent and develop new technologies and displace more economic weight around the world. As a result, they will inevitably demand more authority in the international system, and I believe they will acquire it. China will, in my view, be the country that strips the United States of its current designation of being the world's 'sole superpower'—perhaps within one generation. India will not stride the global stage to that extent, but it will be a significant player in its own region, and through the attraction of its soft power, be hugely influential well beyond its borders. Neither will be—nor has been for some time—a bit player on the global stage.

Both are also currently expanding their hard power. China's military budget has been increasing by a staggering 17 to 18 per cent a year since 2007, rising to $106 billion in 2012. It has launched an unmanned space orbiter, announced a major expansion of its naval and submarine fleet, and conducted a test flight of a new stealth fighter aircraft, the J-20, on the very day (11 January 2011) that the US secretary of defence was calling on President Hu Jintao in Beijing. India is behind but it is heading in the same direction, expanding its defence and space capabilities. (Still, both countries together would have a long way to go before they can compete with the United States, whose defence budget is currently equal to that of the rest of the world put together.)

According to the experts at Goldman Sachs, China is likely to overtake the United States as the world's largest economy by the late 2020s, with India closing in behind them. But let us remember that this would merely be a partial reversion to a historical state of affairs. The economic historian Angus Maddison has told us that back in 1820 China and India together accounted for half of the world's total economic output—India 23 per cent of global GDP, China nearly 27 per cent. Neither is close to those numbers today, but even the most optimistic projections for their rise do not see these two countries accounting for 50 per cent of global GDP in the twenty-first century. So there may be a genuine shift of economic power, but it would not bring these two back to the position they occupied just two centuries ago.

To look at the recent rise of these two countries is, however, remarkably instructive. Those who visited China during Mao's time would not recognize it today. It is a country that remade itself to a point that its visible physical infrastructure is almost entirely new: the extraordinary cities with their dense forest of skyscrapers, their six-lane expressways, studded with flyovers or overpasses, their gleaming modern airports, their large and throbbing ports, and the growing network of high-speed railways. The last is indicative of how significantly China has invested in its infrastructure: the high-speed rail network has gone from zero just six years ago to 8358 kilometres at the end of 2010, and is projected to reach 13,000 kilometres by 2012 and 16,000 kilometres by 2020. It also features trains of a speed and sophistication not widely seen elsewhere in the world. Similar projections about the expressway network, which has gone from zero in 1995 to 66,000 kilometres today, see 100,000 kilometres of six-lane roads by 2015 and 150,000 kilometres by 2020. (The joke used to be that the national bird of China must be the crane, since there were so many of them around the country.)

The transformation has been so dramatic that a little fishing village called Shenzhen has become, in a decade, one of the world's largest and most prosperous modern cities. The rows of massed bicycles across Beijing have given way to choking fleets of spanking new cars; the dull grey Mao tunics have been replaced by colourful clothes of the latest styles and cut, made (or at least copied) in China itself; the supermarkets overflow with consumer goods of every conceivable description, again mainly made in China and exported to the rest of the world, including to those countries that designed these products in the first place. When I first visited Beijing in 1997, I expected to see a version of New Delhi;

I was quite unprepared for the difference of kind, not just of degree, that confronted me there, let alone in bustling, sleek Shanghai. China's prosperous cities are First World conurbations, bearing little resemblance to those of the typical developing country (which is what China's leaders still claim their country is). To an Indian visitor, this is startling, and not a little humbling.

Institutions are acquiring new habits and traditions undreamt of in the Maoist past. A few years ago, I was invited to speak at Beijing University, and was presented with a handsome red-and-white university tie. When I returned to the UN headquarters in New York I made it a point to wear my new tie at a meeting with a senior Chinese official who I knew had graduated from Peking University. He made no comment about the tie, so I was provoked to ask him, 'Don't you recognize what I'm wearing?' No, he replied, and then it struck me: when he had attended Peking University, there had been no such thing as an official university tie, for the simple reason that no one wore one!

Even traditions are being manufactured in the country. Change has come to China, and it's a stunning degree of change. Instead of being hemmed in behind tightly controlled borders, Chinese are now free to travel and study abroad, and almost a million have done so in the last three decades, including some 130,000 who are currently studying in foreign countries, acquiring skills that most will bring back to their native land. The private sector, unknown in Mao's day, bids fair to rival the state-owned enterprises that were the initial engines of China's growth and prosperity. It is not all good news. China is also more polluted than ever before, with air unfit to breathe, visibility in Beijing shockingly limited by smog, and rivers poisoned by toxic effluents. It is also a much more unequal society, an irony for a country that still calls itself a people's republic and is ruled by a communist party.

This is admittedly a sketchy summary of a complex reality, but it serves as a platform for a reflection on two aspects of the rise of China and India: first, the question of commonalities, competition and complementarities between the two of them and, second, the risk of conflict.

First, commonalities, complementarities and competition. It has become rather fashionable these days, in bien-pensant circles in the West, to speak of India and China in the same breath. These are the two big countries said to be taking over the world, the new contenders for global eminence after centuries of Western domination, the Oriental answer to generations of Occidental economic success. Three recent books even explicitly twin the two countries: *Forbes* magazine correspondent Robyn Meredith's *The Elephant and the Dragon: The Rise of India and China and What It Means for All of Us*, Harvard business professor Tarun Khanna's *Billions of Entrepreneurs: How China and India Are Reshaping Their Futures—and Yours* and Raghav Bahl's *Superpower? The Amazing Race between China's Hare and India's Tortoise*. All three books, though different in scope and tone, see the recent rise of India and China as literally shifting the world's economic and political tectonic plates. Some even speak of 'Chindia', as if the two are joined at the hip in the international imagination.

Personally, count me among the sceptics. It's not just that, aside from the fact that both countries occupy a rather vast landmass called 'Asia', they have very little in common. It's also that the two countries are already at very different stages of development—China started its liberalization in 1978, a good thirteen years before India, shot up faster, hit double-digit growth when India was still hovering around 5 per cent and, with compound growth, has put itself in a totally different league from India, continuing to grow faster from a larger base. And it's also that the two countries' systems are totally dissimilar. If China wants to build a new six-lane expressway, it can bulldoze its way past any number of villages in its path; in India, if you want to widen a two-lane road, you could be tied up in court for a dozen years over compensation entitlements. When China built the Three Gorges Dam, it created a 660-kilometre-long reservoir that necessitated the displacement of a staggering 2 million people, all accomplished in fifteen years without a fuss in the interests of generating electricity; when India embarked on the Narmada Dam project, aiming to bring irrigation, drinking water and power to millions, it had to spend thirty-nine years (so far) fighting environmental groups, human rights activists and advocates for the displaced all the way to the Supreme Court, while still being thwarted in the streets by the protesters from non-governmental organizations like the Narmada Bachao Andolan (Save Narmada Movement). That is how it should be; India is a fractious democracy, China is not. But as an Indian, I do not wish to pretend we can compete in the global growth stakes with China.

In fact, if anyone wanted confirmation that twinning India with China is, to put it mildly, premature, one has only to look at the medals tally at the Beijing Olympics. China proudly ranked first, with 51 gold medals and a total of 100. You have to strain your eyes past such twinkling little stars of the global family as Jamaica, Belarus, war-torn Georgia, collapsing Zimbabwe and even what used to be called Outer Mongolia before stumbling across India in 50th place, with precisely three medals, one gold and two bronze.

This is not, in fact, a surprise. Whereas China has set about systematically striving for Olympic success since it re-entered global competition after years of isolation, India has remained complacent about its lack of sporting prowess. Where China lobbied for and won the right to host the Olympics within two decades of its return to the Games, India rested on its laurels after hosting the Asian Games in Delhi in 1982, so that it is now considered further behind in the competition for Olympic hosthood than it was two decades ago. Where China embarked on 'Project 119', a programme devised specifically to boost the country's Olympic medal standings (the number 119 refers to the golds awarded at the Sydney Games of 2000 in such medal-laden sports as track and field, swimming, rowing, sailing and canoeing), Indians wondered if they would be able to crack the magic ceiling of two, the highest number of medals the country has ever won at this quadrennial exercise in international sporting machismo. Where China, seeing the number of medals awarded in kayaking, decided to create a team to master a sport hitherto unknown in the Middle Kingdom, India has not even lobbied successfully for the inclusion in the Games of the few sports it does play well (kabaddi, for instance, or polo, or cricket, which was played in the Olympics of 1900 and has been omitted since). Where China has maintained its dominance in table tennis and badminton, and developed new strengths in non-traditional sports like rowing and shooting, India has seen its once-legendary invincibility in field hockey fade with the introduction of Astroturf, to the point where its team even failed to qualify for the Beijing Olympics.

Forget 'Chindia'—the two countries barely belong in the same sporting sentence.

What's happened at the Olympics speaks to a basic difference in the two countries' systems. It's the creative chaos of all-singing, all-dancing Bollywood versus the perfectly choreographed precision of the Beijing Opening Ceremony. The Chinese, as befits a communist autocracy, approached the task of dominating the Olympics with top-down military discipline. The objective was determined, a programme (Project 119) drawn up, the considerable resources of the state attached to it, state-of-the-art technology acquired and world-class foreign coaches imported. India, by contrast, approached these Olympics as it had every other, with its usual combination of amiable amateurism, bureaucratic ineptitude, half-hearted experiment and shambolic organization.

In China, national priorities are established by the government and then funded by the state; in India, priorities emerge from seemingly endless discussions and arguments among myriad interests, and funds have to be found where they might. China's budget for preparing its sportspersons for these Games alone probably exceeded India's expenditure on all Olympic training in the last sixty years.

But where China's state-owned enterprises remain the most powerful motors of the country's development, India's private sector, ducking around governmental obstacles and bypassing the stifling patronage of the state, has transformed the fortunes of the Indian people. So it proved again in the Olympics: the wrestlers, boxers, runners, tennis players and weightlifters who made up the bulk of the Indian contingent, accompanied by the inevitable retinue of officials, returned with just two bronzes among them, while India's only gold—in shooting—was won by a young entrepreneur with a rifle range in his own backyard and no help from the state whatsoever. Young Abhinav Bindra was, at twenty-five, the CEO of a high-tech firm, a self-motivated sharpshooter who financed his own equipment and training, and an avid blogger. He is, in short, a twenty-first-century Indian. At one level, it is not surprising that he should have won India's first individual gold in any Olympics since a transplanted Englishman competed in Indian colours in the 1900

Games. India is the land of individual excellence despite the limitations of the system; in China, individual success is the product of the system.

Certainly, in absolute numbers, the Chinese are way ahead. Their export of electronic goods now tops $180 billion a year. One out of every three shoes exported in the world is made in China. They make 75 per cent of the world's toys. Foreign direct investment is at the level of $70 billion a year (for comparison, India gets $42 billion). Shanghai alone has nearly 4000 skyscrapers (more than all of India, and exceeding Los Angeles and Chicago combined). China has built an estimated 60,000 kilometres of expressways in less than two decades and will soon outstrip the total length of the US highway network. Per capita income has risen nearly tenfold since 1978 to over $6000, and the number of people living in absolute poverty has dropped from 425 million two decades ago to 26 million today. The population is almost totally literate; life expectancy is reaching developed-country levels. In 2009, China overtook Germany to become the world's third largest economy, behind the United States and Japan; in 2010, Japan was overtaken. It won't stay number two for long.

Against this, though, are a number of factors suggesting that not everything is rosy in China. Economic growth has occurred at breakneck speed, but that means some necks have been broken: the human cost of development has not been negligible (population displacement, farmers thrown off their lands, villages flooded by dams, mounting pollution, low-wage labour in appalling conditions, widening disparities between the rich and the poor, an absence of human rights and few checks on governmental abuses). The Chinese have seen great and rapid improvements in their Internet access, but Beijing employs some 40,000 'cyber-police' to monitor politically undesirable activity on the Web.

Equally important, China's success has not just been China's: a disproportionate share of the benefits goes abroad, to the foreign companies that have set up factories in China. It has been estimated that of the $700 American price of a Chinese-made laptop, only $15 remains in China. Only four of the country's top twenty-five exporters are Chinese companies, according to Robyn Meredith, who adds that in practice 'Made in China' really means 'Made by America [or Europe] in China'.

The Chinese financial system also leaves much to be desired. Where India has been running sophisticated stock markets since the early nineteenth century—and Indians are so skilled at doing so that they got the Bombay Stock Exchange up and running within 24 hours of the terrorist bomb blasts that nearly destroyed the building in 1992—China is new at the game, and not particularly adept at it. The financial information provided by China's companies, especially those in the large governmental sector, is notoriously unreliable, and standards of corporate governance are low. There are no world-class Chinese companies with sophisticated managers to match Tata or Wipro or Infosys. China's capital markets are weak and its banks inefficient: the Chinese banking system carried an estimated $911 billion in unrecoverable loans as of 2006, mainly to government firms.

In his book *Capitalism with Chinese Characteristics*, Professor Yasheng Huang of the Massachusetts Institute of Technology (MIT) argues that the Indian private sector is more efficient and entrepreneurial than the Chinese private sector. State-owned enterprises still account for half of China's economic assets. China has yet to master the art of channelling domestic savings into productive investments, which is why it has relied so extensively on FDI. India, on the other hand, is exporting FDI to member countries of the Organisation for Economic Co-operation and Development (OECD); in other words, India's entrepreneurial capital and management skills are better able than China's to control and manage assets in the sophisticated financial markets of the developed West.

And the world has yet to develop any confidence in China's legal system (where a contract still means whatever the government says it means). In other words, it still lags behind India on the 'software' of development—not just technical brainpower or engineering know-how, but the systems it needs to operate a twenty-first-century economy in an open and globalizing world. The Chinese state is undoubtedly stronger and more efficient than the Indian, but the Indian private sector is not only miles ahead, it is compensating for the inadequacies of the state, whereas in China the state sector can still stifle the private, and both sides know it.

And then there's politics. Whatever you might say about India's sclerotic bureaucracy versus China's efficient one, India's tangles of red tape versus China's unfurled red carpet to foreign investors, India's contentious and fractious political parties versus China's smoothly functioning top-down communist hierarchy, there's one thing you've got to grant: India has become an outstanding example of the management of diversity through pluralist democracy. Every Indian has been allowed to feel he or she has as much of a stake in the country, and as much of a chance to run it, as anyone else: after all, our last-but-one elections, in 2004, were won by a woman political leader of Roman Catholic heritage who made way for a Sikh to be sworn in as prime minister by a Muslim president, in a nation 81 per cent Hindu. And our largest state was ruled till very recently by a Dalit woman, from a community once considered 'untouchable', whose caste and gender would have made her power unthinkable for 3000 years before democracy made it possible. She wasn't promoted by the Brahmin elite in New Delhi; she rode to the top on the ballots of her political base, building her own rainbow coalition along the way.

Contrast this with Beijing, where political freedom is unknown, leaders at all levels are handpicked from the top for their posts and political heresy is met with swift punishment, house arrest or worse. During the 2008 Olympics, under international pressure, China designated a few areas where protesters could, in theory, peacefully gather; but you had to apply for permission to protest, which was never granted, and most of those who applied were arrested and detained, which meant that the authorization of protest became an excellent method for the security police to identify potential troublemakers without having to actually look for them. India's politics means its shock absorbers are built into the system; it has endured major road bumps without the vehicle ever breaking down. In China's case, it is far from clear what would happen if the limousine of state actually encountered a serious pothole. The present system wasn't designed to cope with fundamental challenges to it except through repression. But every autocratic state in history has come to a point where repression was no longer enough. If that point is reached in China, all bets are off. The dragon could stumble where the elephant can always trundle on.

But let us not be complacent. India's problems are enormous and there is still a great deal we need to do internally. Our teeming cities overflow while two out of three Indians still scratch a living from the soil. We have been recognized, for all practical purposes, as a leading nuclear power, but 272 million Indians still have no access to electricity and there are daily power cuts even in the nation's capital. Ours is a culture which elevated non-violence to an effective moral principle, but whose freedom was born in blood and whose independence still soaks in it. We are the world's leading manufacturers of generic medication for illnesses such as AIDS, but we have 3 million of our own citizens without access to AIDS medication, another 2 million with TB, and tens of millions with no health centre or clinic within 10 kilometres of their places of residence. India holds the world record for the number of cellphones sold, but also for the number of farmer suicides (an estimated 17,000 in 2010, because when crops fail, farmers faced with a crippling mountain of debt see no other way out for their families than to take their own lives). We still have a great deal to do before we can meaningfully speak of ourselves in competition with China.

———

But if we can't compete, can we cooperate?

As far back as 1947, even before India and several nations in Asia were yet to throw off the colonial yoke, when China was still in the throes of an uncertain civil war and when Asia got no more than a footnote in any chapter on global politics and economics, the fledgling Indian Council of World Affairs, under the inspiration of Jawaharlal Nehru, organized a visionary 'Asian Relations Conference'. Many of the tenets of that endeavour are closer to being a reality today, since they prefigured the process of Asia's economic integration and increasing interdependence. A hallmark of Nehru's vision was his admiration for the 'other great Asian civilization', and his conviction that, together with India, China would lead the region in a new post-imperial Asian resurgence.

India and China are the most populous nations on the earth, with the arduous task of uplifting millions of our citizens and realizing social harmony and inclusive growth. Given the scale of our economies and the scale of the 'catching-up' required, this is likely to be a long-drawn-out process, in which China is clearly well ahead. Both of us, though, require sustained international cooperation and a peaceful security environment around us in order to fulfil this task. Currently, in a world faced with a rare economic and financial crisis and tenacious new threats and challenges, our job has become all the more difficult. Therefore, as responsible nations with a stake in peace, stability and prosperity of the world, both India and China must strive to tackle the new challenges together while helping the global economy out of a recession that had nothing to do with us. The continued growth of our two economies has proved vital to the health of the world economy, and that in itself is a most eloquent proof of the prospects for the world and Asia of an emerging China and, increasingly, an emerging India.

The Government of India does not view China or China's development as a threat. Indian leaders have always unembarrassedly spoken of the need to develop a friendly and cooperative relationship with China, as a country with which we cannot afford to have a relationship of antagonism. Long before the India–China growth story attracted global attention, we drew upon our joint civilizational wisdom to enunciate the principles of Panchsheel that demonstrated our interest in building peace and friendship. Our relationship has since evolved to a point where we now have a Strategic and Cooperative Partnership for Peace and Prosperity and an agreed 'Shared Vision for the 21st Century' with China. Indeed, our relationships have become so multifaceted, strategic and intricate that the nature of stakeholders in our relations has changed and broadened to include the wider civil society in both nations.

To repeat a point I have made earlier: the basic task for countries like China and India in international affairs is to wield a foreign policy that enables and facilitates their own domestic transformation. By this, as an Indian, I mean that my country's engagement with the world must make possible the transformation of India's economy and society, while promoting our own national values (of pluralism, democracy, social justice and secularism). What I expect from my national leaders is that they work for a global environment that is supportive of these internal priorities, and therefore of a relationship with China that would permit us to concentrate on our domestic tasks. China and India are both engaged in the great adventure of bringing progress and prosperity to a billion people each, through a major economic transformation. At the broadest level, India's foreign policy must seek to protect that process of transformation—to ensure security and bring in global support for our efforts to build and change our country for the better.

India and China have inevitably been directly affected by the global trends of the post–Cold War era. On the one hand, we are both far more globalized economies than most, and more so than we ever were in the days when we raised the protectionist barriers to shield us while we developed our autonomous national capabilities. We are today more connected through trade and travel—much more than ever before—with the international system, and trade and foreign investment accounts for a steadily increasing share of our GDP, China's much more than India's. Today we can admit that our links with the world are one reason for the highest-ever growth rates that our countries enjoyed.

Our two civilizations had centuries of contact in ancient times; thanks mainly to the export of Buddhism from India to China, Chinese travellers came to Indian universities, visited Indian courts, and wrote memorable accounts of their voyages. Nalanda University, which flourished in northern India for seven centuries from 427 CE and attracted students from across Asia, received hundreds of Chinese students in its time, and a few Indians went the other way. My wife and I had the great pleasure of visiting the famous Lingyin Si temple in Hangzhou, established by a Buddhist monk from India in 326 CE. As mentioned earlier, the great admiral Zheng He visited India less than a century later; on his way, in 410 CE, he erected a tablet in Sri Lanka, written in Chinese, Persian and Tamil, calling on the Hindu deities to bless a world of free trade! Kerala's coastline is dotted with Chinese fishing nets, and the favourite cooking-pot of the Malayali housewife is the wok, locally called *cheena-chatti* ('Chinese vessel'). It's been a while, though, since Indians and Chinese had much to do with each other. The heady days of 'Hindi-Chini bhai-bhai' ('Indians and Chinese are brothers'), the slogan coined by Nehruvian India to welcome Chou En-Lai in 1955, gave way, as we all know, to a more difficult period in our relationship, with the humiliation of the 1962 border war, after which it was 'Hindi-Chini bye-bye' for decades. The bitter border dispute between the two countries remains unresolved, with periodic reports of incursions by Chinese troops on to Indian soil and new irritants over the anti-Chinese protests of Tibetan exiles who have been given asylum in India. To speak of a 'trust deficit' between the two countries is arguably an understatement.

And yet, there has been some good news. Trade has increased twelve-fold in the last decade, to an estimated $73 billion in 2011, a figure that is more than 200 times the total trade between the countries in 1990, just twenty-two years ago. China has now overtaken the United States as India's largest single trading partner. The two governments expect trade to keep growing and, in a joint statement of December 2010, have announced a trade target of $100 billion by 2015; if present trends continue, trade with China is poised to reach double the level of US trade with India before the decade is over. Each country's top twenty-five exports are essentially mutually exclusive, making trade relations an easy example of compatibility. There are some 9000 Indian students in China. Tourism, particularly of Indian pilgrims to the major Hindu holy sites in Tibet, Mount Kailash and Lake Manasarovar, is thriving. (However, this is a relative term: after all, the two nations with a combined population of over two and a half billion people exchanged only 570,000 visitors, over half a million of those being Indians with wanderlust while only some 60,000 Chinese tourists travelled to India.) Indian information technology firms have opened offices in Shanghai and Hangzhou; there are many companies and ventures active in the two countries. One can find dozens of Chinese engineers working in (and learning from) Indian computer firms and engineering companies from Gurgaon to Bangalore; Infosys regularly hires mainland Chinese for its Bangalore campus, while Indian software engineers in those and other cities offer research and development support to the Chinese telecom equipment manufacturer Huawei (in turn sending the signal that eavesdropping devices are not integrated into Chinese telecom products). India has become a major market for Chinese engineering and construction project exports, and a vital source of raw materials, from iron ore to chemicals. New Delhi could do more to press China to reduce its non-tariff barriers, however, and promote Indian services exports to its giant neighbour.

By and large, India is good at things that China needs to improve at, notably software; China excels at hardware and manufacturing, which India sorely lacks. So India's Mahindra & Mahindra manufactures tractors in Nanchang for export to the United States. The key operating components of Apple's iPod were invented by the Hyderabad company PortalPlayer, while the iPods themselves are manufactured in China.

Philips employs nearly 3000 Indians at its 'Innovation Campus' in Bangalore who write more than 20 per cent of Philips' global software, which in turn goes to Philips' 50,000-strong workforce in China to turn into brand-name goods.

In other words, the elephant is already dancing with the dragon. The potential for additional cooperation is immense and need not just be in each other's countries. Inevitably, our search for markets, technology and resources to fuel our growth will be key drivers of our international relations. This is why we are both looking far afield, to Africa and Latin America, for opportunities.

There is an instructive comparison to be made between the FDI patterns of both countries. Indian capitalism drives our country's outward investments in a commercial logic of supply and demand, whereas Chinese FDI is largely fuelled by its government and state-owned enterprises. India's FDI is spent mainly in the developed world and is invested mostly in the manufacturing and services sectors, notably information technology and IT-enabled services, whereas Chinese FDI concentrates almost obsessively on the extraction of natural resources from developing countries, through oil and gas exploration and mining, where India has similar needs but a far more modest overseas presence. India's strength—its comparative advantage, if you will—is anchored in its world-class managers, its track record in corporate governance and its exposure to the best global corporate practices, whereas China's comparative advantage lies in the top-down strategic competence of its government and its single-minded economic drive abroad, which often subordinates conventional diplomacy to the pursuit of economic benefit. Whatever one thinks of the two sets of attributes, there is no denying that they are complementary, rather than a recipe for confrontation.

The opportunities for multilateral cooperation between India and China are great. There is, first of all, the regional plane. China and India have notably strengthened their cooperation in regional affairs. China has acquiesced in India's participation in the East Asia Summit and invited India to join the Shanghai Cooperation Organization as an observer, just as India has supported China's becoming an observer at SAARC. While Asia is devoid of meaningful security institutions, their interlocking economic and trade relationships with each other and with other Asian countries will knit China and India closer together.

But multilateral cooperation need not be confined to the Asian region. China and India have broadly similar interests and approaches on a wide range of broader international questions, from most issues of international peace and security to the principles of world trade and the ways and means of coping with globalization. They have already begun working together in multinational forums on such issues as climate change, trade, labour laws, arms control and environment protection, and have no real differences on matters like encouraging biodiversity, promoting dialogue among civilizations, promoting population control, combating transnational crime, controlling the spread of pandemic disease and dealing with challenges from non-traditional threats to security. (Sadly, the two countries have even sometimes made common cause on human rights, with China and India agreeing on countering Western draft resolutions in UN bodies—China because it is usually guilty of the very practices being condemned in others, India because of its allergy to 'country-specific' human rights prescriptions.)

All of these areas provide a realistic basis for further long-term cooperation. One exception, alas, is the issue of combating international terrorism, where China's indulgence of Pakistani terrorist groups at the UN is arguably not in its own long-term interests. But that can change, and China–India cooperation can also improve on the issues of piracy, oil spills and other international environmental issues, nuclear disarmament and arms races in outer space, human trafficking and natural disasters—all of which are issues on which the two countries could play mutually supportive roles, take joint responsibility and contribute to the establishment of new rules in the global system. New areas of cooperation could also emerge—wildlife conservation, for instance, where both countries could cooperate on issues like the smuggling of tiger parts to Chinese customers, or disaster management, where Asia's two giants have much to learn from each other but have made little effort to do so.

Energy is an obvious area for cooperation. The US Department of Energy estimates that China's oil consumption will rise 156 per cent and India's oil consumption will rise 152 per cent by 2025. While both countries are seeking to expand their domestic production, opportunities for growth are limited, and both countries will become more dependent on imported oil, making them more vulnerable to irregularities of supply and price volatility. This makes the quest for reliable sources of supply and secure sea lanes of communication a shared interest. After all, both China and India are relatively new entrants into the global oil system. They are facing fierce competition from much larger, more experienced and arguably more resourceful Western oil companies. Cooperation between Indian and Chinese oil firms is essential.

Prior to 2002, India and China competed aggressively with each other to acquire oil and gas fields abroad. Wisdom dawned, however, with improved energy cooperation starting that year, when India's Oil and Natural Gas Corporation (ONGC) purchased a 25 per cent share of Sudan's Greater Nile Oil Project, operated by the China National Petroleum Corporation (CNPC). The experience has been positive and continued cooperation in the global energy sector, including some examples of joint bids and at least one successful joint acquisition, has occurred. The prospects for further collaboration, to jointly explore and develop oil and natural gas resources in third countries, are high.

To take another example: our demand for food will inevitably rise as well, perhaps by 50 per cent in the next two decades, as a result of our growing population, their rising affluence and the improved dietary possibilities available to a larger middle class. We will need to multiply our sources of food, including acquiring agricultural land abroad, in Africa and even Latin America. Lack of access to stable supplies of water is reaching critical proportions, particularly for agricultural purposes, and the problem will worsen because of rapid urbanization over the next twenty years. We will need skilful and creative diplomacy to ensure that interruptions in the flow of water across our borders do not bedevil relations with our neighbours.

The only question is whether the two countries can prolong the elephant–dragon dance, or whether political tensions could bring the music to a screeching halt. Critics argue that the good news is in fact good only for China. The trade surplus is undoubtedly in favour of Beijing: of the $73 billion in 2011, $50 billion consisted of Chinese exports to India and only less than half of that, $23 billion, of Indian exports to China.

138 · Pax Indica

China conserves it own domestic resources of iron ore by importing this commodity from India and selling finished steel to it. Indeed, some critics have argued that India is largely exporting its primary commodities to China and importing finished products from that country, a pattern of trade relations reminiscent of the exploitation of India's raw materials in the colonial era. A large proportion of Chinese exports involves items that are so much cheaper than Indian alternatives that they are making Indian manufacturing unviable. And the focus on trade, critics suggest, underscores an issue of interest to Beijing, while taking attention away from the broader strategic contest between the two countries, which China's economic interests prompt it to gloss over.

The critics may be right in suggesting that good trade relations do little to help resolve the perennial political problems between countries. But there are two counter-arguments worth making. First, trade contributes to a positive atmosphere between two countries, which at least makes political hostility less likely. More important, in this instance, it ensures that China has far too high a stake in the Indian economy to contemplate engaging in any military adventurism against India. There are some strategic advantages to offering a potential adversary a large market: it is more likely that the Chinese establishment will learn to see Indians as consumers rather than as enemies.

———

This raises the issue of the risk of conflict between the two countries. As all Indians painfully remember, we went to war in 1962—a decisive triumph for China, which wrested 23,200 square kilometres of Indian territory. At the same time, Beijing has taken pains in recent years to remind India that it still claims a further 92,000 square kilometres, mainly in the north-eastern Indian state of Arunachal Pradesh. It doesn't help that the two countries share the longest disputed frontier in the world, since the Line of Actual Control (LAC) has never been formally delineated in a manner accepted by both sides. India's borders were defined by British imperial administrators in the 1913 MacMahon Line, which China rejects (though it accepts that line as its frontier with Myanmar, which was in those days part of British India). With the LAC coming into being in the wake of China's military success in 1962, the situation is even more unclear. Whenever troops from either side build roads, construct or repair their bunkers and other routine fortifications, or conduct patrols close to the LAC, tensions can and repeatedly do flare up. When the two sides are anxious to avoid provoking each other, such activities are kept to a minimum, but it seemed that since 2008 Beijing has taken a conscious decision to keep the Indians on their toes.

Why do I say that? The last three years have witnessed a proliferation of incidents along the 3488-kilometre frontier between the two Asian giants. Nearly 200 have been recorded, including no fewer than ninety-five incursions by the People's Liberation Army in just one sector alone— the evocatively named Finger Area, a 2.1-square-kilometre salient in the Indian state of Sikkim, which shares a 206-kilometre border with Tibet. Intensified Chinese patrolling has been observed both in Ladakh and in the border areas of Arunachal Pradesh. Reports of intrusions into Indian territory included one in which Chinese soldiers entered 15 kilometres into Indian territory in Ladakh and actually burned the Indian patrolling base. While Indian spokespersons are anxious to downplay such reports, and fewer incidents were made public in 2011, they serve to remind us that the border dispute remains unresolved. In a reply to a question in Parliament, Defence Minister A.K. Antony informed MPs in December 2011 that Chinese troops had, in July 2011, damaged a 200-foot (approx. 60-metre) stone wall which was built 250 metres inside Indian territory in the Tawang area of Arunachal Pradesh. Antony said that an attempt by the Chinese People's Liberation Army (PLA) to raze the wall was prevented by the Indian Army. The stone wall was partially damaged by the PLA patrol, but it has been reconstructed, he added.

Arunachal Pradesh has become a rhetorical flashpoint. Chinese notables, including their ambassadors in New Delhi, have publicly laid claim to the state in recent years, describing it as 'Southern Tibet' and publicly objecting whenever an Indian leader (or the Dalai Lama) travelled there. (To India's credit, this has not deterred Prime Minister Manmohan Singh from visiting and campaigning in Arunachal's elections, nor did India prevent the Dalai Lama from ministering to his flock in that state.) China also reacted sharply to the participation by India's Defence Minister Antony in the silver jubilee celebrations of the state of Arunachal Pradesh held on 20 February 2012, with a Chinese foreign ministry spokesperson asking India publicly to refrain from any action that will complicate the border issue. Earlier China had denied a visa to an Indian Air Force official born in Pasighat, Arunachal Pradesh, who was supposed to visit China as part of an Indian tri-services delegation, on the grounds that as an Arunachali he was not entitled to an Indian passport or a Chinese visa! But the quantum of belligerence in the official Chinese media's reporting about India has risen alarmingly; there have been reminders of 1962 and the *People's Daily* has gone so far as to write of India's 'recklessness and arrogance' and urging it to consider 'the consequences of a potential confrontation with China'.

It was also revealed in 2010 that the Chinese authorities had begun a practice of issuing visas to Indian citizens from Jammu and Kashmir on a separate piece of paper to be stapled to their passports rather than on their Indian passports directly, in order to signal that China does not consider residents of that state to be legitimate citizens of India. (This policy has also led to the anomaly that India and China cite different figures for the length of their disputed border, since China refuses to count the 1600 kilometres between Kashmir and Tibet as part of its dispute with India!) The matter was only resolved after Prime Minister Singh took it up with the Chinese premier during his visit to India in December 2010 and after India had suspended defence ties with China upon China's refusal to grant a visa to India's northern army commander on the grounds that he was operating in a disputed state.

Related developments are no less disquieting. With China having established four new airbases in Tibet and three in its southern provinces bordering India, the Indian Air Force is reportedly augmenting its own presence near the Chinese border by deploying two squadrons of Sukhoi-30MKI fighters. Are the two countries bracing for war? What on earth is going on?

Fears of imminent major hostilities are clearly overblown. China, flush from the huge public relations success of the Olympics, and rejoicing in a huge trade imbalance in its favour with India, is hardly likely to initiate a clash, and India has no desire whatsoever to provoke its northern neighbour. But it's clear that China's troubles over Tibet, which first erupted in 2008 and have again arisen in 2011–12 with a seemingly interminable chain of self-immolations, have brought with them unwelcome reminders to Beijing of India's hospitality to the Dalai Lama and his government-in-exile.

Ironically, during the mass protests in Tibet in 2008, one country that was conspicuous both by its centrality to the drama and by its reticence over it was India. On the question of Tibet, India, the land of asylum for the Dalai Lama and the angry young hotheads of the Tibetan Youth Congress, finds itself on the horns of a dilemma. On the one hand, it is a democracy, one that has a long tradition of allowing peaceful protests, including against foreign countries when their leaders come visiting. It provided refuge to the Dalai Lama when he fled the Chinese occupation of his homeland in 1959, granted asylum (and eventually Indian citizenship) to over 110,000 Tibetan refugees, and permitted them to set up a government-in-exile (albeit one that New Delhi does not recognize) in the picturesque Himalayan hill town of Dharamsala.

On the other hand, it has assiduously been cultivating better relations with China. Though their bitter border dispute remains unresolved, and China has been a vital ally and military supplier to India's enemies across the border in Pakistan, the two countries have been warming to each other in recent years. So New Delhi has attempted to draw a distinction between its humanitarian obligations as a country of asylum and its political responsibilities as a friend of China. The Dalai Lama and his followers are given a respected place but told not to conduct 'political activities' on Indian soil. When young Tibetan radicals undertook a march to Lhasa from Indian soil, the Indian police stopped them well before they got to the Tibetan border, and detained a hundred Tibetans. When some Tibetan demonstrators outside the Chinese embassy in New Delhi attacked the premises, the Indian government stepped up its level of protection for the Chinese diplomats. The former Indian foreign minister Pranab Mukherjee—who was noticeably less forthcoming on Tibet than his American counterpart during a press conference in the middle of the Tibet crisis with then secretary of state Condoleezza Rice in Washington—publicly warned the Dalai Lama against doing anything that could have a 'negative impact on Indo-Sino relations'.

The Dalai Lama's curious position has complicated India's dance on the diplomatic tightrope with China. He is simultaneously the most visible spiritual leader of a worldwide community of believers, a role that India honours, and till 2011 the political head of a government-in-exile, a role that India permits but has rejected in its own dealings with him. As a Buddhist he preaches non-attachment, self-realization, inner actualization and non-violence; as a Tibetan he is looked up to by a people fiercely attached to their homeland, most seeking its independence from China, many determined to fight for it. He has been a refugee for nearly five decades, but is the most recognized worldwide symbol of a country he has not seen in half a century. His message of peace, love and reconciliation has found adherents among Hollywood movie stars and ponytailed hippies, Irish rock musicians and Indian politicians; but he has made no headway at all with the regime that rules his homeland, and has been unable to prevent Tibet's inexorable transformation into one more Chinese province. His sermons fill football stadiums and he has won a Nobel Prize, but political leaders around the world shrink from meeting him openly, for fear of causing costly offence to the Chinese.

Indian officials are acutely conscious that, on this subject, the Chinese are easily offended. An interesting instance came when India facilitated the highly publicized visit by Nancy Pelosi, Speaker of the US House of Representatives, to the Dalai Lama in Dharamsala in 2009, but almost simultaneously cancelled a scheduled meeting between him and the vice-president of India, Mohammed Hamid Ansari. When China summoned the Indian ambassador in Beijing to the foreign ministry at 2 a.m. for a dressing-down over the Tibetan protests in New Delhi, India meekly acquiesced in the insult. Though Prime Minister Manmohan Singh has publicly declared the Dalai Lama to be the 'personification of non-violence', India has let it be known that it does not support his political objectives. Tibet, New Delhi says, is an integral part of China, and India lends no support to those who would challenge that status.

The position is not without its detractors within the country. The Opposition BJP (which led the previous government in New Delhi) has criticized the current government for not 'expressing concern over the use of force by the Chinese government' and instead 'adopting a policy of appeasement towards China with scant regard to the country's national honour and foreign policy independence'. Privately, however, few observers believe the BJP would have conducted itself differently had it been in office.

For the stark truth is that India has no choice in the matter. It cannot undermine its own democratic principles and abridge the freedom of speech of Tibetans on its soil. Nor can it afford to alienate its largest trading partner, a neighbour well on the way to global superpower status, which is known to be extremely prickly over any presumed slights to its sovereignty over Tibet. India will continue to dance delicately on its Tibetan tightrope.

But the dangers are real. The fact that Tawang, the birthplace of the sixth Dalai Lama and a major monastery of Tibetan Buddhism, lies in Arunachal Pradesh deprives Beijing of a vital asset in its attempts to assert total control over Tibet. Beijing must hope that the passing of the current Dalai Lama will permit it to identify and indoctrinate a young successor, rather as it has done with the Panchen Lama. But the Dalai Lama has announced that the next Dalai Lama may not be born in Chinese-controlled Tibetan lands; the suggestion is that he could easily emanate either from the Tibetan diaspora or from traditional areas of Tibetan residence now in India, notably the Tawang tract. Reminding New Delhi of China's claims is therefore all the more urgent for Beijing: China would like to take control of Tawang before it is too late.

India, of course, has no intention of obliging Beijing. Tibet has also exposed the limitations of China's claims to constituting an alternative global pole of attraction to that of the United States. China is not the natural leader of the South; its development experience and economic clout are so exceptional that it is difficult for other developing countries to see themselves in the same mirror. More important on Tibet, China's position, while ostensibly anchored in a principle that other southern governments tend to uphold (that of sovereignty and non-interference), is also infused with a strong dash of national chauvinism that leaves even its allies cold. It is perfectly understandable for Chinese to be proud of China and to demonstrate that pride by jingoistic behaviour in the streets of Beijing, but why should such passions inspire anyone who is not Chinese? By contrast, the spiritual teaching and Gandhian pacifism of the Dalai Lama finds a far more universal appeal, especially in democracies like India and Buddhist nations like Sri Lanka and

Thailand. Their governments may be reluctant to offend China, but their hearts are, in many cases, with the Tibetans rather than their sovereign overlords in Beijing.

The recent announcement by the Dalai Lama that he had renounced his political role as head of the Tibetan government-in-exile, and would henceforth seek to confine himself to a purely spiritual and ecclesiastical role, has further confounded the Chinese, who have made it clear that they see it as yet another example of his Machiavellian design. By organizing free and fair elections among the Tibetan diaspora—which elected Lobsang Sangay, a forty-two-year-old Harvard academic, as the new political head of the exiled government—the Dalai Lama has effectively insulated the political leadership of the Tibetan diaspora from the question of his own succession. Even if the Chinese were to identify and indoctrinate a new 'Dalai Lama', that child would only be regarded by Tibetans at large as having succeeded to a religious role, while political authority would continue to inhere in the elected leader, Sangay, or his successors. Sangay, an impressive young man I have met and spoken with at length, is a plausible twenty-first-century political leader, unlike the other-worldly spiritual Dalai Lama. China has unleashed an unrelenting tirade against this development, denouncing the so-called Dalai clique and categorizing the new arrangements, in its idiosyncratic lexicon, as 'splittist'. That India has acquiesced in the new dispensation and allows Sangay to live in, and operate from, its territory remains a sore point for Beijing.

The limitations of China's diplomatic appeal to the world have become apparent in a number of recent diplomatic disasters. Beijing's pronouncement that the South China Sea was an area of core concern for China did not go down well with its neighbours. Several countries spoke against the declaration at the meeting of the ASEAN Regional Forum (ARF) in Hanoi in 2010, leaving the Chinese foreign minister fuming in the meeting at the perceived 'ganging up' against his country. There followed a diplomatic spat with Japan over the Diaoyu/Senkaku Islands, and Beijing's overreaction to the award of the Nobel Peace Prize to Liu Xiaobo, which backfired in worldwide revulsion at China's behaviour. Meanwhile, China's relations with North Korea have increased tensions with both South Korea and Japan at the same time. China's refusal to condemn Pyongyang's outrageous behaviour, such as its sinking of a South Korean naval vessel and the persistent shelling of Yeonpyeong Island, has damaged its relations with Seoul. All these actions have pushed China's East Asian and Southeast Asian neighbours towards American arms purchases and increasingly towards improving their relations with India. The Chinese push in Southeast Asia has resulted in a push back from these countries. Vietnam, for instance, has sought to offset the presence of its Chinese neighbour by developing remarkably good relations with the United States, a former adversary, going so far as to sign a nuclear cooperation agreement with Washington. Malaysia and Indonesia have sought to develop better relations with India.

Behind the unpleasantness between Beijing and New Delhi over Tibet and Arunachal Pradesh, and China's disinclination to resolve the border dispute (as it has resolved its disagreements on all its other land borders, even with Russia and Vietnam), may lie a broader strategic calculation. With the end of the Cold War, Beijing had two options in relation to India: to see the country as a natural ally, together with Russia, in building up an alternative pole to US dominance in the region, or to identify it as a potential adversary to its own aspirations. The emergence of a stronger US–India partnership in recent years appears to have convinced China to place New Delhi in the latter category, even as an instrument of 'containment' of China. Such a perception may have been reinforced by India's frequent military exercises with the United States, Japan and Australia, its cultivation of the former Soviet 'stans' in Central Asia (including sowing the seeds of a potential military presence by establishing an Indian air force unit at the Aini airbase in Tajikistan) and its attempts in recent years to establish strategic ties with countries that Beijing sees as falling within its own sphere of influence (from Mongolia to Vietnam, and including direct competition over Myanmar).

For these reasons, Beijing has signalled that it is in no hurry whatsoever to resolve its frontier issues with India. During his visit to New Delhi in December 2010, Prime Minister Wen bluntly declared that settling his country's border dispute with India 'will take a fairly long period of time'. His government publicly signalled that despite all the good economic developments showcased during Wen's visit, the bilateral geopolitics was still problematic. On the eve of Wen's visit, the

Chinese ambassador to India, Zhang Yan, told the press that 'China–India relations are very fragile and very easy to be damaged and very difficult to repair'. Needling an anxious-to-please New Delhi on its troubled northern borders helps China to keep India guessing about its intentions, exposes the giant democracy's vulnerabilities at a time when internal tensions and dissensions abound and elections in one state or another loom every few months, and cuts a potential strategic rival to size.

The two countries' competition for scarce energy resources and investment opportunities in markets such as Africa, Central Asia, Southeast Asia and Latin America have regularly pitted them against each other, usually to China's advantage. Indeed, India's refusal to condemn the Myanmar junta's crackdown on monks in mid-2007 was directly linked to its competition with China for influence, strategic assets and oil and gas from that unhappy country—because its earlier policy of support for Myanmar's democratic forces had simply allowed China, and its ally Pakistan, to steal a march on India.

Other factors have added to the strains in the relationship. One was a great Indian diplomatic triumph: the Indo-US nuclear deal. China, concerned that the American willingness to create an 'Indian exception' reflected a desire to build India up as a strategic counterweight to China, made its hesitations apparent in the Nuclear Suppliers' Group, thus incurring public statements of disappointment from senior officials in New Delhi. The deal went through nonetheless, but not without reminding Indians that Beijing was fundamentally negative on India's acquisition of a significant strategic capability.

And yet, in the context of the global contention for power and global influence between the United States and China, India may well have an intriguing role: the increasing Indo-US closeness could actually serve to make improving relations with India a higher priority for China than it might otherwise have been, by reminding China of India's potential to serve US interests, perhaps to China's detriment. This could well be one of the less visible motivations for Beijing's recent interest in India.

China's consistent and long-standing support for Pakistan, including military assistance and help for Pakistan's nuclear programme, confirms Indian suspicions that China wishes to use our troublesome neighbour to keep our regional, let alone global, ambitions in check. In addition,

China's development of the port of Gwadar in Pakistan, of the Sri Lankan port of Hambantota and of a Burmese port on the Bay of Bengal, all reflecting its development of a naval capacity on India's flanks, causes understandable concern that the proximity of such a presence is at least partly intended to choke India.

From Beijing's point of view, it is not just New Delhi that has grounds for concern. India's inclusion in the East Asian summit, which was pushed by Japan, Singapore and Indonesia primarily to limit China's influence in intergovernmental Asian institutions, suggests that India may be getting too big for its subcontinental boots, seeking to spread its influence to China's own backyard. China's reluctance to support Indian (and for that matter Japanese) aspirations to a permanent seat in the UN Security Council partially reflects this concern. Beijing has no desire to dilute its own status as a P5 member by sharing it with other Asian powers. Equally, India resents China's reluctance—alone among the current P5—to endorse what it sees as India's self-evident case for such a seat in a reformed Security Council.

Gurmeet Kanwal, director of a Delhi-based military think tank, the Centre for Land Warfare Studies (CLAWS), argues that 'China's foreign and defence policies are quite obviously designed to marginalize India in the long term and reduce India to the status of a sub-regional power by increasing Chinese influence and leverage in the South Asian region.' A Princeton University scholar of Indian origin, Rohan Mukherjee, goes further, writing that 'India's competition with China is not just economic or geo-strategic; in a sense it is existential—a clash of two competing political systems, bases of state legitimacy, and ways of ordering state–society relations.' If the clash is as fundamental as that, it is indeed difficult to imagine any conceivable geostrategic convergence between the two states.

There is also the question of China's view of the world and its own place in it, going well beyond India. In his 2011 book *On China*, Henry Kissinger, architect of the United States' 1971 opening up to that country, portrays this in almost mystical terms. Kissinger's book is replete with genuflections to the Chinese people and their 'subtle sense of the intangible', as he seeks to explain 'the conceptual way the Chinese think about problems of peace and war and international order'. Thus he makes much of the Chinese fondness for playing *wei qi*, a complicated game of encirclement far different from the West's (and presumably India's) preference for chess. In an eight-page account of 'the Himalayan border dispute and the 1962 Sino-Indian war', which is far more sympathetic to the Chinese version of events than the Indian, Kissinger describes the Chinese strategy as 'the exercise of *wei qi* in the Himalayas'. China's war with Vietnam in 1979 'resulted from Beijing's analysis of Sun Tzu's concept of *shi*—the trend and "potential energy" of the strategic landscape'. Kissinger, of course, writes from the point of view of an American Sinophile. Both Washington and Beijing are capitals of countries that consider themselves exceptional. 'American exceptionalism is missionary,' Kissinger writes. 'It holds that the United States has an obligation to spread its values to every part of the world.' China's exceptionalism, on the other hand, is cultural: China does not seek to impart its ways to other countries, but it judges 'all other states as various levels of tributaries based on their approximation to Chinese cultural and political forms'. This is potentially worrying for India (a land which is anything but an 'approximation to Chinese cultural and political forms'), especially when one considers another major potential problem. China has so far shown little interest in concluding an agreement regarding the sharing of river waters with India, which lies downstream of the Brahmaputra and its tributaries. Reports of China damming or diverting these waters have so far proved to be unfounded—China has claimed its river constructions all involve no diversion of waters—but the situation involves a risk of major unpleasantness developing, especially given increasing water scarcity for India's 1.2 billion thirsty people.

And then there is the inevitable worry that the United States might plump for China to the exclusion of all others, including India. Kissinger seems to advocate this in his book. Arguing that a close and cooperative US–China relationship is 'essential to global stability and peace', Kissinger repeats his traditional and oft-iterated preference for 'a rebalancing of the global equilibrium', calling for a 'co-evolution' by China and the United States to 'a more comprehensive framework'. He envisions the emergence of a 'Pacific community' with China, paralleling the Atlantic community that America has created with Europe, under which both countries would 'establish a tradition of consultation and mutual respect', making a shared world order 'an expression of parallel national aspirations'. This sounds alarmingly like the 'G2 condominium' that some Washington strategists would like to see run the world of the twenty-first century—and it doesn't leave much room for the rest of us (though Kissinger, never one to shirk a contradiction, is simultaneously an advocate of close American relations with India too).

Such thinking, which is never far from the surface in Washington, engenders an understandable level of disquiet in New Delhi. But one issue that no longer does is the now-fading enthusiasm for China in India's own left, whose previous zealotry ('China's Chairman is our Chairman', said communist graffiti scrawled on Kolkata's walls in the 1960s and 1970s) had given rise to worries of a Beijing-inspired fifth column seeking to destroy the Indian state from within. China's evolution into a highly capitalist state, accompanied by a thoroughgoing disinclination to foment revolution elsewhere, has cost it the loyalty of India's communist cadres, whose disillusionment with Beijing is now palpable. Indeed, there are more true believers in Maoism in India than in China. The Hong Kong magnate Ronnie Chan once remarked to me that 'China is officially a communist country, but you would have to look very hard to find a communist in China. If you want to find a real communist, you will have to go to Kerala.' The leading Indian communist party, the Communist Party of India (Marxist), which had been the only party in the world to pass a resolution hailing the Tiananmen Square massacre in 1989, displayed great ideological angst in its 2012 party congress over the direction China was taking. Whatever else New Delhi might have to worry about with regard to Beijing, it is no longer its capacity to foment revolution in India.

But all the other factors outlined above mean that the usually complacent elephant is wary of the hissing dragon, and for the first time it has begun showing its distrust. In December 2010, Premier Wen was obliged to sign a joint communiqué which did not explicitly mention India's routine affirmation of 'One China' (an acknowledgement of Chinese sovereignty over Tibet and Taiwan). Though there is little prospect of India changing its policy on either Tibet or Taiwan, failing to reaffirm it—in what had become a ritual the Chinese took for granted— was a clear signal of Indian displeasure with Chinese attitudes on the political issues dividing the two countries. Until the Sino-Indian frontier is satisfactorily demarcated and the dispute ended, bilateral relations are likely to remain mildly frosty.

And yet, there is a lot that India and China can achieve by joining hands, and it will not only be for their interest, but for the common good in Asia and the developing world. India is not an obstacle to China's aspirations, far less an instrument for its 'containment', as was wrongly suggested by some in that country. Even the purported competition for resources between the two countries in Africa and Latin America is, in my view, overblown. The two Asian giants actually have far greater common interests than is generally believed—in keeping open sea lanes, stabilizing overseas markets and securing vital resources from developing countries. Since there are enough resources to go around, this is not a zero-sum game but one where both could cooperate towards the same objectives. But it is true that such a perception is not yet widely shared in the two countries.

It would certainly help if Chinese scholars and commentators broadened and deepened their understanding of India. The liberal Chinese-American scholar Minxin Pei has described how 'ignorance, stereotyping, and latent hostility characterize the views of India held by a large segment of Chinese society'. In his view, 'The combination of under-appreciation of India's achievement and exaggeration of India's role as a geopolitical rival could generate dangerous self-reinforcing dynamics that may make strategic competition between India and China more likely in the future.'

There is statistical evidence for his concerns. A 2006 Pew Global Attitudes Survey found that 43 per cent of Chinese had an unfavourable opinion of India, while 39 per cent of Indians had an unfavourable opinion of China. Looking at specific issues dividing the two countries, 63 per cent of Indians described China's growing military power as a 'bad thing' for their country, while 50 per cent said the same about China's growing economic power. A poll released in 2010 by the respected Chinese private market research firm Horizon Research, which asked respondents to rate their 'friendly feelings' towards twenty-five countries, has demonstrated that the average Chinese citizen views India more negatively than an average Indian views China. While Indians expressed an 'average' level of 'friendly feeling' towards China, the Chinese polled had a much lower level of 'friendly feelings' towards India, higher only than their traditional negativism towards Japan. Whereas more Indians viewed China as a 'partner' than as an 'adversary', Chinese respondents saw India as the number three threat, behind the United States and Japan, and as the 'weakest' of the four BRIC countries—Brazil, Russia, India and China.

Equally, knowledge and scholarship of China in India needs to be augmented: we need to understand China better. Exchanges of scholars and journalists, and a significant improvement in tourism between the two countries, would go a long way towards making this possible. It is striking that only 56,000 Chinese visited India in 2008, a year in which about one million Chinese visited Malaysia. Indian traffic in the other direction is not much better—roughly 380,000 Indians visited China in 2010, fewer than travellers from Mongolia. Till very recently, there was only one non-stop commercial airline service which connects the two countries, and it flew from New Delhi to Shanghai; there was no direct flight between the two major Asian capitals. Chinese carriers have now corrected this anomaly but no Indian airline has yet undertaken a Delhi–Beijing flight. Ironically, there is a daily flight connecting New Delhi with Taipei.

———

If there is one assumption taken for granted by all of us familiar with Chinese sensitivities, it is that of 'One China'—the inflexible policy adhered to by Beijing that requires the world to accept the unity and indivisibility of the Chinese nation, including not only Tibet but also Hong Kong (despite its autonomy, separate administration and currency) and Taiwan (despite its de facto, but not de jure, independence).

Taiwan has tended to go along with the assertion of One China: it still officially calls itself the Republic of China (ROC), claiming descent from the regime established in Beijing by Sun Yat-sen when he overthrew the last emperor of the Q'ing dynasty in 1911. Still, it has been a while since the world took seriously the Taipei government's pretence of speaking for the whole country. Once seen by the majority of members of the United

Nations in the 1950s as the legitimate government of China temporarily displaced by communist usurpers, Taiwan has been marginalized for decades: it was forced to surrender its UN seat to the People's Republic of China (PRC) by an overwhelming vote in 1971, and has been largely ostracized from the global political community since.

At the same time, no one pretends that Beijing speaks for this island nation of 23 million, with its GDP of $460 billion (a per capita income of over $20,000) and its robust democracy. Taiwan has not been ruled from the mainland since 1949, and for all practical purposes it conducts itself as a separate country. Not only is it a major trade powerhouse, out of all proportion to its size, but a significant source of foreign investment. It also has a robust defence establishment, designed to ward off threats from the mainland, and a proactive foreign policy. But it is recognized as a sovereign state by only twenty-three of the 193 member states of the United Nations. As a result, the other 169 nations must deal with it by subterfuge. So the United States, India and other countries maintain quasi-diplomatic relations with Taiwan by assigning foreign office personnel to Taipei in nominally trade-related jobs. The Indian 'ambassador' in Taiwan is officially the director-general of the India-Taipei Association; his Taiwanese counterpart in India rejoices in the designation of representative at the Taipei Economic and Cultural Centre in India.

Seems fair enough. There's only one catch: deal with Taiwan more formally, and China goes ballistic. Any contact that implies official recognition of a 'state' or a government of Taiwan provokes furious outrage and protests on Beijing's part. Thus the president of Taiwan could not set foot on US soil as long as he was president; ministers of countries recognizing Beijing are forbidden from meeting ministers from Taiwan. Taiwanese officials are, of course, banned at the United Nations, where the PRC's sway is confirmed by a General Assembly resolution. I remember, in my UN days, apoplectic Chinese diplomats prompting successive Secretary-Generals to bar entry to Taiwanese representatives who had been invited to address the UN Correspondents' Association. The resultant standoff at the UN gates usually got the Taiwanese diplomats more publicity than if China had simply ignored them altogether, but the bad press was less important to Chinese officialdom than insisting on their rights to prevent the pretenders from sullying the UN's precincts.

The strange thing, as I discovered during a recent visit to Taipei, is that these rules don't apply to China itself. Behind the formal rejection, a thriving and almost incestuous level of contact flourishes. There are 370 flights a week between the mainland and Taiwan; some 3 million Chinese tourists came to the ROC last year. Taiwanese businesses are China's largest investors, with an estimated $300 million pumped into their economy, and one of the largest trading partners, to the tune of over $110 billion. Some 1 million Taiwanese are either living, working or studying in China at any given time. Chinese officials, up to and including governors and ministers, travel happily to Taiwan, and are quite pleased to welcome high-ranking Taiwanese visitors in return; when I was there, the mayor of Taipei (a crucial post, since the last two mayors became the country's presidents) was planning a holiday in China. Obviously, Beijing does not recognize the Taiwanese passport, but it is quite pragmatic and flexible when it wants to be: travel by the two sets of citizens uses informal documentation that implies no recognition of separate sovereignty by either side.

Some think this implies an extended willingness to coexist: rather than the 'One China, Two Systems' formula that applies to Hong Kong, this is almost 'One China, Two Entities'. Others, more cynically, think that what Beijing is doing is enveloping Taiwan in a smothering economic embrace while continuing to isolate it politically, so that Taipei's dependence will inevitably oblige it to submit to a Hong Kong–type merger with the PRC. And then there are the optimists, who think the increased contact will instead change China, making the PRC more like the ROC. 'You know what these Chinese tourists do?' a senior official asked. 'They enjoy a day's tourism, have dinner and then sit in their hotel rooms in front of the TV for hours, watching Taiwanese talk shows. They can't get enough of the cut-and-thrust of our democracy.' 'Imagine,' a mainlander said to me, 'my taxi driver had an opinion on nuclear policy, as if it had anything to do with him.' But in Taiwan, unlike in China, the taxi driver gets to vote on who makes the policy, so it has everything to do with him. Chinese citizens are learning that, and going back to the mainland infected with the taste of freedom. Soon, the optimists aver,

'They will want to be like us. Then Taiwan will have conquered China.'

It's a pity that Indians can't engage more formally with this vibrant land, because China demands that we be more purist than they are. There's a lot we can do to attract more investment, tourism (just 25,000 Taiwanese a year, from a country that sends 1.8 million to Hokkaido alone!) and educational and scientific exchange. But that means greater and higher-level contact in our dealings with Taiwan, not holding its leadership at arm's length. Given the PRC's penchant for needling us on Arunachal and Kashmir, isn't it time we picked up a Taiwanese thimble of our own?

This is not just about self-assertion, or even showing China that we have options. It is also, quite simply, about self-interest.

First of all, Taiwanese companies and government institutions have a lot of money sloshing about, looking for a place to plant itself. Taiwan invests some $300 billion in the economy of mainland China, and many in Taipei wonder whether it is wise to place quite so many eggs in the PRC's basket. Taiwanese investment in India is a measly $1 billion so far, and the potential for more is considerable. Most of it is currently concentrated in a handful of industries in a couple of states (Tamil Nadu and the bits of Andhra Pradesh that are easily accessible from Chennai). Diversification is clearly on the cards; when I was in Taipei in 2011 I met a businessman who was about to buy 10 per cent of a petrochemical industry in Gujarat, and was open to more. Kerala, with its upcoming Technocity in Thiruvananthapuram and Smart City in Kochi, will want to talk to Taiwanese IT firms about setting up shop in its sylvan environs. There are many other examples. Attracting investment isn't just about growing GDP; it generates employment, which is vital if we are to benefit from our 'demographic dividend' (having a young, dynamic workforce at a time when the rest of the world, including China, is ageing).

If India is skittish about opening its arms nationally to Taiwan, why not take advantage of our federal system to allow our states to deal directly with the island nation? In an economy which is already witnessing considerable competition between states for investment (remember the offers flooding into Tata after the Nano pulled out of Bengal?) I see no reason why we shouldn't encourage Kerala and Gujarat to sell their wares to Taiwanese investors. In the end, it is India that will benefit.

Another obvious area of cooperation is educational and scientific exchange. Taiwan is host to some of the best universities in the world, especially in the areas of science and engineering. Degrees earned there are recognized worldwide (even in India). They are also more affordable than university courses in the United States or the United Kingdom, and of comparable quality. There's only one catch: for the most part, the medium of instruction in Taiwan is Mandarin Chinese. But Taiwan is also the best place in the world outside Beijing to learn that language, mastery of which will count for more in the world as China acquires superpower status in the next few decades. So encouraging Indian students to both learn Chinese and undertake advanced study in Taiwan is potentially of double benefit. The Taiwanese minister of education recently came to India, accompanied by twenty-two university presidents from his country. He and his colleagues are keen on opening their portals to young Indians. There are currently 500 Indian students in Taiwan; the minister, and his country's energetic representative in Delhi, Philip Ong, would like to see that figure change to 2000 within two years. The potential is for 10,000, Ong says, in five years. The word just needs to get out.

If we send you students, I joked to the Taiwanese, please send us your tourists! India has been receiving just 25,000 Taiwanese visitors a year, a negligible figure from a country of affluent travellers. As the birthplace of Buddhism, the majority religion in Taiwan, and as a country that has much to offer the East Asian tourist, India should be doing a better job of selling its attractions to Taiwan.

Alongside the development of this relationship, we would need to increase official-level contact between our two countries, encourage journalists and scholars to travel to and write about each other, establish connections between our smarter think tanks, and get parliamentarians to meet to exchange their experiences of fractious democracy in action. Political leaders from various parties could also be welcomed in each other's countries.

All of this, of course, immediately begs the question, won't China object? Will such overt engagement with a 'pariah state' incur Chinese disapproval? It might, but I believe we should stand our ground. No country needs to apologize for doing something that is unambiguously in its own national interest, and that is not gratuitously offensive to the other. So we should stop short of doing anything that implies treating Taiwan as a sovereign state; no prime ministerial namaste for the Taiwanese president, for instance, which would naturally rile Beijing. But inviting an ex-president of Taiwan to deliver a lecture in India, or getting a presidential candidate to familiarize herself with New Delhi before entering the electoral lists, should be possible, indeed desirable.

And we should do it. In addition to the intimate and direct contact China already has with Taiwan, it has also made important international concessions, notably permitting the International Olympic Committee to admit a separate Taiwanese team, albeit under the name 'Chinese Taipei' and without flying the Republic of China's flag. Recently, Taiwanese delegates were allowed to participate in the World Health Assembly, the global gathering of the UN's World Health Organization (WHO), though China ensures they are not treated on a par with governments. If 'one country, two entities' is a viable formula in those two places, it can be contemplated carefully elsewhere.

So let us not be, as the French put it, *plus royaliste que le roi*, placing restrictions on ourselves that the Chinese have long ceased to observe (but insist on imposing on others). After all, China too has its own interests in preserving a good relationship with India—a gigantic market for its products and project exports, and a trade balance weighted hugely in Beijing's favour. The onus should not always be on us to bend over to accommodate their concerns. As long as we draw the line short of political recognition, India should deal enthusiastically with Taiwan. On its own merits—and for our own sake.

———

Though I have laid out a lot of both good and bad news, no serious decision-maker in either Beijing or New Delhi wants the bad news to prevail. There are manifest opportunities for cooperation which India should seize, including involving Chinese companies in the mammoth infrastructure-building tasks needed in our country over the next two decades (though sensitivity to security concerns may continue to limit Chinese involvement in telecom equipment, port building and some kinds of software services). International cooperation is also an obvious win-win, though India should be careful not to let such cooperation mire us in shared responsibility for Chinese policies that are not ours (for example, on climate change, it is odd that India, which has 17 per cent of the world's population but generates only 4 per cent of its emissions, should make common cause with China, which has 17.5 per cent of the world's people but generates nearly 20 per cent of its emissions). There are certainly issues on which cooperation suits both countries, including on anti-piracy, keeping open the sea lanes of communication across the Indian Ocean, progress on fair and free trade at the World Trade Organization (WTO), or the reform of the Bretton Woods institutions. In other cases, India might well be advised to wait and watch while others take the lead in pushing Beijing; this could result in issues being resolved to our advantage, such as the re-evaluation of the yuan or the effective pushback from the East Asian countries to China's assertiveness. We should join issue with China only on matters which directly affect us, whether it is the border, the offensive Chinese practice of issuing stapled visas to some Indian nationals, responsible sharing of river waters or the need to reduce the trade deficit. Here our policy has to be deliberate and finely calibrated, and must involve a palette of options, ranging from conciliation to firmness to the judicious development of our strategic relations with other countries.

Deep disdain for India in Beijing has transformed into grudging admiration in recent years, especially as we have also withstood the global economic recession, despite our chaotic democracy. We need to ensure that complacency does not once again set in in China, by taking proactive steps of our own to strengthen our border infrastructure (woefully deficient by comparison with China's on the other side) and to deepen our maritime capabilities in the Indian Ocean while China is still focused on the northern waters closer to its shores. Such naval capacity building could usefully be buttressed by diplomatic engagement with maritime states in our region, including building up a network of security cooperation arrangements with them. This does not (and should not) imply any belligerent intention; on the contrary, its motive should be purely preventive, for as the old maxim has it, 'if you want peace, prepare for war'. New Delhi's own diplomatic messaging should make it clear to Beijing that it has no hostile intentions in attending to its own security perimeter.

In his book *Rivals*, Bill Emmott quoted an unnamed senior Indian official as saying, 'both of us [India and China] think that the future belongs to us. We can't both be right.' Actually they can both be right—it's just that it will be two very different futures. And there can be room for both: the world is big enough for India and China, together and separately, to realize their developmental aspirations.

Chapter Five

India's 'Near Abroad': The Arab World and the Rest of Asia

During my brief stint as minister of state for external affairs, I had the privilege of being responsible in the ministry for India–Arab relations. It was a welcome challenge. The Arab world constitutes an integral part of India's extended neighbourhood and is a region of critical importance to India in political, strategic, security and economic terms. It accounts for 63 per cent of our crude oil imports, trades with India to the tune of $93 billion and plays host to 6 million Indian expatriate workers who remitted over 65 per cent of the $57 billion that India received in 2011 in inward remittances. Yet, for all its significance, it cannot be said that the full potential of our relationship with the Arab world has yet been explored, let alone fulfilled.

My personal contacts with the Arab people have left me with a deep sense of appreciation of the historic, cultural and civilizational ties that bind India and the Arab countries. As a student of history as well as an ardent believer in the importance of history in shaping our destiny, I am conscious of the extent to which our ties pre-date our emergence as nation states. Not only did Arabs and Indians know each other before the advent of Islam, but it can be said that the Arabs played a crucial role in the emergence of the very notion of 'Hindustan' and even in giving a name to the religion of Hinduism. We can argue about whether it is to the Arabs, the Persians or the Greeks that we owe the concept of the 'Hindu'—the people who live across the river Sindhu or Indus—but there is no doubt that the people of India were referred to as Hindus by the Arabs long before the Hindus themselves called themselves Hindus.

The Arabian Sea, which washes the shores of both our regions, and whose trade winds have carried vessels across since the days of antiquity, has played a crucial role in the cultivation of our relations. India's cultural links with West Asia can be traced to the early years of recorded history. There is evidence, for instance, of trade links between the Harappan civilization and that of Dilmun in the Gulf. In pre-Islamic times, Arab traders acted as middlemen in trade between Bharuch in Gujarat and Puducherry and the Mediterranean through Alexandria, and even (as evidenced in archaeological finds of Roman coins and artefacts in southern India) as far south as through the Palakkad gap in Kerala. Ongoing excavations in and around the Red Sea coast continually produce fresh evidence of even older links. The idea of India has long flourished in the Arab imagination: it is no accident that so many distinguished Arab families in many different Arab countries bear the surname al-Hindi, or that 'Hind', as a term connoting beauty and desirability, is still a name given to many Arab women.

Indian learning was another factor that brought the civilizations together. Indian numerals reached the world through the Arabs (and so became known as 'Arabic numerals'). Islamic scholars from the turn of the eighth century CE to al-Baruni in the mid-eleventh century have, in their writings, documented Indo-Arab cultural links, including Indian contributions to Arab thought and culture. Translations of Indian works were sponsored by the Abbasid Caliphate in Baghdad where, especially under the legendary Caliph Harun al-Rashid, Indian concepts in secular subjects ranging from medicine to mathematics and astronomy were absorbed into the corpus of Arab scientific writing. (Algebra, for instance, was an Indian invention perfected in the Arab world by Muhammad ibn Musa al-Khwarizmi. Working at Baghdad's House of Wisdom around 825 CE, al-Khwarizmi wrote a book entitled *The Book of Addition and Subtraction according to the Hindu Calculation* extolling the virtues of the Indian decimal system that used the zero. He went on to expound the system we now know, in a transmutation of his name, as algebra.)

Indians discovering the new religion of Islam helped develop its philosophies and jurisprudence; some scholars trace Indian studies on the hadith to the early days of the arrival of Islam in India in the South in the seventh century and in the North in the eighth century CE. Scholars have also documented the compilation of a large number of

Indian works in Quranic studies over the last 500 years as also in Islamic jurisprudence over a slightly longer period. Perhaps less remembered today is the contribution of Indians to Islamic scholarship in the medieval period. Among notable scholars was Shah Waliullah of Delhi and his descendants. Indeed, so important were these contributions from India during the centuries of Arab decline that the Lebanese scholar Rasheed Rada observed:

> If our brothers, the Indian Ulema, had not taken care of the science of hadith in this period, the [hadith] would have disappeared from the Eastern countries, because that branch of knowledge had become weak in Egypt, Sham (Syria, Lebanon, Jordan and Palestine), Iraq and Hijaz since the 16th century A.D. and it [had] reached its weakest point at the beginning of the 20th century A.D.

Travellers between India and the Arab world were the vehicles not only for scholarly exchanges but also for cultural interaction at a popular level. Much of the Sufi tradition is the result of Indo-Arab interaction and Khwaja Moinuddin Chisti, whose shrine at Ajmer is visited by people of many faiths, was himself an Arab. Over centuries, stories from the Hindu classic the Panchatantra have been retold across the Arab and Greek worlds, blending with the Fables of Aesop and stories from Alf Laila wa Laila or the Arabian Nights. Some Arab travellers to India, such as the Moroccan Ibn Batuta, occasionally found themselves elevated to positions of power by their hosts; Ibn Batuta was, for a while, made the Qazi of Delhi, even though he was unfamiliar with the school of Islamic jurisprudence used in India. Many Arabic words can be found in several Indian languages, particularly in Hindi and Urdu but also in Malayalam and Gujarati.

The adventures of seafarers who have ridden the waves and tides of the Arabian Sea on their dhows are the stuff of legend. I have even heard the story that it was an Indian seafarer who regularly travelled between Kerala and the Arab settlements on the east coast of the African continent who might have guided Vasco da Gama to the Indian coast at Kozhikode. It is for scholars to debate the accuracy of this tale, but what is not debatable is that these ties have hundreds if not thousands of years of history behind them and are responsible for the civilizational intermixture that all Indians have inherited and thrived in.

In 2010, to recreate the magic of times gone by, a traditional sailing boat, the *Jewel of Muscat*, was built in Oman, in large part by boat builders from Kerala, as a replica of the ninth-century dhows that sailed the waters of the Arabian Sea between our countries. I had the great pleasure of setting foot on the *Jewel of Muscat* and admiring how, in a desire for authenticity, the builders had sewn the planks together with coir fibre, rather than using nails, which were not in general use at the time. The *Jewel of Muscat*'s voyage from Oman to Singapore via Kerala and Sri Lanka, on the route many of our forefathers regularly sailed, was an evocative symbol of the seafaring ties that have united our peoples. It reminded me of the formidable reputation of the Kunjali Maricars in Kerala, whose seafaring prowess was so great that many Hindus believed one had to be a Muslim to be a good sailor. (The Zamorin of Calicut even decreed that every fisherman's family in his domain had to bring up one son as a Muslim, to man his all-Muslim navy.)

The early years of the twentieth century saw a revival of these historic links. Indian soldiers participated (under the British flag) in the arduous military campaigns in Egypt and Palestine in the First World War and in the bloodier battles in Iran, Syria and Iraq during the Second World War. The post–First World War years, marked as they were by the beginning of the end of Western colonialism, witnessed much interest in the fortunes of the Arab and Islamic world within India's own freedom movement. The Khilafat struggle, led by Mahatma Gandhi and calling for the restoration of the Ottoman Caliphate at the end of the First World War, perhaps best exemplified this: it served as a major unifying force within the Indian nationalist movement, even if its thrust was soon rendered irrelevant by the ascent of Kemal Ataturk to power in Turkey. One of India's great nationalist leaders, the Muslim divine Maulana Abul Kalam Azad, who was president of the Indian National Congress in the crucial years leading up to independence, was born in Mecca and studied at the famous al-Azhar University of Egypt. The leaders of our freedom movement closely monitored developments in Egypt and other countries, a trend that was also noticeable after we gained freedom. The struggle of the National Liberation Front (FLN) in Algeria and President

Nasser's nationalization of the Suez Canal and the Suez crisis of 1956 were two important historical developments that found resonance in India's support for what were widely seen as fraternal Arab peoples.

Many Arabs, especially from the Gulf countries, lived and worked in India, developing close relations with the country. Before the post-1973 oil boom dramatically increased Arab incomes and widened educational possibilities, many Arabs, again especially from the Gulf, were educated in India. I have come across Arabs of a certain age from Kuwait, Bahrain, the Emirates and Oman who learned English at schools in India, picked up smatterings of Hindustani and habits (such as drinking Indian tea) which they have preserved in Arabian adulthood. Direct knowledge of India is not, of course, necessary for Arabs to enjoy the popular Indian cinema of Bollywood, which consolidated its hold on Arab viewing publics when the political isolation of Egypt after its peace with Israel in 1977 meant that Egyptian films were banned in many parts of the Arab world. Though that ban has long since been lifted, Indian cinema remains popular. I recall meeting the owner of the major cinema theatres of Oman and being told the principal fare on offer was Hindi movies; asked if that reflected a considerable Indian presence in his country, he replied that over 90 per cent of his audiences were Arab. An Indian diplomat serving in Damascus informed me a decade ago that the only publicly displayed portraits in that city that were as large as those of the then president Hafez al-Assad were posters of the Indian megastar Amitabh Bachchan. Such extensive familiarity continues to predispose many Arabs favourably towards India.

A crucial element in consolidating Indo-Arab relations has been the presence of a large, growing and highly successful Indian expatriate community, particularly in the Gulf. India has been a vibrant presence in the political, economic and cultural evolution of the Gulf. For thousands of years, our ancestors sailed the turbulent waters of the Indian Ocean and exchanged goods, ideas and experiences. This interaction over several millennia has left an abiding mark on our civilizational ethos, giving our peoples a similarity of perceptions and cultural mores. With Gulf Arabs thoroughly accustomed to seeing Indians in their midst, India's presence in the Arab imagination is not just historical or commercial, but involves a far more intimate mutual dependence affecting every sphere of daily life.

This relationship between India and the Gulf has had such sustained resonance primarily because our engagements have been continuously refreshed and revitalized by meeting new needs and requirements. When, in recent years, the Gulf region, awash in new-found prosperity after its discovery of oil and the raising of its price, took up the massive expansion of its infrastructure and welfare institutions, India came forward with its human resources, initially blue collar but increasingly progressing to professionals. The numbers were significant, with Indian workers often exceeding the population of the host countries themselves. It was said in the early 1980s that the largest ethnic group in Bahrain was not Bahrainis but Keralites from India. In the UAE, it is unofficially estimated that 90 per cent of the population is expatriate, and more than 70 per cent of those are Indians. Today, there is no aspect of the UAE economy which has not been touched by an Indian contribution. The people of India in the Gulf and the Arab world have contributed immensely to the economic development of both India and the countries they reside and work in. The remittances that India receives from the nearly 6 million expatriates in the Gulf, many of them from Kerala, in the order of more than $57 billion currently, make a significant contribution to India's economic development.

In view of the large Indian population in the region, a number of issues come up from time to time in our relations with these countries which relate to our people-to-people contacts and to consular matters. Active steps have been taken and are continually being taken, in cooperation with the countries of the region, to promote the welfare of the Indian community, particularly expatriate workers. Many suffer difficult conditions of work and are not always treated with dignity, but they still feel they can send more money back home than if they had never left India. Memoranda of understanding on manpower have been signed with some countries and are under negotiation with others to improve their lot. These and similar arrangements will enable India and the Arab countries to jointly deal with issues relating to the welfare of the expatriate Indian communities in the region, especially the conditions of service of blue-collar workers.

Problems inevitably arise, but they have largely been addressed in a constructive spirit. When I travelled to the region as minister, the well-being of Indian expatriates was a prominent concern in my meetings: as a Lok Sabha MP from the state which dispatches the most migrant workers, I could do no less. Many heart-rending stories have been told about the working conditions of some of the Indian blue-collar workers on construction sites and their residential conditions in labour camps. Though they are undoubtedly there of their own free will, and suffer these difficulties in order to send savings back home, as an Indian politician I was concerned to do what I could to ease their conditions of life and work without seeming to intrude on the sovereign prerogatives of the host countries. While I was in Oman in early 2010, for instance, I met with a number of Indian workers, heard about their problems and sought a meeting with the manpower minister to resolve them. I was gratified by the warm and receptive spirit in which the Omani minister discussed them with me and accepted my suggestions. Mechanisms to institutionalize the welfare of the Indian expatriate workforce in the Arab countries need to be created and strengthened. There was a clear appreciation in all the Arab countries I visited that these Indian workers are an asset to their receiving countries; in turn I suggested that if conditions governing their work and life are improved, it would be a win-win proposition for all concerned.

Trade is undoubtedly a vital aspect of the Indo-Arab relationship. For several centuries, India provided the necessities, comforts and luxuries needed by the people of the Gulf and occasionally re-exported by them to other markets. Well before the invention of the internal combustion engine and the sudden importance of oil and gas from Arabia, Indian foodstuffs, textiles and jewellery constituted the main exports to the Arab world, while India in turn imported huge quantities of dates and pearls.

Later, hydrocarbons entered the equation, boosting both need and quantity. As a result, India's trade with the Arab countries is booming as never before. A look at our figures of trade with the Arab world is illuminating. For instance, the Gulf region has emerged as the most significant trading partner of India in dollar terms. During 2006–07 the total two-way trade was $47 billion; by the year 2010–11 it had reached more than $130 billion. Trade with the non-Gulf Arab countries totalled more than $15 billion. Total trade with Arab countries was about $90 billion in 2007–08 and is nearing $150 billion today. It is clear that commerce with the Arab world has assumed an importance for India that can simply not be jeopardized.

It is also clear that here, too, there is no room for complacency. Both in the foreign and in the trade ministries, India and its trading partners need to identify and focus our work on multipliers and leverages. Negotiations with the Gulf Cooperation Council (GCC) to conclude an India–GCC free trade agreement have, for instance, become bogged down, with little sign of urgency on either side to resolve the impediments to an agreement. The successful conclusion of an FTA would complement our ongoing and rapidly expanding bilateral economic engagement with individual member countries of the GCC, but the talks have proceeded at best fitfully.

India has always shown its willingness to share with our Arab brethren our experience and expertise in institution and capacity building, governance, science and technology (including, especially, information technology), medical research and biotechnology, health care and higher education. This cooperation has also featured the training of Arab officials, diplomats, soldiers and scholars. While the more affluent Arab countries tend to pursue the training of their elites in the developed West, many developing countries in the Arab world are appreciative of the Indian connection.

There are, of course, some areas where what India offers is in no way inferior to competing products or services from the advanced West. While agreements on cooperation in information and communication technology exist with a number of Arab countries, India and Egypt have even concluded an agreement on the peaceful use of outer space. Antrix Corporation, the commercial arm of the Indian Space Research Organisation (ISRO), was awarded a contract in July 2008 for the launch of Algeria's satellites. Antrix has completed a remote sensing project involving setting up of an earth station in Algeria using Indian CARTOSAT imagery.

The fundamentals of India–Arab relations thus both pre-date and transcend the importance of oil and gas, though there is no doubt that Arab countries—as vital sources of hydrocarbons, whether from the Gulf or more recently from Egypt, Sudan and the Maghreb—have become essential to India's energy security needs. Indian companies have secured concessions or have otherwise invested in the oil sector significantly in Sudan, Egypt and Libya. Less publicized, perhaps, is the enormous importance to India's food security of countries such as Jordan, Morocco, Tunisia and Algeria as providers of rock phosphate and phosphoric acid and potash, all of which translate into fertilizer for our farmers.

Besides the hydrocarbon and fertilizer sectors, Indian companies have executed or are in the process of completing a variety of projects, including those financed by concessional lines of credit. Examples include a thermal power plant in Sudan, a cement plant in Djibouti, an architecturally complex bridge in Jordan and a variety of projects in Libya. Egypt has emerged as a significant Indian investment destination with Indian investments estimated at over $500 million. A series of India–Arab investment projects conclaves, starting in 2008, have paved the way for stronger trade and investment relations between the two regions. The conclaves provide an enabling institutionalized platform for businesses and investors from India and the Arab countries to cooperate and build partnerships.

There is much more scope for Arab investment in India; the Arab world's surplus resources have still largely been directed to the West. Indian diplomats have attempted to persuade Arab countries that they should contemplate massive investments in our infrastructure, energy and industrial sectors, but success has been modest (though the UAE's Abu Dhabi Investment Authority and Dubai Ports World have been active in India). India is also seeking Arab investments in its human resources through the upgrading of India's institutions of primary education and higher learning. India's invitation to Arab investors to participate in the new phase of development and prosperity on which we have embarked has not yet found the number of takers New Delhi had hoped for.

The Gulf region and the UAE in particular are key targets for investment promotion. The Gulf Cooperation Council countries are rich in financial resources and in technological capabilities and expertise that have emerged over the last forty years of extraordinary all-round development. The UAE as a country and the GCC as an economic grouping are already among India's top trade partners. India's trade with the UAE touched $67.1 billion in 2010–11 and with the GCC members as a whole it reached $130.9 billion. India now sees the UAE and the GCC as our premier investment partners as well, in the hope that we can, through our joint efforts, build up the projects and institutions that will transform the face of India. Given the long history of our fruitful interaction, Indian ministers, myself included, have sought to portray a potential investment partnership as one more step in the mutually beneficial relationship that has bonded our people over several millennia, which promises, in its implications, to be more extraordinarily transformational and fruitful than any interaction that has gone before.

And yet, it is apparent that the mere fact of having had centuries-old contact does not mean that we do not have to endeavour to sustain and nurture our present-day relations. If anything, past proximity requires more hard work by all concerned so that neither is lulled into complacency.

Partition and the creation of a 'Muslim Indian' state called Pakistan certainly confused some Arab Muslims, who felt their religious affinity should imply a transfer of allegiance to Pakistan. Though this sentiment is mainly aroused only in times of war or conflict on the subcontinent, and the positive image of India has survived above and beyond the idea of Pakistan (especially since Indian expatriate workers of all faiths have a far better reputation for hard work and integrity than their Pakistani counterparts, whether merited or not), it complicates perceptions of the country in some Arab minds. (There are also strategic and security relationships with Pakistan to be considered; a contingent of Pakistani troops long protected the Saudi royal family, and the UAE was, in the 1990s, the only state persuaded by Islamabad to grant full diplomatic recognition to the Taliban regime in Kabul.) Though the bedrock of goodwill between our two regions allows us to build a strong edifice of substantial contemporary relations, it is difficult to argue that these have fully been built. Even though India considers the Arab region very important in shaping our political, economic, defence and security policies at both the regional and global level, it is far from establishing the kind of strategic partnerships essential to give these relations true geopolitical heft. Though India declares often enough that the Arab world is a key part of its strategic neighbourhood and both sides speak desultorily of the importance of strategic cooperation, there have been few, if any, meaningful consultations at a high level to this end.

There have been evident positives: India's approach on issues affecting the Arab world has been consistent, and New Delhi has been able to demonstrate that its policies towards the region are based on principles, not expediency. They are also backed up with tangible action: India is a major troop contributor to United Nations peacekeeping operations in Arab lands, from the United Nations Interim Force in Lebanon to the United Nations Disengagement Observer Force on the Golan Heights. Indian peacekeepers have also served more recently with the UN Mission in Sudan and UN operations in Western Sahara. India has also been a strong supporter of the United Nations Relief and Works Agency for Palestinian Refugees, and a significant aid donor to the Palestinian National Authority (it is among the very few countries to station a diplomat in Ramallah).

The principles animating New Delhi's positions on such issues as the legitimate demands of the Palestinian people, the Suez crisis or the Algerian independence movement have stood the test of time. The overt support of many Arab countries for Pakistan at times of conflict with India has not swayed New Delhi from this course. India has endeavoured to follow the spirit of South–South solidarity and cooperation in its dealings with the Gulf and Arab world and has never failed to bear in mind its fundamental interests in the region. The result has been to promote a pattern of contact, especially at the people-to-people level, that has few parallels. It is not surprising, for instance, to note that the number of flights from Indian airports to the Gulf region far exceeds the total number of flights from India to the rest of the world.

Whereas the world has heard of our 'Look East' policy in Southeast Asia, of which more later, as far as the Arab world is concerned, we are proud that we have a 'Look West' policy too, in which the word 'West', for once, does not refer to Europe or America. Our traditional bonds have been revitalized in recent years. For India the basic constants remain that the Arab world is an important source of our energy security and is home to nearly 6 million Indians. The Arab world's rich resources and the growing demands of India's rapidly expanding economy make us natural partners. In keeping with our desire to strengthen our relations with the countries of the region, India has been trying to put in place a structure of multifaceted cooperation covering all sectors. There is a consistent pattern of exchanging high-level visits between India and the Arab countries, bilaterally manifesting the importance of each relationship, and each seeking to open up new facets for cooperation. Several such visits and joint commission meetings have facilitated many institutional arrangements in the areas of trade and investment, energy cooperation, security cooperation, cultural, scientific and educational cooperation and bilateral arrangements.

One example of such high-level engagement occurred when the then secretary-general of the League of Arab States and my good friend, H.E. Mr Amre Moussa, in 2012 a contender for the Egyptian presidency, visited India in November–December 2008 and signed a memorandum of cooperation between India and the League of Arab States on the establishment of an Arab-India Cooperation Forum. This is a very comprehensive document that looks at deepening Indo-Arab relations in many sectors including energy, education, human resource development and trade and investment. In 2009, the Indian Ministry of External Affairs (MEA) worked with the Indian Council for Cultural Relations (ICCR) and the Federation of Indian Chambers of Commerce and Industry (FICCI) to organize the first Indo-Arab cultural festival in New Delhi with the support of various Arab missions and governments. The Government of the UAE has recently selected Indian books for translation into Arabic to enhance understanding of our country's history and literature. The study of Arabic in India has also made significant strides, with many Indian scholars of Arabic available to provide continuing momentum to the process.

India desires to strengthen cooperation to explore opportunities across the entire spectrum of potentialities that exist in its relationship with the Arab world. We wish to work together today with an eye on tomorrow: to consolidate our ties in emerging sectors of the economy so that we can develop a framework for future generations. Our economies are complementary. In many areas, countries in the Arab world have the capital, while India offers the opportunities, especially for the development of infrastructure. The more the long-term linkages that India and the Arab world develop, the greater will be our mutual stakes and interests in each other's success and prosperity. When in government I used to assure India's Arab friends that it is not only financial investments that we were thinking of: we are invested, I would say, in the future of our relationship.

And yet it should be said that our strategic aspirations have not yet been fulfilled in the region. Few consultations have taken place at a high political level on matters of mutual geopolitical interest—though intelligence sharing and meetings by India's national security adviser with his Arab counterparts have indeed occurred. There has been no serious effort to develop a habit of strategic dialogue with the countries of the region, even though there are obvious implications for India in issues of Gulf security, and developments in the subcontinent can hardly leave the Arab world indifferent. Despite being one of the very few countries with an ambassador in Tel Aviv *and* a political officer in Ramallah, India has not attempted to play a significant role in the Middle East peace process. It named a special envoy for West Asia in 2007, but allowed his role to lapse in 2009 without replacement. As a result, a country which once was an indispensable player in international discussions and conferences on the region—and which still retains credibility with both sides of the Israel–Palestinian divide—has essentially been ignored by the UN-led quartet and has not bestirred itself to exercise its geopolitical influence in favour of a Middle East peace settlement.

Because India's dependence on Gulf oil will increase in the coming decade, the Gulf states will continue to be central in India's foreign policy. This raises the question of what, if anything, India can do to ensure the security of its energy supplies from the region, especially at a time of diminishing Western interest in expending resources for the security of the region (since high oil prices have made a number of alternative sources of oil and gas affordable for the West). India's ability to control and protect the flows of energy that these states supply to India is limited, since it would require a strong 'blue water' navy with effective submarines and long-range aviation to help keep 'choke points' like the Straits of Hormuz open. These are capabilities the Indian Navy must acquire, and is in the process of doing so.

The geopolitical environment of 2012, as these words are written, is fraught with possibilities. The traumatic changes of the Arab awakening (known to the West as the 'Arab Spring') have created new political realities within each of the affected states. New regimes are still in the early stages of consolidating themselves in Tunisia, Egypt and Libya; all have witnessed the rise of Islamist parties, though all also profess to be interested in pursuing their religious agenda within a democratic political space. How the societies around them—and their military and intelligence services, all formed and deployed in more secular times—will react to the new-found prominence of the Islamists is still unknown. The Western countries that led the intervention in Libya (and are clamouring for a similar outcome in Syria) are themselves in the process of becoming less and less dependent on Arab oil and gas, which could reduce the intensity of their fervour for intervention and at the same time give them less to lose in adopting a bold course of action. In all this, the role of non-Arab Iran, whose geopolitical influence across West Asia has increased dramatically after the Iraq war, remains a complicating factor. Its apparent quest for nuclear weapons has raised alarms not only in Israel and the United States but also across the Sunni Arab world. India, which enjoys reasonably good relations with Iran as well as with its Arab neighbours, will have to tread lightly, but it cannot afford to be indifferent to the evolving situation. It does not wish to see another nuclear power in the region, but it rightly fears the regional and global consequences of any military intervention against Iran. Nor can it be insensitive to the concerns of Saudi Arabia, a country it can ill afford to antagonize.

So far India has handled the transformations reasonably well; it managed to avoid antagonizing both sides (the recognized government and the emerging democratic forces) in the convulsions that changed three regimes, and it is proceeding gingerly in advocating accommodation in Syria. The government did a highly commendable job in managing the evacuation of some 18,000 Indians from Libya under 'Operation Safe Homecoming'. India's key interests in the region will undoubtedly continue to be defined along the familiar verities: the promotion, to the extent possible, of security and stability in the region with a view to ensuring a stable supply of hydrocarbon supplies; extensive cooperation and engagement with the countries of the region in order to enhance trade relationships and boost trade and investment levels;

and safeguarding the interests, as well as promoting the welfare, of the 6 million Indians living in the region.

To summarize: there are many dimensions to Indo-Arab relations, some very old and some very new. India and the Arab world share a close and historical relationship marked by similar values. The Arab world has left an indelible imprint on India's history, on our culture and on our civilization. As a student of history I can argue with confidence that the past has built us an excellent platform for the future. There is a genuine partnership and synergy existing between India and the Arab world, which we are collectively endeavouring to strengthen further. The paradigm realignment that has accompanied changes in the global economic order, particularly after the financial meltdown, has compelled both sides of the relationship to move towards a major rethink on how we should cooperate to face the challenges in front of us. Happily for both of us, the framework for cooperation is readily available. The nature and level of our cooperation is constantly deepening and widening. Progress is undeniable. While its pace could be faster, a critical mass has already developed to take us into a qualitatively upgraded relationship.

In today's era of globalization we have to take into account the changing world economic scenario and equip ourselves appropriately. Our endeavour should be to leverage our comparative advantage to build alliances, develop partnerships, create new avenues of growth and development and strengthen the existing ones. We need to enhance our mutual investments, joint ventures and project participation in the region and in India. Our engagement must be multifaceted. Our geopolitical aspirations are entirely compatible with those of the countries of the region. There is no reason why our efforts should not dovetail into each other's.

———

One important aspect of India–Arab relations has been a similarity of views on a number of political questions of global import, notably New Delhi's consistent position on the issue of Palestine. India's solidarity with the Palestinian people and its attitude to the Palestinian question reflects, perhaps more than any other issue, the enduring nature of Indo-Arab ties. It was as early as in 1936 that the Congress Working Committee sent greetings to Palestine and on 27 September 1936 Palestine Day was first observed in India. The 1939 session of the Indian National Congress adopted a resolution on Palestine and looked forward to the emergence of an independent democratic state in Palestine in which Jewish rights would be protected. India was a member of the United Nations Special Committee on Palestine. In 1974, it became the first non-Arab country to recognize the Palestine Liberation Organization (PLO) as the sole and legitimate representative of the Palestinian people. In March 1980, the Government of India announced in Parliament India's decision to accord full diplomatic recognition to the PLO office in New Delhi. It was after this that Yasser Arafat paid a three-day official visit to India, during which he described India as 'an eternal friend'. In 1988, India recognized Palestine as a state. The Indian government has constructed the Palestine embassy building in New Delhi, as a gift of the people and Government of India to the Palestinian people.

India has had an unwavering record of support for the Palestinian cause since the days of our own freedom struggle. In November 1938, Mahatma Gandhi had written on the subject of persecuted Jews seeking a homeland in Palestine:

> My sympathies are all with the Jews. . . . But my sympathy does not blind me to the requirements of justice. The cry for the national home for the Jews does not make much appeal to me. The sanction for it is sought in the Bible and the tenacity with which the Jews have hankered after return to Palestine. Why should they not, like 20 other peoples of the earth, make that country their home where they are born and where they earn their livelihood? Palestine belongs to the Arabs in the same sense that England belongs to the English or France to the French. It is wrong and inhuman to impose the Jews on the Arabs.

This was a more or less consensual position in the Indian nationalist movement, though Jawaharlal Nehru, moved by the treatment of Jews in Germany, proposed in 1936 that they be allowed refuge in India. The belief was that the Jews deserved humanitarian relief for their suffering, but the issue of their mistreatment in Europe could not be solved at the expense of Arabs, by relocating them to Palestine. It was for this reason that India voted against the creation of Israel in the United Nations General Assembly in 1948. Though India subsequently recognized the new state of Israel in 1950, relations were maintained at a low-key consular level for four decades thereafter.

Contemporary India's view of the Israeli–Palestinian question therefore has old roots. Our current policy is in line with United Nations Security Council resolutions 242 of 1967 and 338 of 1973, the Quartet Roadmap and the Arab Peace Initiative of Saudi King Abdullah. India supports a united, independent, viable, sovereign state of Palestine with East Jerusalem as its capital, living within secure and recognized borders side by side at peace with Israel. Despite India's increasing closeness to Israel since 1991—underscored by the two countries' security cooperation in the face of grave terrorist threats to each—India has not hesitated to express concern about the continuing expansion of Israeli settlements in occupied Palestinian territories. India also supports Palestine in a variety of tangible ways, including the contribution of millions of dollars as budget support for the Palestine National Authority and assistance to Palestine in developing its human resources through India's technical cooperation programme.

Such an attitude has nothing to do with prejudice, since Jews have lived in India, according to legend, since the destruction of their First Temple by the Babylonians in 586 BCE prompted several to cross the established trade routes across the Arabian Sea to the south-western coast of India. They were welcomed by the local ruler of Kodungallur in what is today Kerala without conditions, 'as long as the world and moon exist', in one recounting. A delightful anecdote that is part of Kerala's oral history traditions recounts how, when St Thomas the Apostle landed on the coast of Kerala around 52 CE, he was welcomed on shore by a flute-playing Jewish girl. Other waves of Jewish migration created the Bene Israel of Maharashtra in the hinterland of Mumbai, who were accepted as yet another 'Hindu' sub-caste for centuries until a wandering rabbi identified their practices and beliefs as Jewish; and the so-called Baghdadi Jews, largely urban and educated elites from various Ottoman cities who migrated to India in the nineteenth century during the British Raj. None of India's Jews experienced the slightest episode of anti-Semitism at Indian hands; indeed, the only time this diaspora suffered was when the Portuguese arrived in Kerala in the sixteenth century, found a thriving Jewish community and began to persecute it, leading the Jews to flee south to Kochi (Cochin), where they were given refuge and land, and where in the mid-sixteenth century they built one of the finest synagogues in the world. Today, the community known as the 'White Jews of Cochin' has dwindled to the point where it cannot assemble a quorum for a minyan, and their old neighbourhood, tactlessly known as 'Jew Town', has become a quaint curiosity shop for tourists. But their history, and that of the other two waves of Jewish migration, is one of India's willing embrace of the Jewish people and their cultural (but not racial) assimilation into their surroundings—a process that has characterized India's absorption of the many ethnicities that have infused themselves into the national gene pool.

Nonetheless, friendship and hospitality is one thing, political perspective another. Though the peace process in the region after 1977 made it possible for India to sustain its position on Palestine while upgrading and strengthening relations with Israel, the constraints on New Delhi in this area have been largely internal. An important element guiding India's political stance towards Israel has undoubtedly been the strong feelings within the country of India's own Muslim population, which has, perhaps inevitably, looked with suspicion if not hostility at Tel Aviv. The assumption on the part of most Indian political parties that overt friendship with Israel would cost its advocates dearly at the Indian ballot box remains a strong factor, especially when elections loom in states with a significant number of Muslim voters. It did not help that pro-Israeli stances were, in the early years, advocated only by the communally minded Hindu chauvinist party the Bharatiya Jana Sangh, which used support for Israel mainly as an additional stick to beat the Muslims with.

However, a significant change occurred at the end of the Cold War when India re-examined its entire geopolitical posture in the light of the disappearance of the Soviet Union and the subsequent expansion of India's options. As part of a general reorientation of Indian foreign policy, which included changes in India's relations with the United States and with Southeast Asia, the government of Prime Minister Narasimha

Rao decided in 1992 to upgrade diplomatic relations with Israel to full ambassadorial level. The change was managed reasonably well, with the Arab world being assured that it would not affect India's traditional position on Arab–Israel issues or the considerably greater priority accorded to India's engagement with the Arab world. Nonetheless, the last two decades have witnessed a steady strengthening of the India–Israel partnership, particularly in the defence and security areas where the two countries' shared concerns about Islamic extremism have offered common ground for cooperation. The period 1998–2004, when the Bharatiya Janata Party, the successor to the Jana Sangh, headed coalition governments in New Delhi, was particularly productive from the Israeli point of view, and included the only visit of an Israeli prime minister (Ariel Sharon) to India in 2003.

India is now Israel's largest market for defence products and services (it is estimated that fully half of the country's military equipment sales abroad go to India). Despite the huge advantage built up by Russia during the Cold War years as a military supplier to India, the much smaller Israel has, at some $10 billion, become India's second largest defence supplier (and in some reckonings its largest). Israel is apparently willing to offer India equipment and technology unavailable from any other country, and to provide indigenously developed defence technologies that are therefore less vulnerable to third-party pressures. Israel is reportedly also helping with the modernization of some of India's ageing Russian-made weapons systems. Surface-to-air missiles, unmanned surveillance aircraft, training simulators and other sophisticated Israeli defence products are now an indispensable part of India's arsenal. Israel has provided India with vital ground-based missile defence components, but even more important, it has sold India the Phalcon airborne warning and control system (AWACS), which greatly enhances India's early warning, command and coordination capabilities and could seriously alter the military balance with Pakistan in its favour.

In turn, the ISRO has launched at least one Israeli military satellite, and the two countries have intensified intelligence sharing, especially on Islamist threats to both nations. Cooperation in such areas as counterterrorism, border management and the joint training of security forces has grown. India's armed forces have embarked on an intensive series of high-level exchanges, especially involving the two naval and air forces, which have deepened strategic understanding between the countries.

The cooperation has been assessed on both sides as excellent, even though for some years India has had a defence minister who is notably wary of Israel. Inevitably relations with Israel get a boost when tensions between India and Pakistan erupt; it is said that Pakistan's unexpected incursion into Kargil in 1999, which thrust on India a war for which it was unprepared, was partly resisted thanks to an emergency infusion of artillery shells from Israel. At the same time, India is not ready to adopt Israeli methods to deal with terrorism in its own borderlands; it has consistently been critical of Israeli attacks on Gaza and Lebanon, and is unlikely to see Israel as a tutor for its own approaches to similar problems in its neighbourhood.

Non-military commerce has also progressed, with India–Israel trade reaching just under $5 billion in 2010. (Interestingly, India's trade with Egypt is comparable in figures to its trade with Israel.) India is the second largest export market for Israel and Israel is India's seventh largest trading partner. There is talk of a bilateral free trade agreement, though India's turbulent domestic politics will continue to prompt New Delhi to proceed with caution. Israel's advances in agriculture have not escaped the attention of even India's state governments, several of which have sent agricultural delegations to Israel, and there is perennial interest—increasing as India contemplates serious water scarcity—in learning from Israel's ability to make its deserts bloom. Opportunities for collaboration in high-technology aspects of information technology, space technology, nanotechnology and biotechnology are being explored by the private sector as well as by the two governments.

India–Israel relations have been acquiring significant dimensions in a number of less utilitarian areas. Israeli tourism to India has increased significantly in the last two decades, and Hebrew signboards are visible in places like the Kullu valley and Dharamsala in northern India, and in Goa, whose beaches have become a particular favourite for young Israeli vacationers. Some 40,000 tourists from each country travel annually in both directions. There are increasing instances of inter-faith dialogue, including even, on one occasion, a delegation of Indian Muslims travelling to Israel. Indian Jewry is no longer significant enough in numbers to play a part in altering New Delhi's domestic political calculations about the relationship, but interest in diaspora history has grown on both sides, and the success of the Bene Israel community from India, numbering some 25,000 in today's Israel, has given a fillip to Israel's awareness of their original homeland (including in the establishment of some Indian restaurants). The recent migration of some 1500 members of a 'lost tribe' from India's North-East, the Beni Menashe, identified somewhat controversially as a Jewish group that had lost its links to the mother faith but rediscovered them, has added to the connection. Public opinion polls consistently show high regard in each nation for the other, with India often emerging as the world's most pro-Israeli country after the United States in such surveys (and in one 2009 survey conducted by the Israeli foreign ministry, the single most pro-Israeli nation).

Nonetheless, political visits at the highest levels have been relatively infrequent, and the Indian government has tended to treat its Israeli connection with circumspection, both to avoid antagonizing its domestic voter base and to reduce the risk of alienating its important Arab trading partners. The visit to Israel in January 2012 by Indian Foreign Minister S.M. Krishna, more than a decade after his BJP predecessor Jaswant Singh, came after several years during which Israeli ambassadors in New Delhi wondered privately if theirs was 'the love that dare not speak its name'. Invitations to prominent Israeli political personalities have been noticeably infrequent, for fear of a domestic backlash. And yet Israel's willingness to sell India weapons technology it cannot obtain elsewhere, the two countries' shared concerns about Islamist terrorism and largely (though not wholly) compatible strategic interests make this an indispensable relationship for both sides. The Congress party–led United Progressive Alliance (UPA) government has been careful not to repeat the rhetoric of its National Democratic Alliance (NDA) predecessors that spoke of a potential 'alliance of democracies' among the United States, India and Israel. The national security adviser of the previous NDA government, Brajesh Mishra, had declared in a speech to the American Jewish Committee in Washington in May 2003 that democratic nations facing the menace of international terrorism should form a 'viable alliance' to counter this threat: 'India, the United States and Israel have some fundamental similarities. We are all democracies, sharing a common vision of pluralism, tolerance and equal opportunity. Strong India–US relations and India–Israel relations have a natural logic.' Though such an approach has not been explicitly evoked since, such views are never very far from the surface in some influential circles in all three countries.

India and Israel could conceivably develop additional areas of cooperation—nuclear policy, defence systems development and intelligence sharing, for instance. But strategic coordination is likely to be hamstrung by serious differences of perception on Iran, where India does not share Israeli views; by Israel's widening of its options in relation to Pakistan and China, New Delhi's major adversaries; and, perhaps above all, by India's consciousness of its special relationship with the Arab world, including as a source of energy security, as a home for Indian migrant labour and as a potential fount of investments. It is clear that India values its relationship with Israel, but not at the expense of its friendships with Arab and other Muslim states.

A brief look at Iran is necessary before we leave the region. Iran's natural resources, particularly its oil and natural gas, have been increasingly important for India for decades. Many Indian refineries are in fact devised to process the quality of crude oil that Iran supplies, and its gas would be cheaper than most alternatives available. This makes the proposed Iran–Pakistan–India pipeline a serious attraction, despite huge pressure from Washington to resist such an arrangement and India's understandable reluctance to place any portion of its energy security in the hands of Pakistan, through whose territory much of the pipeline would run. India's Iran policy today, however, has to take account of not only its energy dependence, but India's own concerns about nuclear proliferation in its subregion, and the increasing international isolation of the Iranian regime, with resultant pressures on India to reduce or even end its dependence on energy from a reviled government. The United States' increasing exasperation with Iran's attempts to develop a nuclear weapons capacity (if not a bomb itself) has also added to the stress on India, at a time when New Delhi is building an improved and revived relationship with Washington centred on nuclear cooperation. India is anxious to avoid Iran becoming an irritant in its strengthening relations with the United States. On the other hand, India feels the United

States is being unreasonable in not recognizing that trade sanctions on Iran are far easier to impose if you don't need Iranian oil, and next to impossible if a large portion of your energy security is dependent on it. (Nonetheless, it was revealed in May 2012 that India had been quietly reducing the quantity of its oil imports from Iran.)

India sees Iran as a significant partner for other reasons as well: Iran has been a kindred spirit of India's on Pakistan and Afghanistan, where the two share a mistrust of the Sunni fanaticism of the Taliban and the sinister machinations of the Pakistani ISI. This point of convergence adds to Iran's role as a vital source of usable hydrocarbons, a crucial link with Central Asia and the Gulf, and a 'friend at court' in the Islamic world. In turn, Iran sees a good relationship with India as helpful in escaping its diplomatic isolation, and it also sees in India an important trading partner, a useful source of high technology and a reliable customer for its energy exports. The two sets of considerations will ensure that the 'civilizational relationship' with Iran that India's leaders speak regularly about will continue to have genuine substantive content, even as pressure to isolate and sanction Iran remains unrelenting.

This helps explain why India has been noticeably unsympathetic to the rising clamour from the United States and Israel for action to dismantle the Iranian nuclear programme, even though New Delhi has made clear its disapproval of Iran developing a nuclear weapon. There is no doubt that India, while responsive to US and Israeli pressure (and angry about the apparent abuse of India's friendship in an Iranian bomb attack in New Delhi in early 2012 on an Israeli military attaché's car), will not want to be pushed beyond a point into rupturing relations with Tehran. India's stand has been devoid of moralizing on either side of the issue, its pragmatism extending to such measures as bartering Indian gold for Iranian oil, and allowing Iran to trade with India in rupees (with the proceeds held in a Kolkata bank invulnerable to international sanctions because it has no overseas operations).

It is a pity, though, that neither New Delhi nor Washington has seen fit to use India's continuing Iranian connections diplomatically. A still-engaged India might have proved a more useful mediator in Iran's row with the West than the European Union (EU) countries currently engaged in the task, but no such initiative has been pursued.

A different set of conditions explains India's policy on Syria, which has seen New Delhi simultaneously affirm its friendship and regard for the secular regime in Damascus, with which it has long enjoyed good relations, in preference to any likely Islamist alternative. But without comparable economic incentives at stake, India, while opposing any military intervention against the regime, has voted with the West in the UN Security Council to call for the Assad government to negotiate a peaceful transition. In this it differs from Syria's neighbour Turkey, another secular regime in the region, which openly condemned Assad's repression of dissent, the sort of position India has been chronically reluctant to take (both because of its respect for Syrian sovereignty and for fear that such condemnation could be used to justify foreign military intervention, as happened in Libya).

Turkey itself represents an underexploited opportunity for India: a secular democracy with a fast-growing economy, it ought to be a close ally, but has been locked for decades in a pro-Pakistan policy crafted under successive military regimes in both those countries. This is gradually changing, and with burgeoning trade (currently over $7.6 billion and growing), a distinct note of warmth has been creeping into the relationship. This is a story only beginning to unfold, but I see New Delhi's relations with Ankara as having immense potential in the immediate future. The question that comes to mind, as BRICS emerges as a body with an alternative view of the world, is: could Turkey, a NATO member with a mind of its own, join them? There are no signs yet, but no country offers a more natural fit with the incipient new grouping than Turkey. BRICST won't be easy to pronounce, but the entry of Turkey would fill a hole in the geographical centre and enhance the group's geopolitical centre and enhance its potential. It's well worth thinking about.

India's closer ties with the countries of Southeast and East Asia are the result of our 'Look East' policy, first enunciated by the government of Prime Minister P.V. Narasimha Rao at the end of the Cold War in 1991 and pursued faithfully by all his successors. Jawaharlal Nehru had referred, in his classic *The Discovery of India*, to Southeast Asia as

'Greater India', but that heady romanticism foundered amid mutual suspicions during the Cold War, and relations remained sparse. The end of the superpower standoff—and thus of the obligation of states to determine their international allegiances in relation to Cold War loyalties and commitments—widened India's foreign policy options, permitting New Delhi to look beyond the conventional wisdom of its non-aligned years. 'Look East' followed.

Initially aimed at improving relations with the member states of the ASEAN at a time when India had embarked upon economic liberalization, and indirectly at enhancing strategic cooperation with the United States ('looking East to look West', as the author Sunanda Datta-Ray termed it), the policy has succeeded beyond the vision of its initiator. 'Look East' has not just become an end in itself, cementing enhanced economic cooperation with a long-neglected region, but it has signalled India's return—some might say arrival—in a part of the world increasingly anxious about China's overweening influence. That the policy continues to bear fruit two decades after it was launched is reflected in such recent developments as India's admission as a full dialogue partner of ASEAN, its acceptance as a member of the ASEAN Regional Forum and as a full participant in the East Asia Summit (even though by no stretch of the geographical imagination can India be said to be an East Asian power). In 2003 Yashwant Sinha, then India's minister of external affairs, described the 'Look East' policy as having evolved through two phases, the first 'ASEAN-centred and focused primarily on trade and investment linkages' and the second 'characterized by an expanded definition of "East", extending from Australia to East Asia, with ASEAN at its core'. The latter phase, Sinha explained, 'also marks a shift from trade to wider economic and security issues, including joint efforts to protect the sea-lanes and coordinate counter-terrorism activities'.

In the first few decades after 1947, India's establishment, shaped by the long colonial era, was inevitably Western in its orientation (if 'orient'ation is not too paradoxical a term). This was ironic, since India had long had a major impact on Southeast and East Asia. Hinduism and Buddhism spread throughout the Asian continent from India, the former being carried by traders and missionaries across much of Indonesia, Malaysia and Thailand, while Buddhism was taken to and through Tibet to China and Korea, whence it reached Japan and Vietnam (it also flourished, of course, in countries closer to India, such as Myanmar, Sri Lanka, Cambodia and Thailand). As Indian trade (and very limited military conquest) expanded the culture's horizons, the religious message and Indian spiritual practices were not the only export: language (particularly Sanskrit), social customs (including reverence for Brahmins), styles of art and architecture, and dance, music and epic narrative, all travelled from India as well. The Ramayana became an Asian, not just Indian, epic, with versions being told and performed from Indonesia to the Philippines. This was a remarkably peaceful process: aside from the invasion of the Srivijaya kingdom in Sumatra by the South Indian raja Rajendra Chola in the eleventh century CE, India did not evince any imperialist ambitions in Southeast Asia. Instead, as David Malone describes it, 'great Indianized kingdoms arose over the centuries throughout Asia and particularly Southeast Asia . . . [following] Indian court customs, administrative organization on the Indian pattern, and laws based on the Code of Manu, the Indian lawgiver. Indianization also included the alphabetical basis of Southeast Asian scripts, the incorporation of Sanskrit in vocabularies along with the adoption of the Hindu-Buddhist religious beliefs, and an Indian concept of royalty.' The spread of Islam to the region was in its turn facilitated by Indian sources, including Indian Muslim traders and missionaries. Thus Indonesia underwent successive layers of Buddhist, Hindu and Muslim conversion, all intermediated by Indian influences. Even Japan was not immune to Indian cultural influence, having been taken over by the spread of Buddhism that had come from India, as evident in the absorption of the Hindu goddesses Lakshmi and Saraswati into Japanese Buddhism as guardian-deities.

Given this history, it was not surprising that, even prior to independence, the interim government led by Nehru organized in March 1947 a 'Conference on Asian Relations', bringing to Delhi delegates from twenty-nine countries, some still under colonial rule, to promote cooperation among Asian countries and express solidarity with the freedom struggles in other parts of Asia. Nehru's India saw itself as the leader of Asia's progress towards independence, a self-image reflected in its leading roles in both the special Delhi 'Conference on Indonesia' in 1949 and the Bandung 'Afro-Asian Solidarity Conference' of 1955.

But this emphasis was lost in Cold War politics. Nor did the Southeast Asia of the early post-independence years encourage much interest; for the most part, it was just as backward, diseased and conflict-ridden as the subcontinent itself, and slow to unveil its potential. India's own economic policies, shaped in reaction to the fact that the British East India Company had come to trade and stayed on to rule, were protectionist; looking for trade opportunities did not feature high on New Delhi's list of priorities. It did not help either that India's natural overland linkages to Southeast Asia were blocked by post-colonial politics: Myanmar shut itself off from the rest of the world in the early 1960s, while India's natural land routes eastwards ran through the suddenly foreign—and hostile—territories of East Pakistan (later Bangladesh). Neither was particularly inclined to provide transit facilities to Indian goods. Global geopolitics also intervened, with the countries of Southeast Asia clearly choosing a side during the Cold War, while India remained non-aligned, with a pronounced tilt towards the Soviet Union that was looked at askance by much of the region. India's closest Asian political relationship in the 1980s was with communist Vietnam rather than ASEAN.

With all these factors in operation, it took New Delhi some time to recognize that India's economic interests are best served by greater integration with Southeast and East Asia, whose countries are natural trading partners with whom links had flourished millennia ago. This is why 'Look East' took so long in coming into existence. But 'Look East' goes well beyond economics. As Prime Minister Manmohan Singh has declared, the 'Look East' policy is much more than an external economic policy; it reflects a changed understanding of India's role in the world economy and signals a significant strategic shift in India's vision of international affairs. It is instructive that no Indian political party—and several have had turns at government since Narasimha Rao—has questioned either the underpinnings or the manifestations of the 'Look East' policy.

One factor helping drive the policy was undoubtedly China's early interest in the region. During the Cold War, Southeast Asia saw itself threatened by the risk of communist expansion, but once China opened up its economy to the outside world and became a major trading power, the prospects of military adventurism receded. Nonetheless, China's growing economic and military might cast a shadow over a region that had traditionally been wary of Beijing. India's interest in engaging more deeply with them offered the nations of Southeast Asia the prospect of a democratic and non-threatening counterbalance. For years India had been bogged down in its own neighbourhood, and dismissed by most—especially by Beijing—as at best a subcontinental power. 'Look East' began with trade but soon expanded to include diplomatic dialogue and strategic and military cooperation. It helped that both sides of the equation enjoyed a shared colonial experience, cultural affinities going back to antiquity and, despite the estrangement of the Cold War years, a striking lack of historical resentments to come between them.

The India–ASEAN free trade agreement on goods, adopted in August 2009 in the face of critical domestic opposition from farmers in India, is perhaps the most striking evidence of the strategic priority accorded by New Delhi to commercial relations with the region. Part of the Framework Agreement on Comprehensive Cooperation signed with ASEAN in 2003, the FTA was India's first multilateral trade agreement outside GATT/WTO. Indian bureaucrats had wanted to delay signing an FTA on goods until ASEAN members had agreed to conclude an FTA on services and investment, but they were overruled by Prime Minister Manmohan Singh, who was trying to use the FTA to send a political, and not just economic, signal to the region. (These negotiations are making slow progress, since India's overwhelming advantage in the services sector causes some anxiety in Southeast Asia.) Nonetheless, in 2009 only 2.5 per cent of ASEAN's trade was with India, compared to 11.6 per cent with China. In the three years since the FTA was signed, trade with ASEAN has gone up by 30 per cent.

In addition, a host of bilateral agreements has been signed with individual countries: FTAs with Sri Lanka and Thailand, comprehensive economic partnership agreements with Singapore, South Korea, Malaysia and Japan, and an early harvest scheme with Thailand, as well as strong commercial, cultural and military ties with individual ASEAN members, notably the Philippines, Singapore, Vietnam and Cambodia. Relations have been strengthened (and upgraded to 'strategic partnerships') with Japan and South Korea, seen previously as too close to Washington to be of interest to non-aligned New Delhi, and even with Taiwan, a country which India had traditionally kept at arm's length out of skittish deference to Beijing's sensibilities. With Japan, there has been a flurry of high-level exchanges, with every one of the country's succession of prime ministers making a beeline for New Delhi early in his term. Tokyo tends to see the utility of building up India as an alternative Asian centre of attraction, if not quite a counterweight, to Beijing. India, not China, is now the top recipient nation of yen credits. Japan and South Korea clearly began to take India more seriously after the India–ASEAN relationship improved and India began engaging with the region's leaders at summit level.

Japanese FDI in India is continuing to grow and has crossed $5.5 billion; Japan is also a generous purveyor of official development assistance, albeit in the form of loans, not grants, which are focused on infrastructure development (particularly power and transportation). One of the most important current Indo-Japanese projects is the Delhi–Mumbai industrial corridor, calling for an estimated total investment of $90 billion, which will transform a vast stretch of territory between the nation's administrative and commercial capitals, involve a dedicated container freight rail line from the capital to India's western seaports, vastly improved transport links and the creation of greenfield townships along its route. India and Japan elevated their relationship to a 'strategic and global partnership' in August 2007. The regular bilateral naval exercises already alluded to reflect the fact that more than 50 per cent of India's trade and more than 80 per cent of Japan's oil imports transit through the Strait of Malacca, giving both countries a significant stake in the security of the Indian Ocean. The exercises also reflect wariness about the likely need for understanding between the two countries in the event that China's major military expansion begins to acquire unfriendly overtones.

Also in East Asia, South Korea has developed an increasingly important relationship with India, its entrepreneurial multinational corporations having made striking inroads into the Indian market. South Korean brands dominate India's advertising billboards, and have cornered impressive shares of the market for cars and consumer goods. The steel company POSCO even launched a $12-billion project in Orissa, but this has fallen afoul of political and bureaucratic resistance by local tribals and Delhi environmentalists, so that the project's long wait for approvals and clearances has been dragging on since 2005. An active India–Republic of Korea foreign policy and security dialogue has been established, and the prospects for defence cooperation appear bright, especially since India and South Korea decided to enhance their relationship to a strategic partnership in 2010.

These changed relationships offer a striking contrast to the days in the late 1950s when the Thai prime minister complained to an Indian journalist of New Delhi's characterization of his country as a 'Coca-Cola economy', and Nehru's foreign policy ideologue, V.K. Krishna Menon, when approached by Japan's UN Ambassador Matsushima seeking collaboration, 'shooed me [Matsushima] off, remarking that the policies of India and Japan were so different that collaboration was out of the question'. India kept ASEAN at arm's length since its inception, seeing the organization as a surrogate for American interests during the Vietnam War. Its own increasing proximity to the Soviet Union, crystallized in the Treaty of Friendship and Cooperation signed as war clouds with a US-backed Pakistan loomed in 1971, did not help enhance its image in Southeast Asian eyes. The decision of the Indira Gandhi government to recognize the Vietnamese-backed Heng Samrin regime in Cambodia prompted further alienation between ASEAN capitals and New Delhi. India even rejected an invitation to become an ASEAN dialogue partner in 1980. But these difficulties were temporal and not structural ones. The estrangement ended swiftly when New Delhi wanted it to, in 1991.

In India's new pragmatic view of its foreign policy, it was important to improve relations not only with ASEAN but with East Asian lands beyond the association's reach—with Japan and South Korea, for instance, because they are major sources of foreign investment to speed up India's economic development. But equally, New Delhi saw an increasing strategic convergence with these two democracies, in the face of China's impressive rise. 'Look East' has acquired tangible content in such areas as cooperation on counterterrorism and anti-piracy, maritime and energy security, keeping open the sea lanes of communication in the region's waters and joint humanitarian relief operations (notably after the Indonesian tsunami, when the United States asked India, along with Japan and Australia, to constitute the core group of countries to deliver relief).

A military and security dimension to the policy has also been emerging. With more than half of India's trade traversing the Strait of Malacca, the Indian Navy has taken on a role in the joint patrolling of the Strait, and established a Far Eastern Naval Command at Port Blair on the Andaman and Nicobar Islands, Indian territory that lies closer to Sumatra than to Surat. It organizes a gathering of naval fleets, code-named 'Milan', in Port Blair biennially since 1995, to conduct combined exercises with eleven regional navies and also promote social and professional interactions among them. Defence cooperation has strengthened since 1993 with Malaysia—which, with over 2 million persons of Indian origin, is home to one of the largest Indian diaspora communities in the world—and has featured annual meetings of the two countries' defence secretaries, military training and the supply of defence equipment.

Bilaterally, India has cooperative arrangements with several countries stretching from the Seychelles to Vietnam, many of which have acquired security dimensions. Multilaterally, India has been an active participant in the Regional Cooperation Agreement on Combating Piracy and Armed Robbery against Ships in Asia (ReCAAP), and maritime security has begun to loom larger in the consciousness of Indian decision-makers after the terrorists of 26/11 hijacked an Indian ship and transported themselves to Mumbai. A counterterrorism agreement with ASEAN reflects the region's increasing worries about Islamic fundamentalism after the Bali bombings. Joint naval exercises have been conducted with Singapore also since 1993, with Indonesia since 2002 and occasionally, since 2000, with Vietnam; other exercises have featured Malaysia, Thailand and the Philippines. One joint exercise that involved India, Singapore, Japan and Australia sent the alarm bells ringing in Beijing and prompted a nervously Sinophile Canberra to pull the plug. New Delhi has shown little regret about the end of what many had seen as an incipient strategic alliance of these four countries (with a benign United States looking on) in East Asia.

India's diplomats have been kept busy as New Delhi stepped up its active presence in the region. India became a 'sectoral dialogue partner' with ASEAN in 1992, a full dialogue partner in 1995, a member of the Council for Security Cooperation in the Asia-Pacific the following year;

it participated in the ASEAN Ministerial Meeting, the Post Ministerial Conference and the ASEAN Regional Forum in July 1996. India became a 'summit level partner' (a status accorded previously only to China, Japan and South Korea) in 2002. 'ASEAN+3' became 'ASEAN+6' to include India (in order, Japan made clear, to balance China's strength in the +3 format); and India was made a full member of the East Asia Summit by leaders in Singapore and Indonesia who shared much the same concerns. (India is not yet in the Asia-Pacific Economic Cooperation forum, APEC, despite the best efforts of Japan and the United States, because China stubbornly persists in pointing out that New Delhi doesn't actually have any visible connection to the Pacific.)

In all this, it is difficult to see the same India that had failed—indeed refused—to get in on the ground floor when ASEAN was created in 1967. In the ARF, India has focused on a number of key activities such as peacekeeping, maritime security and cyber security, where its undeniable strengths are of great value to the other members. India has also involved itself in several infrastructure projects that serve to tie it closer to Southeast Asia: the UN Economic and Social Commission for Asia and the Pacific's plans for an Asian highway network and a trans-Asian railway network, and the intermittent attempts to reopen the Second World War–era 'Stilwell Road' which would link Assam with China's Yunnan province through Myanmar. While such ventures are still largely schemes on the drawing board, the government has been kept busy hosting India–ASEAN business summits, pursuing its obligations under ASEAN's Treaty of Amity and Cooperation in Southeast Asis (to which India acceded in 2003) and arranging a series of high-level visits to and from ASEAN countries. Trade with the region accounts for some 45 per cent of India's foreign trade, and remains vital for the country's future prosperity.

The Stilwell Road may in fact be a somewhat premature idea, given that a road link with a China that still does not recognize Arunachal Pradesh as a part of India would open our country up further to Chinese irredentist claims, not to mention flooding the region with Chinese products at a time when Indian goods are struggling to reach north-eastern Indian markets. A bigger priority ought to be to connect the rest of India better to the state and to the north-eastern region as a whole, which will require New Delhi to do much more to develop infrastructure in the state than to establish a road link with China. If India starts thinking strategically about its North-East, it will have to make some investments in domestic infrastructure before it thinks of expenditure abroad.

Nonetheless, India has played a crucial role in developing multilateral organizations in the region, notably the Mekong–Ganga Cooperation (MGC), the IOR-ARC and BIMSTEC, the latter pair of which we will discuss in greater detail below. Such associations of countries around a common purpose have two attractive features: they permit progress to be made on developmental, environmental and security issues, while benefiting from the exclusion of strategic rivals like Pakistan and China. Pakistan has systematically obstructed all of India's efforts to forge meaningful progress in SAARC, as noted in Chapter Three. Despite China being an Upper Mekong riparian country, it has been omitted from the MGC, giving credence to Beijing's view that India's intentions in devising this organization are deliberately to counterbalance China's influence in the area. (In all fairness, however, it should be pointed out that China refuses to be part of the Mekong River Commission, claiming that it is not an Upper Mekong riparian state.)

As Prime Minister Manmohan Singh made clear when speaking about the strategic shift embodied in India's 'Look East' policy, 'most of all it is about reaching out to our civilizational neighbours in Southeast Asia and East Asia'. This outreach was essential if India was to avoid being confined to its immediate subcontinental environs and establish itself as a regional power; it was also necessary if India was to take advantage of the huge economic advances made by the Southeast Asian nations, whose successes in many respects pointed the way for India's own progress and prosperity. Six of the twenty members of the G20, as the Indian prime minister noted—Australia, China, India, Indonesia, Japan and South Korea—belong to the East Asia Summit. With talk of the twenty-first century being the 'Asian Century' as the twentieth was America's, Prime Minister Manmohan Singh's vision of an integrated Asia stretching from the Himalayas to the Pacific Ocean, in which one could travel, trade and invest freely throughout the region, is an admirable objective, if still—given geopolitical realities—largely a dream.

For despite all the encouraging developments, there is still a long way to go. India–ASEAN trade is not yet at $50 billion; with a few exceptions like Singapore, the visa regime between India and ASEAN members remains complicated and difficult; despite the liberalization of air services agreements with ASEAN members, India's airlines still do not enjoy a comprehensive open skies policy with ASEAN and vice versa; and tourism from ASEAN (and for that matter from East Asian countries like Japan, Korea, China and Taiwan) to India does not begin to compare to that in the opposite direction, reaching barely 10 per cent of Indian travellers to the East. It is startling that the land that gave birth to Buddhism has not been able to attract more Buddhists to places like Bodh Gaya, Sarnath and Nalanda (or for that matter to the much else that India offers, from the Taj Mahal to golden beaches, nature parks and resorts and places of historical interest, none of which has been marketed well in the region). Visa restrictions continue to apply on both sides; tentative moves to promote visas on arrival in India were scuttled after the terrorist attacks of 26/11 revealed the country's vulnerability to malign outsiders. The kind of cooperative projects being discussed— launching an India–ASEAN health care initiative aiming to provide low-cost drugs, or creating an India–ASEAN Green Fund for Climate Change projects—are underwhelming. In contrast, the China–ASEAN FTA is the third largest regional agreement in terms of economic value, after only the EU and NAFTA. India has also been seen to be considerably less active than China or Japan across the ASEAN region.

There are, however, some evident Indian comparative advantages that can be leveraged through its 'Look East' policy. The excellence of its institutions of higher education, notably the famed Indian Institutes of Technology (IITs) and of Management (IIMs) have given it a reputation in human resource development that makes it an attractive resource not just for developing countries like Cambodia, Laos or Timor-Leste, but even for relatively advanced nations like Indonesia, Malaysia and Singapore, each of which has solicited the establishment of Indian educational institutions on their territories. Information technology remains a key selling point, but by no means the only one.

While India has never shown a great deal of enthusiasm for exporting its democracy, it remains willing to offer technical assistance in such areas of democracy promotion as public administration and the conduct of free and fair elections. As the motherland of much of Southeast Asia's culture and the crucible of the Buddhism widely practised across the region, India begins with a storehouse of respect that it has sometimes seemed to squander. Where imagination has been allied to public policy and governmental support, the results can be spectacular, as in the Nalanda project, which revives a fabled international university in Bihar, a lodestar for students from the Far East for centuries before Oxford and Cambridge were even dreamed of. The active participation of China, Japan and Singapore in Nalanda's revival is a noteworthy example of the use of culture to strengthen political relations across the region.

On the other side of the ledger is the failure to use the scattered Indian diaspora in the region as levers of Indian policy. Unlike the Chinese diaspora, the Indian is less cohesive, more generally working class in origin (going back to the importation of plantation labour by the colonial regime) and less influential in their societies—there is no Indian equivalent of the ethnic Chinese generals in Indonesia or prime ministers in Thailand. The Indian diaspora in Southeast Asia, differing visibly from the indigenes around them, also tends to be more anxious to demonstrate their loyalty to their countries of residence, overtly eschewing any political affinity to their cultural motherland in India. This is gradually changing, though, as India itself is seen as more acceptable to the countries of the region; some prominent Singaporean Indians, for instance, who at one time went out of their way to criticize India sharply and publicly, now speak openly in misty-eyed terms of their Indian origins—a clear reflection of the changing esteem in which the new, post-1991 India is held.

This discussion of Asia has omitted Australasia and the Pacific, which must be briefly mentioned. India has a complex relationship with Fiji in view of the endemic tensions between the indigenous majority there and the large population of Indian descent (some 44 to 46 per cent of Fijians, a number declining with increasing emigration). Fiji has often been quick to accuse successive Indian high commissioners in Suva of interference in the country's internal affairs, while India has lobbied hard for sanctions against Fiji after the two coups there against elected Indian-dominated governments in 1987 and 2000. Relations have settled into an uneasy truce, with India providing some aid to Fiji and Fijian Prime Minister Qarase making a successful visit to New Delhi in 2005.

New Zealand has modest defence links with India, featuring pleasant interaction between their navies, with ship visits and naval exercises; India posted a former navy chief as its high commissioner in Wellington till 2012. Canberra's is a more important relationship that can grow manifold, given the converging interests of both nations, reflected in a series of agreements in 2006 and 2007 (on joint naval exercises, increased maritime security cooperation, more frequent military exchanges, and joint training of the two nations' armed forces) complemented in 2009 by the announcement of a 'strategic partnership'. Australia has become the second most favoured destination for Indian students after the United States, with over 120,000 Indian students enrolled in 2009 (reflecting an average annual increase of 41 per cent since 2002). Though this has declined somewhat following the spate of attacks on Indian students in Australia in 2009–10, the reversal of that trend, and the positive portrayal of Australia in a number of Hindi films, may again see Indians flocking to the sunshine, cricket, nubile youth and job opportunities that a student visa to Australia gives access to.

Central Asia is also an increasingly important region within India's 'near abroad'. It is a region with which India has rich historic links and one that offers a wealth of natural resources, abundant transit options and a new geopolitical arena. The oil and gas resources of the region are of particular interest, having prompted ingenious proposals like the US-backed Turkmenistan–Afghanistan–Pakistan–India (TAPI) pipeline, which remains on the drawing board as long as the territories of Afghanistan and Pakistan are insecure. Tajikistan, which shares borders with both Afghanistan and China, has emerged as an important strategic Central Asian partner for India, and has provided India its first external military airbase at Ayni. Several Central Asian governments, worried about Islamic radicalism and understandably suspicious of the close ties between Pakistani militant organizations and their counterparts like the Islamic Movement of Uzbekistan (IMU), see in India a plausible sympathetic ally against violent Islamism. The potential of such alliances helps explain India's intense interest in the Shanghai Cooperation Organization (SCO), launched in 2001 by China with Kazakhstan, Kyrgyzstan, Russia, Tajikistan and Uzbekistan, in which India has been given observer status but not yet full membership.

The SCO has so far done little more than hold summit meetings, but its importance should not be underestimated. Two regional organizations in which India has a far more central role—BIMSTEC and the IOR-ARC—are discussed in more detail below.

———

BIMSTEC is an international organization founded in 1997 and initially named BIST-EC, for economic cooperation among its original four members, Bangladesh, India, Sri Lanka and Thailand. Its membership now also includes Bhutan, Myanmar and Nepal; Myanmar's admission changed the acronym to BIMSTEC, and with Bhutan and Nepal coming in, the acronym was retained but its meaning altered (this is the kind of clever wordplay in which Indian diplomats specialize).

BIMSTEC offers an interesting opportunity to demonstrate my central thesis of foreign policy serving to benefit domestic publics, because its success will help transform India's neglected and underdeveloped north-eastern states. India's North-East is the bridge between two subregions of Asia—South Asia and Southeast Asia. Both regions are in the midst of tremendous positive change, spurred by economic growth and development. For various reasons, India has not so far been able to leverage the various opportunities that this subregion of India offers for the well-being and prosperity of the people who live here. Among the opportunities we should seize are not only the geographical factor of being a bridgehead between South Asia and Southeast Asia, but also the trade potential emerging from the natural and human resources of the seven sisters of the North-East. Today's challenge is to harness these opportunities to ensure that growth and development does not bypass this region but passes by this region. BIMSTEC's objectives as an organization will involve it in truly linking this region not only to other parts of India but beyond.

If the most clichéd slogan about India is 'Unity in Diversity', there are places in the country that vividly demonstrate diversity within India's unity. The north-eastern states of the Indian Union, populated mostly by people ethnically kin to their neighbours to the east and south of them, have been bountifully endowed by nature. The region features rich biodiversity; its hydro potential is unparalleled; it has petroleum and natural gas along with other minerals; and it also has great forest wealth. But more than these rich natural endowments, the region is blessed with great (and underdeveloped) human resource wealth, emerging from the confluence of various ethnic, linguistic, religious, cultural and educational currents.

Although industrialization was brought to this region by the British East India Company in the early nineteenth century with the cultivation and first export of tea way back in 1839, the rapid development of industry has not taken place here. Even coal was found here soon thereafter and exploited, which led to the development of the railways. The first oil refinery of Asia was set up in 1901 in Digboi following the discovery of oil in Upper Assam. It is also important to remember that in the past, during times of acute foreign exchange scarcity, Assam's tea and jute exports were sources of much-needed foreign exchange for India. So it is all the more ironic and disheartening that today this region is yet to benefit fully from the industrialization and economic development of post-liberalization India, and that significant differences in terms of some development indicators have emerged with other parts of India. Happily, various initiatives are in place to correct the discrepancies and BIMSTEC is a key part of these efforts. New Delhi must give the organization greater support as part of its strategic obligation to bring economic development to this geopolitically crucial region of India.

With the paradigm shift that has been taking place in New Delhi from a state-centred approach to one of interdependence and global and regional cooperation, we have become all the more aware of the geo-economic potential of the north-eastern region as a gateway to East and Southeast Asia. I am convinced that by gradually integrating this region through cross-border market access, the north-eastern states can become the bridge between the Indian economy and what is arguably the fastest growing and most dynamic region in the world. While we live with the geographic fact that our north-eastern region is landlocked, the geographical location of the North-East makes it the doorway to Southeast and East Asia and vice versa, a doorway for these economies into India.

Let us consider some basic facts. A glance at the map of the north-eastern region reveals that the region is almost entirely surrounded by foreign states and the seven sisters of the region are internally landlocked with concomitant locational disadvantages, despite the fact that each of these states has at least one international border. The north-eastern region is cradled by five Asian states—China, Nepal, Bhutan, Myanmar and Bangladesh—and connected to India only by a narrow strip of territory, 21 to 40 kilometres in width, running north of Bangladesh, the so-called Chicken's Neck. Arunachal Pradesh, Manipur, Mizoram and Nagaland share a 1643-kilometre-long border with Myanmar; Assam, Meghalaya, Tripura and Mizoram share a 1880-kilometre border with Bangladesh; Arunachal Pradesh, Assam and Sikkim share a 468-kilometre border with Bhutan; Arunachal Pradesh and Sikkim share a 1325-kilometre border with the Tibet Autonomous Region of the People's Republic of China. The region's difficulties following from the loss of connectivity and market access as a result of Partition in 1947 are well known, though recent discussions with Bangladesh augur well for changing that narrative of deadlock and denial. Traditional transportation routes—rail, road and river, linking the Chittagong and Kolkata ports—suddenly became unavailable in the 1960s and alternative routes were prohibitively costly. To cite an example, the distance between Agartala and Kolkata port is 1700 kilometres, whereas earlier it was just about 375 kilometres through the territory of what became East Pakistan, now Bangladesh. The result, therefore, was massive market and logistical disruption, from which the North-East of India still suffers.

The Manmohan Singh government has taken a number of initiatives which will have a long-term economic impact on the region, including the launching of a 'North-Eastern Region Vision 2020' by the prime minister himself in 2008 and the setting up of a coordinating ministry dedicated to the development of the north-eastern region, focusing particularly on important infrastructure tasks, such as rail and road development and power projects, the development of services in sectors like hotels, adventure and leisure sports, nursing homes and vocational training institutes. Considering the rich biodiversity of the region, biotechnology has been brought under the purview of the new policy.

This may sound like an internally focused approach, but it is part of a larger picture. India's 'Look East' policy, as explained earlier in this chapter, was not merely a matter of external policy; it was also a strategic shift in India's vision of the world and India's place in the evolving global economy. Most of all, it was about reaching out to our civilizational neighbours in the region and availing of the economic opportunities presented by these countries for our own domestic development.

Several projects have been proposed, and some beginnings undertaken, under the aegis of the 'Look East' policy, specifically to uplift North-East India. Among these are the Asian Highway, the proposed Asian Railway link and various schemes for a natural gas pipeline across the area. The Kaladan Multimodal Transit Transport facility is aimed at establishing connectivity between India and Sittwe port in Myanmar (formerly Akyab) through river and road links from Mizoram. With the Mekong–Ganga initiative, the intention is to permit direct flights between Guwahati in Assam and Ho Chi Minh City in Vietnam, and between Imphal in Manipur and Hanoi. When completed, the Asian highway project is expected to provide a land route from Singapore to New Delhi through Malaysia, Vietnam, Laos and Myanmar. India has already taken the first step in this direction and has built the road linking Tamu in Manipur to Kalemyo, a key communication junction in the centre of Myanmar.

As an earnest gesture of its intent to improve linkages between India's North-East and Southeast Asia, India organized an India–ASEAN car rally in 2004, which started in Guwahati and ended in Indonesia's Batam Island off Singapore after crossing Myanmar, Thailand, Laos, Vietnam, Cambodia, Malaysia and Singapore. The event was greeted with much enthusiasm in all of India's north-eastern states, with mini rallies held in all the seven sisters to great public acclaim. Though the initiative sparked hopes of ending the North-East's isolation from the rest of India and their immediate neighbours to the east, it was not followed up with concrete policies and the implementation of many schemes outlined earlier remained inordinately slow. Projects to create a Delhi–Hanoi rail link and a trilateral highway linking India, Myanmar and Thailand have made little headway; had they done so, they could also have encouraged Bangladesh to join the bandwagon, instead of remaining a sole obstacle to India's eastern connectivity. Given the continuing political sensitivities in Bangladesh over seeming to be giving in too much to India, it might be easier for Dhaka, too, to cooperate on issues of transit not as a purely bilateral matter but as part of an overall regional arrangement.

For once, the Government of India recognizes that it does not have all the answers: the Vision 2020 document makes it clear that private-sector investment is indispensable for the long-term economic development of the North-East. It does not go far enough, however, to assure the private sector that the government will create the infrastructure, or the conditions of security in the face of insurgency, to make their investments worthwhile. It remains an axiom that the private sector will move in only where the government has first established the basic platform for them to pursue their profits. This remains a huge challenge.

Nonetheless, India's engagement with BIMSTEC is a key component of our 'Look East' policy. Indeed, BIMSTEC is a forum where New Delhi's 'Look East' policy meets Bangkok's 'Look West' policy. BIMSTEC is a unique link between South Asia and Southeast Asia. From the very beginning, it has been considered a powerful mechanism to promote opportunities for trade, investment and tourism between these two regions. Since its inception with just four members in 1997, the combined GDP of the BIMSTEC countries has almost tripled, reaching nearly $2 trillion. At present, connectivity among the members is far more than it was in 1997, and intra-BIMSTEC trade turnover and investment and people-to-people exchanges have multiplied. A free trade agreement within the BIMSTEC framework is being discussed.

If India takes advantage of the experiences and strengths of the member countries in a concerted way, it is possible to have a far-reaching impact on poverty reduction and on the overall development of the region. For this to happen, tremendous effort and investment will have to be made in the north-eastern states to benefit from the doors that are being opened. There needs to be greater focus on capacity building, especially in building up human resource capacity, by preparing the people of the seven sisters for the opportunities that will open up in the commerce, tourism and services sectors. As already suggested in Chapter Three, major new projects to rebuild the overland linkages between this region and neighbouring countries will help create the physical integration from which economic integration will flow.

The overlap between the internal and the international makes it also essential that we dovetail the development strategies of the north-eastern region with the BIMSTEC initiative. Pursuance of the 'Look

East' policy for over fifteen years has put in place certain diplomatic and political structures. There is now need to make these structures work for the north-eastern region. Diplomatic initiatives urgently need to be converted into commercial, touristic and investment opportunities. This will require greater coordination than we have seen so far between the Ministry of External Affairs and the Ministry of Development of North-Eastern Region, the Planning Commission, the assorted economic ministries and the seven state governments.

Bilateral relationships are also vital in strengthening our collective efforts. The increased momentum of the strengthening of India's relations with countries like Bangladesh and Thailand will inevitably contribute to our effective cooperation within BIMSTEC as well. This is a mutually reinforcing process.

However, practical progress will require much more by way of the development of transportation and communication linkages and greater connectivity among the members. Tackling constraints and bottlenecks in transportation and communication identified by the Asian Development Bank (ADB) is essential. As part of the 'Look East' policy, India strongly supports the various initiatives taken to improve comprehensive physical connectivity between countries in the region. From our perspective, the most critical link would be to create road connectivity from the North-East of India through Myanmar into Southeast Asia. A trilateral highway project between India, Myanmar and Thailand is under construction. Thailand and India in fact have completed construction of the link roads on either side. Some portions of the internal road connectivity in Myanmar remain to be completed, and Myanmar has made requests for grants and funding to enable this project to proceed. Once this road is completed, it would conveniently link us with the Asian highway network and the new East-West highway project running from Vietnam through to Myanmar.

India is involved in a variety of cross-border development projects with Myanmar in diverse fields such as roads, railways, telecommunications, IT, science and technology and power. These initiatives are aimed at improving connectivity between north-eastern India and western Myanmar and are expected to give an impetus to the local economies as well as bilateral trade. Probably among the most important is the

Kaladan Multimodal Transit Transport facility already mentioned, which envisages connectivity between Indian ports on the eastern seaboard and Sittwe port in Myanmar and then through riverine transport and by road to Mizoram, thereby providing an alternative route for transport of goods to India's North-East. In fact, given the importance that the Government of India attaches to this project, New Delhi has decided to fund it completely. Several projects are on the anvil to provide road, rail and river transportation routes from the north-eastern states through Myanmar into Thailand and the rest of ASEAN. Once these are completed—which would require energy, political will and commitment from all BIMSTEC countries and most of all from India—one can truly turn the term 'landlocked' into 'land-linked'.

In any case, 'landlocked' is a geographical concept whose applicability in the twenty-first century is contestable. In today's IT age, land is not necessary for countries to be linked. That is why India must put more effort into enhancing digital connectivity with this region, starting with an optical fibre cable link between the towns of Moreh in Manipur and Mandalay in Myanmar.

Similarly, India's excellent relations with Bhutan and its involvement in the development and growth of Bhutan's economy also translate into direct benefits for the north-eastern states. Recent increases in the export of raw material and agricultural produce from this region to Bhutan have meant better opportunities for agriculturists and industries in the North-East. In fact, Jaigaon on the Indian side of the border across from Phuntsoling on the Bhutan side has grown and become prosperous with its position as the nodal point for trade with Bhutan. Mutually beneficial development of water resources between India and Bhutan has already been described earlier in this chapter, and most of the hydroelectric power that is being generated as a result is for the use of the eastern and north-eastern states of India.

BIMSTEC is an important vehicle to promote regional cooperation and economic integration in a range of areas in our region. I would like to see BIMSTEC develop as a vibrant organization effectively making the North-East our country's gateway to Southeast Asia. I have often argued that in today's globalized world the distinction between the national and the foreign is increasingly irrelevant. BIMSTEC provides an opportunity for India to advance its national developmental priorities in this region and its foreign policy interests in the wider region in one seamless approach. Given the obvious political and security interests that are also at stake, it is an opportunity that must be seized in our fundamental national interest.

———

All is not unrelievedly good news. The limitations of India's 'Look East' policy are nowhere more apparent than in Timor-Leste (formerly known as East Timor), the former Portuguese colony which won its independence from Indonesia in 2000. 'Embassy Row' in the capital, Dili, occupies much of the capital's sparkling seafront. All the embassies have majestic views of the Indian Ocean. The imposing US embassy is set far back from the street in fear of possible truck bombers; the Chinese one practically hugs the pavement; the Japanese and Koreans appear to jostle with the Portuguese and the Australians for the most desirable oceanfront space. Now Pakistan has announced it is opening an embassy in Dili. Of India, there is no sign: the newest member country of the United Nations is covered from Jakarta by our ambassador to Indonesia, whose brutal twenty-five-year occupation, ending in 2000, has not yet been forgotten in Timor-Leste. The fact that the only Indian flag flying in Dili was one placed in the foyer of my hotel, in honour of this visiting MP, reflects our country's inexcusable failure to engage with the great potential of Southeast Asia's youngest nation.

I was in Dili in early 2011 at the invitation of my good friend and then president Jose Ramos-Horta, whom I had first met a decade and a half ago as a Gandhian-minded human rights activist, whose advocacy of his people's freedom won him the Nobel Peace Prize in 1995. Ramos-Horta has held every position of international heft in his country—foreign minister, prime minister and president—but retains a disarming modesty. My wife and I were astonished to be picked up by him personally at the airport and driven (by him, not a chauffeur) to our hotel in his quaint six-wheel Mini Moke. His message was clear: an Indian visitor, even one far removed from the corridors of power, was a welcome indication of interest, to a nation uncomfortably being wooed by both China and Pakistan.

That Timor-Leste should be the object of so much international courtship is hardly surprising. This small country of just over a million people sits on an enormous quantity of oil and natural gas, whose revenues have already helped build a reserve fund of $6 billion, growing every year. The half-island nation (its other half is Indonesian West Timor) is also home to significant quantities of gold and manganese, and its shores teem with fish. But it's not just Timor-Leste's natural resources that attract outsiders. Its needs are significant as well. The country, once dirt-poor, was devastated by a vengeful Indonesian withdrawal that left much of the capital in ruins. The task of building infrastructure—including support for the country's exploitation of its own offshore oil and gas—is enormous, and calls for enterprising investors. Given its own increasing prosperity, Dili is not looking for handouts, but for help.

Timor-Leste is the kind of place in which one would imagine India being far more active than Pakistan, and yet it's Islamabad that has leapt at the prospect, not New Delhi. Our woefully understaffed foreign service has been noticeably reluctant to open new missions without the qualified and experienced personnel available to run them. Despite a Cabinet authorization two years ago to double the strength of our diplomatic corps, little progress has been made to increase available numbers, given the unwillingness of the establishment to open itself up to mid-career recruitment from outside the foreign service. This means that a number of pending recommendations for new missions are still languishing, and new recommendations simply aren't being made.

But if Delhi won't stir itself, Dili will. President Ramos-Horta had already won Cabinet approval to open an embassy in India and was about to embark on the necessary procedures to implement it. He was grateful for China's huge contributions to his nation—Beijing has already built the foreign ministry building and the presidential palace in Dili, as well as a headquarters building and staff quarters for the military—but remained wary of being enveloped solely in the dragon's embrace. Timor-Leste hopes to join ASEAN soon, and would like nothing better than for China's blandishments to be balanced by an attentive India. Non-alignment between two big powers is still, after all, the wisest option for a small and newly independent nation.

The Indian private sector has been quick to wake up to the

possibilities. Reliance Petroleum is spending a million dollars a day drilling in an exploratory block off the country's southern coast, and if it strikes oil, the proceeds could be astronomical. Builders, road developers and exporters are also beginning to take interest. Timor-Leste imports almost everything: its trade imbalance is startling, featuring imports of $828 million and exports of just $8million (consisting entirely of what President Ramos-Horta insists is the world's best coffee). Opportunities abound, and it won't be the first time Indian entrepreneurs take initiatives before our government does.

Not that South Block has been entirely asleep at the switch: there are uniformed Indians, both military and police, in the United Nations mission in Timor-Leste, and our government has offered Timorians a number of scholarships for study in India. For the most part, though, the scholarships have gone abegging, since Timorese students don't have the grounding, or the English, to take them up. The President would love to have Indian help in building up his country's human resource capacities. An Indian IT training centre in Dili, he says, would be a wonderful start.

India has started putting diplomatic and financial energy into its traditional talk of South–South cooperation; we are offering foreign aid, grants and loans, to a number of African countries. Timor-Leste is a more self-reliant nation than most, so we will not need to be out of pocket much to help it. But if we send a few experts over to train young Timorese to take advantage of all that the twenty-first century offers them, we can make an impact out of all proportion to its cost. When the prime minister, the heroic Xanana Gusmao, developed cervical pain, he had to fly to Singapore to be treated: a good Indian hospital would be welcomed by every Timorese. Agriculture, mining and the development of small and medium enterprises are also things we are good at that the Timorese sorely need. It's time for New Delhi to plant an Indian flag in new Dili.

———

The story of Admiral Zheng He, with which I began Chapter Three, is a marvellous evocation of cultural eclecticism, but it is also a wonderful illustration of the age-old cosmopolitanism of the Indian Ocean region, centuries before the word 'globalization' had ever been coined.

Zheng He's travels six hundred years ago stand as a reminder of the economic potential of the vast waters of the Indian Ocean, which wash the shores of dozens of countries large and small that straddle half the globe, account for half of the planet's container traffic and carry two-thirds of its petroleum. But far more interesting, perhaps, are the strategic implications of the Indian Ocean region. The American writer Robert Kaplan's premise, in his 2010 book *Monsoon*, is that the 'Greater Indian Ocean', from the Horn of Africa to Indonesia, 'may comprise a map as iconic to the new century as Europe was to the last one' and 'demographically and strategically be a hub of the twenty-first century world'. As an American analyst, he argues that this makes the Indian Ocean 'the essential place to contemplate the future of U.S. power'. Perhaps that is what President Obama was doing in early November 2010, as he flew from India to Indonesia and contemplated the vastness of the Indian Ocean beneath. But surely it is even more vital for India to see its eponymous ocean as the locus of its own strategic power calculations.

From an Indian point of view, though, the strategic importance of an ocean, at whose central point our subcontinent stands, is easy enough to grasp. The Indian Ocean is vital to us as the place through which most of our trade is conducted; keeping it safe from the depredations of pirates or the dominance of hostile foreign navies is indispensable for our national security. Our coastlines represent both points of engagement with the world and places of vulnerability to attack from abroad (as we saw most recently on 26/11). What should we be doing about it?

One way of dealing with the Indian Ocean is to see it through a security prism, and that, I am sure, our defence ministry and our navy, in particular, are already doing. The creation of an 'Indian Ocean Naval Symposium' that brought together over fifty countries to talk about the ocean is testimony to that. Another way, though, is to see the Indian Ocean's potential for constructive diplomatic action. I am a believer in doing this through a subregional organization that India did a great deal to start, and needs to do a lot more to sustain.

What international association brings together eighteen countries straddling three continents thousands of miles apart, united solely by their sharing of a common body of water? That's a quiz question likely to stump the most devoted aficionado of global politics. It's the Indian Ocean Rim Association for Regional Co-operation, blessed with the unwieldy acronym IOR-ARC, which bids fair to be the most extraordinary international grouping you've never heard of.

The association manages to unite Australia and Iran, Singapore and India, Madagascar and the UAE, and a dozen other states large and small—unlikely partners brought together by the fact that the Indian Ocean washes their shores. As India's minister of state for external affairs in 2009, I have attended their ministerial meeting in Sana'a, Yemen, and despite being used to my eyes glazing over at the alphabet soup of international organizations I've encountered during a three-decade UN career, I find myself excited by the potential of this one.

Regional associations have been created on a variety of premises: geographical, as with the African Union; geopolitical, as with the Organization of American States; economic and commercial, as with ASEAN or Mercosur; security driven, as with NATO. There are multi-continental ones too, like IBSA, which brings together India, Brazil and South Africa, or the better-known G20. And even Goldman Sachs can claim to have invented an intergovernmental body, since the 'BRIC' concept coined by that Wall Street firm was reified by a meeting of the heads of government of Brazil, Russia, India and China in Yekaterinburg in 2009, and has continued since, with South Africa joining the grouping in 2011. But it's fair to say there's nothing quite like the IOR-ARC in the annals of global diplomacy.

For one thing, there isn't another ocean on the planet that takes in Asia, Africa and Oceania (and could embrace Europe, too, since the French department of Reunion, in the Indian Ocean, gives Paris observer status in IOR-ARC, and the Quai d'Orsay is considering seeking full membership). For another, every one of Huntington's famously clashing civilizations finds a representative among the members, giving a common roof to the widest possible array of worldviews in their smallest imaginable combination (just eighteen countries). When the IOR-ARC meets, new windows are opened between countries separated by distance as well as politics. Malaysians talk with Mauritians, Arabs with Australians, South Africans with Sri Lankans, Iranians with Indonesians. The Indian Ocean serves as both a sea separating them and a bridge linking them together.

Regional associations have a wide variety of uses, and it's fair to say they have not all been successful. Many would argue we haven't fully exploited the potential of IBSA (India–Brazil–South Africa), or that BRIC, despite annual meetings of the leaders of Brazil, Russia, India and China, and the 2011 admission to it of South Africa, remains little more than a clever idea of an analyst at Goldman Sachs. So why try and make much of the IOR-ARC?

Well, I can't think of many other groupings in which Madagascar can exchange experiences in such a small forum with the UAE, and both with India. For another, the potential of the organization—as a forum to learn from each other, to share experiences and to pool resources on a variety of issues—is real. There are opportunities to learn from each other, to share experiences and to pool resources on such waterborne issues as blue-water fishing, maritime transport and piracy (in the Gulf of Aden and the waters off Somalia, as well as in the straits of Malacca). But the IOR-ARC doesn't have to confine itself to the water: it's the member countries that are members, not just their coastlines. So everything from the development of tourism in the eighteen countries to the transfer of science and technology is on the table. The poorer developing countries have new partners to offer educational scholarships to their young and training courses for their government officers. There's already talk of new projects in capacity building, agriculture and the promotion of cultural cooperation.

The IOR-ARC was, in many ways, India's brainchild. To let it languish is not just to write off another bureaucratic institution; it is to give up on our leadership of a region that, whether we like it or not, is indispensable to us. To engage with it and seek to revive it will take time, effort, energy and some resources—not more than twenty-first-century India can afford. The IOR-ARC could be the diplomatic arm of a two-pronged strategy to make Indian Ocean security and political, economic and cultural cooperation two sides of the same glittering coin.

This is why we should not write off its immense possibilities. India, its chair as of 2012 (for a two-year term), must pledge itself to energizing and reviving this semi-dormant organization. As vice-chair I persuaded Australia to agree to be next in line, thus giving two active democracies a combined four-year stretch leading the IOR-ARC.

We haven't made much of it so far. The IOR-ARC has been treading water, not having done enough to get beyond the declaratory phase that marks most new initiatives. The organization itself is lean to the point of emaciation, with just half a dozen staff in its Mauritius secretariat (including the gardener). I visited the rather forlorn-looking headquarters in Port Louis and was concerned at the staff's perception that the member states had not yet accorded adequate priority to the association.

It is clear that the IOR-ARC has not yet fulfilled its potential in the decade that it has been in existence. As often happens with brilliant ideas, the creative spark consumes itself in the act of creation, and the IOR-ARC has been neglected by its own creators. Indian policy-makers have remained focused on the immediate challenge of Pakistan and the headline-grabbing relationships with the United States and China rather than spend time on an area they see as complex, inchoate and anything but urgent. The IOR-ARC's formula of pursuing work in an academic group, a business forum and a working group on trade and investment has not yet brought either focus or drive to the parent body.

But such teething troubles are inevitable in any new group, and the seeds of future cooperation have already been sown. Making a success of an association that unites large countries and small ones, island states and continental ones, Islamic republics, monarchies and liberal democracies, and every race known to mankind, represents both a challenge and an opportunity. This very diversity of interests and capabilities can easily impede substantive cooperation, but it can also make such cooperation far more rewarding. In this diversity we in India see immense possibilities.

The brotherhood of man is a tired cliché; the neighbourhood of an ocean is a refreshing new idea. The world as a whole stands to benefit if eighteen littoral states can find common ground in the churning waters of a mighty ocean.

Chapter Six

Red, White, Blue and Saffron:
The United States and India

As presidential elections loom in the United States of 2012, perhaps the most striking aspect of them from an Indian point of view is that no one in New Delhi is unduly concerned about the outcome. There is now a widespread consensus in Indian policy-making circles that, whoever wins, India–US relations are more or less on the right track.

Democrats and Republicans in the White House have both been responsible for this development. President Obama's successful visit to India in 2010 and his historic speech to a joint session of Parliament capped the most significant recent milestone in India–US relations. This was his sixth encounter with Prime Minister Manmohan Singh in various forums since his assumption of office eighteen months previously, but his first in New Delhi, and it set the seal on the consolidation of a relationship that has changed dramatically over the last decade.

Throughout the Cold War, the world's oldest democracy and its largest were essentially estranged. America's initial indifference was best reflected in President Harry Truman's reaction when Chester Bowles asked to be named ambassador to India: 'I thought India was pretty jammed with poor people and cows round streets, witch doctors and people sitting on hot coals and bathing in the Ganges . . . but I did not realize anybody thought it was important.' If that was bad enough, India's political orientation was worse. The American preference for making anti-communist allies, however unsavoury, tied Washington to a series of increasingly Islamist dictatorships in Pakistan, while the non-aligned democracy drifted towards the secular Soviet embrace. Non-alignment was regarded with distaste in Washington; the views of Eisenhower's secretary of state, John Foster Dulles, cited in Chapter One, were simply blunt expressions of general sentiment. In a world divided between two uncompromising superpowers, India's temporizing seemed like appeasement at best, and providing aid and comfort to the enemy, at worst. Pakistan, on the other hand, became an essential element in the United States' containment of the Soviet Union and in its later opening to China. From India's point of view, the United States' indulgence of Pakistan turned into overt hostility when Washington sent the Sixth Fleet into the Bay of Bengal in support of Pakistani genocide in Bangladesh in 1971. Tempers cooled soon enough after that, but New Delhi was always regarded as tilting towards Moscow in its general inclination, hardly a recommendation for India in American eyes.

With the end of the Cold War and India's reorientation of its foreign policy, as well as its increasing integration into the global economy, a thaw set in, but India's explosion of a nuclear device in 1998 triggered a fresh round of US sanctions. Bill Clinton began to turn things around with a hugely successful India visit during his last year in office, in 2000. The Bush Administration took matters much further, with a defence agreement in 2005 and a landmark accord on civil nuclear cooperation in 2008 that remains the centrepiece of the transformed relationship.

The nuclear accord simultaneously accomplished two things. It admitted India into the global nuclear club despite our principled refusal to sign the Nuclear Non-proliferation Treaty. More important, it acknowledged that US exceptionalism had found a sibling. Thanks to the United States, which strong-armed the forty-five countries of the Nuclear Suppliers' Group into swallowing their concerns that special treatment for India could constitute a precedent for rogue nuclear aspirants such as Pakistan, North Korea and Iran, there is now an 'Indian exception'. Few things could have been more gratifying to a deeply proud nation that was tired of being constantly hyphenated by Washington with its smaller, dysfunctional neighbour Pakistan.

Under Obama, nothing quite so dramatic was possible: there were no spectacular breakthroughs conceived or executed, nor could many have been imagined. But Obama, who as a senator had displayed a photograph of Mahatma Gandhi in his office, carried a locket of the Hindu god Hanuman in his pocket and spoke often of his desire to build a 'close strategic partnership' with the world's largest democracy, knew how to strike all the right symbolic chords. (His familiarity with India precedes his presidency: when my friend Arun Kumar attended an Obama campaign meeting with a small group of South Asian supporters, he told them that he 'could cook a mean daal, but the naan, I will leave to someone else'. He introduced himself as a 'desi', pronouncing the 's' in just the right way. The person who taught him to make daal, his room-mate at Occidental College, Vinai Thummalapalli, is currently US ambassador to Belize.)

So on Obama's visit to India in November 2010, he hit all the right notes in his speech to Parliament. The references to Mahatma Gandhi, Swami Vivekananda, and even Dr Ambedkar, the quotes from Tagore, the Panchatantra and the Upanishads (though he wisely didn't attempt to pronounce the ancient Puranic dictum 'vasudhaiva kutumbakam', contenting himself with saying it in English, 'all the world is one family') and the game utterances of 'bahut dhanyavad' and 'Jai Hind' won over many a sceptical Indian heart. And the President's speech conveyed two substantive assurances: support for India's aspirations to a permanent seat on the UN Security Council and an unambiguous declaration that safe havens for terrorists in Pakistan were 'unacceptable'.

The latter was particularly welcome. The Obama Administration's understandable concerns in Afghanistan have made Pakistan loom much larger in the US consciousness than India. Obama understands that there is no successful outcome in Afghanistan possible without Pakistan, and his administration has therefore been attentive to Islamabad's priorities in ways that New Delhi finds occasionally irritating. This statement went a long way towards reassuring India that Washington is conscious of the fundamental danger to Indian security emanating from that side of the border and is committed to addressing it with its friends in Pakistan.

Over the last year, there has also been progress on other fronts—the small but significant steps that add up to strengthening the sinews of a relationship. Agreements on seemingly mundane subjects like agriculture, education, health and even space exploration and energy security testify to enhanced cooperation, and the two governments have also proclaimed 'initiatives' on clean energy and climate change as well as educational linkages between American and Indian universities.

The Obama visit consolidated all these gains, and the announcements in Mumbai of significant trade and investment deals confirmed that each nation is developing a more significant stake in the other than ever before. The United States is India's largest trading partner, if you take goods and services together. American exports to India have, in the last five years, grown faster than to any other country. The Confederation of Indian Industry (CII) estimates that services trade between the two countries is likely to grow, despite the recent global financial crisis and the US recession that sparked it, from the present $60 billion to over $150 billion in the next six years.

We will return to these aspects in greater detail, but it is useful to note not just the geopolitical background against which much of the relationship has evolved, but the policy advocacy in Washington that has underpinned it. India has come a long way, in American eyes, from the days when I went there as a graduate student in 1975. I recall watching a three-hour NBC television special that year on 'America and the World': after long sections on the United States and the Soviet Union, the United States and Europe, and so on, a series of shorter sections on less important parts of the world followed. I kept waiting for 'the United States and India': it never came. India, in those days, did not even figure on the US radar screen, let alone its television screens. Today, it's a different story: high-level visits proliferate in each direction, stories from and about India can be found everywhere on the US media and, as the well-heeled, 3-million-strong Indian-American community flexes its political muscles, few US political candidates can afford to be indifferent, let alone hostile, to relations with India.

The Indian diaspora in the United States, some 3 million strong and thriving, is a huge factor in the relationship. The first Indian to set foot in the country was a sailor in the 1770s, whose presence aroused much curiosity, and in the 1890s shiploads of Sikhs settled on the Pacific coast and established thriving farming communities in California, but racist immigration restrictions (prompted by such events as anti-Indian riots in the state of Washington in 1907) kept Indian migration low till the 1960s. A thin trickle of students made their way to the United States after the 1920s, but most returned to India; indeed, as late as 1935, signs on the doors of certain California establishments declared, 'No Jobs for Japs or Hindus'. It was only with the opening of the sluice gates under the liberal Immigration Act of 1965 that a larger number of Indians began to arrive, mainly as students, an increasing proportion of whom stayed on, bringing high levels of academic attainment and valuable scientific and engineering skills to their new country. By the early 1970s the still-small Indian minority had the highest per capita income of any ethnic group in the United States, and even today the median family income of Indian-Americans exceeds that of white Americans. Working-class Indians found their way into the United States for the first time from the end of the 1970s, toiling on construction sites and as farm labour, taking over newspaper kiosks, operating rundown motels, cooking and serving in Indian restaurants, and driving taxicabs. Many arrived (or stayed on) illegally, but as the numbers grew, a pair of 'amnesties' in the 1990s gave them the legal status they needed to bring their families over, and today this 'third wave' of Indian immigrants accounts for perhaps half the desi diaspora in the United States.

Though there are Indian-American doctors and scientists of considerable renown (including three Nobel Prize–winners born and brought up in India), the newer Indian immigrants are demonstrating an entrepreneurial spirit that has created a wider impact on the community's fortunes. The spirit of enterprise has also affected the professional classes, especially the Indian engineers who brought from India a solid grounding in their field and excelled in the freedom afforded to them in the United States. An Indian invented the Pentium chip, another created Hotmail, a third started Sun Microsystems, and Indians have been involved in some 40 per cent of the start-ups in Silicon Valley. Over time, the Indianness of engineers and software developers began to be taken as synonymous with mathematical and scientific excellence. Today, Americans speak of the IITs—the elite engineering schools from which many of these migrants came—with the same reverence they used to accord to MIT. The image of India has changed from that of a backward developing country to a sophisticated land that produces engineers and computer experts.

The prosperity this engendered has also translated into political activism. Indian-Americans are among the most prominent fund-raisers in both major parties, and their active involvement in politics is now translating into elective office at various levels, including two state Governors, Bobby Jindal of Louisiana and Nikki Haley of South Carolina.

But neither has chosen to identify much with their Indian origins or Indian causes; indeed, their acceptability to their right-wing political base has hinged on de-emphasizing their foreign origins. Indian-Americans have found greater success in influencing mainstream non-immigrant American politicians by sensitizing them to issues of importance to the Indian diaspora. The rising financial clout of the community and its collective willingness to flex its political muscles has seen many non-Indian candidates for political office running targeted campaigns aimed at Indian-American voters and donors. The pole positions held by Indians in the boardrooms of corporate America are also a tangible source of influence at high levels of the country's decision-making processes. The result of all this is apparent in the size and strength of the India Caucus on Capitol Hill; the political desiderata for many American Congressmen now includes the need to demonstrate interest in Indian-American issues and goodwill towards India.

So India is now undoubtedly an important country to US policy-makers; but what, from a US point of view, are the main 'drivers' of the India–US relationship? One can quickly dismiss the typical tendency of some American politicians to see geopolitical relationships in crude transactional terms. Some US senators have had a pronounced inclination to demand quid pro quos in relation to any act of seeming US generosity—if Washington supported New Delhi's claims to a permanent seat on the UN Security Council, would India support the US policy on sanctions against Iran? Such questions are not easily answered at all, let alone in a simple affirmative, since a country like India would always reserve the right to take its own decision on such issues, on a case-by-case basis. If India–US relations had to be judged by such old-fashioned yardsticks as counting the number of UN votes on which New Delhi agreed with Washington, the partnership would never get off the ground. Blatant reciprocity—expecting that, as a beneficiary of US goodwill, India would, for instance, favour US aircraft in its defence procurement (a subject to which we will return)—is simply untenable in evaluating relations between two large, complex and proud nations.

A better place to gauge the new American approach to India would be the views of two members of the Washington policy community who have been associated with an increasingly influential school of thought that recognizes the strategic utility of the two nations' shared political values and advocates a broadly pro-Indian policy for the United States in the first two decades of the twenty-first century. These two prominent American strategic analysts, both at the Carnegie Endowment for International Peace, argue for two distinct approaches to relations with India. One, George Perkovich, puts his views most clearly in an essay published in the *Washington Quarterly* in 2003. Perkovich, recognizing both New Delhi's modest military and strategic capacity and its traditional disinclination to seem to be acting on anyone else's behest, acknowledged that India does not 'have the interest or power to augment US interests in many areas'. Yet India was 'too big and too important in the overall global community to measure in terms of its alignment with any particular US interest at any given time'. In other words, support for India promoted US strategic goals not by direct support of American aims but rather by a general congruence of approaches on issues of global order. As Perkovich put it, 'It matters to the entire world whether India is at war or peace with its neighbors, is producing increasing prosperity or poverty for its citizens, stemming or incubating the spread of infectious diseases, or mimicking or leapfrogging climate-warming technologies. Democratically managing a society as big, populous, diverse, and culturally dynamic as India is a world historical challenge. If India can democratically lift all of its citizens to a decent quality of life without trampling on basic liberties and harming its neighbors, the Indian people will have accomplished perhaps the greatest success in human history.'

This argument seems to assume more American altruism than many realist Indian analysts find plausible. In such an analysis, the United States would essentially leave India alone to pursue its own interests, so long as these upheld a liberal world order; when, in Perkovich's view, they did not, as (in his view) with the US–India civilian nuclear agreement, Washington should oppose India (as Perkovich himself did in advocating rejection of the deal). In such a reading of Washington's interests, any attempt to cajole India into a 'strategic partnership' would of course clash with India's own view of its strategic autonomy and fierce independence on the international stage, but it would also be unnecessary. What would be best, therefore, would be a loose partnership on global issues, rather than anything resembling an alliance, with the only litmus test on each issue being the contribution that India would make to the kind of world order the United States sought to build.

An alternative view that embraces many of the same premises but goes beyond them was that of the Indian-American scholar Ashley Tellis, also at the Carnegie Endowment, who advocated in Washington that the United States should support India in a 'calculated contribution to creating, in Condoleezza Rice's famous phrase, a "balance of power that favours freedom"'. As Tellis argued, 'assisting India to develop its national capabilities is intended not merely to uplift its humanity' but rather 'to advance the vital US interest in preserving a stable geopolitical balance in Asia and globally'. He goes on:

> To the degree that the American partnership with India aids New Delhi in growing more rapidly, it contributes—along with Japanese, Australian, and Southeast Asian power—towards creating those objective structural constraints that discourage China from abusing its own growing capabilities, even as Washington preserves good relations with Beijing and encourages all its Asian partners to do the same. American strategic generosity towards India, thus, remains an investment in its own geopolitical well being.

In this view, the United States should support policies to strengthen India—including the nuclear deal—even if India remained wilfully independent on certain issues, because it would be good for the United States to do so. To Tellis, 'the real issue boiled down to how Washington could assist the growth of Indian power so as to secure its larger global aims at lowest cost to itself'.

Neither scholar succumbs to the crude 'what can India do for us?' reasoning of many American politicians; Tellis, in effect, suggests that the United States has a stake in India's success even when no direct benefits to Washington accrue from it—since a successful India is an asset for the United States' own geopolitical vision of the future world order and 'itself becomes New Delhi's strategic bequest to Washington'. Tellis's only caveat is that his argument for backing Indian success applies 'so long as it is not used to undermine America's vital interests'. In turn, Tellis 'expects that New Delhi would see cooperation with Washington as being fundamentally in its own interest—and, by extension, act in ways that confirm this expectation whenever possible. Such responses would materialise not so much out of gratitude to the United States but because aiding the preservation of the American-led global order, in contrast to, say, acquiescing to the rise of a Chinese alternative, is necessarily consistent with India's own vital national interests.'

Tellis served as an adviser to the Bush Administration and to its ambassador in New Delhi, Robert Blackwill, and it is safe to accept that his view both informed and reflected the administration's thinking on relations with India. It helped, of course, that Indian economic reforms since 1991 had transformed the land of the tortoise-like 'Hindu rate of growth' into a rising economic power by the time Bush was elected, and a decade of post–Cold War geopolitics had ended all traces of the sympathy in New Delhi for the Soviet Union that the Republicans used to despise. India's democracy was itself a source of deep fascination for President Bush, as was the country's pluralist way of dealing with its own diversity (he was known to have remarked with admiration upon the fact that in 2004 India's elections were won by a woman of Italian Catholic background who made way for a Sikh to be sworn in as prime minister by a Muslim President). Bush could see no reason why the two giant democracies could not make common cause in pursuing compatible global interests, and he had little patience for the non-proliferation orthodoxies that had ostracized India after the 1998 nuclear tests. The Indian exception was born.

In Tellis's telling, Washington under Bush perceived a 'strong compatibility in values' which was 'reinforced by the growing recognition that India's interests increasingly converged with those of the United States'. Abstract considerations of a global balance of power favouring 'freedom' were supplemented by far more hard-headed considerations of both countries' targeting by the forces of Islamist terrorism, especially after 9/11. Tellis puts it well when he suggests that 'American and Indian interests were similar even if they were not always perfectly congruent'. As an Indian-American, he probably had a higher tolerance for the areas of policy difference between the two states than many of his Washington colleagues, but his President, too, was quite willing to cut India some slack in this area. And there were, with the end of the Cold War, the new Indian relationship with Israel and the pragmatic recalibration of relations with Southeast Asia embodied in the 'Look East' policy, no longer any major differences on issues that the United States would have seen as affecting its own vital interests. In President Bush's view, therefore, Tellis avers, 'having India in the stable of America's friends and allies was preferable to being without it'.

India undoubtedly preferred being considered a friend rather than an ally—a distinction that matters in New Delhi since alliance politics implies a logic of commitment that few Indian policy-makers would find acceptable. India's preference to support or oppose American policies depending on India's own assessment of the issues involved is one that successive administrations in Washington have found difficult to swallow, but Bush seems to have done so, provided India was supportive on the transcendent issue of Islamist terrorism, which it was.

Ironically a key issue that cemented Washington's new thinking about India in the Bush years was one in which the two countries did not in fact necessarily share the same perception. The Bush Administration saw India and the United States as kindred nations threatened by the inexorable rise of Chinese power, and assumed a shared interest in containing Beijing, a perception of which India did not fully partake. Washington was happy enough to promote China's economic integration into the global order but less content to see it grow too large for its geopolitical breeches; a democratic state in Asia of comparable size, military strength and economic capacity would, many American policy-makers thought, help place some checks on Chinese assertiveness on the regional and world stage. India, while conscious of China's potential to disrupt the geopolitical status quo, felt its relations with China should follow a strictly bilateral logic, independent of any American desire for an Asian counterweight to China. India's chronic resistance to being seen to be doing anyone else's bidding, or to any perception of encroachments on its strategic autonomy, made it, in any case, an implausible participant in any third country's strategic logic, including America's. This has become steadily apparent to Washington over the years, and may have helped diminish the ardour with which India is courted, though not the basic underpinnings of the relationship.

At the same time, this thinking helped explain the Bush Administration's enthusiasm for arranging an 'Indian exemption' on the nuclear deal, as well as its willingness to strengthen defence cooperation, agree to high-technology transfers and even to promote partnership in space exploration. The Obama Administration, in turn, built on these foundations, adding to it the largely symbolic declaration of support for India's efforts to obtain a permanent seat on the UN Security Council, as well as welcoming and even promoting India's membership in assorted non-proliferation arrangements.

This kind of relationship, accepted in these terms across influential policy-making circles in both Washington and New Delhi, falls well short of a traditional alliance, something to which India is generally presumed to be allergic. But it justifies strong American support for India as a player on the global stage, as a sound investment for Washington that advances both countries' strategic aims.

This was broadly the approach of the Bush Administration, given its profound misgivings about the rise of Chinese power. A somewhat more benevolent view of China on the part of the Obama Administration might have diminished the intensity with which such an approach was advocated in Washington, leading some Indian analysts to write of a state of 'drift' in the relationship. But it was amply compensated for by the President's own considerable regard for Indian Prime Minister Manmohan Singh, whom he even publicly described as the first of the three world leaders he most admired and had good relations with. In sum, each country could afford to take a benevolent view of the pursuit by the other of its own interests, secure in the belief that that pursuit would not fundamentally be incompatible with its own core national objectives on the world stage.

———

But in fact there is more to the India–US relationship than that. As far back as 2005, Prime Minister Manmohan Singh had declared: 'I believe we are at a juncture where we can embark on a partnership that can draw both on principle as well as pragmatism.' That practical benefits are available to both sides in the relationship is readily apparent: as the Canadian diplomat David Malone observed, 'US demand for information technology and other services has been extremely helpful to India, and India's capacity to absorb American exports has greatly strengthened American commerce (at a time when much militates against continued unfettered global US economic dominance).' The question is how to build on those basic trade-offs in order to accomplish a more substantial partnership. The two nations are busily working on this.

So President Obama's 2010 visit, with which we began this chapter, resulted in significant new agreements across a wide range of subjects, from civil nuclear cooperation to food security issues. The two governments have followed up by developing a collection of consultative mechanisms to improve and strengthen the trade and investment relationship. To take an illustrative list, there are meetings of the US–India Economic and Financial Partnership at finance minister level, the US Trade Representatives' Trade Policy Forum, and the Department of Commerce's Commercial Dialogue; perhaps most important to India, a High Technology Cooperation Group has been working to reduce barriers to trade in sensitive cutting-edge high technology.

But governments do not determine every aspect of an economic relationship. US–India business ties have emerged as particularly crucial drivers of the relationship; despite the bureaucratic and domestic political impediments to faster growth, delays in upgrading India's shoddy infrastructure and the unavoidable transaction costs of doing business in India (including the prevalence of corruption), American firms rightly see the country's long-term potential as one worth being invested in. According to the McKinsey Global Institute, 80 per cent of the Indian infrastructure of 2030 has yet to be created, and US businesses will have the opportunity to provide the goods and services needed to build or upgrade India's railways, airports, power plants and IT infrastructure (laying fibre optic cables, for instance). India projects a need to invest some $143 billion in health care, $392 billion in transportation infrastructure and $1.25 trillion in energy production by 2030 to support its rapidly expanding population; many of these contracts could come America's way.

India's demographic advantages are particularly attractive: with 65 per cent of its population under thirty-five, India should have a dynamic, productive and youthful workforce when the rest of the world, including

China, is ageing. This would give India, according to one study, 25 per cent of the world's working population by 2025 (provided India does enough to educate and train its young people to take advantage of this demographic opportunity). India is also a market of 1.2 billion actual and potential consumers, with McKinsey estimating that its middle class could number 525 million by 2025 (though not all would have the purchasing power of the American middle class). Given that the United States is India's principal export market for its services (and has only just been overtaken by China as a trading partner in goods), the scope for collaboration is huge.

The figures are impressive, and reveal a pattern of increasing economic interdependence. Between 2002 and 2009, US goods exports to India quadrupled, growing from $4.1 billion in 2002 to over $16.4 billion in 2009, while US services exports to India more than tripled, increasing from $3.2 billion in 2002 to over $9.9 billion in 2009. More striking than absolute numbers is the fact that US exports to India grew faster than exports to almost all other countries in the world. In 2010, US exports of goods to India shot up 17 per cent and US goods imports from India went up 40 per cent, making India, at $48.8 billion in goods trade, the United States' twelfth largest goods trading partner. Preliminary figures for 2011 confirmed the positive trend. Nor is the traffic all one-way. The overall trade relationship is a balanced one, and there are some departures from the norm: while overall FDI into India declined over 2009–11, Indian companies continued to invest in the United States, growing at a compound annual growth rate of 35 per cent between 2004 and 2009. In addition to India's role in providing services to US businesses and consumers, from medical transcriptions to call centres, India has also become a significant source of tourist revenue for the United States, with some 650,000 Indian visitors in 2010, making India the tenth largest source of tourism to America.

India's biggest asset in its economic relationship with America lies in its national penchant for innovation. Already, multinational giants like GE and Philips are employing more researchers in India than in the United States or Europe, and Indians are doing cutting-edge work designing aircraft parts for Boeing and doing biotech research for US and Indian pharmaceutical companies. The Indian IT revolution, its huge base of trained scientific manpower, entrepreneurial skill honed in adversity, and Indians' special talent, amid scarcity, for improvising on a shoestring have helped create new, cheaper and more imaginative versions of products Americans first devised, from cardiograms to automobiles. A Google search for 'frugal innovation' returns mainly Indian results; the University of Toronto has established an India Innovation Centre to study the phenomenon; and 'Indovation' is becoming the new buzzword. As the high costs of manufacturing make the United States more and more a knowledge economy, India seems a natural partner, one that can complement America's economy and help meet its needs.

Where are things not quite so amicable? One sometimes fraught area has been cooperation on security issues of vital importance to India. The United States was understood to have been initially helpful in the aftermath of the 26/11 terrorist attacks in Mumbai, both with intelligence sharing and in placing pressure on the Pakistani military establishment to back off from the militants it had sponsored. But subsequent revelations that a US citizen of Pakistani descent, Daud Gilani, calling himself David Coleman Headley, had visited India several times to reconnoitre the terrain for the attacks, and that he may have been a US double agent, led to a great deal of recriminations in the Indian strategic community. Indian commentators alleged that, in effect, the United States had allowed the 26/11 attacks to happen, rather than revealing information in their possession to India, merely in order to protect Headley's cover. Subsequent disagreements over the level of access to Headley required by Indian investigators of 26/11 became public in India, further poisoning the atmosphere and adding to the mistrust that often finds receptive ground in certain Indian circles.

Indians are chronically suspicious that US dependence on Pakistan over the years—as a staging base for attacks on Soviet troops in Afghanistan earlier, now as an ally and logistical partner of US troops in Afghanistan—always vitiates its broader strategic interests in India. Differences have also emerged between Washington and New Delhi in recent years over a number of issues: the two nations' different reactions to the Arab Spring, in particular the revolts in Libya and Syria; incompatible views about the implementation of one key follow-up provision to the nuclear deal, the Nuclear Liability Law, where American companies are seeking exemptions from liability in the event of accidents, which New Delhi judges politically impossible to push through the Indian Parliament (where memories of the Bhopal disaster caused by an American multinational have not faded); and significant disagreements about sanctions on Iran for its nuclear programme, one which India is also concerned about but disinclined to back, given its own dependence on Iranian oil supplies. While these are issues that have played out over months, even years, one specific issue that caused some heartburn between the two countries related to India's rejection of a US bid to sell the country a large number of combat aircraft.

American officials have been particularly alive to the opportunities afforded by the much-needed (and long-delayed) modernization of India's ageing military and weapons systems, with estimates of some $35 billion of expenditure likely to be incurred in the next decade. US Assistant Secretary of State Robert Blake told an Indian audience in 2011 that 'the [Indian] Cabinet Committee on Security's approval of the purchase of C-17s from the U.S. is just a sample of the sales that we expect will occur over the next several years'.

In this context, India's decision in 2011 not to purchase American planes for its $10-billion-plus fighter aircraft deal—the largest single defence tender in the country's history—stirred considerable debate in strategic circles in both countries. The two US contenders, Boeing's F/A-18 Superhornet and Lockheed's F-16 Superviper, were deemed by the Indian Ministry of Defence not to fulfil the technical requirements New Delhi was looking for in a medium multirole combat aircraft (MMRCA). With the Russian MiG-30 and the Swedish Gripen also eliminated at the preliminary stage, two European planes, the Eurofighter Typhoon and the French Rafale, were the only aircraft still in the fray for an expected order of 126 planes (the Rafale finally got the nod, though at this writing that decision had been placed in suspense).

The Indian decision was immediately denounced by pro-American commentators as a setback to bilateral relations. India had never previously purchased an American fighter plane, and Washington had hoped its doing so would signal India's determination to cement an emerging strategic partnership with a hefty cheque. US officials from

President Obama on down had lobbied for the deal, which would have pumped money and jobs into the ailing US economy. The 'deeply disappointed' American ambassador in India, Tim Roemer, promptly announced his resignation from his post in New Delhi. In a typical comment, Ashley Tellis observed trenchantly that India had chosen 'to invest in a plane, not a relationship'. The implication was that India should have sold its technical requirements short out of a desire to reward the US politically for its goodwill.

The notion that a major arms purchase should be based on broader strategic considerations—the importance of the United States in India's emerging *weltpolitik*—rather than on the merits of the aircraft itself, has struck Indian officials as unfair. Sources in New Delhi are quick to deny that the decision reflects any political bias on the part of India's taciturn but left-leaning defence minister, A.K. Antony. Instead the choice, they aver, is a purely professional one, made by the Indian Air Force, and only ratified by the ministry. The two European fighters are generally seen as aerodynamically superior, having outperformed both American aircraft in tests under the adverse climatic conditions in which they might have to be used, particularly in the high altitudes and low temperatures of northern Kashmir. Experts suggest the American planes are technologically ten years behind the European ones, and it doesn't help that Pakistan, India's likely adversary were the aircraft ever to be pressed into combat, has long been a regular client of the US warplane industry.

In addition, Indian decision-makers could not help but be aware that the United States has not, over the years, proved to be a reliable supplier of military hardware to India or other countries. It has frequently cut off contracted supplies, imposed sanctions on friends and foes alike (including India), and reneged on the delivery of military goods and spare parts, as well as been notoriously unwilling to transfer its military technologies. The current Indian fleet of mainly Russian and French planes has suffered from no such problems, and the existing ground support and maintenance infrastructure, geared to service them, would have needed major changes to handle the US aircraft. (It is likely that the eventual winner of the bid will be required to enter into a joint production arrangement with India, which the US companies would not have done.)

As if all this was not enough to drive the choice away from Boeing and Lockheed, the final clincher might well have been the Government of India's desire to avoid any further procurement controversy at a time when allegations of corruption have beset it from all sides. A decision made unarguably on technical grounds, many felt, would be easier to defend than one skewed in a particular direction on political grounds. Defence Minister A.K. Antony even postponed a US–India strategic dialogue (scheduled originally for mid-April 2011) for which Secretaries Hillary Clinton and Robert Gates were planning to travel to New Delhi, in order not to come under pressure from his American visitors to weigh political factors in making his technical decision.

Against this are the unarguable advantages of pleasing a major new ally for whom an Indian decision would have meant a great deal, and developing a pattern of mutual cooperation in supply, training and operations which has yet to evolve between the two militaries. At a time when US nuclear reactor purchases—made possible by the historic deal negotiated by the Bush Administration and sold by Washington to the forty-eight other members of the Nuclear Suppliers' Group—have been held up by US insistence on exemptions from supplier liability in the event of an accident, the rejection of US aircraft is seen by some as New Delhi gratuitously spurning an opportunity to demonstrate that friendship with India is in Americans' interest too.

Is India being its old prickly non-aligned self again? Is appeasement of India's notoriously anti-American politicians more important to a beleaguered Indian government than winning Washington over? Is India's traditional obsession with preserving its own strategic autonomy always going to limit its usefulness as a partner to the United States?

The questions are unfair. Surely India–US relations are greater than any single arms purchase. Why should the financial value of one deal be the barometer of a strategic partnership? It is simply narrow-minded to reduce American policy towards India to the bottom lines of US defence salesmen.

Nor is there any military estrangement between the two countries. Even if this deal didn't work out for the United States, it is still a leading arms supplier to India, having won bids to provide ships, reconnaissance aircraft and advanced transport planes. The Indian Army, Navy and Air

Force still conduct more exercises with US defence forces than with those of any other power. The two countries' worldviews on the big issues confronting the planet are not incompatible.

In any case, the strategic traffic is not merely one-way. Washington too has a national interest in Indian strategic autonomy, which would be buttressed by a wider range of external partnerships, including with the European states that will be the beneficiaries of the aircraft tender. Though India is rightly allergic to being seen as a US-supported counterweight to a rising China, in practice it is avidly courted by Southeast Asian countries anxious to balance Beijing, a development which suits Washington's interests. President Obama's 2010 visit cemented a perception that the two countries shared an increasingly convergent worldview, common democratic values and a thriving trade. None of this will cease to be relevant if India buys a European fighter plane.

In fact the potential for India–US collaboration in a variety of areas— military and non-military—would probably be enhanced by this decision. Turning the United States down this time actually frees the hands of the Indian government to pursue other aspects of the partnership, immune from the charge that it is too responsive to US pressures. So New Delhi hasn't foreclosed its options; it has in fact enlarged them.

The MMRCA deal was, however, only one of several issues that arose between the two states that created the impression of a downturn in India–US relations after the heady days of the Bush Administration, when Prime Minister Manmohan Singh had even publicly declared to the American leader, 'Mr President, the people of India love you.' India's positions on the MMRCA order and its rejection of the nuclear liability legislation advocated by Washington remain what Americans like to call the 'poster children' for the argument that the relationship with India is not yielding the rewards its advocates had predicted, or at least implied. But those who make this point in Washington fail to see that neither is specifically anti-US in conception—both involve India taking positions based on its own understanding of its own national and security interests within a specific domestic political context, exactly what democracies tend to do. The same is true of the more general disappointments that are being voiced in Washington, notably over India's timidity in pursuing economic reforms that would open its market further to US firms—something that affects all potential foreign investors and not just Americans. (And yet it is US companies, more than others, that could conclude that the Indian market is less attractive than they had imagined, since Americans are quickest to complain that the lure of the potential of the Indian market needs to be matched by its performance.)

Meanwhile, the reality of extensive defence cooperation is masked by the rejection of one American combat aircraft. In fact India relies significantly on American platforms for its long-range maritime patrol aircraft, very heavy lift transport aircraft, advanced special operations tactical transport aircraft and heavy attack helicopter requirements— all implying a degree of Indian dependence on American defence technology, and American willingness to supply it, that would both have been inconceivable just two decades ago. And India's attitude to the American troop presence in its own neighbourhood—which has gone from outright rejection during the Cold War to publicly welcoming American troops in Afghanistan as a source of security and stability and seeking their prolongation—is proof of an astonishing metamorphosis in Indian perceptions of America.

At the same time, if American analysts can point to the aircraft deal and the nuclear liability legislation as evidence of India not trying hard enough, there is just as much cause for disappointment on the other side of the equation. Many Indians had expected more from the new strategic partnership with the United States than has been forthcoming. Major irritants from an Indian point of view include America's excessive generosity to the Pakistani military—some $11 billion since 2001, ostensibly for security against terrorism but much of it spent on weapons aimed at India—its continuing sale of conventional arms to Pakistan, US inattention to Indian interests in Afghanistan, the Obama Administration's assiduous cultivation of China and the continuing reluctance in Washington to transfer cutting-edge defence technology to India. On China, Indians saw a clear contrast from the start with the Bush view of Beijing as a power to be contained; on Obama's inaugural visit to Asia as President in November 2009, he spent four days in China and left after signing a joint statement that declared Beijing to be the key to 'peace, stability, and development in South Asia', a distinction that surely ought to have been accorded to India. The visit was accompanied by some suggestions that this was a far more important relationship to Washington than the one with India, and even loose talk of a 'G2' condominium between the United States and China to manage the world. India was kept waiting another year for a visit.

There were, of course, various reasons for a change in the priority that had been accorded to India under Bush, apart from Obama's diagnosis of China's importance to American interests. The huge pressures of America's domestic financial problems were always bound to loom larger than foreign policy concerns to the beleaguered Obama Administration, while the economic choices underpinning enthusiasm for India (support for free trade and the advantages to the American consumer of outsourcing and offshoring to India, for instance) were diluted by a more protectionist American approach focused principally on generating jobs in the United States. The Democrats are also more reflexively anti-nuclear and less likely to share Bush's enthusiasm for the India–US civil nuclear deal; they are also more evangelical on climate change issues than the Republicans, making them less predisposed towards India's position. On Afghanistan, too, both the logistical indispensability of Pakistan for the resupply of NATO forces and the domestic compulsions to bring the troops home were always going to weigh more heavily in US policy-makers' minds than India's interests.

Within US policy-making circles, two constituencies have been less than helpful in building India–US ties—the so-called non-proliferation ayatollahs, whose attitude towards India is predicated entirely upon hostility to its nuclear programme, and the 'hyphenators', who view India entirely through the lens of US relations with Pakistan and 'hyphenate' the two subcontinental neighbours, subordinating US interests in New Delhi to the logic of its strategic focus on Pakistan. Pakistan had been a vital Cold War ally, a member of both CENTO and SEATO, the take-off point for Gary Powers' famous and ill-fated U-2 spy flight over the USSR in 1962 and for Henry Kissinger on his epoch-changing clandestine opening to China in 1971. Years of Cold War policies have given Washington a 'Pakistan-centric' bureaucracy, at the State Department, the Pentagon and the CIA, who have long links to their counterparts in Islamabad and argue that closeness to India undermines traditional US objectives in the region. Their arguments—in a nation which is still run largely by institutions and policies set up in the Cold War era—have been buttressed by the US dilemmas in Afghanistan and the conviction that the road to peace in Kabul lies through New Delhi, and in particular to forcing Indian concessions to Pakistan on Kashmir. The result has been some active bureaucratic resistance in Washington to the attempts to change US policy in a more India-friendly direction.

Of course it is true that the impact of such resistance can be exaggerated in Indian minds. In any case the tendency in India to overreact to every development, real or imagined, in the US–Pakistan relationship reflects an anxiety that many in Washington see as paranoia and does the country no favours. Instead there ought to be a recognition in New Delhi that US interests in India are driven by a logic of their own, independent of Pakistan, just as we would wish the United States to understand that our relations with China have little or nothing to do with our relations with the United States. Indians have perhaps been too sensitive to the perception that the Obama Administration offers India symbolic gestures like the first state dinner of his administration for Prime Minister Manmohan Singh, while reserving substance for China and aid for Pakistan. Some Indian commentators scoffed at what they saw as empty symbolism: 'We get the state dinners, while Pakistan gets $11 billion worth of weapons.' Though events like the first US–India strategic dialogue (started years after a similar dialogue was initiated with China) were initiated, critics felt they offered sound bites, not solid actions. The United States, in this reading, could have done better had it seized the opportunity afforded in 2009 by the end of Prime Minister Manmohan Singh's dependence for parliamentary survival on the support of communist parties to offer something major to New Delhi. That is hardly fair, since both countries have been increasingly looking inward, and opportunities have been missed by both sides.

Still, things have moved a very long way from the estrangement of the Cold War years. Today, the basic forward thrust of the relationship is not in dispute, and momentum is strongly supported by the influential Indian-American community in the United States. Americans should not expect as much from India as they would from a close ally like Israel, but they are no longer the recipients of non-aligned diatribes from India, and New Delhi has voted with the United States more often than had once seemed likely on key issues before the UN Security Council, notably backing a US resolution on Syria in early 2012 rather than joining Russia and China in their opposition. Even when they disagree, as they did on Libya and Iran, there is much more mutual understanding than before, and a respect for Indian ways of thinking on world issues that did not previously exist in Washington. On Myanmar, for instance, the United States, a staunch critic of India's appeasement of its generals (so much so that Obama even mentioned India's unsatisfactory Myanmar policy in his otherwise laudatory speech to the Indian Parliament), has gradually veered around to the Indian point of view favouring engagement with Naypyidaw. The two countries consult each other on a wide range of subjects and at a significantly high level, in ways that simply were inconceivable a couple of decades ago. And when things go wrong for one country, the other one tends not to fish in troubled waters, as New Delhi's refusal to be drawn into the recent US–Pakistan tensions testifies.

This is not to suggest that the relationship is perfect, or could not be improved. Many Indians feel that the United States could be doing more to give its friends in New Delhi ammunition in their efforts to resist the reflexive suspicion of 'imperialist' Washington in many influential circles in India. Many in Washington despair at what they see as India's reluctance to oblige the United States tangibly on issues that matter to it. One can also point to India's own seeming reluctance to take domestic decisions (from economic reform to market access issues to military realignments) that would make it a more worthwhile partner for the United States. The sympathetic Ashley Tellis is probably fair in saying that India's positive gestures towards the United States

are often hesitant, precarious, incomplete, and at constant risk of backsliding—dangers that are exacerbated by the currently troubled state of Indian domestic politics, the discomfort with the United States still persisting among elements of the Indian political class, the native Indian conservatism with regard to doing anything to 'shape' the world, and the still significant limitations in analytic, bureaucratic, and decisional capacity affecting the Indian state.

Tellis concludes that 'as India's capacity and confidence grows, New Delhi's ability to more effectively partner with the United States will only increase further'.

For India to continue to be regarded as an important friend in the United States, however, it is not enough to rely on an American interest in helping India to displace sufficient weight in the world as to balance, or help constrain, less friendly powers. The two countries will have to develop the habits of substantive cooperation that make each turn naturally to the other on issues engaging both. Indian public opinion is generally more favourably disposed to the United States than influential political leaders are, and this is particularly true of the younger generation, which has grown up without the anti-imperialist rhetoric of earlier years and sees much to admire in America's free-enterprise culture. The shared values of democracy, the two countries' use of a common language (with Indian English becoming increasingly Americanized) and congruent strategic goals should strengthen these ties. India's increasing economic opening will help, as will policies that provide more incentive to US businesses to invest in, and trade with, a market whose middle class is estimated by McKinsey as likely to reach 525 million by 2025. The social links between Indians and Americans have also been deepening over the years, especially with the integration of the thriving Indian diaspora into the American mainstream, and the corresponding increase in American interest in the land of their forebears. (That diaspora is particularly prosperous—the median income of an Indian-American family is almost 79 per cent higher than the national median—and therefore disproportionately influential.) Economic engagement in the era of globalization has reinforced these bonds, as more and more categories of people in both societies interact with and learn from each other.

The two countries' affinities also transcend their domestic politics. In New Delhi, Congress party rule has witnessed a continuation and strengthening of openings doggedly pursued by the BJP-led government (notably in the extensive dialogues conducted between then foreign minister Jaswant Singh and the US deputy secretary of state Strobe Talbott, who chronicled the talks in affectionate detail). In Washington, Clinton, Bush and Obama were all broadly on the same page; gone are the days when only Democrats were thought to be interested in improving ties with India. The right-of-centre American commentator Mary Kissel has observed tartly that India's still-socialist Congress party, in power again since 2004, has a 'kindred spirit' in Obama: 'a left-leaning big spender who thought that America should take a back seat in foreign affairs and stop dictating terms to its friends, both new and old'. Polemics aside, though, if Democrats see that kind of affinity with India, today's Republicans, unlike their Nixonian predecessors, have even more strategic assumptions in common with India, whether run by the Congress party or its opponents. The increasingly significant informal relationships between power brokers in the United States and business leaders in India are another manifestation of this trend. Indian business leaders often attend the exclusive Bohemian Grove retreats, for instance, and the Aspen Institute has done an effective job of promoting strategic dialogue between the countries' elites. The US India CEO Forum, set up by the two countries' heads of government, is an example of harnessing the power of such relationships.

These factors underlie the comfort—some might say complacency—with which Indians are regarding relations with the United States in the lead-up to the 2012 presidential elections. And yet there remain some potential flies in the proverbial ointment. One is undoubtedly the notoriously short-term American attention span to foreign affairs issues that do not appear to impinge directly on the country's immediate security or welfare. A more inwardly focused domestic orientation, a more benign relationship with China and a post-Afghan-withdrawal indifference to South Asia could all lead Americans to forget the enthusiasm for India of the Bush years. President John F. Kennedy once memorably said, 'The cost of freedom is always high, but Americans have always paid it.' The problem for many Americans is that in recent years it seems that cost has been paid with a credit card. Many are understandably unwilling to keep racking up the bills internationally when debt and unemployment are mounting at home. But it would be disingenuous to think that increased 'America-first'ism would not have consequences for Washington's bilateral relationships with countries whose economies have become increasingly dependent on it, especially India's.

There is also the ever-present risk of competing US priorities clashing with the Indian relationship; a desire to accommodate China, along the lines advocated by Henry Kissinger, could again prompt the United States to steer a more Pacific course. Washington does not always appreciate that India cannot move faster on certain issues than it is currently doing, however frustrating that might seem to Americans (the nuclear liability issue is a case in point). India's own stubborn emphasis on its independence of thought and action, while respected in principle by Washington, can sometimes grate there: as became apparent on the issue of sanctioning Iran, Washington may not always understand or fully appreciate India's inability to agree with it, leading many to think of India as a false friend. And there is always the risk of complacency on the other side: the notion that the United States need not make more of a special effort with India since it has nowhere else to go but towards Washington, and that in any case it is too cussed to go far enough to make additional attention worthwhile.

There is an additional risk. America's own gradual transformation from a globe-straddling superpower to something less could have an impact on the relationship. An America in decline, if that is indeed what transpires, will both have less interest in India and be of less use to it in the world as a partner in its own rise. This may not be a likely scenario in the foreseeable future, since even America's loss of sole-superpower status is unlikely to mean its ceasing to be a global power in the imaginable future. But it is something else that cannot be ignored.

———

So the current scenario suggests that the transformation of India–US relations that began with the end of the Cold War is continuing its gradual course towards the evolution of a 'special relationship' between New Delhi and Washington. But the overall report card remains mixed.

There are strong reasons for congruence and powerful arguments for continued closeness. India is clearly going to join the United States among the top five world powers of the twenty-first century. Both nations are anchored in democratic systems, and are committed to the rule of law, diversity and pluralism, and the encouragement of innovation and enterprise. The engagement of the two countries with each other is reinforced by the growing Indian presence in America—the 100,000 Indian students (who form the largest foreign student community there) supplementing the flourishing and influential 3-million-strong Indian-American community, who enjoy the highest median income of any American ethnic group and who are playing an increasingly prominent role in politics and government.

The way in which the two countries are economically useful for each other's basic objectives was crisply brought out in a recent speech in Washington by India's National Security Adviser Shivshankar Menon, who declared that 'the US is a crucial partner in our enterprise to abolish mass poverty within a democratic framework and open society, while respecting human rights and rule of law'. In turn, he added, 'India offers a large and growing market for the US, creating jobs in both economies, adding competitiveness to US firms, and synergy in innovation and technology.'

Nonetheless, there is a perception among critics, not just in India, that these are 'soft' and 'feel-good' aspects of the relationship that mask a lack of substantive progress on the hard strategic, political and security issues that analysts here consider more important. How understanding is the United States of India's security concerns, especially vis-à-vis Pakistan? Here President Obama's statements, particularly in Delhi, have inspired confidence that the United States does indeed pay serious attention to India's core national security interests. But some hard content still needs to be defined. One example lies in the continuing restrictions on the sale of US high technology to India; New Delhi's endeavours to seek the liberalization of US export controls have encountered significant delays and obstruction in Washington, inevitably having a dampening effect on the publicly announced plans to cooperate in nuclear and space technology.

There has been some American appreciation for India's role in Afghanistan but greater receptivity to Pakistani objections than New Delhi considers reasonable. New Delhi remains seriously concerned about the possibility of a US withdrawal from Afghanistan that implicitly leaves the country to the mercies of the Pakistani ISI, which has been known to foment and guide terrorist actions against India. Cooperation between India and the United States on counterterrorism has improved after 26/11, but the two countries have not gone much beyond information sharing (though the access somewhat belatedly granted to the Pakistani-American terrorist enabler David Coleman Headley helped overcome Indian misgivings about the depth of this cooperation). This is one area where real teeth could be added, not least to reassure Indians that the United States' understandable desire to cut its losses in 'Af-Pak' would not leave our country more vulnerable to the depredations of those who stand to gain from an American departure.

The United States could also show more interest in resisting China's irredentist claims to Indian territory, particularly its habit of dubbing Arunachal Pradesh as 'South Tibet', an issue on which the United States has stayed conspicuously neutral. The question of the strategic content of the relationship goes beyond the subcontinent. Obama's support in the Indian Parliament for New Delhi's claims to a seat on a reformed Security Council has not been followed by any instructions to American diplomats around the world to execute this commitment or even to pursue this objective. The suspicion remains that what Indians saw as a substantive triumph during Obama's visit in fact amounted to little more than a rhetorical flourish.

Strategic partnerships are tricky to conceive and implement. There is, to begin with, a definitional challenge for Washington: what does the US national security apparatus understand by the concept of a 'partnership' such as the one it touts that it enjoys with India? Clearly, New Delhi is not going to sign on to anything resembling a traditional Cold War–era 'ally', but if the 'partnership' means anything, it has to amount to something more than the two countries merely being not hostile to each other. The need to define a suitable mid-point between 'friend' and 'ally' could not be more acute, but equally important is the need to give the term 'partner' some real operational content, and to create the necessary bureaucratic architecture to sustain such a partnership.

To take one instance, the Bush Administration had appeared to envisage the emergence of a quartet of the United States, Japan, Australia and India to cooperate together in the Indian and Pacific Oceans, but this idea has languished since one round of joint naval exercises was conducted. Maritime security is an obvious area for cooperation, since these four countries (together with a couple of ASEAN powers) could easily construct a credible security architecture for the Indo-Pacific region. But there is a serious asymmetry in the relations among the various countries in such a configuration: Washington enjoys long-established treaty relationships with Tokyo and Canberra, but there is nothing comparable with India, or between New Delhi and the other capitals. A serious effort would have to be made to create new linkages, but none has been forthcoming, and Washington is arguably at least as much to blame as New Delhi.

The still-lacking substantive definition of India's place as a 'partner' of Washington's—despite the realization after 26/11 that both sides have a common global adversary—impedes the creation of effective mechanisms for intelligence sharing, joint military operations and collaboration in high technology, the very things that India seeks. The commentator Nikolas K. Gvosdev has suggested some benefits that a 'partner' like India might be accorded: 'full participation in a number of counterterrorism initiatives, an expedited export control process for space technology, and invitations to participate in selected research and development projects with the Department of Defense'. That is a useful list to begin with, and India will be delighted if it were to happen. But it would need to be accompanied by operational mechanisms: urgent policy reviews, working groups that met frequently and against real deadlines, and possibly organizational changes in the national security apparatuses of both countries. Thanks to the estrangement of the Cold War years, New Delhi and Washington have not built the habits of trust and confidence between their bureaucracies, and this will take both time and political will. Neither is an indefinitely stretchable commodity.

Similarly, the economic relationship between the two countries has been a source of satisfaction, but it is no longer without concern. India has thrived on US outsourcing to its IT-enabled services sector, and there has been an assumption that the recession will only drive up the demands for outsourcing by cost-conscious American corporations. Unfortunately, however, instead of greater market access in this sector, Indians have been facing signs of an American political backlash, ranging from state-level decisions not to outsource major government contracts to the imposition by the US Congress of punitive visa fees on white-collar Indian experts working for Indian technology providers. The United States has facilitated the globalized world by proselytizing for the very policies (capitalism, open markets, globalization and international institutions) that it now seems to be abandoning. You don't have to watch Lou Dobbs on TV (though many foreigners did, until CNN International mercifully took him off-air) to conclude that the United States is acting as if it is now suspicious of the economic policies it has traditionally advocated—free markets, trade, immigration and technological change. In other words, Indians are not the only ones to fear that, just as the world is increasingly opening up, America may be closing down. The India–US relationship would suffer seriously if, beset by internal preoccupations, America turns inwards and forgets its responsibilities to the well-being of others.

As David Malone put it, 'The entente between the two nations is not so much an alliance as a "selective partnership" based on specific shared interests in some areas and quid pro quo arrangements in others, all underscored by strong economic interdependence. As long as their interests are aligned, India and the United States will seem locked in a wider strategic embrace. But perceptions of interests can change rapidly.' That is a sobering thought, and a wise reminder that complacency is never sensible in international relations.

Obama also spoke of a 'global partnership'. What could this mean in practice? Both countries share a responsibility for preserving a rule-based, open and democratic world order and for the management of the global economy. Both are active in the G20 as the world's premier institution for dealing with international economic questions. Both could work together on global development initiatives—USAID has famously deployed in Africa and elsewhere the India Mark II hand pump, devised for agriculture in India, which has revolutionized water supply in rural areas around the world. India and the United States could also act together to preserve the global commons—the environment, the high seas, human trafficking, outer space and cyberspace—all areas in which the two democracies, one the world's richest, the other still emerging from poverty, have different but not irreconcilable approaches. Cooperation on the innovative development of green energy technologies, for instance, and on space exploration or combating cyber crime are obvious examples of issues that did not even exist before the twenty-first century dawned.

Other possibilities for cooperative action could cover joint responses to natural disasters in South and Southeast Asia, agricultural research and development, and even nuclear proliferation, now that India is no longer lumped together with the 'bad guys' on that issue. But the United States must rein in the fulminations of its own 'non-proliferation ayatollahs', who are prepared to live with a nuclear China and take for granted a nuclear Britain or France, but cannot abide the thought of Indians with nukes. Washington must lift the export controls and restrictions on sharing high technology with India that understandably are seen by many in New Delhi as an affront. Obama's visit made a positive beginning in this area, but some restrictions remain.

Globally, India is looking for a more inclusive multilateralism, and would not accept, as some foreign observers have suggested, a G2 condominium of America and China. There is a consensus in our country that India should seek to continue to contribute to international security and prosperity, to a well-ordered and equitable world, and to democratic, sustainable development for all. This means that, in the wake of the global economic crisis, we must work to redistribute power in the international financial institutions like the IMF and World Bank, as well as in the political organs of global governance such as the UN Security Council. This is an area where New Delhi expects greater understanding from Washington.

But Indians must beware of seeing the US relationship in terms of a checklist of Indian expectations alone. Former US ambassador Robert Blackwill was once reported to have said: 'India wants the US to invest, India wants the US to keep its markets more open, India wants more visas for its professionals, India wants us to be helpful on Kashmir and in dealing with Pakistan, India wants US support for membership of the UN Security Council, India wants this and India wants that. Tell me what will India give in return?' This is not elementary transactionalism alone, since Blackwill was very much an exponent of the support-India-for-its-own-sake school of American foreign policy making. Rather, it reflected a genuine level of exasperation. The fact is that Washington has reason to feel that New Delhi has not done enough to define its own sense of its role as an emerging great power, and consequently has no settled vision of what it wants from a strategic partnership with the United States. India is gradually moving from its traditional obsession with preserving its own strategic autonomy in the face of external pressure to a broader acceptance of its own responsibilities in shaping the world in which it wants to thrive. But there is not yet a full-fledged consensus on what that entails and how far it permits the two countries to flesh out the meaning of the expression 'natural allies' first used by both governments in the current decade.

Part of the success of the India–US relationship will lie in how effectively the two countries manage the differences that inevitably will arise between them. Diplomats like to pretend that there are no difficulties or misunderstandings, when it fact several have arisen in the recent past. An illustrative list would include different priorities on terrorism and mismatched threat perceptions, incompatible views on Pakistan as a credible partner for peace and continued disagreements on aspects of trade relations, none more evident than in their duelling positions on the Doha Round. There are also issues of style—American insensitivity and Indian preachiness have tended to rub each other the wrong way. But on geopolitical fundamentals, there is no real clash of interests. On no issue of vital national interest to either country (with the possible exception of Iran) is the other arraigned on the 'wrong' side.

The United States has to come to terms with a world whose centre of gravity has clearly moved away from the Atlantic to Asia, and to determine where it sees itself in relation to the incontestable rise of China and the growing prowess of India. If the relationship with India is going to become as important to American security as Europe's once was, wouldn't America need to revise its own positions on the threats and challenges faced by India?

And yet the fundamental driver for long-term relations between the United States and India remains the importance of America—the nation, not just the government—as a partner in India's own remaking. As I have argued in Chapter One, the basic task for India in international affairs is to wield a foreign policy that enables and facilitates the domestic transformation of India. The relationship with the United States is part of an effort to make possible the transformation of India's economy and society through our engagement with the world, while promoting our own national values (of pluralism, democracy, social justice and secularism) within our own society. The India–US partnership contributes towards a global environment that is supportive of these internal priorities, and that facilitates our energy security, our food security and our environmental future. When we succeed in our national transformation, we will be including more and more of our people in the great narrative of hope that has been the narrative of social and economic development in America over the last two hundred years. That is why President Obama's visit was a hugely important step in the building of an enduring edifice of cooperation.

The transformation of the India–US relationship from estrangement to strategic partnership is well on its way, and the relationship has clearly acquired a depth that goes beyond the utilitarian measurement of successful transactions. The twenty-first-century world is one in which an emphasis on the shared values of both countries—democracy and pluralism, tolerance and transparency, and respect for personal liberty and human rights—has greater salience than ever. For the first time in human history, the majority of the world's population lives in democracies. The idea that the two principal ones have special interests and responsibilities is not a fashionable one, but it could become one of the defining features of the new era.

As democracies, India and the United States have the additional responsibility of establishing and running international structures to cope with the myriad challenges of the twenty-first century that go beyond the capacity of any one state or alliance to resolve. These include terrorism and nuclear proliferation, but also less conventional threats: state failure, transnational organized crime, the spread of pandemics, piracy in international waters, the management of cyberspace and the military misuse of outer space, to name a few. The threat of Islamist fanaticism and the rise of an authoritarian China also pose specific national security challenges to the United States and India that, if handled well and in cooperation, could assure a safer world.

The possibilities are vast. As they say in America, Obama stepped up to the plate in India, and in his speech to Parliament, he hit a home run. To turn to a more Indian sport, let us make sure that, well after his departure, we keep the ball in play.

Chapter Seven

Familiar Lands and Uncharted Territories: Europe, Africa and Latin America

The rest of the world presents India with an intriguing mix of underdeveloped opportunities and unexplored potential.

Europe is a case in point. India has had a very long history of relations with the Old Continent, going back to the days of the Roman Empire. The south-western state of Kerala boasted a Roman port, Muziris, for centuries before Jesus Christ; excavations are going on now that are revealing even more about its reach and influence. The discovery of ancient amphorae has confirmed that products such as olive oil, wine and glass used to be imported into India from there, in return for more exotic items like ivory and spices from India. Interestingly, an ivory statue of the Hindu goddess Lakshmi dating back to the first century BCE was found in the ruins of Pompeii in south Italy during excavations.

After centuries of languishing, trade is once more a major determinant of the relationship. The EU is no longer India's second largest trading partner, with its trade in 2011 having dropped to 41 billion euros in 2011 from 68 billion in 2010, somewhat below 20 per cent of India's global trade. This is in addition to services exports from Europe worth 10 billion euros, and services imports valued at a little over 8 billion euros. But Europe's contribution to India's overall global trade has been shrinking: the percentage of India's total trade made up by imports from and exports to EU member states has in fact been decreasing even while the Indian economy grows. Differences persist on tariff barriers and on climate change.

241

India has a number of affinities with Europe and with the EU, not least since it, too, is an economic and political union of a number of linguistically, culturally and ethnically different states. Both are unwieldy unions of just under thirty states, both are bureaucratic, both are coalition-ridden and both are slow to take decisions. But in practice these affinities have not translated into close political or strategic relations. Though India was one of the first countries (in 1963) to establish diplomatic relations with the European Economic Community, and the India–EU Strategic Partnership and Joint Action Plan of 2005 and 2008 offer a framework for dialogue and cooperation in the field of security, it will take time for the EU to develop a common strategic culture, which is essential for meaningful strategic cooperation between the EU and India. The India–EU Joint Action Plan covers a wide range of fields for cooperation, including trade and commerce, security, and cultural and educational exchanges. However, as David Malone has observed, 'These measures lead mainly to dialogue, commitments to further dialogue, and exploratory committees and working groups, rather than to significant policy measures or economic breakthroughs.'

Indians have an allergy to being lectured to, and one of the great failings in the EU–India partnership has been the tendency of Europe to preach to India on matters it considers itself quite competent to handle on its own. As a democracy for over six decades (somewhat longer than several member states of the EU), India sees human rights as a vital domestic issue. There is not a single human rights problem about India that has been exposed by Amnesty International or Human Rights Watch or any European institution, which has not been revealed first by Indian citizens, journalists and NGOs and handled within the democratic Indian political space. So for the EU to try to write in human rights provisions into a free trade agreement, as if they were automobile emissions standards, gets Indian backs up. Trade should not be held hostage to internal European politics about human rights declarations; the substance of human rights is far more important than the language or the form. On the substance, India and the EU are on the same side and have the same aspirations.

Once this irritant is overcome, the negotiations for an FTA, which has been long in its 'final' stages, should be concluded and should transform trade.

Of course there are structural impediments that will not disappear. Ironically, given its human rights professions, the EU has long favoured China over India, and China is clearly the preferred investment destination: for every euro invested in India from the EU, 20 euros is invested in China. (This is partly India's fault, in not creating a comparably congenial climate for foreign investment.) An EU ambassador to India, quoted by Malone, observed that 'each has a tendency to look to the most powerful poles in international relations rather than towards each other, and each spends more time deploring the shortcomings of the other rather than building the foundations of future partnership'.

A major element in the equation is India's well-advertised preference for bilateral arrangements with individual member states of the EU, over dealing with the collectivity. This is arguably necessary, given the lack of cohesion in European institutions on strategic questions. Since Maastricht in 1992, Europe has claimed to have a 'common foreign policy', but it is not a 'single' foreign policy. (If it were, EU member states would not need two of the five permanent seats on the UN Security Council, and be clamouring for a third.)

The case for India–EU cooperation could be strongly made, since the bulk of the problem areas in the world lie between India and Europe (or, as Sweden's Foreign Minister Carl Bildt once put it, between the Indus and the Nile). To take two examples: more people have been killed in Europe by drugs coming in from Afghanistan than the total number killed in two decades of fighting in that country. India's security interests in Afghanistan and its greater proximity to that country offer important intersections with Europe's interests. India's increasing salience in the geopolitics of the Indian Ocean, and especially in the security of the Gulf, the source of much of Europe's energy, suggests another area of cooperation.

And yet the prospects for institutional cooperation between India and the EU—despite all that they have in common, the long history of contact between the Old Continent and the subcontinent, and the contemporary relevance of the challenges and opportunities they confront—remain negligible. India–EU relations currently lack substance and strategic weight, despite the conclusion of a strategic partnership in 2004. The oxymoronic lack of European unity undermines the credibility of the collectivity; policy-makers in New Delhi will not be able to find many instances of the EU, rather than its individual member states, engaging with or standing up to the United States, Russia or China on any major issue. The ongoing eurozone crisis has also not served to enhance India's confidence in Europe. So New Delhi strengthens relationships with a number of individual European countries that it considers reliable partners, but fails to think of Europe collectively as one of the potential poles in the evolving multipolar world. A European observer, Karine Lisbonne de Vergeron, characterizes the thinking of the Indian elite as follows: 'Europe lacks a strategic vision and ranks at the bottom of the list of partners in India's multipolar understanding of the future geometry of world affairs.' This assessment is not far off the mark.

Conceptually, the foreign policy establishment in independent India sees the nation as a modern state founded on and sustained by strong ideas of sovereignty, territoriality and raison d'état. In contrast, the EU is a post-modern construct, with diminishing regard for sovereignty within its territorial space and a growing desire for extraterritoriality in its aspirations. This basic difference between the conceptual outlook of India and that of the EU might help explain the inherent discomfort of modern India in engaging with a post-modern entity like the EU. In principle and in practice, too, India is wedded to non-interference in the internal affairs of states, whereas the EU is the land on which Bernard Kouchner propounded his theory of a '*droit d'ingerence*' and its soil has offered fertile ground for initiatives revealing a penchant for intervention beyond sovereign boundaries. India and the EU may have democracy and diversity in common, but in their basic orientation towards statecraft, they diverge fundamentally.

For all these reasons, India has consistently revealed a greater sense of comfort in dealing with individual European nation states; New Delhi sees an affinity with London, Berlin or Paris that it cannot bring itself to imagine with Brussels or Strasbourg. As a result, as my former colleague, the Indian diplomat Sandeep Chakravorty, has observed about Europe, 'it may not be an exaggeration to state that India's relationship with the parts is more substantive than with the whole'. It does not help that India also considers Europe with its multiplicity of complex organizations to be over-institutionalized and over-bureaucratized and, therefore, far more complicated and less attractive to engage with than national capitals.

The boot is not entirely on one foot. Where Europe and India have divergent approaches to addressing security issues, for instance, Indian deficiencies are arguably to blame. For instance, the EU has formalized an elaborate Common Foreign and Security Policy, a European Security and Defence Policy, and even a European Security Strategy (by the European Council in 2003), while India has not yet even formally articulated a national security strategy. While Europe may desire closer security cooperation with India, India is really in no position to reciprocate except in terms of generalities. On the other hand, of course, Indian decision-makers could point out that there is no European defence ministry, army headquarters or intelligence service, and so security cooperation is in any case better conducted with individual states.

It could also be argued that the EU adds very little value to India's efforts to overcome its principal security challenges. In the immediate priority areas of strategic interest to India—its own neighbourhood, the Gulf region, the United States and China—the EU is almost irrelevant, and the story does not get better if one extends India's areas of security interest to Central and Southeast Asia. On the big global security issues—nuclear proliferation, civil conflict and terrorism—the problem is the same, while the EU has almost nothing to contribute to India's search for energy security. Even in India's quest to be part of the global decision-making architecture, including a permanent seat on the UN Security Council, it is not the EU but the existing European permanent members, the United Kingdom and France, which bring more value to the table for India. India certainly needs European cooperation in counterterrorism and European remote surveillance technology, but it would obtain these from European nation states, not from the EU.

If security is therefore a marginal area for EU–India cooperation, there certainly is scope in the fields of food security, the response to climate change and the protection of the environment, where Europe could share with India its advances in 'green technology'. In the sphere of science and technology, India's participation in both the International Thermonuclear Reactor Project (ITER) and the GALILEO satellite programmes came through the EU. But beyond these, there are few visible 'wins' in India–EU cooperation. There is certainly room for enhanced technological cooperation, where India's abundant and inexpensive scientifically savvy brainpower and its burgeoning record in 'frugal innovation' offer interesting synergies with Europe's unmatched engineering traditions and capacity. But the Arcelor-Mittal affair, in which a takeover bid by an Indian steel firm of a European one was challenged in a manner that can only be described as racist ('Europeans are like a delicate perfume, Indians a cheap eau de toilette' was only one of the many unpleasantries bandied about) showed India the limits of doing business with and in Europe.

The notion that Europe could collectively emerge as a new 'pole' in a multipolar world order has its adherents, but progress in this direction is difficult to discern, especially given the choice of low-profile leaders for the principal European institutional positions, the presidency and the high representative for foreign and security policy. The danger remains that New Delhi will write Europe off as a charming but irrelevant continent, ideal for a summer holiday but not for serious business. The world would be poorer if the Old Continent and the rising new subcontinent did not build on their democracy and their common interests to offer a genuine alternative to the blandishments of the United States and China.

And yet, within Europe, some bilateral relationships have never been stronger. That with France, for instance, has witnessed increasingly close military cooperation and intelligence sharing, creating a level of trust that may also have played a role in the decision to award Dassault's Rafale the multi-billion-dollar fighter plane contract. France's willingness to offer India an unprecedentedly generous level of 'offsets' in exchange for its decision, as well as to transfer technology, suggests the basis for the kind of close partnership that India is yet to enjoy with the United States. There is active bilateral engagement on specialized defence-related fields such as counterterrorism—the Indo-French Working Group on Terrorism has met every year since 2001—as well as on nuclear non-proliferation and disarmament.

France has also developed an important level of energy cooperation with India, especially following a 2008 agreement between the two countries that has paved the way for the sale of nuclear reactors to India. French interest in Indian culture and a sustained level of scholarship on the country, as reflected by the impressive work of its Centre de

Sciences Humaines in New Delhi and the prestigious Institut Français de Pondichéry, testify to the intellectual depth of the engagement. (This has only modestly been reciprocated by India, which has posted a succession of non-Francophone ambassadors to Paris.)

France enjoys a limited historical basis for its relationship with India, since its colonial presence was limited to a few enclaves and left no lasting mark on society as a whole. The opposite, of course, is true of Britain, India's colonial master for two centuries and the source of both its Westminster-style parliamentary democracy and its obsession with cricket, not to mention the provenance of the English language that has been India's calling card to the world. India's relations with Britain come with an extraordinary amount of historical baggage, compounded by the presence of some 3 million immigrants of Indian origin in the United Kingdom (numbers comparable to those of Indians in the United States, but representing both a higher proportion of the population—some 5 per cent, as against 1 per cent in the US—and a very different demographic profile). Recent developments appear, however, to have reversed the historical pattern; it is now Britain that is seen as the supplicant, seeking to please an often-indifferent India.

The importance given to India in the foreign policy priorities of British Prime Minister David Cameron is striking: he visited the country to burnish his international credentials soon after being elected leader of the Conservative Party, and India became the second country (after the United States) that he made an official visit to upon becoming prime minister. Barely eight weeks after taking office, Cameron travelled to India with an unusually large delegation of key ministers, including the Chancellor of the Exchequer, several well-heeled businessmen and a motley crew of MPs and academics in his entourage. His homage to the new India began with his arrival in Bangalore, at the headquarters of Infosys Technologies, the shining example of India's success in conquering world markets, where he also took the opportunity to lecture Pakistan on the need to abjure terrorism against India. Apart from pleasing his hosts, Cameron was signalling a departure from what Indians had too often seen in the past as a patronizing and arrogant tone about India from British political leaders. He could not have begun his journey better.

At the same time, the substance of the relationship had been stagnating for some time, with trade showing little improvement from a plateau of $11 billion in 2008–09. Cameron's visit signalled a spurt of some 20 per cent in the next fiscal year, which has led to talk of bilateral trade heading to $20 billion by 2015. Other areas also show both progress and setbacks. Despite the signing, also in Bangalore, of an $800-million deal between British Aerospace and Hindustan Aeronautics Ltd for fifty-seven advanced jet trainers, the potential for stronger defence ties remains largely unexplored, as would become apparent a year and a half later in Britain's dismay when it too (like the United States) was rejected in India's choice of a fighter aircraft. The operationalization of the civilian nuclear agreement signed during Cameron's visit also remains to be tested in practice.

The media outcry in early 2012 over Britain's modest development aid to India, which broke out when the fighter deal was announced, reflected many of the complexities that still bedevil the relationship. After two centuries of presiding over the systematic impoverishment of the Indian people, Britain arguably has a historical and moral responsibility towards the well-being of its former subjects, and it provides India annually with some $400 million of developmental assistance, mainly targeting beneficiaries in three of India's poorest states. (This is perfectly reasonable: if the United Kingdom is to have an aid programme, it would make little sense *not* to aid poor Indians.) When India picked the Rafale over the British-backed Eurofighter, however, the British media resurrected a two-year-old statement by Indian Finance Minister Pranab Mukherjee that British aid was 'peanuts' that New Delhi could do without, and created a national uproar over Indian 'ingratitude', not to mention profligacy. Even sober commentators saw the decision as a setback to Cameron's efforts to establish Britain as a 'partner of choice for India'. It did not help that India had dawdled for over six months in replacing its retiring high commissioner to the United Kingdom, suggesting that Britain figured low in New Delhi's strategic priorities.

This is where a distinction would be worth drawing. Don't aid the Indian government—the cumulative aid it receives amounts to little over half of 1 per cent of the country's GDP, and the finance minister is not alone in wishing it away. But *do* aid poor Indians; they need it, because however much the Government of India is doing for them, their poverty is so dire that it can never be enough. So don't give the aid to the same people who are buying fighter aircraft; channel it instead through charitable NGOs, British or Indian, working directly with the poor. That would not only help people in need, it would avoid a revival of this invidious debate, and ease the journey towards a more equal, and less contentious, relationship between the two countries.

A more recent but arguably closer European relationship that is undergoing reinvention is that of India with Russia. Beginning with the Indian nationalists'—and particularly Jawaharlal Nehru's—fascination with an idealized Soviet state in the 1920s (though Nehru, in particular, had few illusions about the nastier excesses of Stalinism), Russia enjoyed a privileged place in the Indian imagination. A celebrated pair of visits in 1955—Nehru's to Moscow in June and Khrushchev's return trip in November—inaugurated a particularly warm phase in the relationship, with steadily increasing Soviet technical assistance to India's public sector, peaking with the decision in 1962 to transfer technology to manufacture the MiG-21 fighter jet in India. In 1965 the Soviets were still seen as neutral enough to broker a ceasefire in Tashkent at the end of the India–Pakistan war; but when tensions arose with Pakistan in 1971 over what would become the secession of Bangladesh from that country, Moscow clearly chose sides. A letter from Chairman Mao implying support for Pakistan in the event of conflict prompted India to jettison its non-aligned principles and sign a treaty of friendship and cooperation with the Soviet Union in August 1971. During the remaining two decades of the Soviet Union, successive Indian governments relied heavily on Russian military supplies (which accounted for over 70 per cent of Indian defence imports) and were broadly sympathetic with Russian objectives in Afghanistan and in Southeast Asia.

The collapse of the Soviet Union helped prompt the significant reorientation of Indian foreign policy already described in earlier chapters—the advent of the 'Look East' policy, the new opening to Israel and a much more serious engagement with the United States. Despite this, Russia and India remained important foreign policy partners for each other, as the continued frequency of high-level exchanges of visits demonstrated. The economic relationship underwent a downturn as

India opened up its trade with China and the West, but the defence and security relationship continued, with Russia remaining India's top military supplier well into the first decade of the twenty-first century (when, in some accountings, it was overtaken by Israel). India is still Russia's second largest customer for conventional weapons exports, after China. Russia continues to be seen by India as a faithful and reliable supplier of sophisticated, yet relatively inexpensive, weapons systems. Indians were conscious (and grateful) that Russian military cooperation did not merely constitute a buyer–seller relationship but included joint research and development, servicing contracts, and training, including joint exercises. But the abrupt cancellation of a pair of scheduled exercises in 2011 (in the wake of India's rejection of the Mikoyan MiG-35 as a suitable combat aircraft, the same decision that also dismayed the United States and the United Kingdom), and continued delays and cost escalations in the refurbishing of the aircraft carrier Gorshkov for the Indian Navy, did not suggest that all has remained quite well in the military relationship.

The somewhat misty-eyed view of Russia born during the struggle against British imperialism was never wholly absent from Indian thinking, though. When India's President Pratibha Patil visited Moscow in 2011, her then counterpart Dmitry Medvedev declared somewhat conventionally that 'our mutual ties of friendship are filled with sympathy, and trust, and openness', but his Indian visitor gushed: 'We are confident that India lives in the hearts of every Russian. In the same way, I can assure you that Russia also lives in our souls as a Homeland, as people who share our emotions, our feelings of mutual respect and constant friendship.' Such sentiments were never wholly absent in New Delhi's attitudes, even though the nature of the Russian state had visibly undergone major changes since the Soviet era and the priorities of both sides meant that neither loomed quite as large in its foreign policy consciousness as before.

Nonetheless, though bilateral trade (at $8.5 billion in 2011) remained insignificant, the fact that Russia (and the Soviet Union) had contributed to the creation of India's capacity in the nuclear, defence, space and heavy industry sectors when no other country was willing to do so has not been forgotten. Partly as a result of this legacy, Russia's current cooperation with India continues to occur in a number of vital strategic sectors (including nuclear development and space exploration, and the joint development of the highly sophisticated BrahMos missile), ensuring that Russia remains a factor in India's contemporary *weltpolitik*.

New Delhi also has, over the last two decades, actively pursued Russian sources of energy, both oil and gas and nuclear. Russia is a useful partner for India in its quest for energy security in its extended neighbourhood, since India hopes to work with Russia to secure greater influence in Central Asia (which comprises several former Soviet republics). As mentioned in Chapter Five, this region could well constitute the route for several major potential oil and natural gas pipelines which would, if built, terminate in India.

It remains true that in every fundamental particular Russian and Indian interests do not clash. The two countries meet in the context of the trilateral Russia–India–China meetings of foreign ministers, at the East Asia Summit, in the Shanghai Cooperation Organization and as members of the newly emerged BRICS grouping. The opportunities to share compatible views of the world also arose at the UN Security Council during India's stint as a non-permanent member in 2011–12, even if the two countries did not always vote in sync (with New Delhi agreeing with Moscow on Libya but voting in favour of the Syria resolution that Russia vetoed).

The changing global environment has had an inevitable impact on India–Russia relations. Russia's startling opening to the NATO alliance, its warming relationship with China and its much-improved relations with Pakistan have all moved Moscow away significantly from the logic that had underlain its approach to New Delhi in the Cold War years. Indian policy-makers continue to see Russia as a friend whose sympathy and support for Indian objectives is time-tested, especially in India's moments of need, such as in 1971 or in international discussions on Kashmir. Russia is the only country with which India maintains an institutionalized defence cooperation mechanism featuring annual meetings of defence ministers, and while Indo-US nuclear cooperation has been hamstrung over supplier liability issues, Russia is proceeding with the construction of two nuclear power reactors on Indian soil. And yet the absence of widespread people-to-people contacts, the barriers of language and the fact that each country has greatly diversified its global relations mean that talk of a 'special relationship' is sounding increasingly hollow. The two countries are much more equal than they ever were; India's is the larger economy and Russia's will not long remain the much more developed one. Finding a new logic for the 'special relationship' remains a task in progress, and not one pursued with any great energy or enthusiasm, it would seem, on either side. In David Malone's trenchant words, 'Russia will remain a trusted interlocutor, if only out of habit. Economic relations can be conducted unsentimentally on the basis of mutual interest. But the parties are definitely out of love, if they were ever smitten.'

India shares a satisfactory relationship with Turkey but there is considerable scope for improvement, since neither side has reached out to the other fully. Military regimes in Turkey and Pakistan were close to each other, and Ankara made common cause with the supposedly kindred spirits in Islamabad, leading to a certain distance between New Delhi and Ankara. The volume of bilateral trade is modest, at under $5 billion. There has been an FTA deal in the offing for quite some time, but negotiations have dragged on for a while now and are far from nearing completion. High-level visits had not occurred for nearly a decade when President Abdullah Gül came calling in 2011; the last time a Turkish prime minister visited India was in 2003. Turkey is therefore undeniably a land of unexplored potential for India.

As for the part of Europe rarely discussed these days in India— Eastern Europe—the tale can be briefly told. While a considerable amount of rhetoric was expended on celebrating ties with the states of Eastern Europe during the era of India's special relationship with the Soviet Union, they are no longer a significant preoccupation for India today. This is especially true of India's most important old friendship in East Europe, the old non-aligned affinity with Yugoslavia now lying in the rubble of the Yugoslav civil war, the collapse of Titoism and the dawning of what one might mischievously dub 'the Brussels Consensus' in the Balkans.

A more promising narrative emerges from India's relationship with an older continent—albeit one made up of newer states—Africa. Africa is increasingly emerging as a central plank in Indian foreign policy. The India–Africa partnership has deep roots in history. Linked across the Indian Ocean, Indians have been neighbours and partners of East Africans for thousands of years. There was regular interaction between communities and traders, especially from the West coast of Gujarat and parts of South India with Abyssinia, Somalia, Mombasa, Zanzibar and even as far south as Mozambique. These communities and groups played significant roles in the histories of both India and Africa; an Abyssinian warlord rose to political prominence in medieval India, and groups of African descent still populate parts of western India. The advent of the Europeans and the era of colonial rule disturbed these interactions but could not disrupt them: indeed they added to them the painful experience of indentured labour, shipped from India to work on African plantations.

In many ways Indians and Africans trod a common path. As colonization came, our contacts acquired different dimensions, some of which remain with us. Both India and Africa shared the pain of subjugation and the joys of freedom and liberation. In the period of decolonization and the struggle against apartheid, we stood shoulder to shoulder in the fight against apartheid and racial discrimination; India godfathered the entry of an increasing number of African countries into the international comity of nations. Satyagraha, non-violence and active opposition to injustice and discrimination were first devised by Mahatma Gandhi on the continent of Africa. The Mahatma always believed that so long as Africa was not free, India's own freedom would be incomplete. Our first prime minister, Jawaharlal Nehru, was also a firm believer and practitioner of the principle of Afro-Asian solidarity and of support to the struggles of the people of Africa against discrimination and apartheid.

After India achieved independence, we embarked on a path of close cooperation with the newly independent nations of Africa that shared similar problems of underdevelopment, poverty and disease. India's cooperation with Africa was based on the principle of South–South cooperation, on similarities of circumstances and experiences. India believes that Africa holds the key to its own development but it needs support, facilitation and durable partnerships. We have always been willing to share our development experience with Africa. In India we have sought to empower our people by investing in their capabilities and widening their development options, and we are happy to help apply that approach to Africa. Transfer of knowledge and human skills, going beyond government-to-government interactions and embracing civil society, will help strengthen our mutual capabilities. India is always open to sharing its strengths, its democratic model of development and its appropriate technologies, which many Africans found are low cost, resource efficient, adaptive and suitable to help identify local solutions to local problems.

There was also a continuous high level of interaction between the political leaderships of India and African nations, with scarcely a year going by without some African head of state or government visiting New Delhi. A startling number of African leaders, particularly but not exclusively from former British colonies, have studied in some Indian university, among the tens of thousands of African students who then returned home to contribute to the economic and social development of their respective countries. Indian officials visiting Africa have often been pleasantly surprised to discover that their interlocutors in high positions shared an alma mater with them.

Mahatma Gandhi also expressed the belief that 'commerce between India and Africa will be of ideas and services, not of manufactured goods against raw materials after the fashion of the western exploiter'. Here, though, the Mahatma cannot be credited with great prescience, since ideas and services play only a modest role in the growing Indian–African relationship, while manufactured goods and raw materials still dominate their trade links. Western-style colonial exploitation is, however, mercifully absent.

In the first few decades of our independence, Africa became the largest beneficiary of India's technical assistance and capacity building programmes. India extended over $3 billion worth of concessional lines of credit to be used in those infrastructure and other development projects that were determined by African countries, a welcome change from the more top-down assistance extended by other donors, whether Western or communist. These cooperation programmes laid the foundation of the political and economic partnership between India and Africa in the twentieth century. It was against this background that India sought to re-engage in the twenty-first century, by redrawing our framework of cooperation and devising new parameters for an enhanced and enlarged relationship commensurate with our new role in a changing world. The challenge of globalization and the need to identify new opportunities for mutually beneficial cooperation led to a renewed vigour in the India–Africa relationship.

On the old foundations, a new architecture for structured engagement and cooperation for the twenty-first century was designed and launched at the first India-Africa Forum Summit hosted by India in April 2008 in New Delhi. The summit provided an occasion for the leaderships of India and Africa to come together to chart out the roadmap for a systematic engagement. As Prime Minister Manmohan Singh said in his address to the summit, 'Africa is our Mother Continent. The dynamics of geology may have led our lands to drift apart, but history, culture and the processes of post-colonial development have brought us together once again.' The India-Africa Forum Summit adopted two historic documents, the Delhi Declaration and the India-Africa Framework for Cooperation—the first a political document covering bilateral, regional and international issues (such as common positions on UN reforms, climate change, WTO and international terrorism) and the second spelling out the agreed areas of cooperation, from human resources and institutional capacity building to agricultural productivity and food security, and (perhaps inevitably) information and communications technology. These were all areas in which African countries had great interest in what India had to offer.

The 2008 summit received a commitment by the Government of India for up to $5.4 billion in new lines of credit in a five-year period—a quantum leap in governmental commitment to support the economic growth of Africa, which helped act as a stimulus package when the global financial crisis erupted shortly thereafter. Under this programme, India has committed about $1 billion every year, mainly in the form of soft loans at extremely low interest rates (around 0.75 per cent in most cases) that barely cover the costs of servicing the loans. The loans are 'tied', in that 80 per cent has to be spent on purchasing Indian goods and services, though it is the African country itself that will decide on the choice of

Indian supplier. The lines of credit lead to asset creation in Africa and help catalyse confidence in the Indian economic partnership.

The model of cooperation emerging from the first India-Africa Forum Summit has governed India's approach since. The Delhi Declaration made clear that:

> This partnership will be based on the fundamental principles of equality, mutual respect, and understanding between our peoples for our mutual benefit. It will also be guided by the following principles: respect for the independence, sovereignty, territorial integrity of states and commitment to deepen the process of African integration; collective action and cooperation for the common good of our states and peoples; dialogue among our civilizations to promote a culture of peace, tolerance and respect for religious, cultural, linguistic and racial diversities as well as gender equality with the view to strengthening the trust and understanding between our peoples; the positive development of intra-regional/sub-regional integration by complementing and building upon existing/sub-regional initiatives in Africa; recognition of diversity between and within regions, including different social and economic systems and levels of development; and further consolidation and development of plural democracy.

Beyond the diplomatic rhetoric, the strength of the Indian model of cooperation with Africa has lain in its non-prescriptive nature. India has made it clear throughout that it seeks mutual benefit through a consultative process. Indian diplomats do not instruct, impose or even demand certain approaches or projects in Africa, but offer to contribute to the achievement of Africa's development objectives as they have been set by our African partners. Besides the consultative process and the spirit of friendship, both of which are clearly linked to our desire to fulfil the developmental aspirations of African countries rather than to prescribe them ourselves, there is also the element of a sharing of knowledge and experience for which many African countries often want to relate to us. India's multicultural, multi-ethnic, multiparty pluralistic democracy has emerged as an attraction to many African countries moving in the same direction. So are our parliamentary institutions and procedures, and our manner of conducting free and fair elections. Our ability to work with the non-governmental sector and civil society in our quest for inclusive growth is also an important lesson which many African countries have wanted to share with us. This sharing of experiences on political cooperation is, therefore, another aspect of our non-intrusive support to the development of democratic institutions in our partner countries.

Similarly, areas of human resource development and capacity building have been at the forefront of our partnership with Africa. Both India and Africa are blessed with young populations. At the first India-Africa Forum Summit, India announced a grant of $500 million specifically to undertake projects in human resource development and capacity building. It is only by investing in the creative energies of our youth that the potential of our partnership will be fulfilled. Tens of thousands of African students have received education and training in Indian institutions; at any time there are at least 10,000 to 15,000 African students studying in various parts of India. The African students at present in India, nearly 1000 of them on Government of India scholarships but a larger number on a self-financing basis, add to the experience of many African countries with Indian teachers and professors. Long-term scholarships for undergraduates, postgraduates and higher courses have been doubled and the number of slots under the Indian Technical and Economic Cooperation (ITEC) programme has increased to 1600 every year. This partnership in human resource development has been augmented by the tele-education component of the Pan African e-Network project which is visionary in its appeal and impact. The role of information and communications technology (ICT), science and technology, and research and development has contributed to the enhancement of our engagement with Africa in this important area of human resource development.

The 1600 training positions offered under India's technical cooperation programme to Africa have also become important avenues of capacity building. India is in the process of establishing nineteen institutions on African soil jointly with the African Union Commission and the member states, including an India-Africa Institute of Information Technology, an India-Africa Institute of Foreign Trade, an India-Africa Institute of Educational Planning and Administration, an India-Africa

Diamond Institute, ten vocational training centres and five human settlement institutes in Africa to contribute to capacity building. Such endeavours to invest in human capital and sustainable political systems have made human resource development a vital aspect of India's model of cooperation with Africa.

Technology has of course been a particularly valuable Indian calling card. The Pan African e-Network project that seeks to bridge the 'digital divide' between Africa and the rest of the world is one of the most far-reaching initiatives undertaken by India anywhere in the world. Already nearly fifty countries have joined this programme, which is intended to provide e-services (with priority for tele-education and telemedicine services) and VVIP connectivity by satellite and fibre optic network among the heads of state of all fifty-three countries. The project would give major benefits to Africa in capacity building through skill and knowledge development of students, medical specialists and for medical consultation.

India has also offered to share with African nations its experience in using remote-sensing and satellite-imagery for weather-forecasting, natural resources management, land use and land-cover mapping and a variety of other applications.

What has not always worked as well as it might is the pace of implementation of many Indian projects in Africa. It is true that as a democratic country we have to have consultations and build consensus. Sometimes our overly strong bureaucracy takes too literally its obligation to act as a check and balance on decision-making. But if the government is sometimes accused of being slow, once it takes a decision to go forward, progress is steady.

There is an undoubted need, however, for more careful management and audit of disbursements made through the government's lines of credit for Africa. In 2009, several reports appeared of questionable transactions relating to the export of rice at subsidized prices to several African countries, but these were never fully investigated and the allegations have largely petered out. Given that these lines of credit amount to considerable sums of money—more than $5 billion, or ₹25,000 crore—there is a fundamental need for greater transparency in the allocation of funds, the choice of projects, the drawing up of the requirements for bidders and the selection of contractors. This should not be allowed to slow the process down, but it is essential that India's relations with Africa not be reduced in the eyes of some critics to an unsavoury boondoggle.

One way of compensating for the deficiencies of the governmental sector in this model of cooperation is India's increased reliance on its burgeoning private-sector investment in Africa, which has acquired much greater visibility in the last few years. This has been more manifest ever since India liberalized its own economic system in 1991 and, in the twenty-first century, private Indian investment in Africa is giving the relationship a new vigour and impetus. Indian companies have made large investments in Africa running into several billion dollars in industry, agriculture, infrastructure and human resource development.

An illustrative example of an Indian private-sector success story is Vedanta Resources' turnaround of Zambia's copper mining industry— which had been nationalized in the late 1960s, driven into ruin, resold to the former owners, Anglo American PLC, the South African mining giant, which failed to revive them and were then essentially abandoned. Vedanta, an FTSE 100 Indian metals and mining group, came in 2004 to buy a majority shareholding in Konkola, the jewel in the crown of the Zambian mines, and other properties, and made them hugely profitable: its CEO, Anil Agarwal, likes to boast that he is '26 per cent of Zambia's GDP'. Other examples, big and small, abound: Tata Steel's $1.5-billion joint venture in an iron project in Cote d'Ivoire, Apollo Tyres' manufacturing plants for rubber automobile tyres, and many ventures in the continent's fastest-growing region, East Africa, which has the oldest historical links with India, and some of the largest communities of Indian origin.

Indian private investment is largely not government led or government subsidized but governed by the logic of commercial opportunities. And yet they are able to make a serious contribution to development. I never tired of telling my African interlocutors about the magnificent work being done by Indian entrepreneurs who have introduced low-cost Kirloskar irrigation pump sets in West Africa. These pump sets have made a significant impact in increasing the food production capacities of some African countries, particularly Senegal. It is a good example of appropriate technological and investment intervention, something which serves the felt needs of African communities without requiring them to make huge investments. This can be a good example for others to emulate.

Indian investors are respected across Africa because they are reputed to be effective in the local environment, to ensure the highest employment generation, to not be reticent on transfer of technology and to be quite willing to live among Africans and employ African managers. Their entrepreneurship and business skills—attributes for which the Indian private sector has long been well known—have been buttressed by India's growing economic clout, which has added to the respect with which they are received. It helps, too, that they leave behind trained Africans well equipped to use the newly created assets.

The combined net flows from India to Africa emerging from governmental credits and private-sector investment, therefore, form another part of our sustainable model of cooperation with Africa, which has in turn given a huge incentive to many Indian companies to seek opportunities in Africa. Cumulative Indian investments in Africa rose to $90 billion in 2010 and are likely to grow significantly in the years ahead. Indian investment in Africa is contributing to the fulfilment of domestic demand in African countries, intra-African trade and foreign exchange earnings through exports. The pharmaceutical sector is a good example. Indian pharmaceutical companies like Ranbaxy and Cipla are not just supplying low-cost generic drugs, particularly anti-retroviral drugs to combat AIDS, across the African continent; many also have production facilities in Africa. The Indian pharmaceutical industry has established such a significant reputation for providing Africans with urgently needed health care, at affordable prices, that Chinese knock-offs of Indian drugs have been found smuggled into several African countries, with fake Indian packaging. If imitation is the best form of flattery, counterfeiting is the ultimate confirmation of the indispensable role Indian pharma is playing in Africa.

Indian investment in agriculture and horticulture, on the other hand, contributes mainly to exports, with Indian firms increasingly attracted by the large tracts of fertile land available in many African countries, especially in regions blessed with abundant rainfall and sunshine. The idea that Africa could become a breadbasket for India, as Indian domestic demand outstrips the country's capacity to produce the food it needs, has begun to make Africa an important element in Indian thinking about long-term food security.

This has led, perhaps inevitably, to what Ethiopian Prime Minister Meles Zenawi described as 'ill-informed and even ill-intentioned loose talk' about Indian farming companies conducting 'land-grabbing' in his country, charges that had indeed been aired in the Indian press. When I met Zenawi in 2010, he was quite open about the fact that Ethiopia has 3 million hectares of unutilized land, which it intended to lease out to foreign agricultural enterprises. An Indian investor, Krishna Karaturi, had already made a reputation for himself by growing roses in Ethiopia for export to Europe, and in 2011 he was awarded a lease of 300,000 hectares in the Gambela province to produce maize. 'We want to develop our land to feed ourselves rather than admire the beauty of fallow fields while we starve,' Zenawi declared, adding, 'I want to reassure Indian companies that they are welcome here. We want them to come and farm what is virgin land.' Similar offers from Mozambique, Liberia and other countries indicate a productive future for Indian investment in agriculture, horticulture and floriculture in Africa.

All these investment flows are matched by a multi-tiered cooperative partnership which involves, almost uniquely, a major engagement with pan-African institutions, notably the African Union (AU). While India has had successful bilateral partnerships with most African countries over decades, its willingness to inject multilateralism into its relations with Africa has been broadly seen as reflecting a more complete partnership and greater respect for Africa than other partners offer. A substantial amount of the funds committed for capacity building in Africa is being channelled through the AU in a joint action plan involving shared decision-making on the allocation of resources. In West Africa, India has devised a regional initiative called the Team-9 framework for cooperation, which has brought in a regional focus for its development projects and concessional loans; African countries in the region have been clamouring to be included. This co-equal multilateralism is an important feature of India's new model of engagement with Africa.

India's trade with Africa has been growing rapidly. Two-way trade rose from some $5.5 billion in 2001–02 to over $46 billion in 2010–11, which represents an almost ninefold increase in as many years. There is even talk of aiming for $70 billion by 2015. Even so, the true potential is much greater and the spread and the composition of the trade have to be substantially diversified. With a view to increasing trade flows between India and Africa, India has also extended a duty-free tariff preferential scheme for the fifty least developed countries, thirty-four of which are in Africa. This covers 94 per cent of India's total tariff lines and provides preferential market access on tariff lines for 92.5 per cent of the global exports of all least developed countries.

India and Africa are also engaging closely on trade policy; there has been systematic coordination with African countries on the Doha Round of negotiations, especially on agriculture. India has been particularly close to South Africa in concerting positions on international issues of global interest, a process that has been accentuated with the establishment of IBSA, which launched the India–Brazil–South Africa Dialogue Forum, a gathering of three large developing countries aiming to reify South–South cooperation. IBSA negotiated successfully together in the Doha Round and at other trade talks, and the three countries meet regularly, though insufficient progress has been made on concluding trilateral trade agreements among themselves. IBSA has set up its own cooperation fund, launching initial projects in Equatorial Guinea and Haiti, though the need for individual country branding of aid projects may still limit the possibilities for IBSA development projects. India also supported the inclusion of South Africa in the BRIC grouping, thus making that Goldman Sachs creation into 'BRICS'. But so far both BRICS and IBSA have been forums for meetings rather than incipient international organizations; no institutional structures have been created for either group.

In case most of this chapter seems to provide too economics-oriented an analysis, it is worth pointing out that India has also been extensively involved in peacekeeping efforts in Africa over the past six decades. At present, India has over 7000 peacekeepers serving in Africa, including a 5000-strong contingent in the Democratic Republic of Congo. The fourth batch of India's first all-female formed police unit is currently deployed in Liberia. In addition to peacekeeping, this unit has been successful in reaching out to the most vulnerable sections of society—

women and children—and in inspiring women who have so often been victims of war to see themselves also as sources of succour and strength in this recently war-torn society. President Ellen Johnson Sirleaf, the first woman elected President on the continent, told me when I met her that the Indian women police had inspired many young Liberian women to volunteer for their country's security service.

The presence of Indian-Africans adds an intriguing element to the relationship, especially when their numbers are a significant percentage of the population, as in Mauritius, disproportionately influential, as in South Africa or Nigeria, or visible and sometimes contentious, as in East Africa. I had the pleasure of visiting Mauritius in 2010 to participate in the Aapravasi Diwas—a historic date steeped in poignant memory, which marked the arrival of the first Indian labourers to that country. History is unforgiving to those who do not remember the forefathers and foremothers who sacrificed so much to convert a new, rocky, inhospitable land—in the face of both nature's fury and human cruelty, and through lives of unimaginable torment and drudgery—into a flourishing paradise. Commemorating the Indian connection reifies *le devoir de mémoire* ('the duty to remember') and of course unites the mother country with its diaspora. Similar stories can be told of the Indian presence in South Africa.

There are, on the whole, an estimated 2 million people of Indian origin living in Africa. Indian businessmen, teachers and even missionaries can be found in every African country. Though there have been no incidents of racial tension in recent years to mirror the dark days of 1972 when President Idi Amin threw ethnic Indians out of Uganda, the Indian diaspora has tended to remain distinct, engaging with but often not integrating into the political and cultural environment of their host countries. There is all too little intellectual or cultural exchange between India and Africa; journalists and academics from each are rarely to be found in the other. One point of cultural contact, amusingly enough, is the popular cinema of Bollywood. I have lost count of the number of African leaders I have met who spoke to me with nostalgia of growing up in small towns or villages in Africa, looking forward to the arrival of the latest Bollywood movie in the nearest town. This is an affinity India can, and should, build on.

A vibrant India and a resurgent Africa are thus witnessing an intensification of relations and growing convergence of interests in their common quest for sustainable economic growth and development. Our partnership encompasses priority sectors integral to the developmental goals of Africa in the twenty-first century. The potential for growth and development in this relationship is considerable. There is a growing demand in Africa for developing infrastructure, new technologies, engineering services and manufacturing capabilities for local value addition. These offer excellent opportunities to Indian businesses in Africa, and to millions of young people in Africa who can be employed in the manufacturing and services sectors.

Some suggest that India and Africa have little in common. Nothing could be further from the truth. We face emergent common challenges of food security, energy security, pandemics, terrorism and climate change. Africa and India also share a common societal commitment to pluralism, to inclusiveness across distinctions of region or religion, tribe or clan, language or class, and to the creation of a world that is fair to all its inhabitants. Our shared vision of the world should enable us to work together on the vital challenges facing our peoples, and for the world as a whole, whether in our bilateral relations or multilaterally. In my own experience, I have found that African leaders look at India not the way they look at the West or China—with admiration bordering on awe, and with gratitude admixed with resentment. Rather, they see India as a sort of kindred spirit—a country that has faced problems very similar to those confronted by most African countries, and which has managed in no small measure to overcome them through methods which strike African leaders as replicable in their own lands. From an African point of view, the successes of America and China may be intimidating; those of India seem accessible. The queue of African heads of state and government seeking to visit India is extraordinarily large, given India's limitations in accommodating more than a modest number of state visits every year.

Ironically for a country focused on capacity building in Africa, India suffers from its own capacity limitations in the continent, with far too few embassies in crucial countries, and the existing ones far too thinly staffed. At a time when I was spearheading a major thrust into improving relations with Liberia—newly emerging from civil war but overflowing with minerals (notably iron ore) and large tracts of lush agricultural land, to name just two assets—India relied there entirely on an intrepid businessman who served as our honorary consul-general, while our official diplomacy covered the country through an embassy situated in the French-speaking Cote d'Ivoire. Indian companies and citizens need the reassurance of a supportive embassy presence if they are to be encouraged to work in a new country. There is also a case to be made for India's embassies in Africa to be staffed by a larger number of young and energetic diplomats anxious to establish their reputations, rather than by those promoted from the ranks or at the tail end of their careers, who might tend to regard an African posting as a punishment and who are disinclined to develop much interest in the local language or culture.

On frequent visits to Africa in pursuance of the many consultative mechanisms that have been established with New Delhi, Indian officials have made it clear that India envisions an Africa that is self-reliant, economically vibrant and at peace with itself and the world. In saying this they could look to a familiar source of inspiration. While highlighting the vitality of the African continent, Jawaharlal Nehru had said, 'Of one thing there can be no doubt, and that is the vitality of the people of Africa. Therefore, with the vitality of her people and the great resources available in this great continent, there can be no doubt that the future holds a great promise for the people of Africa.'

It is this promise that our partnership with Africa seeks to fulfil. It has become fashionable these days to ask openly what we expect of each other. This perhaps overlooks the fact that India and Africa have been close to each other over so many centuries that our relationship is not one of immediate give and take but has been that of a family where each one provides the best advice, the best support and the best sharing of experience, so that when we walk the same path, we learn from each other and do not make the same mistakes. India will offer its fullest cooperation to harness the great potential of the African people for the cause of Africa's progress and development. As I stated when addressing the UN General Assembly in 2009 on the New Partnership for Africa's Development: 'The objective of our partnership is to cooperate with all the countries of Africa, within the limits of our capacities and capabilities, in their efforts towards achieving economic vibrancy, peace, stability and self-reliance. Towards this end, it is our intention to become a close partner in Africa's resurgence.'

In the process, a global debate has arisen as to whether India and China—the other Asian power that has made major inroads into Africa in recent years—are engaged in a new 'scramble for Africa', reminiscent of the one among European powers in the nineteenth century. Africa's mineral wealth and energy resources are undoubtedly of interest to both countries, but the notion of a competition for Africa, let alone a scramble, is considerably exaggerated. While it is true that each country has sought advantages for itself across the continent, they have also cooperated with each other; India and China are jointly exploring and developing a Sudanese oilfield, for instance. And when China decided to set up an embassy in Liberia, it was India's honorary consul-general, a long-standing presence in Monrovia, who facilitated the Chinese ambassador's efforts to establish his embassy.

African leaders are mildly insulted by Western attempts to describe their relations with either country in language borrowed from the colonial era. In any case, the core competencies of each country are actually complementary rather than competitive, with China's huge edge in the sale of manufactured goods, in the construction of large infrastructure projects and in the gift of everything, from buildings to vehicles, to African elites, versus India's somewhat more modest focus on capacity building, education and training and of course its strengths in information technology. The Chinese have been known to move into certain nations and practically buy up their governments; democratic India has neither the capacity nor the inclination to try anything remotely like that. On the other hand, Indians are active in sectors like agriculture and floriculture from which the Chinese are virtually absent.

There is a broader strategic dimension as well to the alleged rivalry in Africa—India's reported discomfort with the growing Chinese presence on the African rim of the Indian Ocean and its corresponding desire, if London's Royal Institute of International Affairs at Chatham House is right, to strengthen its countervailing presence there. There is no doubt that the security of the Indian Ocean sea lanes is an area of major concern for India, as it is for China. But analysts such as those at Chatham House seem to overlook the fact that both China and India have compatible interests in this area, since both depend heavily on the Indian Ocean for the movement of goods, especially vital energy supplies through those waters. India has discreetly provided security to certain East African nations through offshore naval patrols when requested to do so, and the Indian Navy regularly calls at a number of African ports. But there is no credible reason to believe that any policy-maker in New Delhi would lose any sleep if Chinese ships were to drop by as well.

One interesting area of difference between the two countries' roles in Africa is that the Chinese inroads have prompted something of an African backlash, with Zambia, in 2011, electing a President who had campaigned on an openly anti-Chinese platform. India, by contrast, is seen as low key and assimilative, willing to leave behind more than it takes out of Africa. The management styles of Indians and Chinese are a study in contrast: Indians handle their African employees better, with greater communication, trust and respect, as well as willingness to train, so that even non-Indian companies often hire Indian managers for their African operations. There is no doubt that in strictly dollar terms, China is way ahead of India in Africa, and the gap is likely to widen. But India's own strengths and successes in Africa suggest that there is more than enough room for both to flourish in the Oldest Continent.

So what is the future for India's presence in Africa? The second India-Africa Forum Summit in Addis Ababa in 2011 confirmed that India's development assistance programme, its long record of political engagement and the effectiveness of its private-sector enterprises have contributed effectively to strengthening its role in Africa. As Africa continues to grow steadily—the continent has even been described, by the OECD's Javier Santiso, as 'the new frontier of emerging markets'—the opportunities for an older emerging market, one which President Obama declared has 'emerged', remain considerable.

Energy is moving increasingly to the forefront of India's strategic objectives in Africa. With some 70 per cent of India's oil supply imported, mainly from the Middle East, the need to diversify the country's sources of supply is self-evident. According to International Energy Agency (IEA) estimates, India's current growth patterns will require an annual increase of some 3.6 per cent in its energy consumption. This will oblige India to import 90 per cent of the petroleum it needs to meet its energy requirements, making Africa a key geographical focus for the Indian government's oil and gas exploration and production company, ONGC, and its foreign arm, ONGC Videsh. Nigeria already supplies about 15 per cent of the Indian requirement, ranking as India's second largest supplier, and it has sold shares in oil exploration ventures to ONGC Videsh. The Indian public-sector giant has also made substantial investments in the hydrocarbon sector in other African countries, notably Libya, Sudan (mainly in the new Republic of South Sudan) and off the coast of Cote d'Ivoire. The Indian private sector is not absent from the energy field either: Reliance Industries is active in such countries as Angola and Nigeria, and continues to explore farther afield. Despite such ventures, India has been unable to shake off the widespread perception that it lacks the hard-nosed strategic drive for energy resources displayed by its Asian neighbour, China, on the African continent. While the two countries' oil corporations have cooperated in Sudan, they have made competing bids elsewhere in Africa, and China has always prevailed. (Indians would respond, of course, that there is enough for both countries' needs in Africa.)

Another key area for future progress is telecommunications, with Indian companies investing heavily in Africa, notably Bharti Airtel, whose acquisition of Zain has given it a presence in fifteen African countries. Despite the failure of Bharti's negotiations in 2009 to acquire a controlling share in South Africa's Mobile Telephone Networks, the largest mobile-phone operator in Africa, it remains interested in expansion across the continent. Providing a low-cost telecom model to a growing African population where mobile telephony has already vastly outstripped fixed-line communications is a 'natural' for Indian telecommunications firms, which have already demonstrated the effectiveness of their model at home.

Mineral resources will also be essential to the growing Indian economy. Africa's enormous natural resources, including iron ore, copper and coltran, and its rich agricultural lands, swathes of which have been lying fallow because of civil conflict, neglect or simple economic mismanagement, are of obvious interest to India. India will undoubtedly add to its burgeoning presence in these areas, though it will have to be particularly attentive to ensure that extraction does not slip over into exploitation.

African opinion has also largely been welcoming of the Indian presence, while understandably stressing that care must be taken to avoid exploitation. For instance, a prominent online journal from Uganda, *New Vision*, wrote not long ago that Africa had a lot to gain from deeper links with India: 'there are lessons to learn from its strengths in agriculture, technology, financing and land tenure systems, and its development path offers a highly relevant example for Africa.' My former United Nations colleague K.Y. Amaoko, then the executive director of the Economic Commission for Africa, declared in 2008: 'There is much we could learn from India on improving the African business environment for private sector investment, public-private partnership as well as strengthening capital markets. India has been especially successful at developing its small- and medium-scale enterprises, an area where we lag behind terribly in Africa.' He added a point not made often enough, that Indian democracy could serve as a model for the continent: 'India is the world's largest democracy and has a proud record of regular elections. Many African countries have recently reverted from one party or military to multiparty systems of governments. On our continent, we are grappling more severely with strengthening the rule of law and the divisions of power between the legislative, executive and judiciary arms of governance, as well relations between citizens and state institutions. We can learn from India.'

Africa is visibly moving from being a relatively modest priority in India's foreign policy—far less important in commercial or political terms than the Middle East or Southeast Asia—to a significant area of focus. New Delhi has rightly eschewed any temptation to concentrate its attention principally on the major powers even as it develops a global role as a major player on the twenty-first-century stage. But as India cultivates this globe-striding presence, Africa has emerged as a vital area for its own 'rebranding'—a continent where it has begun effectively positioning itself as a visionary benefactor, a source of investment, a partner in development efforts, a donor in humanitarian need and a guide on the new information highway that will lead the developing world into the knowledge economy of the twenty-first century.

———

Latin America has long been the Forgotten Continent in India—a region with which India might have found much in common but did not, separated as the two were by distance, language and the lack of any common history of interaction. Yet, with a population of 580 million, a GDP of $4.9 trillion (four times larger than India's) and 6 per cent of global merchandise trade, Latin America is clearly a part of the world Indian policy-makers cannot afford to neglect. At 20 million square kilometres, Latin America also has a larger land surface than Russia or Canada, the largest biodiversity and the biggest freshwater reserves on earth; it is also largely democratic and peaceful, far removed from the interstate wars that have bedevilled the rest of the world. And most important, over the past decade, it has managed to grow at an average of 5 per cent despite the global recession, with figures of 6.1 per cent in 2010, and about 4.5 per cent in 2011. This performance makes it a global success story to rival India's own, and suggests a natural fit in an era in which modern communications has ensured that geography is now history.

It is not that India has been neglecting the region. As one who briefly served as the minister responsible for the region in the Ministry of External Affairs, I am conscious of the increasing salience of Latin America in the government's thinking. Latin Americans are also waking up to the potential of relations with India. A recent report by the United Nations' Economic Commission for Latin America and the Caribbean (ECLAC) titled 'India and Latin America and the Caribbean: Opportunities and Challenges in Trade and Investment Relations' (LC/L346, November 2011) followed hard on the heels of one from the Inter-American Development Bank the previous year—'India: Latin America's Next Big Thing?' by Mauricio Mesquita Moreira—and another on the same subject by the Sistema Económico Latinoamericano y del Caribe (SELA). It is clear that India is well on the way to becoming the 'next big thing' in Latin America.

The trends are encouraging. Trade between India and the region of Latin America and the Caribbean (abbreviated for convenience to LAC) increased nearly ninefold between 2000 and 2010, reaching about $21 billion. While these numbers are relatively modest given the number of countries involved, the Chilean academic and diplomat Jorge Heine has outlined the case for 'the New Latin America'—solid macroeconomic and fiscal management, as well as prudent financial and banking supervisory practices, sustained growth and poverty reduction—strengthening and enhancing trade relations with 'the New India'—a land of 'high savings and investment rate, and rapidly expanding middle class, whose demands for western consumer products is growing in leaps and bounds'. (To these factors could be added the LAC's impressive public finances, current account surplus and substantial reserves, and India's increasing outreach to the world.)

The case is a strong one. Though Latin America's exports to India are largely of natural resources and products based on them, its import basket differs from the usual stereotype. Unlike Chinese exports, which have tended to flood the market at prices at which domestic manufacturers cannot compete, at least half of India's exports (as Heine and the Indian diplomat R. Viswanathan point out in a recent article in *Americas Quarterly)* 'consist of raw materials and intermediate goods such as bulk drugs, yarn, fabrics, and parts for machinery and equipment, which can help Latin American industries cut production costs and become globally competitive'. The worry that increased trade could become a net negative for Latin America, by reducing it to a purveyor of agricultural products and an importer of finished goods (leading even to possible 'deindustrialization'), therefore does not apply to trade with India. Of course, India's food security needs will require it to continue to import ever larger quantities of such natural-resource products from the region—oil, copper, soya and iron ore feature prominently—but LAC countries could, in turn, develop more sophisticated and better targeted farm products which would be of interest to Indian consumers in the years to come.

In his Inter-American Development Bank study, Moreira concluded that while 'the fundamentals exist for a strong trade relationship between the two regions', economic cooperation is being hampered by tariffs and other non-tariff trade barriers. The answer to this, of course, is more trade and less protectionism. 'More trade is likely to strengthen the virtuous circle in which trade boosts incentives for cooperation while cooperation creates even more opportunities to trade,' argues Moreira. The $20 billion in India–LAC trade is highly concentrated in a few countries, with Chile, Brazil, Argentina and Paraguay providing the bulk of the region's exports to India, and Brazil, Peru, Colombia and

Nicaragua a large chunk of the imports. India has, however, concluded preferential trade agreements with Chile and with Mercosur which have contributed to improving trades with the countries concerned, and there is no reason why a similar approach could not be applied to the currently underserved countries of the LAC.

Indian investments in the region are also increasing, amounting to some $12 billion since 2000, with Indian companies present and active in six key LAC economic sectors: agrochemicals, energy, IT and IT-enabled services, manufacturing, mining and pharmaceuticals. Some of India's bigger companies are already an established presence in the region, including ONGC Videsh, the IT majors Tata Consultancy Services (TCS) and Wipro, and the agrochemical giant United Phosphorus. Indian investment is helping Latin America to diversify its sources of economic growth, making the region less dependent on its traditional source of economic strength, commodity exports. Smaller Indian ventures are also making inroads in the region, thanks to individual entrepreneurs who have challenged convention by making new lives in the region. I met a young Sikh in Colombia who has established a flourishing Ayurvedic practice in Bogota, helping fuel high-level interest in India's alternative health systems.

As in Africa, additional investments are likely in the relatively unexplored area of agriculture. In its quest for food security, India cannot help but notice that many LAC countries possess exactly what India is looking for beyond its own borders: in the words of Heine and Viswanathan, Brazil, for instance, has 'a large and fertile land mass with abundant water that can significantly increase the production of food—something India will always need, be it soybean oil, legumes or sugar'.

History has also planted the seedlings of a literary connection. When I published my first novel, *The Great Indian Novel*, in the United States, the then UN secretary-general, Peru's Javier Pérez de Cuéllar, told me how enamoured he was of Indian literature and poetry as a young man, especially the work of Tagore, evocatively translated by Argentina's legendary Victoria Ocampo, Tagore's special friend. Tagore and Ocampo, it is said, inspired each other to write beautifully, leaving behind a poetic legacy that is part of the Indo-Latin heritage. The legacy was broadened by the work of Octavio Paz, whose service as Mexico's ambassador in

India witnessed the flowering of profoundly evocative poetry and prose about the land he saw around him. His books *The Monkey Grammarian* and his valedictory *In Light of India* are both testaments to a sophisticated affair with India that may yet animate a new generation of Latin American intellectuals. Tagore's appeal lingers, but more contemporary Indian writers, some of whom have been translated into Spanish, have not made a comparable impact. On the other hand the magic realism of Gabriel García Márquez has seeped into the sensibilities of many Indian readers, including in translation into Malayalam, making him one of Kerala's most beloved novelists.

There are other affinities: a Gujarati businessman in Medellin runs a Mahatma Gandhi Foundation, which is devoted to propagating Gandhian teachings, in that violence-prone city. Che Guevara's two-week visit to India in 1957, during the course of which he met Nehru and wrote to him to offer Cuban aid in the Kashmir earthquake that year, is fondly remembered, even though no aid was actually sought or received. The most popular 'telenovela' in Brazil in the first decade of the twenty-first century was a soap opera set in India, with Brazilian actors portraying Indian characters. These are all cultural connections waiting to be developed and built upon, which could one day give people-to-people contact more depth and meaning.

Another area with huge potential for growth is information technology. In Latin America as elsewhere, India's IT and IT-enabled services industry has played a significant role in expanding India's presence. Latin America clearly welcomes this and is looking to greater Indian involvement in these areas, including some significant technology transfers. As Indian IT companies establish themselves in the LAC, hire locals, train them in Indian ways and expose them to the opportunities generated by providing IT-enabled services in a globalized world, this sector is likely to be seen increasingly as India's unique contribution to the development and prosperity of the region. On another note, when I was in Peru, the mayor of Lima had a one-point agenda for my meeting: he wanted me to persuade the Tatas to open a Nano factory in Lima. (I took the message back to India but failed. Perhaps Tata's priorities might yet change in the years to come.)

The recent growth of trade and investment ties between India and Latin America has also encouraged much closer diplomatic relations.

Today, LAC countries have nineteen diplomatic missions in New Delhi, while India has fourteen missions in the LAC region, both representing significant increases from twelve and seven, respectively, in 2002. In 2010 India opened a new embassy in Guatemala to cover Central America, but pending invitations from countries like El Salvador and the Dominican Republic to do the same have been deferred solely because of a lack of human resources in India to staff new establishments adequately. Inadequate attention to Spanish-language training in the Indian Foreign Service has also given New Delhi far too few diplomats ready, equipped and inclined to interact with Latin America in the language with which it is most comfortable.

Spanish is, of course, not a factor in the noticeable warming in the bilateral relationship between India and (Portuguese-speaking) Brazil, each of which is the largest economy and most populous country in its region. The two countries have already expanded the scope of their bilateral dialogue to go well beyond trade issues alone, and there are hints that defence and security cooperation are also on the anvil. The former Brazilian president Lula de Silva visited India three times during his eight years in office, more than any other head of state. The creation of IBSA, referred to earlier, came out of the Brasília Declaration of 2003, which launched the India–Brazil–South Africa Dialogue Forum to promote enhanced trilateral cooperation on issues such as trade, investment, education, poverty reduction and the environment. All this did not, however, prevent the two countries from disagreeing with each other during the fraught WTO negotiations in 2008. South–South cooperation is all very well, but national interests must inevitably prevail.

As in Africa, comparisons with China are inevitable. The extraordinary increase in China's trade with Latin America is the greatest bilateral spurt in any trade relationship in the world—an astonishing nineteenfold rise over the past decade, to a staggering $150 billion in 2010. That figure dwarfs India's $20 billion, but it also gives rise to some disquiet in the LAC countries, which fear dependence on Chinese manufactured goods and the extractive (some would say exploitative) nature of China's interest in the region, which (again unlike India's) is largely government led and not private-sector driven. As to investment, as *The Economist* noted a few years ago, Chinese FDI in Latin America 'has hitherto amounted to less than meets the eye'. That Indian companies have begun to make significant investments is welcomed by many who are hoping to see the South Asian country balance China's impressive presence in the LAC, but it would again be idle to see the two in competition—not least because the two systems are different and India is never likely to match the Chinese government's single-minded strategic drive abroad.

And yet the narrative of the last decade is sufficiently impressive to augur well for a significantly transformed relationship. The time has clearly come to look beyond the relatively modest figures for India–LAC trade (a little over $20 billion in 2010) or of Indian investments in the region (some $12 billion) to the direction of current and future trends. The current occasional (and relatively infrequent) visits of policy-makers have to be augmented in both directions, and the success of the handful of existing trade agreements needs to be built upon with systematic efforts to conclude similar agreements with more countries. It is time to take India–LAC ties to the next stage: institutionalizing regular contacts (from foreign office consultations to state visits), signing new trade agreements, offering more incentives to both the public and the private sectors, and putting more energy and vision into trade and investment promotion (for instance, offering governmental support to small and medium enterprises from one region to explore market access in the other). High-level policy dialogues on improving relations should not merely take place but, as Heine suggests, become part of the regular agenda of governments on both sides.

The India–LAC relationship could be the most interesting example of the transformation of the underdeveloped concept of South–South cooperation—from the rhetorical days when both regions advocated the statist concept of a new international economic order and clamoured for more resource transfers from the developed world to an era in which the indigenous private sectors of both have become powerhouses driving their growth and prosperity. In India, where rhetorical genuflections to socialism have persisted stubbornly for longer than in Latin America, the pursuit of the unexplored potential of the region should and will transform the Forgotten Continent into the Continent of Opportunity. That requires a vision and energy that I believe to be incipient but in need of encouragement from the highest levels in New Delhi.

Chapter Eight

The Hard Challenge of Soft Power and Public Diplomacy

I am partially guilty for having introduced the idea of the importance of India's 'soft power' into the public discourse of our country. My rationale for applying Joseph Nye's ideas to India (initially in a series of speeches at the dawn of the new millennium) lay in the excessive international focus on the country's rising power in conventional terms: our consistent economic growth in the last two decades has prompted too many to speak of India as a future 'world leader' or even as 'the next superpower'. The American publishers of my 2007 book, *The Elephant, the Tiger and the Cellphone*, even added a gratuitous subtitle suggesting that my volume was about 'the emerging 21st century power'. (The Indian subtitle was the more modest 'Reflections on India in the 21st Century'.) India, assorted foreign commentators claimed with a breathlessness that began to grate a few years ago, is heading irresistibly for 'great power' status as a 'world leader' in the new century.

And yet I have a problem with that term. The notion of 'world leadership' is a curiously archaic one; the very phrase is redolent of Kipling ballads and James Bondian adventures. What makes a country a world leader? Is it population, in which case India is on course to top the charts, overtaking China as the world's most populous country by 2034, or even, in some recent estimates, 2026? Is it military strength (India's is already the world's fourth largest army) or nuclear capacity (India's status having been made clear in 1998, and then formally recognized in the Indo-US nuclear deal)? Is it economic development? There, India has made extraordinary strides in recent years; it is already the world's fourth largest economy in PPP terms and continues to climb, being poised almost certainly to overtake Japan for the third spot in 2012, though too many of our people still live destitute, amid despair and disrepair. Or could it be a combination of all these, allied to something altogether more difficult to define—its 'soft power'?

Many of the conventional analyses of India's stature in the world rely on the all-too-familiar economic assumptions. But we are famously a land of paradoxes, and among those paradoxes is that so many speak about India as a great power of the twenty-first century when we are not yet able to feed, educate and employ all our people. So it's not economic growth, military strength or population numbers that I would underscore when I think of India's potential leadership role in the world of the twenty-first century. Rather, if there is one attribute of independent India to which I think increasing attention should now be paid around the globe, it is the quality which India is already displaying in ample measure today—its 'soft power'.

The notion of soft power is relatively new in international discourse. The term was coined by Harvard's Joseph Nye to describe the extraordinary strengths of the United States that went well beyond American military dominance. Nye argued that 'power is the ability to alter the behaviour of others to get what you want, and there are three ways to do that: coercion (sticks), payments (carrots) and attraction (soft power). If you are able to attract others, you can economise on the sticks and carrots.' Traditionally, power in world politics was seen in terms of military power: the side with the larger army was likely to win. But even in the past, this wasn't enough: after all, the United States lost the Vietnam War, the Soviet Union was defeated in Afghanistan, and the United States discovered in its first few years in Iraq the wisdom of Talleyrand's adage that the one thing you cannot do with a bayonet is sit on it. Enter soft power—both as an alternative to hard power and as a complement to it. To quote Nye again: 'the soft power of a country rests primarily on three resources: its culture (in places where it is attractive to others), its political values (when it lives up to them at home and abroad), and its foreign policies (when they are seen as legitimate and having moral authority)'.

I would go slightly beyond this: a country's soft power, to me, emerges from the world's perceptions of what that country is all about. The associations and attitudes conjured up in the global imagination by the mere mention of a country's name is often a more accurate gauge of its soft power than a dispassionate analysis of its foreign policies. In my view, hard power is exercised; soft power is evoked.

For Nye, the United States is the archetypal exponent of soft power. The fact is that the United States is the home of Boeing and Intel, Google and the iPod, Microsoft and MTV, Hollywood and Disneyland, McDonald's and Starbucks, Levi's jeans and Coca-Cola—in short, of most of the major products that dominate daily life around our globe. The attractiveness of these assets, and of the American lifestyle of which they are emblematic, is that they permit the United States to persuade others to adopt the US agenda, rather than relying purely on the dissuasive or coercive 'hard power' of military force.

Of course, this can cut both ways. In a world of instant mass communications enabled by the Internet, countries are increasingly judged by a global public fed on an incessant diet of Internet news, televised images, videos taken on the cellphones of passers-by, email gossip. The steep decline in America's image and standing under the Bush Administration after 9/11 is a direct reflection of global distaste for the instruments of American hard power used by that government—Iraq invasion, Guantánamo, Abu Ghraib, torture, rendition, Blackwater's killings of Iraqi civilians.

The outpouring of goodwill for Washington in the wake of 9/11 (think of Le Monde's famous assertion, 'we are all Americans now') and its squandering by America's over-reliance on hard power in the invasion and occupation of Iraq, and the related 'global war on terror', are instructive. The existing soft power assets of the United States clearly proved inadequate to compensate for the deficiencies of its hard power approach: fans of American culture were not prepared to overlook the excesses of Guantánamo. Using Microsoft Windows does not predispose you in favour of extraordinary rendition. The misuse of hard power can undermine your soft power around the world.

But this discussion today is not about the United States. In his book The Paradox of American Power Nye took the analysis of soft power beyond the United States; other nations, too, he suggested, could acquire it. In today's information era, he wrote, three types of countries are likely to gain soft power and so succeed: 'those whose dominant cultures and ideals are closer to prevailing global norms (which now emphasize liberalism, pluralism, autonomy); those with the most access to multiple channels of communication and thus more influence over how issues are framed; and those whose credibility is enhanced by their domestic and international performance'.

At first glance this seems to be a prescription for reaffirming the contemporary reality of US dominance, since it is clear that no country scores more highly on all three categories than the United States. But Nye himself admits this is not so: soft power has been pursued with success by other countries over the years. When France lost the war of 1870 to Prussia, one of its most important steps to rebuild the nation's shattered morale and enhance its prestige was to create the Alliance Française to promote French language and literature throughout the world. French culture has remained a major selling point for French diplomacy ever since. The United Kingdom has the British Council, the Swiss have Pro Helvetia, and Germany, Spain, Italy and Portugal have, respectively, institutes named for Goethe, Cervantes, Dante Alighieri and Camoes. In recent years, China has started establishing 'Confucius Institutes' to promote Chinese culture internationally, and the Beijing Olympics were a sustained exercise in the building up of soft power by an authoritarian state. The United States itself has used officially sponsored initiatives, from the Voice of America to the Fulbright scholarships, to promote its soft power around the world. But soft power does not rely merely on governmental action: arguably, for the United States, Hollywood and MTV have done more to promote the idea of America as a desirable and admirable society than any US governmental endeavour. Soft power, in other words, is created partly by governments and partly despite governments; partly by deliberate action, partly by accident.

What does this mean for India? It means acknowledging that India's claims to a significant leadership role in the world of the twenty-first century lie in the aspects and products of Indian society and culture that the world finds attractive. These assets may not directly persuade others to support India, but they go a long way towards enhancing India's intangible standing in the world's eyes.

The roots of India's soft power run deep. India's is a civilization that, over millennia, has offered refuge and, more important, religious and cultural freedom to Jews, Parsis, several varieties of Christians, and Muslims. Jews came to the south-western Indian coast centuries before Christ, with the destruction by the Babylonians of their First Temple, and they knew no persecution on Indian soil until the Portuguese arrived in the sixteenth century to inflict it. Christianity arrived on Indian soil with St Thomas the Apostle ('Doubting Thomas'), who came to the Malabar coast sometime before 52 CE and was welcomed on shore, or so oral legend has it, by a flute-playing Jewish girl. He made many converts, so there are Indians today whose ancestors were Christian well before any Europeans discovered Christianity. In Kerala, where Islam came through traders, travellers and missionaries rather than by the sword, and which boasts the oldest mosque, church and synagogue on the subcontinent, the Zamorin of Calicut was so impressed by the seafaring skills of this community that he issued a decree obliging each fisherman's family to bring up one son as a Muslim to man his all-Muslim navy! The India where the wail of the Muslim muezzin routinely blends with the chant of mantras at the Hindu temple, and where the tinkling of church bells accompanies the Sikh gurdwara's reading of verses from the Guru Granth Sahib, is an India that fully embraces the world. Indeed the British historian E.P. Thompson wrote that this heritage of diversity is what makes India 'perhaps the most important country for the future of the world. All the convergent influences of the world run through this society. . . . There is not a thought that is being thought in the West or East that is not active in some Indian mind.'

That Indian mind has been shaped by remarkably diverse forces: ancient Hindu tradition, myth and scripture; the impact of Islam and Christianity; and two centuries of British colonial rule. The result is unique. Though there are some who think and speak of India as a Hindu country, Indian civilization today is an evolved hybrid. We cannot speak of Indian culture today without qawwali, the poetry of Ghalib, or for that matter the game of cricket, our de facto national sport. When an Indian dons 'national dress' for a formal event, he wears a variant of the sherwani, which did not exist before the Muslim invasions of India. When Indian Hindus voted a few years ago in a cynical and contrived competition to select the 'new seven wonders' of the modern world, they voted for the Taj Mahal constructed by a Mughal king, not for Angkor Wat, the most magnificent architectural product of their religion. In the breadth (and not just the depth) of its cultural heritage lies some of India's soft power.

One of the few generalizations that can safely be made about India is that nothing can be taken for granted about the country. Not even its name: for the word India comes from the river Indus, which flows in Pakistan. (That anomaly is easily explained, of course, since what is today Pakistan was hacked off the stooped shoulders of India by the departing British in 1947.) Indian nationalism is therefore a rare phenomenon indeed. It is not based on language (since our Constitution recognizes twenty-three and there are thirty-five, according to the ethnolinguists, that are spoken by more than a million people each—not to mention 22,000 distinct dialects). It is not based on geography (the 'natural' geography of the subcontinent—framed by the mountains and the sea—has been hacked by the Partition of 1947). It is not based on ethnicity (the 'Indian' accommodates a diversity of racial types, and many Indians have more in common ethnically with foreigners than with other Indians: Indian Punjabis and Bengalis, for instance, are ethnically kin to Pakistanis and Bangladeshis, respectively, with whom they have more in common than with Poonawalas or Bangaloreans). And it is not based on religion (we are home to every faith known to mankind, with the possible exception of Shintoism, and Hinduism—a faith without a national organization, no established church or ecclesiastical hierarchy, no Hindu Pope, no Hindu Mecca, no single sacred book, no uniform beliefs or modes of worship, not even a Hindu Sunday—exemplifies as much our diversity as it does our common cultural heritage). Indian nationalism is the nationalism of an idea, the idea of an ever-ever land—emerging from an ancient civilization, united by a shared history, sustained by pluralist democracy. Pluralism is a reality that emerges from the very nature of the country; it is a choice made inevitable by India's geography and reaffirmed by its history.

We are a land of rich diversities: I have observed in the past that we are all minorities in India. This land imposes no narrow conformities on its citizens: you can be many things and one thing. You can be a good Muslim, a good Keralite and a good Indian all at once. So the idea of

India is of one land embracing many. It is the idea that a nation may endure differences of caste, creed, colour, culture, cuisine, conviction, costume and custom, and still rally around a democratic consensus. That consensus is around the simple principle that in a democracy you don't really need to agree—except on the ground rules of how you will disagree. Part of the reason for India's being respected in the world is that it has survived all the stresses and strains that have beset it, and that led so many to predict its imminent disintegration, by maintaining consensus on how to manage without consensus.

The world of the twenty-first century will increasingly be a world in which the use of hard power carries with it the odium of mass global public disapproval, whereas the blossoming of soft power, which lends itself more easily to the information era, will constitute a country's principal asset. Soft power is not about conquering others, but about being yourself. Increasingly, countries are judged by the soft-power elements they project on to the global consciousness, either deliberately (through the export of cultural products, the cultivation of foreign publics or even international propaganda) or unwittingly (through the ways in which they are perceived as a result of news stories about them in the global mass media).

India produces various kinds of culture, notably including the films of Bollywood, now reaching ever wider international audiences. The triumph of *Slumdog Millionaire* at the 2009 Oscars both reflects and reinforces this trend. Bollywood is bringing its brand of glitzy entertainment not just to the Indian diaspora in the United States or the United Kingdom but around the globe, to the screens of Syrians and Senegalese. I have lost count of the number of senior African officials, ministers and even heads of state who have mentioned to me their pleasure at growing up watching Indian films in their childhood. A Senegalese friend told me of his illiterate mother who takes a bus to Dakar every month to watch a Bollywood film—she doesn't understand the Hindi dialogue and can't read the French subtitles, but these films are made to be understood despite such handicaps; she can still catch their spirit and understand the stories, and people like her look at India with stars in their eyes as a result. When I met the owner of the principal cinema theatres in Oman, he told me that he showed mainly Bollywood films. When I assumed that meant that he catered to an expatriate Indian clientele, he corrected me: 90 per cent of his customers, Bollywood fans to a man, were Omanis.

So Arabs and Africans are swayed by films made for Allahabadis and Agrawalas. Indian art, classical music and dance have a similar effect. So does the work of Indian fashion designers, now striding across the world's catwalks. Indian cuisine, spreading around the world, raises our culture higher in people's reckoning; as the French have long known, the way to foreigners' hearts is through their palates. The proliferation of Indian restaurants around the world has been little short of astonishing. When I was invited, as a United Nations peacekeeping official, to testify before the German Constitutional Court in the modest town of Karlsruhe in 1994, I wondered what, as a vegetarian, I would do for a meal in a small Mitteleuropean town that was far from being a cosmopolis. The German Foreign Office, satisfied with the day's proceedings, duly invited me to a slap-up meal in Karlsruhe—at an Indian restaurant! A few years later, exploring Victorian wine-country in Australia, I drove through a tiny settlement in the countryside famous for two wine-tasting establishments; the only restaurant on its single main street was an Indian one. Indian restaurants have clearly become to the world what Chinese laundries were in the United States at the turn of the previous century. In England today, Indian curry houses employ more people than the iron and steel, coal and shipbuilding industries combined. (So the Empire can strike back.)

Globalization has both sparked and allayed many Indians' fears that economic liberalization will bring with it cultural imperialism of a particularly insidious kind—that *Baywatch* and burgers will supplant Bharatanatyam and bhelpuri. Instead, India's recent experience with Western consumer products demonstrates that we can drink Coca-Cola without becoming coca-colonized. Indians will not become any less Indian if, in Mahatma Gandhi's metaphor, we open the doors and windows of our country and let foreign winds blow through our house—because Indians are strong enough not to be blown off their feet by these winds. Our popular culture has proved resilient enough to compete successfully with MTV and McDonald's. Besides, the strength of 'Indianness' lies in its ability to absorb foreign influences and to transform them—by a peculiarly Indian alchemy—into something that belongs naturally on the soil of India.

Indeed, from the export of Bollywood to bhangra dances, India has demonstrated that it is a player in globalization, not merely a subject of it. India benefits from the future and the past—from the international appeal of its traditional practices (from Ayurveda to yoga, both accelerating in popularity across the globe) and the transformed image of the country created by its thriving diaspora. Information technology has made its own contribution to India's soft power. When Americans in Silicon Valley speak of the IITs with the same reverence they used to accord to MIT, and the Indianness of engineers and software developers is taken as synonymous with mathematical and scientific excellence, it is India that gains in respect. Sometimes this has unintended consequences. I met an Indian the other day, a history major like me, who told me of transiting through Schiphol airport in Amsterdam and being accosted by an anxious European crying out, 'You're Indian! You're Indian! Can you help me fix my laptop?' The old stereotype of Indians was that of snake-charmers and fakirs lying on beds of nails; now it is that every Indian must be a software guru or a computer geek.

In the information age, Joseph Nye has argued, it is often the side which has the better story that wins. India must remain the 'land of the better story'. As a society with a free press and a thriving mass media, with a people whose creative energies are daily encouraged to express themselves in a variety of appealing ways, India has an extraordinary ability to tell stories that are more persuasive and attractive than those of its rivals. This is not about propaganda; indeed, it will not work if it is directed from above, least of all by government. But its impact, though intangible, can be huge.

To take one example: Afghanistan is clearly a crucial country for India's national security, as it is for the United States'. President Obama has spoken of reinforcing American and NATO military capacity there. But the most interesting asset for India in Afghanistan doesn't come out of a military mission: it doesn't have one. It comes, instead, from one simple fact: till a couple of years ago, you simply couldn't try to telephone an Afghan at eight-thirty in the evening. Why? Because that was when the Indian TV soap opera *Kyunki Saas Bhi Kabhi Bahu Thi*, dubbed into Dari, was telecast on Tolo TV, and no one wished to miss it. It was reportedly the most popular television show in Afghan history (at least until the onset of *Afghan Idol* in 2009), considered directly responsible for a spike in the sale of generator sets and even for absences from religious functions which clash with its broadcast times. (This has provoked visceral opposition to the show from the mullahs, who clamoured for it to be shut down.) But until the series ended in 2010, *Saas* so thoroughly captured the public imagination in Afghanistan that, in this deeply conservative Islamic country where family problems are usually hidden behind the veil, it was an Indian TV show that had come to dominate society's discussion of family issues. I have read reports of wedding banquets being interrupted so that the guests could huddle around the television for half an hour, and even of an increase in crime at 8.30 p.m. because watchmen are sneaking a look at the TV rather than minding the store. One Reuters dispatch in 2008 recounted how robbers in Mazar-i-Sharif stripped a vehicle of its wheels and mirrors during the telecast time and wrote on the car, in an allusion to the show's heroine, 'Tulsi Zindabad' (long live Tulsi). That's soft power, and India does not have to thank the government or charge the taxpayer for its exercise. Instead, Indians, too, can simply say, 'Tulsi Zindabad.'

Of course, official government policy can also play a role. Pavan Varma, a former head of the Indian Council for Cultural Relations, has argued that 'culturally India is a superpower' and that cultural diplomacy must be pursued for political ends. So India is highly visible at cultural shows around the world, and the ICCR is rather good at organizing Festivals of India in assorted foreign cities. That's good, but I'm not a fan of propaganda, which most people tend to see for what it is. I believe the message that really gets through is that of who we are, not what we want to show.

For soft power is not just what we can deliberately and consciously exhibit or put on display; it is rather how others see what we are, whether or not we are trying to show it to the world. To take a totally different example: politically, the sight in May 2004—after the world's largest exercise in democratic franchise (but then every Indian election is the world's largest exercise in democratic franchise!)—of a leader of Roman Catholic background (Sonia Gandhi) making way for a Sikh (Manmohan

Singh) to be sworn in as prime minister by a Muslim (President Abdul Kalam), in a country 81 per cent Hindu, caught the world's imagination and won its admiration. (This is not a Congress MP's insight: I was travelling in the Gulf on behalf of the United Nations at the time, and the reactions of my Arab interlocutors to what had happened in India could not have been more gratifying.)

So it is not just material accomplishments that enhance India's soft power. Even more important are the values and principles for which India stands. After all, Mahatma Gandhi won India its independence through the use of soft power—because non-violence and satyagraha were indeed classic uses of soft power before the term was even coined. Jawaharlal Nehru was also a skilled exponent of soft power: he developed a role for India in the world based entirely on its civilizational history and its moral standing, making India the voice of the oppressed and the marginalized against the big power hegemons of the day. This gave the country enormous standing and prestige across the world for some years, and strengthened our own self-respect as we stood, proud and independent, on the world stage. But the flaw in Nehru's approach was that his soft power was unrelated to a significant acquisition of hard power; as the humiliation of the military defeat by China in 1962 demonstrated, soft power has crippling limitations in national security terms. Instead of Theodore Roosevelt's maxim 'speak softly and carry a big stick', Nehru's India spoke loudly and carried a rather slender stick. But in a tough neighbourhood, the rhetoric of peace can only take you so far. Soft power becomes credible when there is hard power behind it; that is why the United States has been able to make so much of its soft power.

Recent Indian history offers a somewhat mixed picture when it comes to the effective use of hard power. The 1971 war with Pakistan, leading to the emergence of Bangladesh, remains the pre-eminent example, but there are few others—the eviction of the Portuguese from Goa in 1961, the annexation of Sikkim in 1975, the repelling of Pakistani intruders from the Kargil heights in 1999 and a swift paratroop intervention in the Maldives to reverse a coup against President Gayoom in 1996 providing rare instances of hard power success. Against these examples are the 1962 China war, the spectacular failures of the Indian Peace-Keeping Force in Sri Lanka in 1987 (which withdrew after incurring heavy casualties in an unplanned war with the Tamil insurgents), the hijacking of an Indian Airlines aircraft to Kandahar in 1999 resulting in the craven release of detained terrorists from Indian jails, the repeated 'bleeding' of the country through terrorist incidents planned and directed from Pakistan, and innumerable unprovoked incidents on the Bangladesh border involving Indian loss of life. India is often caught in a cleft stick on such matters: it often treads softly in its anxiety not to come across as a regional bully, and in so doing it emboldens those who are prepared to test it. As a result it has been noticeably reluctant to evolve a strategic doctrine based on hard power; there is a sense in which most Indians still think that would be unseemly.

This helps explain India's growing consciousness of its soft power. I do not argue that hard power will become irrelevant, merely that its limitations are apparent, whereas soft power lasts longer and has a wider, more self-reinforcing reach. For China and Russia, kung-fu movies or the Bolshoi Ballet will win more admirers internationally than the People's Liberation Army or Siberian oil reserves, even if in each case the latter is what the state relies on. But of course New Delhi knows that its soft power cannot solve its security challenges. After all, an Islamist terrorist who enjoys a Bollywood movie will still have no compunction about setting off a bomb in a Delhi market, and the United States has already learned that the perpetrators of 9/11 ate their last dinner at a McDonald's. To counter the terrorist threat there is no substitute for hard power. Hard power without soft power stirs up resentments and enmities; soft power without hard power is a confession of weakness. Yet hard power tends to work better domestically than internationally: an autocratic state is not concerned about having a 'better story' to tell its own people, but without one, it has little with which to purchase the goodwill of the rest of the world. Whether it is the Americans in Guantánamo, the Chinese in Tibet or the Russians in Georgia, it can in each case be said that a major military power won the hard power battle, and lost the soft power war. Where soft power works in security terms is in attracting enough goodwill from ordinary people to reduce the sources of support and succour that the terrorists enjoy, and without which they cannot function.

But this means that India also needs to solve its internal problems before it can play any role of leadership in the world. We must ensure that we do enough to keep our people healthy, well fed and secure not just from jihadi terrorism but from the daily terror of poverty, hunger and ill health. Progress is being made: India can take satisfaction from its success in carrying out three kinds of revolutions in feeding its people—the 'green revolution' in food grains, the 'white revolution' in milk production and, at least to some degree, a 'blue revolution' in the development of our fisheries. But the benefits of these revolutions have not yet reached the third of our population still living below the poverty line. We must ensure they do, or our soft power will ring hollow, at home and abroad.

At the same time, if India wants to be a source of attraction to others, it is not enough to attend to these basic needs. It must preserve the precious pluralism that is such a civilizational asset in our globalizing world. Our democracy, our thriving free media, our contentious civil society forums, our energetic human rights groups and the repeated spectacle of our remarkable general elections, all have made of India a rare example of the successful management of diversity in the developing world. It adds to India's soft power when its NGOs actively defend human rights, promote environmentalism, fight injustice. It is a vital asset that the Indian press is free, lively, irreverent, disdainful of sacred cows.

But every time there are reports of sectarian violence or a pogrom like the savagery in Gujarat in 2002, or a nativist attack like those by a fringe group in 2010 on women drinking at a pub in Mangalore, India suffers a huge setback to its soft power. Soft power will not come from a narrow or restricted version of Indianness, confined to the sectarian prejudices of some of the self-appointed guardians of Indian culture ('Bharatiya sanskriti'). It must instead proudly reflect the multi-religious identities of our people, our linguistic diversity, the myriad manifestations of our creative energies. India must maintain its true heritage in the eyes of the world.

And that will mean acknowledging that the central battle in contemporary Indian culture is that between those who, to borrow Walt Whitman's phrase, acknowledge that we are vast, we contain multitudes, and those who have presumptuously taken it upon themselves to define (in increasingly narrower terms) what is 'truly' Indian. Pluralist India must, by definition, tolerate plural expressions of its many identities.

To allow any self-appointed arbiters of Indian culture to impose their hypocrisy and double standards on the rest of us is to permit them to define Indianness down until it ceases to be Indian. To wield soft power, India must defend, assert and promote its culture of openness against the forces of intolerance and bigotry inside and outside the country.

It helps that India is anything but the unchanging land of timeless cliché. There is an extraordinary degree of change and ferment in our democracy. Dramatic transformations are taking place that amount to little short of an ongoing revolution—in politics, economics, society and culture. Both politics and caste relations have witnessed convulsive changes: who could have imagined, for 3000 years, that a woman from the 'untouchable' community of outcastes (now called 'Dalits') would rule India's largest state, Uttar Pradesh, as Kumari Mayawati did for five years with a secure majority? It's still true that in many parts of India, when you cast your vote, you vote your caste. But that too has brought about profound alterations in the country, as the lower castes have taken advantage of the ballot to seize electoral power.

These changes are little short of revolutionary. But the Indian revolution is a democratic one, sustained by a larger idea of India—an India that safeguards the common space available to each identity, an India that celebrates diversity. If America is a melting pot, then to me India is a thali, a selection of sumptuous dishes in different bowls. Each tastes different, and does not necessarily mix with the next, but they belong together on the same plate, and they complement each other in making the meal a satisfying repast. India's civilizational ethos has been an immeasurable asset for our country. It is essential that India does not allow the spectre of religious intolerance and political opportunism to undermine the soft power which is its greatest asset in the world of the twenty-first century. Maintain that, and true leadership in our globalizing world—the kind that has to do with principles, values and standards—will follow.

This will require the more systematic development of a soft power strategy than India currently has. So far, such strategic advantages as have accrued from India's soft power—goodwill for the country among African, Arab and Afghan publics, for instance—have been a largely unplanned by-product of the normal emanations of Indian culture. Such goodwill has not been systematically harnessed as a strategic asset by New Delhi. It is ironic that in and around the 2008 Olympics, authoritarian China showed a greater determination to use its hard power strengths to cultivate a soft power strategy for itself on the world stage. India will not need to try as hard, but it will need to do more than it currently does to leverage its natural soft power into a valuable instrument of its global strategy.

Some commentators have pointed to the irony that while communist China avers its allegiance to Confucius, democratic India comes across as wary of projecting its culture for fear that doing so might seem insufficiently secular. Foreign Indophiles—especially in the scholarly community—have no such qualms. A German writer settled in India since the 1980s, Maria Wirth, wrote in the *Garhwal Post* in late 2011 about her dismay at the Government of India's decision in 2005 to refuse to sponsor the World Sanskrit Conference in Bangkok, which had been initiated by Thailand's crown princess, a Sanskrit scholar. (In Wirth's recounting, once an expatriate Indian businessman had risen to the occasion and filled the sponsorship breach, an Indian government minister insisted on inaugurating the conference.)

'India has the deepest philosophy still expressed in a vibrant religion, a huge body of literature, amazing art, dance, music, sculpture, architecture, delicious cuisine and yet Indians are in denial mode and wake up only when foreigners treasure India,' wrote Wirth. 'They don't seem to know the value and, therefore, don't take pride in their tradition, unlike Westerners who take a lot of pride in theirs, even if there is little to be proud of.' (She ascribed this principally to the ignorance of Anglophone Indians and the inability of non-Anglophone ones to make their voices heard, though I know many English-educated Indians who are far more deeply steeped in an erudite appreciation of ancient Indian culture than many overtly chauvinist Hindi-speaking nativists. But that's another matter.)

The charge that India has been reticent about its cultural diplomacy and noticeably unenthusiastic about leveraging its soft power is, therefore, one that is convincing. Despite my reluctance to indulge in comparisons with China, Beijing's performance in this domain has been revealing. China devised the concept of Confucius Institutes only in 2004 but has already established 350 of them at universities across the world (with 260 more in the pipeline, awaiting Chinese government funding to follow suit). To these Confucius Institutes it has added 430 'classrooms' affiliated with secondary schools in 103 countries. According to Chinese education ministry figures, 7000 teachers are recruited every year from Chinese universities and sent abroad to impart Chinese language and cultural instruction for two-year stints. They have reached some 100 million foreigners who are currently, according to official Chinese estimates, learning Mandarin.

By contrast, Indian governmental backing for the development and dissemination of culture has been largely formalistic. The ICCR, established as far back as in 1950, has thirty-five centres abroad and is in the process of creating eight more around the world. It also supports ninety-five academic chairs for Indian studies in universities abroad, though at very modest levels that usually require supplementing by the host institution. For the rest, it sends out travelling troupes and runs festivals of Indian culture from time to time in foreign countries. The ICCR has done good work, but at a modest level of ambition, and it has appeared to its well-wishers to be in serious need of additional resources, both financial and creative, if it is to make a serious global impact.

It is, of course, true that China's extensive outreach is not matched by commensurate benefits in terms of goodwill because its culture is being projected by an authoritarian state that is known to impose considerable restrictions on freedom of expression. As Joseph Nye observed in the *New York Times*:

The 2008 Olympics were a success, but shortly afterwards, China's domestic crackdown in Tibet and Xinjiang, and on human rights activists, undercut its soft power gains. The Shanghai Expo was also a great success, but was followed by the jailing of the Nobel peace laureate Liu Xiaobo and the artist Ai Weiwei. And for all the efforts to turn Xinhua and China Central Television into competitors for CNN and the BBC, there is little international audience for brittle propaganda. What China seems not to appreciate is that using culture and narrative to create soft power is not easy when they are inconsistent with domestic realities.

My earlier observations about the limitations of government propaganda have been borne out by the Chinese experience. But India's failure to leverage its soft power lies in its inability to exploit its own democratic traditions of freedom. The ICCR could serve as a framework organization and a source of catalytic funding support for principally private-sector initiatives, buttressed by the reach and enthusiasm of non-resident Indians (NRIs), the 25-million-strong Indian diaspora. In my book *India: From Midnight to the Millennium* I suggested that the term NRI could equally stand for 'Not Really Indian' and 'Never Relinquished India'. The Not-Really-Indians are, for the most part, prone to an atavistic nostalgia that makes them yearn to rediscover their mother country, while the Never-Relinquished-Indians chronically seek to be of service to India, and are usually well heeled enough to make a difference. What is lacking is a policy to channel their enthusiasm, their commitment and their resources to the promotion of India's image and the showcasing of Indian culture. If India sought to do that, it would find both categories of NRIs to be 'Now-Required-Indians'.

It must be admitted, however, that in one major area of soft power failure, India has only itself to blame. If soft power is about making your country attractive to others, the Indian bureaucracy seems determined to do everything in its (not inconsiderable) power to achieve the opposite effect, in the way in which it treats foreigners wishing to travel to or reside in India. Visa processes, already time-consuming, unnecessarily demanding and expensive, have become far more cumbersome as a result of the government's reaction to 26/11. Travellers on tourist visas may now not return to India for a period of at least two months after a previous visit—a restriction designed, it would seem, to curb a future David Coleman Headley, whose frequent trips to India (interspersed with trips to Pakistan) were aimed at 'scoping out' or reconnoitring the venues for the 26/11 attacks. Aside from the fact that Headley travelled on a business, not a tourist, visa, the new policy has made victims of a wide range of legitimate travellers, from tourists planning to base themselves in India while making brief forays to neighbouring countries, to frequent visitors with personal or cultural interests in India. The initial application of the new visa regulation pointed to its obvious absurdity: a man who had been in India to attend to his gravely ailing mother was not allowed to re-enter to attend her funeral because two months had not elapsed since his previous visit; a couple who had left their bags at a Mumbai hotel to make an overnight visit to Sri Lanka were not allowed to come back even to collect their luggage; in another case, an NRI who had come to India to get engaged was not permitted to return for his own wedding! Such stories, recounted by the ambassadors of the nations whose passports were held by these victims, made me cringe with embarrassment, but their wide repetition around the world certainly did India's image a great deal of harm and therefore diminished its soft power.

If all this is bad enough, it is even worse when it comes to those who, like Headley, are of Pakistani descent or were born in that country. Visa regulations are already severely restrictive for Pakistani passport holders, but a similar level of scrutiny is now applied to other passport holders with a Pakistani connection. Not only is their wait interminable, but clearance in each case is required from India's home ministry, rather than at the discretion of the Indian embassy official dealing with the applicant (an obvious case of closing the stable door after the horse has bolted). When the visa is granted, onerous restrictions are placed on the holders of Pakistani passports, including regular reporting to police stations and limitations on the places where they can travel. A markedly sympathetic Pakistani journalist was denied a second visa to India because, while officially confined to New Delhi on her first visa, she had ventured into the adjoining township of Gurgaon (which for all practical purposes is a Delhi suburb)! The objective of 'winning friends and influencing people' is clearly not part of the ethos of India's visa bureaucracy.

Though some halting progress has been made by extending visa-on-arrival facilities to a handful of foreign nationalities, even these carry restrictions on the Indian airports where a visa-on-arrival can be availed of, so that tourists from the right countries arriving in the wrong airport can be (and have been) summarily sent home. The alienation and antagonism this generates among people who, for the most part, start off being generously well disposed to India is considerable, and entirely unnecessary. The same is true of the severe difficulties undergone by journalists and scholars wishing to write about India, whose visa issuance requires jumping several unreasonable hurdles (unreasonable, that is, for a democracy with a notoriously free press). Journalists and even academics deemed to be insufficiently friendly to India are often denied visas or required to produce so much documentation, or fulfil so many conditions, that they give up the effort. Some who have expressed criticisms of India in the past, whether or not these criticisms are well founded, are placed on a negative list and denied visas when they apply. Such practices are disgraceful in principle in a democracy; worse, since they are intended to avoid negative views about India appearing abroad, they ensure precisely what they are trying to prevent.

India's ability to promote and leverage its soft power in the world will receive a major boost only if and when the country's visa policy is thoroughly re-examined and, ideally, revised.

I must stress, of course, that hard power will continue to have its place in our world. Nonetheless, the world's respect will no longer be accorded merely to the strongest and richest countries. Those who tell the most persuasive stories—and those about whom the most positive stories are told—will fare better in the public's reckoning than those who win the wars. But it is essential to remember that the 'better story' is not merely the story that can be told; it is the story that is heard and seen (and repeated), whether or not one is trying to tell it.

In any case, the need to develop and exploit India's considerable soft power is clear. Pursuing a soft power strategy will mean we must spend smartly on improving our infrastructure and reforming our markets to attract outsiders materially, while developing support systems and adequate financing support for artistic products. It is essential to understand that focusing more on internal investment can lead to gains in the external diplomatic front. Within the MEA, the leveraging of soft power must be done by making its promotion integral to the work of the substantive territorial divisions, rather than leaving it solely to umbrella entities like ICCR and the public diplomacy division. This will mean taking Indian literature, culture, music and dance abroad as an adjunct to Indian diplomacy, and doing so within a context of a coherent public diplomacy strategy that weaves together many institutions that currently function separately. I have made this case extensively in my other writings and speeches. In bringing my arguments together in this book, I urge the development and implementation of a soft power strategy for India.

This is where public diplomacy comes in. I once asked a distinguished senior diplomat what lay behind all the hostility I heard expressed towards the Government of India in a particular foreign country: were we not getting our message across, didn't our critics understand what we were doing—was it ignorance or was it apathy? He replied: 'I don't know, and I don't care' (which rather explains the Indian government's earlier public diplomacy problem).

And yet we know that none of the government's goals can be met without the support of ordinary people around the world—the informed publics who sustain the political will of their governments. This is what makes public diplomacy necessary.

So what is public diplomacy? Our first challenge is definitional. I know that many communications experts in the West draw a distinction among the terms public diplomacy, public affairs and public relations. The United States is the country where these three terms first came into official use. Simply put, from a US government point of view, *public diplomacy* seeks to engage, inform and influence foreign publics in order to promote sympathy and goodwill for the United States and for American policies; *public affairs* seeks to encourage domestic public understanding and support of US government policies and activities; and *public relations* seeks to win the support of a target audience, domestic or foreign, for the work or objectives of a specific US organization or project. Though the Government of India does not use the term 'public affairs' at all, rarely admits to 'public relations' in its own dealings, and has only started speaking of 'public diplomacy' quite recently, the fact is that the government engages in public diplomacy, public affairs and public relations all at the same time, every day.

It is the responsibility of any government to seek to gain the support of people around the world, by reaching out to them through the media, NGOs, and other institutions of civil society as well as, where feasible, directly to the public. While the Wikileaks scandal has demonstrated anew the importance of private diplomacy—the transmission of confidential communications between governments—public diplomacy consists of what governments want the public to know and are prepared to say publicly. Ultimately, both public diplomacy and the more conventional kind have the same ultimate objective, which is to promote a country's national interests, including the well-being and security of the people in whose name the government concerned is acting.

Public diplomacy, of course, is neither as old as Grotius, nor as new as 9/11, though both have shaped its practice. The term was coined at my alma mater, the Fletcher School of Law and Diplomacy, in 1965, and it was during my time at Fletcher a decade later, in the mid-1970s, that I first came to study the subject at the Murrow Center for Public Diplomacy.

Unnamed, and then named, public diplomacy was a keystone of US Cold War foreign policy from the 1950s into the 1980s—when Voice of America, Radio Free Europe, Radio Marti, WorldNet TV and the United States Information Agency (USIA) were treated as important elements of Washington's strategic foreign policy mix. But before we hold the United States up as an exemplar of how to get public diplomacy right, it's also important to recall that with the success of the Solidarity Movement in Poland, and the collapse first of the Berlin Wall and then of the Soviet bloc, US government interest in public diplomacy slumped, and this was inevitably followed by a reduction in resources—and even the abolition of the USIA. It was only in the aftermath of 9/11, and the ongoing battle for hearts and minds in the Islamic world, that we again witnessed a sudden renewal of interest in public diplomacy in the United States. India may have been slower to wake up to the potential of public diplomacy, but in recent years, helmed by a visionary and skilled diplomat heading the MEA's public diplomacy division, Navdeep Suri, India has displayed a new willingness to seek to 'influence public attitudes to the formation and execution of foreign policy'—to use the Fletcher School's definition.

So public diplomacy is the framework of activities by which a government seeks to influence public attitudes with a view to ensuring that they become supportive of foreign policy and national interests. It differs from traditional diplomacy in that public diplomacy goes beyond governments and engages primarily with the general public. In India, at least the way the MEA uses the term, 'public diplomacy' embraces both external and domestic publics, that is what Americans would call 'public diplomacy' and 'public affairs'. I think this is fine, since it is clear that in today's world you cannot meaningfully confine your public diplomacy to foreign publics alone; in the current media environment, whatever message any government puts out is also instantly available to its domestic audience on the Internet.

Public diplomacy is not just about communicating your point of view or putting out propaganda. It is also about listening. It rests on the recognition that the public is entitled to be informed about what a government is doing in international affairs, and is also entitled to responsiveness from those in authority to their concerns on foreign policy. Successful public diplomacy involves an active engagement with the public in a manner that builds, over a period of time, a relationship of trust and credibility. Effective public diplomacy is sometimes overtly conducted by governments but sometimes seemingly without direct government involvement, presenting, for instance, many differing views of private individuals and organizations in addition to official government positions.

Public diplomacy should also recognize that, in our information-saturated world of today, the public also has access to information and insights from a wide and rapidly growing array of sources. This means that government information must be packaged and presented attractively and issued in a timely fashion if it is to stand up against competing streams of information, including from critics and rivals of the government. Your public diplomacy is no longer conducted in a vacuum; you are also up against the public diplomacy of other countries, sometimes on the very same issues.

This is all the more so in the era of the Internet. How does information reach people, particularly young people, today? In recent years, the emergence of Web 2.0 tools and social media sites like Facebook, Orkut, Twitter, YouTube and Flickr—to name just a few of the more popular ones—offer governments a new possibility not only to disseminate information efficiently through these channels but also to receive feedback and respond to concerns. Countries like the United States, United Kingdom and Canada consider Web 2.0 a boon for their public diplomacy and have been quick to embrace and deploy a wide array of Internet tools. They also proactively encourage their diplomats to blog, so that they can populate the discussion forums with sympathetic points of view. In doing so, they are acutely aware of the effectiveness with which terrorist groups like Al Qaeda and many other militant organizations have harnessed the full power of Web 2.0 tools to propagate *their* message.

I believe the MEA has begun to do well to rise to this challenge. The MEA is on Twitter and Facebook, though the extent to which transparency is encouraged remains quite limited. But the very fact that the public diplomacy division has gone beyond seminars in Delhi, and the production of coffee table books, documentaries, and the *India Perspectives* magazine, is welcome. In my brief stint as minister I used to argue that foreign policy is too important to be left to the MEA alone. The nation needs an informed and engaged citizenry to face up to the responsibilities of being a global player in the twenty-first century. This is why I applauded the valuable nationwide lecture series conducted by the public diplomacy division. Even better is the government's willingness, however tentative this may be, to start using Web 2.0 tools. A lively and candid presence on the Internet will have the impact of a force multiplier in terms of the efficacy of our outreach efforts, far in excess of the current reach of the relatively anodyne press releases and statements the government puts out every day.

India cannot be unaware of the global perspective. The role of social media websites—such as Facebook, Twitter, Google, YouTube and Skype—in the 2011 'Jasmine Revolutions' in Tunisia, Egypt and Libya, with ripples elsewhere in North Africa and the Middle East, has given new impetus to the discussion of social media on world politics. The eminent American journal *Foreign Affairs* recently debated the issue. One analyst, Clay Shirky, argued eloquently that 'these tools alter the dynamics of the public sphere. Where the state prevails, it is only reacting to citizens' ability to be more publicly vocal and to coordinate more rapidly and on a larger scale than before these tools existed.' On the other hand, the author Malcolm Gladwell responded that, for Shirky's 'argument to be anything close to persuasive, (he) has to convince readers that in the absence of social media, those uprisings would not have been possible'.

My own position is somewhere between them. Of course, uprisings can occur (and have occurred) without Twitter or even Google, but media always has an impact on the reach and spread of word about an uprising, and therefore has an impact on its intensity and sustainability. In this case, I would argue that satellite television—notably Al Jazeera and its imitators—as well as mobile phones and SMSes, had probably more of an impact on the unrest across these North African Arab countries than Facebook or Twitter. But impact is undeniable. As the American commentator Peter Osnos puts it:

> It is pointless to dispute that digital advances have played an enormous role in recent years in the speed of communications, and, in some situations, Egypt and Tunisia certainly among them, these technologies have played a meaningful part in the rallying of crowds and in garnering international recognition. A global generation of mainly young people will continue to refine and use the capacity to reach out to each other. Turmoil reflects the conditions of the era in which it occurs, and social media are very much a factor of our age.

This is why China has paid particular attention to censoring the Internet, employing 40,000 cyber police to monitor blogging sites, shutting down any sites that get out of line and banning Twitter. When a US-based Chinese-language site called for a Jasmine Revolution in China, the Great Firewall of China blocked all searches for the word 'Jasmine', even if you were merely looking for jasmine tea! Clearly, the authoritarians in Beijing are quite aware of the enormous potential of social media to disrupt even their politics.

The reach of social media has been facilitated by rapid technological developments as well. When we speak of social media we do not mean only media running on a desktop computer or a mainframe server. In a recent study, Nik Gowing of the BBC highlights how in a moment of major, unexpected crisis the institutions of power—whether political, governmental, military or corporate—face a new, acute vulnerability of both their influence and effectiveness thanks to new media technologies. In the twenty-first century, it is impossible to ignore the issue of the uncontrolled impact of instant news on the workings of society and more generally on the impact of new media technologies on political affairs. As Gowing points out:

> It was a chance video taken by a New York investment banker that dramatically swung public perceptions of police handling of the G20 protests. Those 41 seconds swiftly exposed apparently incomplete police explanations of how and why a particular protestor, Ian

Tomlinson, died. They alone forced a level of instant accountability from the police about their orders, behaviour and operation.

When US-led NATO warplanes bombed villages in Afghanistan's Azizabad village, US forces initially claimed only seven people died. NGOs said the bombing killed up to ninety. Only after mobile phone video emerged two weeks later did US commanders accept they had to re-examine evidence. In a reinvestigation, the United States had to revise the death toll up to fifty-five. As Gowing argues:

Such examples confirm how new information technologies and dynamics are together driving a wave of democratisation and accountability. It shifts and redefines the nature of power in such moments. It also creates a new policy vulnerability and brittleness for institutions, who then struggle even harder to maintain public confidence.

In India, as in much of the world, it is evident that most major institutions of power still do not appreciate the full scale and implications of the dramatic new real-time media trend and its profound impact on their credibility. Increasingly, a cheap camera or mobile phone that is easily portable in a pocket can undermine the credibility of a government despite the latter's massive human and financial resources. The new lightweight technologies available to almost anyone mean that they enjoy a new capacity for instant scrutiny and accountability that is way beyond the narrower, assumed power and influence of the traditional media. More people than ever access the videos on mobile phones; while most Indian cellphones are not yet video enabled, the trend is irresistibly moving in that direction. Today, about 300 million people a day watch videos on their mobile phones, four times the number of a year ago.

On any given day, people are sending 150 million Twitter messages, nearly a billion tweets every week. There are two ways to look at this: that it's symptomatic of information overload, or that it represents a huge audience of information generators and consumers that people in positions of public responsibility ignore at their peril. My own sympathies are very much towards the latter view.

The world is full of examples of what Gowing calls 'non-professional information doers': hundreds of millions of amateurs with an electronic eye who can now be found anywhere. As many as 4 billion people worldwide—including 84 per cent of Americans, more than 65 per cent of Chinese and perhaps 60 per cent of all Indians today—now use mobile phones worldwide. They all get messages out. And they do so more rapidly than the official mechanisms can. Their strength is that they enable people to issue and disseminate material, including raw footage and compellingly authentic images, before the mainstream media, or for that matter governments, can do so. Inevitably, this means they shed light where officialdom would prefer darkness, as China learned when video footage of a shootout involving Uighur separatists in 2008 made it to the world media despite Beijing's denials.

The core implications are striking. We have all heard about the so-called 24/7 news and information cycle, but with social media the pressure of the news cycle can build up not just over a few hours but often in no more than a few minutes. As images, facts and allegations emanating from cellphones and digital cameras go viral, they undermine and discredit official versions, present an alternative reality in the face of government denials and, fuelled by dissenters and expatriates, rebound on to the evolution of the situation itself. Twitter and digital cameras had a huge impact on the Iranian protests after the disputed re-election of President Mahmoud Ahmedinejad. Despite Tehran's attempts to manage the crisis, social media kept the protests alive for far longer, and with more prolonged intensity, than they could have survived without that digital fuel.

With such instant scrutiny, governmental power is rendered more vulnerable. In the old days, governments assumed they could command the information high ground in a crisis. That is simply no longer true.

It is fair to say that India has been slow to recognize the potential of social media in dealing with its own domestic challenges and opportunities. But the case for social media has been gaining ground. We are already one of the world's leading countries in the use of Twitter, and social media is bound to gain as the prospects for e-government improve by the day. Indeed, the first draft of the Electronic Delivery of Services Bill, 2011, has proposed that all ministries and government departments will have to deliver services electronically, whether through the Internet or mobile phones. So India is not just on the right track, but bids fair to become a model of e-governance in the developing world.

And yet the recent controversy over the government's alleged desire to censor Facebook, Twitter and other leading lights of the social media has obscured our progress in this area and also raised some genuine and urgent questions we need to address about free speech in our society—not to mention dented India's image as a bastion of freedom abroad, and so undermined our soft power in the eyes of the Internet community.

The problem arose when the *New York Times* reported that our telecom minister, Kapil Sibal, had called in senior social media executives from Facebook, Microsoft, Google and Yahoo and allegedly asked them to prescreen disparaging, inflammatory or defamatory user content from India 'and to remove it before it goes online'. Such a request inevitably sparked off a firestorm of Internet protest against the minister, without waiting to hear his side of the story. Facebook pages sprang up to denounce him; web-boards overflowed with nasty comments against the minister, the ruling party and the government, suggesting they were trying to protect a political leader; and the hashtag '#IdiotKapilSibal' started 'trending' on Twitter. All a bit over the top, a reflection of the gradual coarsening of public discourse thanks to the anonymity that the Internet provides (the very anonymity that protects activism in repressive dictatorships allows irresponsibility to thrive in democracies).

As a frequent recipient of 'disparaging, inflammatory or defamatory content' myself, I'm no great fan of unpleasantness on any media, social or otherwise, but I'm strongly opposed to censorship. Freedom of speech is fundamental to any democracy, and many of the most valuable developments in India would not have been possible without it. Freedom of speech is the mortar that binds the bricks of our democracy together, and it's also the open window embedded in those bricks. Free speech keeps our government accountable, and helps political leaders know what people are thinking. Censorship is a disservice to both rulers and ruled.

But—and free speech advocates hate that 'but'!—every society recognizes some sensible restraints on how free speech is exercised. Those restraints almost always relate to the collectivity; they arise when the freedom of the individual to say what he wants causes more harm to more people in society than restricting his freedom would. Justice

Oliver Wendell Holmes, in the United States, put it memorably when he said that freedom of speech does not extend to the right to shout 'Fire!' in a crowded theatre. (After all, that could cause a stampede, in which people could get trampled upon, injured and even killed, and the theatre's property destroyed—all consequences that outweigh the individual's right to say what he likes.)

Since societies vary in their cultural and political traditions, the boundaries vary from place to place. Free speech absolutists tend to say that freedom is a universal right that must not be abridged in the name of culture. But in practice such abridgement often takes place, if not by law then by convention. No American editor would allow the 'n' word to be used to describe Black Americans, not because it's against the law, but because it would cause such offence as to be unacceptable to use. Just as the commonplace practice of women taking off their bikini tops at St Tropez, Copacabana or Bondi Beach could not be replicated on the beaches of Goa, Dubai or Karachi without risking assault or arrest, so also things might be said in the former set of places that would not pass muster in the latter. It's no use pretending such differences (of culture, politics and sensitivity) don't exist. They do, and they're the reason why free speech in, say, Sweden isn't the same as free speech in Singapore, or even in Surat.

The problem is particularly acute on social media, because it's a public forum for the expression of private thoughts. The fact is that social media's biggest asset is also its biggest problem. Its strength is that social media enables ordinary people (not just trained journalists) to 'report' news and opinions before any other source, including governments or traditional media, can do so. Even more, any individual with the basic literacy needed to operate a keyboard can express his or her opinion, create information, whether video or text, and communicate it immediately, without the delays necessarily wrought by editorial controls, cross-checking or even the synthesizing that occurs in a 'mainstream' media newsroom.

That gives social media an advantage over regular media as a disseminator of public opinion. If you wanted to express your views in, say, a newspaper, you would have to write something well enough to pass editorial muster; your facts and opinions would be checked, vetted and challenged; your prose might be cut for space reasons (or mere editorial whim); and you might have to wait days, if not weeks, to see your words in print. None of that applies to social media. You can write all you want, as you want, in the words you want, on a blog or a Facebook page, put it up with a Twitter link, click a mouse and instantly watch it all go viral. It's a twenty-first-century freedom that no democratic political leader would wish to confront.

And yet this very freedom is its own biggest threat. It means anyone can say literally anything, and inevitably, many do. Lies, distortions and calumny go into cyberspace unchallenged; hatred, pornography and slander are routinely aired. There is no fact-checking, no institutional reputation for reliability to defend. The anonymity permitted by social media encourages even more irresponsibility: people hidden behind pseudonyms feel free to hurl abuses they would never dare to utter to the recipients' faces. The borderline between legitimate creative expression and 'disparaging, inflammatory or defamatory content' becomes more difficult to draw.

Minister Sibal's main concern, as he explained it to me, was not with politics, but with scurrilous material about certain religions that could have incited retaliatory violence by their adherents. People say or depict things on social media that might be bad enough in their living rooms, but are positively dangerous in a public space. The challenge of regulating social media is that the person writing or drawing such things does so in the privacy of his home but releases them into the global commons. My own yardstick is very clear: I reject censorship. Art, literature and political opinion are to me sacrosanct. But publishing or circulating inflammatory material to incite communal feelings is akin to dropping a lighted match at a petrol pump. No society can afford to tolerate it, and no responsible government of India would allow it. Personally, I'd rather stub out that match than close down the petrol pump.

But I'm far from sure that prosecuting Facebook or Google is the right way to go about it. After all, could you sue the phone companies for someone sending a defamatory or obscene SMS? The analogy to a newspaper is wrong—these social network sites are more like the postman carrying the newspaper to your door. You would prosecute the newspaper for publishing legally actionable material, but you would not prosecute the postal service. Our learned judges are now examining the matter but I hope they will take into account these realities of the Internet era. In the meantime, there is an urgent need for senior government officials to recognize the realities of the Internet age and the huge damage that can be done to India's soft power if, as a judge fatuously and irresponsibly remarked, India chooses to go the way of China.

———

I suppose I was the first government official in India who engaged with the general public online on Twitter, though in all fairness, BJP leader L.K. Advani's web page had already created a lot of buzz during the last elections. More and more politicians are online today, including Sushma Swaraj and Narendra Modi of the BJP, and Digvijay Singh, Anil Shastri, Naveen Jindal, Manish Tewari and Hamdullah Sayeed of the Congress, with politicians issuing their own bulletins and actually answering individual questions online. Sometimes this creates its own challenges: Sushma Swaraj has already blamed Twitter's 140-character limit for an imprecisely worded message about the prime minister that created political ripples within the BJP. Of course, there is the safety net that politicians can always type, delete and retype before pressing enter— but Ms Swaraj, by her own admission, dictates her Twitter messages, so perhaps that is more difficult for her.

Bureaucrats are following suit, with the best-known example probably being former Foreign Secretary Nirupama Rao, who opened and operated a Twitter account while still in office (a practice her successor has, alas, abandoned). She in turn may well have been inspired by the success of the MEA's public diplomacy division, whose officials, led by Navdeep Suri and with my active encouragement, have set up a Twitter page and have been pursuing social media strategies, including a Facebook page and a YouTube channel, to let people know about what the ministry and diplomatic missions do. This has enabled them to promote India's soft power (even within the country) by creating goodwill among social media users, whether in India or abroad. To me the MEA's initiative was excellent: it puts India on a par with the Western democracies which have already adopted social media sites as an instrument of outreach.

Of course, India must examine the advantages—and possible pitfalls— of using social media as a tool for diplomacy. The advantages are clear. India acquires a new, young, literate and global audience for our foreign policy initiatives and positions. By being accessible to Internet searchers, we earn goodwill. By providing accurate and timely information, we eliminate the risks of misrepresentation or distortion of our position.

The pitfalls of using social media are the ever-present risk that something said on a social network could itself be taken out of context or misused by our critics. Responses to questions are particularly vulnerable to being issued in haste and without the usual careful vetting that more formal statements undergo. The nature of the medium calls for speedy issuance of information and instant reaction, neither of which government processes are designed for. India was excoriated on the Internet for having failed to issue a reaction to bomb blasts in Mumbai's Jhaveri Bazaar in 2011 before the Pakistani foreign office did so, even though the tragedy had taken place on Indian soil. MEA officials were, however, unrepentant, pointing out that it is precisely because the events took place in India that New Delhi had a greater responsibility to measure its words.

Such challenges persist. Social media is a tool for disseminating a message, not one for making policy. When the policy is not ready, the message will inevitably lag. But the existence of social media should prompt the injection of a new urgency into the government's traditional ways of doing business.

Of course, the MEA is not alone in using social media to reach out to the public. The Delhi Police has a Facebook page, India Post helps people track parcels through Twitter, the Municipal Corporation of Delhi and the Pune city council provide information on garbage disposal, the Census authorities have an extensive Internet presence. For domestic ministries, the use of social media both provides useful public information (as the Twitter sites of the Delhi Police and the Indian Post Office attest) and adds to the sense of public accountability that is invaluable in a democracy.

The principal lesson of this experience is that it works, provided you are willing to make the effort required. And that means having a team in place to deal with all the questions, comments and complaints that come your way, because a non-responsive social media site could be seriously counter-productive. As the Indian blogger Mahima Kaul wrote, 'If you are not in it, you are out of it.' This young lady puts it well when she says that the Indian government 'will have to trust its people, and it will have to trust its own ability to respond to the people'.

There is no good reason why an IT powerhouse like India should not be in the forefront of public diplomacy efforts using twenty-first-century technologies and communications practices. Not to deploy social media tools effectively is to abdicate a channel of contact not only with the millions of young Indians who use Facebook, Twitter and Orkut, but also to the huge Indian diaspora that tends to have such an active presence on the Net on Indian issues and in turn wields a disproportionate influence on international perceptions of India. To place matters in perspective, Facebook alone currently has over 500 million subscribers, 50 per cent of whom access the site on any given day, and a unique ability to disseminate information virally among its system and beyond through its networks of friends, fans and those who share their information. The average Facebook user has 130 friends, and each of those has 130 more, and so on. When President Obama delivered his famous Africa address in Ghana, the state department deployed a full range of digital tools and some 250,000 Africans posed questions or made comments on the address—and most received responses from dedicated staff assigned to respond!

My own experience with Twitter has had its positive and negatives, but in my view the positives outweigh the negatives. It is an extraordinary interactive broadcast medium—an interactive Akashvani. With one message today, I can reach more than 1.3 million people, and that number keeps expanding every day. As I discovered during my time in government, I can also use it to put out information the mainstream media may not be interested in. My visit to Liberia, for example, was the first ministerial visit in thirty-eight years. It was ignored in India by the media, but through my updates and a couple of links I posted, India's Africa diplomacy got more widely known because of Twitter. A similar phenomenon occurred when I interrupted a tour of Latin America to travel to Haiti after its tragic earthquake in early 2010, becoming both the first Indian minister to set foot in that country ever and also one of the first foreign officials to express solidarity with the victims of that disaster. Once again, the Indian media's lack of interest in world affairs meant that the visit went unreported in India but for my Twitter updates from the spot.

I believe that during my ten months in government, I was able to use social media to demystify governance and sensitize people to the daily life of a minister. And after leaving office I have been able to expand my conversation with politically engaged people around the globe. Of course, I haven't shared any sensitive information from any political or government meetings on Twitter, but politicians all over the world are tweeting. President Obama has millions of 'followers' on Twitter and Hillary Clinton was tweeting eight to ten times a day when she was on an official visit to India. The UK government encourages frequent use of Twitter and even issues guidelines on effective tweeting. The former Australian prime minister Kevin Rudd and Canada's ex-leader of the Opposition Michael Ignatieff tweet regularly. A whole slew of foreign ministers—Rudd himself, Norway's Jonas Store, Bahrain's Khalid al-Khalifa (who did so, he declared, inspired by me) and many others—are regular tweeters.

In my view, a democratic politician should not resist a new communications medium. The name Twitter initially put me off, and has led people to suggest that it is not a suitable medium for a serious politician—the BJP's Venkaiah Naidu even presciently warned me that 'too much tweeting can lead to quitting'. But I suppose his colleagues have, like me, come to realize that Google and Yahoo were also silly names that are now household terms. I am convinced that a large number of politicians in twenty-first-century democracies—including India—will be tweeting within ten years from now. Those who are ahead of the curve are rarely appreciated.

Twitter is only a vehicle—the message is the issue, not the medium. I believe that the Government of India should understand that using social media brings into the government's ambit a large number of people who would otherwise be indifferent to India's diplomacy. We just need to take care to ensure that the message is not misunderstood, without becoming so anodyne as to not attract an audience. The idea has always been to inform and engage, rather than to merely issue press releases.

Social media is also critical for connecting the world's younger generation on a single platform, thus strengthening bonds between them across borders and cultures. Young people from different geographic and economic backgrounds can be brought together in a positive direction. Students who attended the India-Pakistan Youth Peace Conferences have started using digital media to stay connected and have even invited others from their campuses to join the conversations.

But there is a long way to go, and it would be idle to pretend there isn't resistance, both from traditionalists and on grounds of security risks. But we can be encouraged, perhaps, by the fact that the practice is spreading, and that governmental organizations have started to make full use of the possibilities offered by the new social media tools. They are receiving a positive response to such initiatives. Whatever traditionalists might say, the same logic does apply to India's external affairs. The government just needs to recognize that social media is here to stay, and we need to live with it. Quite simply, we will not be able to live without it.

———

So much for what public diplomacy is, why it is needed and how it can be deployed. The one issue that remains, though, is the substance of the message. A bad decision or a weak policy can rarely be salvaged by good public diplomacy alone. 'Incredible India!' is a great campaign for the department of tourism, but in public diplomacy what you need is Credible India. There is a need for a positive and forward-looking strategy that projects a vision of India in the world, that helps define and shape what is increasingly being called—in the new buzzword these days about our country—'Brand India'. It's an idea, says the subtitle of a recent book, whose time has come. There's already a foundation to Brand India, and the phrase trips lightly off the tongues of assorted pontificators.

But what is that idea? What, for that matter, is Brand India? A brand, the marketing gurus tell us, is a symbol embodying all the key information about a product or a service: it could be a name, a slogan, a logo, a graphic design. When the brand is mentioned, it carries with it a whole series of associations in the public mind, as well as expectations of how it will perform. The brand can be built up by skilful advertising, so that certain phrases or moods pop up the moment one thinks of the brand; but ultimately the only real guarantee of the brand's continued worth is the actual performance of the product or service it stands for. If the brand delivers what it promises, it becomes a great asset in itself. Properly managed, the brand can increase the perceived value of a product or service in the eyes of the consumer. Badly managed, a tarnished brand can undermine the product itself.

So can India be a brand? A country isn't a soft drink or a cigarette, but its very name can conjure up certain associations in the minds of others. This is why our first prime minister, Jawaharlal Nehru, insisted on retaining the name 'India' for the newly independent country, in the face of resistance from nativists who wanted it renamed 'Bharat'. 'India' had a number of associations in the eyes of the world: it was a fabled and exotic land, much sought after by travellers and traders for centuries, the 'jewel in the crown' of Her Britannic Majesty Victoria, whose proudest title was that of 'Empress of India'. Nehru wanted people to understand that the India he was leading was heir to that precious heritage. He wanted, in other words, to hold on to the brand.

For a while, it worked. India retained its exoticism, its bejewelled maharajas and caparisoned elephants cavorting before the fabled Taj Mahal, while simultaneously striding the world stage as a moral force for peace and justice in the vein of Mahatma Gandhi. But it couldn't last. As poverty and famine stalked the land, and the exotic images became replaced in the global media with pictures of suffering and despair, the brand became soiled. It stood, in many people's eyes, for a mendicant with a begging bowl, a hungry and skeletal child by his side. It was no longer a brand that could attract the world.

Today, the brand is changing again. As India transforms itself economically from a lumbering elephant to a bounding tiger, it needs a fresh brand image to keep up with the times. The government even set up, with the collaboration of the Confederation of Indian Industry, an India Brand Equity Foundation. They were tasked with coming up with a slogan that encapsulated the new brand in time for the World Economic Forum's 2006 session in Davos, where India was guest of honour. They did. 'India: Fastest-growing free market democracy' was emblazoned all over the Swiss resort. Brand India was born.

But though it's a great slogan, is it enough? Coca-Cola, for years, offered the 'pause that refreshes': it told you all that you needed to know about the product. Does 'fastest-growing free market democracy' do the same? India's rapid economic growth is worth drawing attention to, as is the fact that it's a free market (we want foreigners to invest, after all) and a democracy (that's what distinguishes us from that other place over there, which for years has grown faster than us). But isn't there more to us than that?

In fairness to the smart people who coined the phrase, the more attributes you try to get in, the clunkier and less memorable the phrase becomes. It's easier for smaller countries that aim for one-issue branding. Regions of ancient India enjoyed branding before the term was coined— the 'Spice Coast', for example, for the stretches of Kerala to which European and Arab traders came, looking for pepper and cloves; or the 'Silk Route' passing through manufacturing and trading centres of silk across northern India. Such terms highlight the importance of getting the basics right, so the brand encapsulates what you want to be your core appeal to outsiders. What do we want the world to think of when they hear the name 'India'? Clearly we'd prefer 'fastest-growing free market democracy' to replace the old images of despair and disrepair. But surely there are other elements we want to build into the brand: the exquisite natural beauty of much of our country, encapsulated in the 'Incredible India!' advertising campaign conducted by the tourism department; the glitz and glamour of Bollywood and Indian fashion and jewellery designs; the unparalleled diversity of our plural society, with people of every conceivable religious, linguistic and ethnic extraction living side by side in harmony; and the richness of our cultural heritage, to name just four obvious examples. Yet it would be impossible to fit all that into a poster, a banner or even a TV commercial. (And we'd still have left out a host of essentials, from Ayurveda to IT.)

The NDA government led by the BJP tried out a different kind of branding in the 2004 elections with the slogan 'India Shining'. The question that inevitably arose was: who was India shining for? Those who felt that the still-incomplete transformation of India had not brought lustre into their lives were quick to react adversely to the slogan. The NDA lost the election, and the slogan was quietly buried. Good advertising copy cannot make a brand by itself; it must speak to a reality that everyone recognizes.

The importance of Brand India lies in the fact that India's claims to a significant role in the world of the twenty-first century lie in the aspects and products of Indian society and culture that the world finds attractive.

As I have already argued, our strength lies in our soft power, which lends itself more easily to the information era. Soft power is not about conquering others, but about being yourself. A country's brand is judged by the soft power elements it projects on to the global consciousness, either deliberately (through the export of cultural products, the cultivation of foreign publics or even international propaganda) or unwittingly (through the ways in which it's perceived as a result of news stories in the global mass media). National brands, in other words, are not merely created by governments; they emerge from a variety of sources, conscious and unconscious, planned and unplanned. Branding isn't just what we can deliberately and consciously put on display; it's rather how others see what we are. With many of the examples I have provided earlier in this chapter, we weren't trying to impress the world, but the world said 'wow—that's India'. There's your branding.

As I have argued, in the information age, it's not the side with the bigger army, but the one with the better story, that wins. India must remain the 'land of the better story'. To be a source of attraction to others, it must preserve the democratic pluralism that is such a civilizational asset in our globalizing world. An India that is open, accessible, diverse and creative, and that succeeds at creating a more decent life for its citizens, is always more likely to remain a positive force in the eyes of the world than its less admirable neighbours.

I believe that the India that has entered its seventh decade as an independent country is one open to the contention of ideas and interests within it, unafraid of the prowess or the products of the outside world, wedded to the democratic pluralism that is India's greatest strength, and determined to liberate and fulfil the creative energies of its people. Such an India will tell stories the rest of the world wants to hear and is glad to repeat—and that will offer it an inestimable advantage in the global mass media of our information age. Today's India truly enjoys soft power, and that may well be the most valuable way in which it can offer leadership to the twenty-first-century world.

But one essential fact remains: what really matters is not the image but the reality. If we can make India a healthy and prosperous place for all Indians, the brand will be burnished all by itself. Then, and only then, might we even return to 'India Shining'.

Chapter Nine

'Eternal Affairs': The Domestic Underpinnings of Foreign Policy

Back in 1977, as a doctoral student aged twenty-one, I found myself prowling the corridors of the Ministry of External Affairs at South Block in New Delhi for the first time, researching the thesis that was to become my first book, *Reasons of State*. I was callow, curious and opinionated—a useful combination of attributes in one who hopes to break new ground in scholarship—and my analysis was, with hindsight, overly critical of the received wisdom about Indian foreign policy making. Thirty-two years later, I found myself, after an election victory, seated in South Block as a minister of state, with an insider's view of the issues I had written so boldly about. It was instructive to realize how much had changed, and how little.

In *Reasons of State*, a study of how foreign policy was made during Indira Gandhi's first stint as prime minister (1966–77), I was struck by the fact that while formal institutionalization existed in the Indian political system, official processes and decision-making channels were significantly modified in their operation to accentuate Mrs Gandhi's personal, and her advisers' informal, dominance over institutions. It did not help that in her stints in office, the logic of the parliamentary system was inverted in a way that has not been seen since: the concept of a prime minister as *primus inter pares* in a Cabinet, accountable to a political party and responsive to the demands of a parliamentary system, was not realized in actual practice, which instead concentrated powers in the executive along presidential lines. This is simply no longer true in Indian politics, but it prefigured a continuing tradition of wide leeway for the prime minister's office (PMO) in foreign policy making, which persists to this day.

Studying the domestic underpinnings of Indian foreign policy making, I found that public opinion hardly factored in it in those days: there was inadequate articulation of mass views on foreign policy, both urban and rural, underscored by the restricted nature of political communication, and such elite articulation as did take place was largely ineffective. The result was that public pressure on foreign policy—whether through the opinions of the general public, their votes in elections, the activities of interest groups, the arguments of the press, or the positions of intellectuals through or outside the media—failed to influence the creation of foreign policy, even though public opinion always had a major impact when it came to domestic policy formulation. Equally, the organized political Opposition in Parliament, even when it was in power in some of the states, had very little demonstrable impact on foreign policy making, despite paying voluble, if in several ways limited, attention to it. Policy-makers made policy with very little regard to the constraints of elite or mass public opinion. This is noticeably less true today, though again policy-makers have more freedom to disregard, or go beyond, public opinion on foreign policy issues than they do in the domestic arena.

Finally, the principal governmental instrument for the formulation and execution of policy—the MEA—struck me at the time as a flawed institution staffed by superbly qualified and able diplomats. I concluded in 1977 that problems of structure, coordination, personnel and planning in the ministry prevented the bureaucracy from developing the professional expertise and authority that could compensate for the failings of individual dominance by the prime minister in policy-making. That was an unduly critical judgement, which even at the time needed to be somewhat qualified. But three decades later, many of the weaknesses I had spotted in the ministry as a student came back to strike me as surprisingly still relevant.

Under Nehru, many observers had already discerned the marked influence of one individual's view of the world and its reaffirmation by an exclusive but largely powerless elite entrusted with its implementation. This trend continued, I had argued, under Mrs Indira Gandhi, leading to the inadequate development of institutions to organize and conduct foreign policy; the low salience of foreign policy concerns in public opinion; the weakness of popular political and legislative inputs; and the low correlation between foreign policy as conceived and articulated by decision-makers and national interests in security and geopolitical terms.

There is no doubt, of course, that in a democracy it made sense to pay attention to the domestic background, support structures and constraints within which foreign policy is made. Jawaharlal Nehru bequeathed to his successors a conception of a foreign policy as not the prime minister's or the Congress party's but the nation's, transforming opposition to its fundamentals into opposition to India's very independence. Nehru's brilliance at giving conceptual shape to that policy and expressing it in terms of the national zeitgeist rendered his own place at the peak of the foreign policy elite secure. But this also meant that foreign policy, unlike other arenas of action in the nascent Indian democratic polity, was not formulated by the same process of pluralistic bargaining and interest reconciliation that marked domestic politics in the same period. It became the preserve of a few men who elevated the national genius above the national interest and were rarely checked by popular pressure or public opposition. This chapter seeks to examine the contemporary reality, while anchoring itself firmly in this heritage.

———

All those years ago, while ferreting into the interstices of India's foreign policy making, I learned that recruits to India's diplomatic corps were given a picture of the 'ideal foreign minister' during their training lectures. I have no idea if that is still the case—and I thought it politic not to ask, given my own recent departure from the ministry—but the earlier conventional wisdom struck me as pretty sound. According to the 1977 lecture notes of a distinguished (and already then retired) ambassador, I.J. Bahadur Singh, it stated that the ideal foreign minister (and in those days it was assumed it had to be a 'he') must possess the following attributes:

(1) His position in the party and the Lok Sabha must be strong. (2) He must enjoy the confidence of the Prime Minister and his voice must carry weight within the Cabinet. (3) He must not be too immersed in

Party affairs to devote his full attention to his office. (4) He must be the kind of politician who can temper the professionals beneath him, by knowing enough about foreign policy to assess advice, by having a mind of his own and making his views clear to the bureaucracy and by being self-assured enough to delegate responsibility. (5) Finally, he must possess the temperament and stamina required for success in the world of diplomacy.

As with most ideals, such a picture bears little resemblance to the empirical reality during much of independent India's existence. While India's ministers of external affairs have almost always been senior figures in the ruling party, thereby fulfilling the first two requirements in the list, the remaining criteria have rarely been met. As a result, few foreign ministers can truly be said to have been in a position to challenge prime ministerial dominance of foreign policy making. While this was evidently true during Mrs Indira Gandhi's occupancy of the highest office, when the prime minister, as by far the strongest figure in the party and the government, brooked no challenge, it has been no less true under a succession of later prime ministers of considerably less political heft. Far too many foreign ministers were individuals whose seniority in the ruling party was their principal qualification for office, a quality not necessarily matched by an interest in, time for or expertise at the time-consuming mastery of international issues. As a result, many were seen as little more than relay systems for the views of their professional bureaucrats, reading out the speeches and talking points presented to them. In one or another respect, therefore, India's ministers of external affairs, with very few exceptions, never quite emerged as credible and autonomous sources of policy-making, let alone strategic thinking, in their own right, and in their failure to do so they vacated the policy-making arena to the prime minister.

When I first studied Indian foreign policy making, I discovered that a decade earlier, Mrs Gandhi had inherited a ministry of external affairs acknowledged in her predecessor's day to be in complete disarray. One typical critique of the ministry in the days of Prime Minister Lal Bahadur Shastri catalogued a long list of woes. The MEA was described as being in woeful shape: civil servants, the critique ran, had neither expertise nor courage, and proffered as advice what they thought the politicians wanted to hear. There was no coordination in policy-making, least of all in the MEA itself, where three Secretaries shared responsibility. The Indian Foreign Service (IFS) was short staffed and demoralized by the most sought-after diplomatic positions going to non-career appointees. The MEA's publicity division clashed with the information and broadcasting ministry, and foreign service recruits refused to speak to information service officers at several posts. The MEA itself was 'misorganized', with a cumbersome administration, an irrational division of labour and a dilatory decision-making mechanism. In general, it suffered from lack of consultation among those making policy and a lack of coordination among those implementing it.

To remedy these ills, Mrs Gandhi's predecessor, Prime Minister Lal Bahadur Shastri, appointed a committee on the foreign service, headed by a retired MEA secretary-general, N.R. Pillai, in June 1965. The Pillai committee was asked 'to review the structure and organisation of the Indian Foreign Service, with particular reference to recruitment, training and service conditions, and to consider any other matters conducive to the strengthening and efficient functioning of the service at headquarters and abroad, and to make recommendations to Government'. The committee circulated a comprehensive questionnaire, took oral depositions, and held seventy-seven meetings before submitting its report to the Indira Gandhi government in October 1966. It is startling how, more than forty-five years later, so many of its concerns and recommendations are still worth repeating in any discussion of the MEA's structure and functioning.

The Pillai report discerned four basic weaknesses in the Indian Foreign Service and the MEA. The diplomatic corps, then 300-strong, was not large enough and did not draw on wide professional experience; coordination within the MEA was poor; coordination with other ministries which dealt with foreign policy was almost non-existent; and, finally, professional training was limited and, where it existed, inadequate. (Every one of these conclusions could be repeated today.) Among other recommendations to redress these limitations, it urged increased recruitment and the selection of older professionals; the revival of the post of secretary-general, abolished by Shastri upon the appointment of a full-time foreign minister (Nehru had been his own foreign minister, a practice Shastri wisely eschewed), to facilitate coordination of policy and administration within the MEA and with other ministries; and better training facilities as well as increased specialization in the foreign office. The Pillai report also stressed the importance of the non-political aspects of diplomacy, calling particularly for greater economic and commercial expertise.

M.C. (Mohammed Currim) Chagla, who assumed the foreign ministry soon after the submission of the report, made every effort to consider its recommendations earnestly. He went over it every morning with his three Secretaries in an attempt to utilize its workable provisions. Those minor suggestions that could be implemented directly by the MEA were put into practice, but the prime minister and the Cabinet revealed a singular reluctance to act on the report's other recommendations. The Pillai report died of inattention even where (and this was not always the case) its suggestions constituted useful responses to a crying need. And yet, except perhaps in the area of training, which has seen modest improvement—with some mid-career opportunities available to Indian diplomats to improve their skills and international exposure—everything that Pillai said in 1966 remains oddly relevant in 2011.

———

The recruitment, training and orientation of the generalist bureaucracy called the Indian Foreign Service provide a useful indication of how foreign policy is made and executed. The quality of the diplomatic corps provides significant clues to its efficacy in meeting the goals of the system. In India, this is particularly relevant because the elite Indian bureaucracy originated in the pre-independence days and traced its expertise to the colonial vision. The consequent strains of adjustment to imperfect political direction, and the subjugation of the 'supremacy of administration' to the 'sovereignty of politics', has constituted the stuff of many a political developmentalist's view of India. Yet while the bureaucrats submitted themselves to political direction, they were also given the means for their own perpetuation. This went back to the days when the shaping of the post-independence foreign service was left almost entirely in the hands of pre-independence Indian Civil Service

(ICS) men—Sir Girija Shankar Bajpai, M.J. Desai, K.P.S. Menon, R.N. Bannerji, N. Pillai. The service they created made its mark on the nature, direction and style of Indian diplomacy.

The problems persisting from the earliest days are compounded by the crippling affliction of severe understaffing in the MEA. India is served by the smallest diplomatic corps of any major country, not just far smaller than the big powers but by comparison with most of the larger emerging countries. At just about 900 IFS officers to staff India's 120 missions and forty-nine consulates abroad, India has the fewest foreign service officers among the BRICS countries. (In addition, there are some 3000 stenographers, cyber experts and clerks in the IFS 'B' service that provides support staff to the MEA.) This compares poorly not just with the over 20,000 deployed by the United States, and the large diplomatic corps of the European powers—UK (6000), Germany (6550) and France (6250)—but also to Asia's largest foreign services, Japan (5500) and China (4200). The picture looks even more modest when compared to the 1200 diplomats in Brazil's foreign ministry. It is ironic that India—not just the world's most populous democracy but one of the world's largest bureaucracies—has a diplomatic corps roughly equal to tiny Singapore's 867. The size and human capacity of the IFS suffers by comparison with every one of its peers and key interlocutors. While this may partially be a tribute to the quality and the appetite for work of the 900 who staff the foreign service, it lays bare some obvious limitations. I remember the frustrations of the nineteen LAC ambassadors in New Delhi at the near-impossibility of getting an appointment with the sole joint secretary (assisted by one mid-ranking professional) who was responsible for all their countries. At a time when India is seen as stretching its global sinews, the frugal staffing patterns of its diplomatic service reveals a country punching well below its weight on the global stage.

A few examples will suffice. The joint secretary in charge of East Asia has to handle India's policies regarding China, Japan, the two Koreas, Mongolia, Taiwan, Tibetan refugees, and the disputed frontier with China, in addition to unexpected crises like those relating to India's response to the Japanese earthquake, tsunami and nuclear disaster. Inevitably China consumes most of his attention and relations with the other crucial countries within his bailiwick are neglected or assigned to one of the five junior officials working under him. Another joint secretary is responsible for India's relations with Pakistan, Afghanistan and Iran, while a colleague of equivalent rank handles Bangladesh, Sri Lanka, Myanmar and the Maldives, all countries of significant diplomatic sensitivity and security implications. One more joint secretary has been assigned the dozen countries of Southeast Asia, with Australia, New Zealand the Pacific thrown in! It is instructive that the US embassy in New Delhi, with a twenty-person political section, has more people following the MEA than the MEA has to deal with the US embassy—in its own country.

As the *Times of India*'s Indrani Bagchi pointedly wrote:

MEA's mandarins can be the smartest people alive, but it's impossible to expect them to ruminate on policy [and take] strategic initiatives, all the while fighting fires every day, several times a day, pushing files, answering parliament questions, receiving dignitaries, assisting the PM during summits, and then greeting returning Indians evacuated from the latest disaster zone in the world at 2 am in the morning before reporting for work at 9 am. And to then work out where India's global footprint should be a decade from now.

Another acute observer, David Malone, wrote that the MEA's

headquarters staff work punishing hours, not least preparing the visits of the many foreign dignitaries laying siege to Delhi in ever growing numbers as India's importance has expanded . . . India's overburdened Foreign Service is, on average, of very high quality, but because it is stretched so thin, its staff spends too much of its time conducting India's international relations through narrow diplomatic channels, managing ministerial and other visits, negotiating memoranda of understanding of no great significance, and by other means that reflect only a fraction of the rich reality of international relations today and of official Delhi's actual international interests.

The problem has not escaped the attention of the professionals. In 2008, Foreign Secretary Shivshankar Menon moved a Cabinet note proposing a doubling of his effective diplomatic strength. The government agreed to increase the cadre by 520 personnel (320 in the IFS category and 200 additional support staff), but the hierarchy-minded bureaucracy immediately stepped in to forestall any dramatic expansion which would have required, for instance, the infusion of external professional talent at all levels of the MEA by mid-career recruitment from the other services or even (perish the thought!) from the private sector. Instead of reaching beyond the government to people who could fill the gaps in the service—more French and Spanish speakers, for instance, or more professional journalists for public diplomacy positions—the implementation of the Cabinet decision was stretched out over ten years by simply increasing the annual intake into the IFS (including promotions from the clerical grades of the IFS 'B') by thirty-two a year. Even this has not materialized, since the MEA has not found thirty-two worthy candidates in each of the three years since the Cabinet approved Menon's proposal. Lateral entrants have not been encouraged; a circular to the other government departments soliciting candidacies have turned up few whom the MEA is excited about. The chronic understaffing is therefore likely to continue for more than another decade.

The Indian diplomatic corps has long enjoyed a justified reputation as among the world's best in individual talent and ability. It includes men and women of exceptional intellectual and personal distinction who have acquired formidable reputations in a variety of capitals. Indian diplomats over the years have won in print the admiration of Henry Kissinger, Strobe Talbott and other distinguished memoirists who have dealt with them professionally; several have distinguished themselves not only in India's service but in international organizations and conferences. The critique developed in these pages is not in any way meant to reflect on any member of this capable and widely respected corps. It seeks instead to examine institutional failings which are evident despite the quality of the individuals who operate within them.

The IFS is recruited by competitive examinations held by the Union Public Service Commission across the country, followed by a personality test. The diplomatic corps is selected from the same examinations from which emerge the domestic services, like the Indian Administrative Service (IAS), the Indian Police Service, the Indian Revenue Service, and so on. The examinations have always been firmly grounded in the generalist tradition, the only three compulsory subjects being an essay, general English and general knowledge. There are five additional papers, three out of twenty-four broad options (such as Indian history, chemistry, etc.) and two requiring slightly more advanced knowledge (British constitutional history was a popular example). The top cumulative scorers are invited to appear before an interview board which tested their knowledge, behaviour and presence of mind and the eventual selection sought to produce 'bright young men (or women) of 21 to 24 years, who have the requisite intellectual ability, breadth of mind and mental discipline' for diplomatic service. (The age limit has now been relaxed to twenty-eight.)

For decades the cream of the examination crop opted for the IFS: in the years after independence, when resources and foreign exchange scarcities made travel abroad a rare privilege, a job that took you abroad frequently was prized by the middle-class families whose sons (and sometimes daughters) took the civil service examinations. From the 1950s to the 1970s, it was customary for the foreign service to draw its entrants almost exclusively from the top ten finishers in the annual examinations. This has now changed dramatically. Not only has the far more powerful Indian Administrative Service supplanted the IFS as the service of choice, but even the more lucrative Indian Revenue Service—which places officers in the customs and tax administrations, where financial incentives are considerable—is preferred over the IFS by many applicants. As a result it is now common for the IFS to find itself selecting officers ranked below 250 in the examinations, something that had been unthinkable to the officers currently heading the MEA. (The decline in prestige of the foreign service has also been enabled by the relative ease of foreign travel, which has negated what used to be seen as the IFS's principal perquisite, and the widespread perception that diplomats neither wield as much clout nor have as many opportunities to salt away a retirement nest-egg as their domestic counterparts.) The further complication of this problem is that several civil service aspirants are thrust unwillingly into the MEA while their real ambition is to serve elsewhere—a far cry from the glory days but one that does not produce a dedicated and proud foreign service.

The recruits are then trained at the National Academy of Administration in Mussoorie, Uttarakhand, for three months, and then at the Foreign Service Institute (FSI) in New Delhi for about a year, attending courses on such subjects as the Indian Constitution, international law, international relations and diplomacy. The stint at FSI includes a month-long district attachment, visits to India's borders, a tour of the country ('Bharat Darshan', or literally 'seeing India'), a brief exposure to the working of an Indian mission abroad followed by a six-month-long MEA desk attachment. Then there is a final language-training stint of one or two years at a mission abroad. The total amounts to a three-year training period, less than half of which is related to the direct concerns of the professional on the job.

The IFS has at least managed to overcome its earlier deficiencies in language training. Indian universities had at best limited facilities in European languages, and even less in African, Asian and Middle Eastern ones. Formal linguistic training was poor by international standards; this has now improved, with greater emphasis on learning languages in the countries where they are spoken. Even the coursework IFS recruits underwent was mediocre in such subjects as area studies, for which the Indian academic infrastructure was inadequate, and far too focused on pablum like (in the bad old days) 'promoting Indo-Soviet friendship'. Opportunities for mid-career sabbaticals were limited to the occasional year in the United States or Britain, the two countries about which the average IFS officer was already well informed. These are still the favoured destinations for those who take the time to go and study abroad, but the choice is now wider.

Not every diplomat emerges from the training process well enough equipped in the 'soft skills' required in international diplomacy to function effectively, though their mastery of their assigned foreign language is now usually impressive. But then language training, too, is not always reflected in assignments: I have frequently come across Indian diplomats in non-Anglophone European capitals whose foreign language was Chinese, a series of ambassadors in Paris who could not speak French, and (as I pointed out in a Parliament question in 2011) not one of India's nine ambassadors stationed in the countries of the Gulf at that time spoke or had learned Arabic. Surely we can aim at a time when every national language is spoken by at least one Indian officer and an eventual time when every one of our missions is headed by an ambassador who knows the language, be it Khmer or Korean, Spanish or Swahili?

The effect of the foreign service's bureaucratic stranglehold on the MEA merits attention, particularly because the Pillai committee too recommended a broader-based recruitment process that would seek out professionals in various fields, between the ages of twenty-eight and thirty-five, for mid-career employment in the foreign service. The idea was to compensate for the lack of experience and the consequently more restricted vision of the standard process which recruited only twenty-one- to twenty-four-year-olds, who 'grew' in the MEA within the norms and confines of the foreign office bureaucracy. The Pillai report suggested that 15 to 20 per cent of the annual recruitment be set aside for older recruits 'to permit entry of persons with specialized knowledge of international relations and area studies, experience in management and administration and public relations'. The recommendation was never implemented and the thinking behind it continues to be strongly resisted by the entrenched bureaucracy. Ironically the need is even greater today than when Pillai did his work nearly half a century ago. In today's multilateral diplomacy, for instance, the MEA needs expertise that it cannot provide from its own ranks. For instance, climate change has become a hot-button diplomatic issue that needs to be discussed and negotiated in multilateral forums where other delegations rely on technical and scientific expertise that they find indispensable, but which the MEA eschews because it is unwilling to look beyond its own ranks (or those of its retired grandees). In an era when a certain level of specialization is considered essential by many foreign ministries, Indian diplomacy still abounds in talented generalists. Concomitantly, there is no threat to officialdom's established way of doing things.

That 'way' originated in the ICS under the British, when Indian officials functioned under the obligation of proving their worth to their white colleagues, and accordingly placed a premium on individual brilliance and success. The first generation of senior MEA officers, raised in this tradition, institutionalized the ego in bureaucratic procedure, undercutting rivals, sheltering behind seniority and seeking self-advancement as the principal priority in their careers. Under Nehru, these tendencies had received full play: he was less interested, as a critic noted, in institutionalizing a policy-making ministry than in creating a body to reflect his views. Originality in thought and action was thus at a discount. This was augmented by the political culture's emphasis on a 'non-political' bureaucracy primarily responsible for implementation of policies made elsewhere; deprived of ultimate authority, officials were largely content to concentrate on their own advancement. While some of this remains true of any bureaucracy, the increasing clout of the foreign service—as the repository of precedent, the storehouse of experience and the legatee of diplomatic practice—in relation to increasingly underprepared political masters, has improved matters considerably. In all fairness, it is essential to state that there are many efficient, achievement-oriented men and women of vision in the MEA—some of whom helped frame this analysis. But their impact was circumscribed by several of the attitudinal and institutional factors traced above.

These limitations on effective professional performance were underscored by other factors, notably inadequate specialization and training. The IFS recruits' initial three-year training included little of direct applicability in a diplomatic situation. Academic coursework was no substitute for professionalism, and a few months spent in those days in the Indian countryside did not compensate for poor grounding in foreign life and customs. Paradoxically there was greater need for IFS recruits to be exposed to Indian conditions in order to make them more representative of their nation than they were; but a few weeks in a village as visiting government officials were hardly enough. At the same time, the ersatz Westernization of the urban elite was no better preparation for international diplomacy than it was for rural uplift. But advocates of a year's training at a foreign institution (such as selected entrants received at the Fletcher School of Law and Diplomacy in the early 1950s) were defeated by the domestic bureaucrats, whose anxiety to maintain a par between the IAS and the IFS was matched by their desire to be involved as much as possible in India's external affairs. This too has finally changed, with stints at institutions abroad becoming much more widely available at various stages of a diplomat's career. But as one retired ambassador observed, 'Training at any level in the IFS means listening to a series of lectures. These vary in quality and usefulness. At no time is any training given for two of the most important functions expected of officers at every level: political and economic reporting and recording of conversations [or record of discussions (RODs), as this is known in MEA parlance].' The neglect of these basics has created a service that, at its junior levels, is woefully underprepared for the obligations of international diplomacy.

The training process has been strengthened with the establishment of the Foreign Service Institute, which provides some induction as well as mid-career training, but reports of its efficacy are mixed. Assignment to the FSI is not prized by the best of the MEA's professionals, who tend to regard a stint there as the equivalent of being sidelined, and this in turn has had a direct bearing on the way the fresh crop is tended. Although the FSI has acquired impressive new premises close to Jawaharlal Nehru University (JNU), the physical infrastructure has not been matched by faculty development or even by the development of a standardized and modern curriculum (much depends, one recent trainee told me, 'on the whims and fancies of the dean'). The FSI has no institutional or accreditation links with JNU or any other university and is yet to develop into a centre of excellence in its own right.

Mid-career training is still a blight on the MEA's performance. The IFS is the only service in India's bureaucracy which does not have an effective, well-structured mid-career training programme (or MCTP, which the department of personnel and training of the Government of India encourages all branches of the All India and Central Services to devise). While most services have well-organized training programmes spread over various phases of an official's career—which includes training in the relevant service institute and a foreign component—the MCTP for IFS officers is rather limited in scope and design. It is confined to two phases, the first of which (required to be completed for promotion from the rank of director to joint secretary) includes only answering some assignment questions and writing a monograph. (Given the years the average director must have spent on writing policy documents, Cabinet notes and *notes verbales*, this is hardly a training exercise, since the skills needed should have been acquired on the job anyway.) The second phase (required for promotion from joint secretary to additional secretary) includes a week's training in a management institute and one week at the FSI—negligible in comparison with global standards and hardly adequate to keep up with the worldwide revolution in the concepts and practices of foreign policy planning and implementation. IFS officers are also systematically denied exposure to how other diplomatic services and foreign policy establishments work, on the specious grounds that IFS officers do not need foreign exposure as they are in any case serving around the world. Despite the occasional authorized stint (often at the individual officer's own initiative) in a foreign institute's seminar or course, there is little world-class training imparted to the mid-career diplomatic professional. It is clear that the training programmes of IFS officers are not on a par with what other diplomatic services are providing and not even with what other domestic services are doing for their officers.

Moving to a different aspect of organizational culture, Indian diplomats have too often acquired a reputation for being more interested in the amenities than in tasks of their jobs. The scramble for the plum assignments continues to be facilitated by the classification of posts as 'hard' or 'soft', not in accordance with the political importance of the nation but on the basis of the facilities available. Postings continue to be dictated by the comfort or hardships endured in a previous assignment rather than by the skills and expertise of a diplomat for a particular region or task. The lobbying involved is often deleterious to morale; as retired ambassador T.P. Sreenivasan put it in 2009:

There are no established criteria for selection and the competition is most often unequal and unfair. A recent tendency is to blur the gradation of posts in relation to the grades to which officers belong. A grade I officer can be replaced by a grade III officer [rather than the post itself bearing the grade]. Promotions become irrelevant as both in terms of work and compensation, stations matter rather than grades.

The rot sets in much earlier. The mandarin-style approach to recruitment—which requires all entrants to come through one-size-fits-all civil services examination, the same one that produces generalist administrators, tax officials and police officers—has evident limitations. Since working abroad for the government has lost some of its allure, this is no longer the best way to find the most suitable diplomats; indeed, for many applicants the IFS is a third or even fourth preference among the career options available to those who do well in the exams. I feel strongly that a diplomat should not be someone who fell short of his or her 'real' goal of becoming an administrator, a customs official or a crime-busting sleuth. We need internationalist-minded young Indians who see the chance of serving the country abroad not only as a privilege, but as something indispensable to India's growth and prosperity. A separate foreign service exam is one possibility; another would be to recruit bright students, with an extrovert orientation, adaptability and curiosity about the world, directly from universities, and then train them in diplomatic skills before gauging their aptitude and confirming their appointments. Whatever is decided, the time for reform is desperately overdue—though little of the urgency required is visible in the corridors of South Block, once known, in the early 1960s, as the 'Ministry of *Eternal* Affairs'.

In my short stint as minister of state I nonetheless found much to admire in the MEA—many able, smart and overstretched staff, fine traditions of diplomatic practice, and in some cases a sense of the nobility of serving the nation on the world stage. But some matters were less admirable. Administrative procedure runs along lines that, except by Indian bureaucratic standards, were extraordinarily cumbersome. I still recall with fondness admixed with horror the many files that reached my desk, their contents still tied, literally, with the proverbial red tape that has become the symbol of Indian administration. Though the advent of email in the late 1990s permitted more direct and rapid written communication on routine matters than had previously been possible, the official files still rule the roost, and the stranglehold of antediluvian bureaucratic norms (and attitudes) generally hold sway throughout South Block, as they do throughout the Government of India. Yet my friends in the MEA assure me that bureaucratic efficiency is high in their ministry compared to other government departments, so I shall let that pass.

One important area of progress in the MEA is that bureaucratic rivalries do not affect the MEA's functioning as much as they were alleged to in the past. In the 1960s, the three co-equal Secretaries used to meet once a week to discuss policy problems, but in Shastri's time they were more concerned with one-upmanship than coordination. The Pillai report had found it essential to revive the post of the Secretary-General; the creation and strengthening of a foreign secretary position has worked well enough in this respect, with the 'FS' the unchallenged kingpin of the MEA bureaucracy, whose word is law whether in relation to transfers and postings, discipline or political judgement. At the official level there is clearly, at the head of the ministry, someone who not only helps devise and pursue an integrated policy across the board but also can speak with authority for the ministry as a whole.

But the MEA's problems of coordination went deeper than that, into fundamentals of both organization and attitude. The territorial divisions, for instance, were drawn up according to somewhat eccentric principles with little geopolitical logic, but sanctified over the decades by the level of interest in them on the part of the powers-that-be. Thus there were four territorial divisions dealing with India's neighbours, but only one for all of non-Arab Africa (subsequently divided into two, but without regard to the Anglophone–Francophone divide). The responsibility for promoting India's 'soft power' assets remains dispersed among different entities—the public diplomacy division, the external publicity division, the ICCR, the Indian Council on World Affairs, and so on—with no coordinating arrangements among them below the level of foreign minister! The post of special secretary for public diplomacy, a recent (and somewhat occasionally filled) creation, although often manned by very capable officers, is not being functionally utilized to achieve this coordination. The organizational dysfunctionality thus epitomized was compounded by bureaucratic inertia, rigid adherence to procedure and hierarchy (it is striking how Indian diplomats feel obliged to call everyone slightly senior to them 'sir', in a striking contrast with the collegiality of other foreign services) and an informal caste system that set the IFS officers apart from and above the IFS 'B', including the 'promotees' who had attained senior positions but were sneered at behind their backs by officers who had entered the elite service by examination. (Other things, however, have improved considerably over the years: gone are the days when Foreign Minister Chagla discovered that his Secretaries turned up at South Block each morning only at 10.30 a.m.—after their round of golf!)

The government's solution to the coordination problem in the 1960s was to create a coordination division with a director and a staff, to oversee the economic and political divisions in subjects that involved other ministries. This meant that frequently they had, in effect, to coordinate the work of their superiors, a task that scarcely ensured their success. De facto coordination now takes place at the level of the foreign secretary himself—an official with a span of control so impossibly large (including substantive responsibility for India's relations with all the major powers) that he would need to be Superman to do justice to all the tasks incumbent upon him. One outside observer, Daniel Markey of the Council of Foreign Relations in the United States, suggested that the position needed to be split in two, to have a political head of the service and an administrative one. But no senior Indian official is prepared to relinquish control over the promotions and postings that represent his ultimate control over the bureaucracy below, and the idea was given short shrift when it was floated.

To make matters worse, problems of internal coordination are multiplied externally, since from the very start the MEA, as the newest and least entrenched of the government's bureaucracies, faced stiff competition from the established ministries regarding their respective areas of jurisdiction. In the Indian gerontocratic tradition, the older ministries won the administrative battle; and in addition to being burdened with an irrational divisional structure, the MEA found that it had to look elsewhere for inputs into several vital areas of foreign policy. UNCTAD, the EU and similar organizations came within the bailiwick of the Ministry of Commerce, and Mrs Gandhi herself admitted to me that in her time commercial foreign policy generally originated there; however, the foreign minister would, she noted, 'be kept closely in touch'. (This is still the case in 2012.) In practice even that elementary courtesy was rarely adhered to, and in other instances even the intent did not exist. Matters relating to Indian businesses abroad, trade missions and agreements were the province of the Ministry of Commerce as well (or that of foreign trade, in the years when that designation existed), rather than a foreign trade division within the MEA. UNESCO, the ICCR (India's foremost arm for 'cultural diplomacy') and exchanges of scholars remained for years the business of the ministry of education, though in a 1970 reorganization the ICCR did pass into the MEA's hands. The ministry of food and agriculture decided upon India's participation in conferences regarding agriculture, relations with the Food and Agriculture Organization and foreign food agreements. The ministry of health and family planning dealt with WHO and medical training abroad. The ministry of labour determined India's participation in the International Labour Organization; the ministry of works and housing kept UNIDO to itself. The department of atomic energy determined technical aspects of nuclear policy and dealt with the International Atomic Energy Agency (IAEA). There were also the well-known involvements of the information and broadcasting ministry, whose information service officers once functioned virtually as a parallel diplomatic corps; the defence ministry, with its paramountcy on national security matters; and the finance ministry, which in addition to dealing exclusively with foreign investment, foreign aid and foreign exchange questions, controlled the budget of the MEA. Finally, foreign intelligence was first in the hands of the home ministry and then of the prime minister's secretariat (later, since 1977, redubbed 'PM's Office'), which undercut the already limited information resources of MEA officials by offering an alternative channel for analysis and judgement to the political decision-makers, bypassing their nominal superiors in the diplomatic system under whose cover the intelligence officers did their work.

This administrative heterogeneity not only made coordination a chimera; it undercut such internal MEA divisions as those relating to the UN, most of whose logical responsibilities were apportioned to a variety of other ministries. Even such matters as the selection of delegations was largely out of the MEA's hands. South Block effectively chose the delegation of India to the UN General Assembly, which was largely staffed on political considerations anyway. The hostility of various domestic bureaucracies towards enhancing the privileges of the diplomatic corps also undermined the MEA's effectiveness. For instance, foreign training was for many decades rendered virtually impossible by the opposition of IAS officers, who would largely be ineligible for it, and their tacit acquiescence in parliamentary demagoguery against such training for their IFS colleagues. (This has mercifully ceased to be the case.) Even postings abroad are not the sole privilege of the MEA.

The ambassadorship to the European Union in Brussels alternates between the IAS and the IFS, though diplomatic skills are essential in this multilateral assignment, and that to the World Trade Organization in Geneva remains the exclusive preserve of the commerce ministry. On the only occasion a prime minister (the NDA's Atal Bihari Vajpayee) appointed a competent IFS officer to be the Indian ambassador to the WTO, the powerful IAS lobby fired from the shoulders of the then commerce minister, Murasoli Maran, a coalition ally of the prime minister's, to get the appointment scuttled.

Though in that instance the prime minister came off second best, in general the increasing concentration of power in the hands of the prime minister, his or her advisers and the PMO could not but diminish the role of the MEA. As one veteran diplomat lamented:

> The centre of gravity, always a rather shifting entity in the Ministry of External Affairs, now seems to be capable of making frequent long weekend visits to other habitats. Nothing could be more deleterious to the operation of our foreign policy than that it should be devised and manipulated from outside the Foreign Office. The right course to adopt when a Foreign Office does not deliver the goods is not to order the goods from elsewhere, but to overhaul the Foreign Office.

No meaningful change could be attempted, however, since every prime minister has understandably chosen to dominate the foreign policy making process, a natural tendency exacerbated by the era of summitry in which we live. Prime ministers who are frequently in contact with heads of state and government across the world and are running into them every other month (and receiving phone calls from them every day) tend naturally to preserve the major foreign policy issues for themselves, leaving the foreign ministry to deal with the more mundane details. India, for the reasons described, is a classic example of this. In general, it remains true that the MEA is considered most useful in the implementation of policy rather than in its formulation, except on matters of low priority to the prime minister. Major decisions—such as India's decision in 2007 to break with precedent and vote against Iran on the board of governors of the IAEA, or that in 2012 to set a new precedent by voting against Sri

Lanka at the UN Human Rights Council—were taken in the PMO and not by the MEA.

The tragedy of 26/11 confirmed yet again how much we need greater coordination among the many programmes and players in government involved with security and other international issues, and how essential is the modernization of our domestic and international instruments to keep Indians safe. We will have to work harder in government, and with Indians from all walks of life—including business groups interested in foreign markets and in international investors—to ensure that we break down the 'narrow domestic walls' that Tagore wrote about and promote a coherent, visible Indian approach to the world, backed with sufficient resources to take action and to get our messages across clearly. This will help ensure that India remains influential on issues of concern in an increasingly competitive world.

Within this broad picture, there are a number of positives. The foreign service has become much better at the 'non-political' aspects of diplomacy, a welcome change from the days when pinstriped diplomats schooled in the niceties of political relations disdained economic issues as the preoccupation only of shopkeepers. Today IFS officers are made acutely conscious of the fact that promoting business opportunities and facilitating trade and investment are as much a part of their job as writing cables about the political insights gleaned from their last state banquet. The notion of an IFS officer as a travelling salesman for 'India Inc.' has gained ground to a degree that was literally inconceivable when I was a doctoral student.

Relations between the ministers and bureaucrats in the diplomatic service also appear to be generally satisfactory. All foreign ministers have conducted frequent consultations with their senior officials, though most have been seen as in thrall to them, except on the rare occasions, such as during the tenure as minister of K. Natwar Singh, a former IFS diplomat himself, who in addition to his political rank also benefited from the traditional habits of bureaucratic deference to his career seniority on the part of his officials. In general, however, the ministers appeared to prefer to leave matters in the hands of their Secretaries; while this betokens the kind of receptivity to the advice of the MEA professional that I called for in *Reasons of State*, it sometimes goes much further than is entirely healthy in a political democracy, with some foreign ministers seen as accepting bureaucratic judgements uncritically.

Receptivity to ideas from outside has also improved dramatically since my earlier study of the phenomenon. I believe foreign policy is much too important an issue to be left to the foreign ministry alone. Discussion of international relations should not be confined to the seminar rooms in Delhi, and that is why I was delighted, when I was minister, to lead a seminar on Indo-Arab relations in Kochi, another on 'Look East' in Shillong, and to lecture on 'why foreign policy matters' at Aligarh Muslim University. All Indians, even 2000 kilometres away from the nation's capital, have a vital stake in the development of our foreign policy. While progress has certainly been made since the days when, in *Reasons of State*, I had observed the MEA disregarding almost all opportunities to draw upon intellectual and academic resources available to it from outside the ministry, much more could usefully be done. I would welcome much greater and more spirited exchanges between MEA officials and academia, the corporate sector and civil society—in person, through regular meetings and even email—respecting confidentiality but not fighting shy of ideas or opinions that challenge entrenched mindsets.

One major contrast between the era I first studied and the one of today relates to the willingness of the government to entrust bureaucrats with politically sensitive assignments. All too frequently in the past, Mrs Gandhi used to bypass the MEA in sensitive diplomatic missions, as in 1971 when she used politicians and academics like D.P. Dhar in Moscow and 'JP' Narayan and Sisir Gupta on a global conscience-stirring crusade, while MEA officials remained in the dark on the unfolding of policy. It was, indeed, while Indira Gandhi was in sole charge of the MEA (during an interregnum between foreign ministers) that she denounced India's 'generalist' bureaucrats who, in the absence of authoritative government, had 'developed a mystique both of infallibility and of transferability of talent'. In recent years, the number of political appointees in key diplomatic assignments has dwindled, and the majority of them have in fact been retired diplomats, kept on after their retirement date on a contractual basis as 'political' appointees by prime ministers they had impressed in the course of their careers. Even special envoys—a designation used in the past to send politicians or eminent academics on diplomatic assignments to specific countries for particular purposes—are now overwhelmingly, if not exclusively, serving or retired diplomats. Even a purely political controversy such as the dispute in 2012 over a Norwegian court taking two Indian children away from their parents— the sort of problem that in the United States a Jesse Jackson might have flown in to resolve—saw a Secretary in the ministry being sent to Oslo as special envoy. The presumption of 'infallibility and of transferability of talent' seems to be back in full swing.

Other changes have cut both ways. Factors of both recruitment and size had, in the initial decades, rendered the IFS an elite cadre in a country where the top civil services still attracted many of the most promising minds in the country. But the foreign service's elitism went beyond merely intellectual or educational snobbery. A socio-economic study in the late 1960s found that IFS recruits spanned a very narrow social range, hailing almost exclusively from a very thin upper stratum of Indian society. The criteria for the selection to the IFS, stressing as they did fluency in English and social graces, placed a premium on the Westernized urban India, and almost half the IFS recruits were the children of civil servants. Though the tyranny of the Raj-era ICS—the subject of a memorable twenty-one-page deposition by Ambassador Dhamija before the Pillai committee—subsided with attrition, the IFS officers who rose to replace them acquired many of the same colonial-era attitudes to their profession, to the point where many Indian diplomats were described by a critic as 'foreign even to their own country's culture, history and problems'. For many years and all too frequently, it was the exceptional rather than the average diplomat who could relate to and speak for the Indians he claimed to represent.

This has changed dramatically with the democratization of recruitment and the IFS becoming a noticeably less elitist service, including in its ranks many entrants who do not speak English fluently at the time of recruitment, an unthinkable attribute till the 1980s. But whether these young people are also the best to represent India in a world where articulation in English is almost a basic qualification (and one that used to be taken for granted in Indian diplomats) is another matter. As former ambassador T.P. Sreenivasan observed, 'Of late, even proficiency in English is not insisted upon. When it was suggested that those who did not write their papers in English should not be considered for foreign service, some argued that it would be unconstitutional to be discriminatory! We will soon have diplomats without proficiency in English.' When political pressures for greater democratization and the use of the vernacular come up against the diplomatic case for Anglophone sophistication, there is little doubt in India that the former will prevail.

———

The MEA's financial resources are also far from commensurate with the globe-spanning tasks with which it is saddled. The ministry's revised budget for the year 2011–12 was ₹7836 crore ($1.56 billion), of which the amount actually budgeted for 'external affairs' (as opposed to administration, overseas aid, etc.) was ₹3814 crore (about $762.8 million, or 48.6 per cent of the budget). The rest was largely allocated to technical and economic cooperation with foreign countries. The cost of running India's embassies and overseas missions was ₹1464 crore ($292.8 million, or 18.6 per cent). The MEA's overall budget in 2012–13 was slated to go up to ₹9661 crore ($1.93 billion), but again most of the budgeted increase was earmarked for additional aid to Afghanistan, Bhutan and African countries. Not every year witnesses an increase: indeed, in 2005–06 and 2009–10, the MEA's actual expenditure patterns showed negative growth (−3.42 per cent and −5.12 per cent respectively). It is not unreasonable to conclude from these figures that the MEA does not dispose of adequate resources for the challenges of global diplomacy.

Early conceptions of Indian diplomacy had required that India's global presence be wide but inexpensive, a real challenge for a country whose diplomacy spread itself too thin and not too efficiently. Indian diplomats had long tried (with uneven success) to maintain standards of style and hospitality on limited resources while avoiding the appearance of either miserliness or vulgarity. Yet while on the one hand the India of the 1970s could not afford a direct system of communication between the MEA and the embassies, and had to rely on commercial telegrams (on which ambassadors were regularly advised to economize), it also permitted colossal waste in the allocations of such resources as it did not possess. For instance, in a perverse genuflection towards the former colonial masters, India House in London in the early 1980s was overstaffed (with nearly 400 employees), overpriced (it operated on a budget that amounted to a seventh of the total expenditure on all Indian embassies) and maladministered (security guards assigned from India were paid a pittance and not permitted to bring their families with them, while a 'medical adviser' earned twenty-five times as much even though, as a non-registered practitioner in Britain, he could not legally fill a prescription). Though the resources available to today's MEA have gone up considerably with the country's two decades of booming economic growth, such anomalies in the allocation of resources persist, despite India having had to open a slew of new embassies in the former Central Asian Republics of the Soviet Union, and needing considerably to augment its presence in Latin America and in Africa.

On a more positive note, however, the efforts of Indian diplomats are being actively augmented by the Indian private sector, which in recent years has demonstrated a considerable penchant for playing a diplomatic role. The major business associations, particularly the Confederation of Indian Industry and the Federation of Indian Chambers of Commerce and Industry, have been significant players at events such as the World Economic Forum in Davos or the annual meetings of the Aspen Institute. They have also conducted 'strategic dialogues' between titans of Indian industry and influential opinion-makers in countries like the United States, Japan and Singapore, and organized important trade delegations, such as a major group that made a breakthrough visit to Pakistan in 2012. The private sector has already convincingly demonstrated the capacity and the talent to serve as a 'force multiplier' for Indian diplomacy, particularly in its public diplomacy efforts and in national image building overseas.

Aside from tight budgets, another legitimate concern about the MEA's conduct of India's international affairs relates to India's inadequate foreign policy planning and research facilities. As far back as 1965, the reactive rather than anticipatory nature of Indian diplomacy had prompted the creation of the policy planning and review division of the MEA. The division, first headed by a joint secretary, reported to a policy planning and review committee, chaired by the foreign secretary. In theory the committee was to receive the division's recommendations and suggest, on their basis, guidelines and directives for future policy, but in practice the committee paid little attention to the division, which after submitting a few disregarded papers rapidly fell into desuetude. It was reactivated during the Bangladesh crisis, when it served as D.P. Dhar's base of operations and masked his great authority as the fulcrum of Prime Minister Indira Gandhi's Bangladesh policy; but once the war was over and Dhar moved on, the unit reverted to its earlier insignificance. It was revived again in 1974 under former ambassador G. Parthasarathy, whose eminence won him regular meetings with the prime minister and the foreign minister, and then collapsed again with Mrs Gandhi's defeat in the elections of 1977, never to be resurrected as a formidable force. The fundamental weaknesses in policy planning therefore remain; the ascendancies of Dhar and Parthasarathy were a function largely of their personal influence with the prime minister, rather than of enhanced institutionalization of a policy-planning process in the MEA. When I came to the ministry and found myself assigned overall supervision of the policy planning and research division, I was dismayed to find it was a backwater largely used to park officials for whom a more challenging assignment could not be identified. Perhaps the only tangible output of the division is the MEA's annual report, that too prepared by it on the basis of inputs from the other divisions of the MEA. The government's traditional 'political' interests and congenital disregard for strategic thought; MEA officials' limited access to widespread sources of information, their lack of time and opportunity for reading and the narrowness of their functional data base; the nature of the power structure and prime ministerial supremacy; and, above all, the bureaucratic imperatives in favour of immediate and evident results rather than long-term dividends, all militate against the creation of effective policy-planning structures.

Inevitably the MEA tends to place a greater premium on pragmatic ad-hocism than futuristic projections. The top policy-makers largely function on the basis of single-page assessments. Senior Indian policy planners and MEA officials tend to be a little defensive on the subject; several suggest that responsibility for policy planning should reside in the substantive territorial divisions, rather than be assigned to a separate entity with no particular expertise in the areas for which policy needed to be planned. It is not unreasonable to argue, as well, that policy planning is never missed in most governments until a crisis erupts and people start frantically seeking a plan. Inevitably, though, the substantive divisions are too busy with the immediate preoccupations of their daily in-boxes to have time for the luxury of long-term thinking. The result is that hardly anyone in the MEA is able to create policy plans that are anything but extrapolations from past policy.

Ashley Tellis, too, has lamented India's failure to develop state institutions that 'enable the development of rational-purposive strategies and the mechanisms for undertaking the appropriate implementing actions'. Shorn of academic jargon, his argument echoes my own. The conspicuous shortcomings of our policy-planning and national security decision-making institutions, the absence of reform in our defence establishment, and the limited size (and therefore capacity) of the foreign service have unavoidably, in Tellis's words, 'undermined India's ability to make the choices that advance its own interests'. It has also, he argues somewhat more contentiously, 'left the country unable to respond to various American (and other international) overtures of cooperation'. David Malone makes the same point: 'India's foreign policy has tended to be reactive and formulated incrementally, case-by-case, rather than through high-minded in-depth policy frameworks.'

Our conclusion is clear. India has evident, and significant, global responsibilities: these require it to review and reform the capacity, structure, functioning and reach of its foreign policy apparatus and its national security establishment. The challenge of engaging credibly with the global community is no trifling matter. It involves dealing with the wide range of issues involved in conducting relations with the rest of the world from the position of a serious, indeed major, power: political and strategic issues, economic and trade-related questions, cultural exchanges and public diplomacy. And it requires a country like India to be staffed and equipped to take initiatives, not merely react to world events. The MEA has to bear the brunt of the blame when Indian foreign policy is criticized in Parliament and abroad for lacking vision and failing to develop a unified strategy for India's role in the world.

Numbers are an essential part of the reforms needed. It is absurd that in South Block only five officers (some very junior) are assigned to cover all of the Americas, or that the number of Indian diplomats at our embassy in Washington has not changed since the days of our estrangement from Cold War America, or indeed that India has more diplomats posted in West European capitals than in East Asian ones. This situation, replicated ad infinitum across the geopolitical map, has prompted analysts like Daniel Markey to suggest that India lacks the institutional structures to even become, let alone conduct itself as, a global power.

In his landmark 2009 paper, 'Developing India's Foreign Policy "Software"', Markey outlined what he saw as 'significant shortcomings in India's foreign policy institutions that undermine the country's capacity for ambitious and effective international action'. These accord largely with the ones I had identified three decades earlier, in *Reasons of State*. They include the modest size of the IFS, its inadequate selection process, stunted mid-career training and reluctance to avail of external expertise; the absence of compensatory 'high-quality, policy-relevant scholarship' by India's few, under-resourced foreign policy–oriented think tanks; the very modest output of our 'poorly funded, highly regulated' universities, which have few worthwhile international relations programmes (on which more later); and the inadequacy of our media and private-sector companies in promoting foreign policy issues. He went on to propose 'steps that both New Delhi and Washington should take, assuming they aim to promote India's rise as a great power'. These include: expanding, reforming, paying for and training the IFS to attract and retain high-calibre officers who could make a real difference to India's engagement with the world; bringing external recruits into the MEA; encouraging world-class international studies in Indian universities; and building capacity for foreign policy research and policy advocacy in India's think tanks. No reasonable person would dissent from any of these prescriptions.

Markey is undoubtedly correct that the intellectual and institutional infrastructure for foreign policy making in India is still—three and a half decades after I first formulated the case in *Reasons of State*— 'underdeveloped, in decay, or chronically short of resources'. Unusually for a foreigner, Markey comments on the IFS itself, painting a portrait, in the words of former foreign secretary Salman Haidar, 'of a service wrapped up in its own ways, insufficiently responsive to change and mired in outdated methods'. Markey notes practices like the almost automatic promotion system, which involves no weeding out of dead wood before people become senior enough to do real damage; and the extent to which senior policy-makers are bogged down by daily operational responsibilities. His observations on the administrative shortcomings of the MEA prompted a former ambassador to wax indignant about the skewed careers of the 'blue-eyed boys' with which the MEA is said to be replete: 'Those who have remained in neighbouring countries or in multilateral posts [the most desirable foreign postings] for long have done so by hook or by crook, not by the government's deliberate design.'

This clearly has to change. There is room for additional ideas that such studies have overlooked, such as doing unto the MEA what India does unto other nations—outsourcing some of its tasks and functions (especially routine protocol matters) to lesser, lower-paid entities in the private sector. Some of the needed reforms, if implemented, would beget other reforms; if the recruitment policy were changed, for instance, even if it simply involved a doubling or tripling of the annual intake, as India's place in the world would justify, there would be an inevitable promotion logjam in a couple of decades as the number of entrants would vastly outstrip the number of senior positions available. This would itself oblige the MEA to create a more rigorous evaluation and promotion policy that would reward efficiency and effectiveness, rather than mere seniority.

Some other proposals, however, face difficulties going beyond the terms of the argument Markey makes: India's few think tanks, for instance, have to struggle to have access to any official documentation or reliable inside information, so that their studies, in Salman Haidar's mordant words, 'tend to be at a remove from official preoccupations'. This may be gradually changing, for instance with the establishment in Mumbai of Gateway House, a foreign affairs think tank seemingly modelled on New York's Council on Foreign Relations, but without (yet) the resources, the convening power or the clout of its comparator. But there is for now no equivalent of the Council in India. There is no shortage of seminars and discussions, however, including some—such as the annual India meetings of the World Economic Forum—which serve as a platform and a location for policy discourse as well as for international networking and image building.

The lack of a coherent and effective declassification policy compounds this problem. It is difficult for analysts to understand Indian foreign policy making from Indian sources, as the analysts have no legitimate access to such sources or to any documentation at all, other than material of historical value (though even many in that category have not been declassified, including material relating to the wars of 1962 and 1971). Other ideas, like improved pay to make diplomacy a more attractive career option, cannot be pursued in the IFS alone; as Haidar points out, some of the reforms suggested by the likes of Markey or myself 'cannot be undertaken without much broader reform within the civil services as a whole: the MEA is not an island to itself.'

In India, therefore, some changes in essential areas will be slow to come because they cannot be pursued in other areas. There is a mountain to be climbed before the IFS and the MEA become more effective instruments of India's global interests in a globalizing world.

———

'Much is written, even more spoken, every day about India's foreign policy,' commented a former diplomat towards the close of Mrs Gandhi's reign. 'In Delhi, in particular, especially after the establishment of Jawaharlal Nehru University, dons, area specialists and others wax eloquent on it. They participate in public seminars, give radio and television talks and interviews and publish articles. Their zeal for educating the public and drawing attention to themselves is astonishing.' Even more astonishing, perhaps, was the barrenness of that activity, its seeming unrelatedness to the empirical realities of Indian foreign policy making and its virtual inability to make the slightest dent in the armour of the establishment, of which it was a major component. Every one of a wide variety of Mrs Gandhi's top aides and a number of senior MEA officials interviewed by this author in 1977 testified to their disregard of the self-appointed elite public on foreign policy; the only intellectuals who made any impression on foreign policy were those who went beyond co-optation and actually joined the decision-makers. It is hard to argue that things are that different in 2012.

'I have no doubt,' Mrs Gandhi acknowledged early in her rule, 'that our present administrative system uses the expert inadequately and indifferently.' As it proved, there was little she could do about it; the anti-intellectualism of the entrenched bureaucracy was too intractable. The concept of the non-governmental expert as a legitimate addition to established channels of policy was not a popular one among either politicians or bureaucrats. Nor did it find much support in India's sociocultural evolution.

Indian intellectuals are heirs to one of the most elitist intellectual traditions of the world. The post-Vedic Brahmins sought exclusive intellectual distinction in principle, and the caste system confirmed their elitism in practice. Increasingly, however, that elitism became a hallmark of all Indian intellectualism. The search for knowledge, and in turn the entire realm of ideas, was detached from the everyday concerns of the rest of society. Over the years—from the earliest simple divisions between the (priestly and scholarly) Brahmins and the (martial and kingly) Kshatriyas, to the gulf that separates the twentieth-century academic from the politician—intellectuals abandoned worldly affairs to those qualified to act rather than to analyse. In modern India they remained aloof from the quotidian concerns of governmental policy, but this distance no longer bespoke Brahminical superiority. Instead intellectuals were a deprived breed, shorn of that which made their elitist forebears respected: influence over the wielders of power. An increasingly populist politics and a career bureaucracy took over the symbols of state authority. In the new formulation, those who could did; those who could not theorized.

The value preference of middle-class India inevitably reflected these norms. 'Society' had come to accord more respect to the lowliest IAS/ IFS trainee than it did the most qualified academic or savant. (The rates in the country's unofficial but pervasive dowry market could confirm this empirically.) Intellectuals, therefore, formed a segment of the educated class from which sprang the country's rulers, but they did not constitute (in Mosca's sense) members of the 'ruling class'. This, many intellectuals came to regret. In independent India they sat in judgement all too frequently on those whose seats they would gladly have occupied, if they could. Far from constituting a jury of peers in a people's court on governmental performance, intellectuals are—as the subjects of their prescriptions realized—by and large passing verdicts on their betters. Sentenced to a lower social status, his livelihood subsidized by government grants, the Indian intellectual is a poor relative of the Indian bureaucrat, and he knows it.

The result is, as the sociologist Edward Shils noted, that government officials 'do not learn to benefit from criticism emanating from the universities; instead, they maintain a secretiveness and touchiness which is injurious to efficiency in economic life and to political democracy'. K. Subrahmanyam, who, as a government official appointed to head the scholarly Institute of Defence Studies and Analyses, operated in the twilight zone between bureaucracy and academics, found to his dismay that even government-sponsored academic institutions were disregarded by the MEA in policy formulation. Subrahmanyam attributed this to the MEA's insecurity about its own competence, and fear that ministers would soon bypass officialdom altogether. Whatever the reason, academics received short shrift in the MEA. A plan briefly mooted by then foreign minister Dinesh Singh to attach a consultative committee of a dozen scholars to the MEA was quickly shot down. One academic on the list suspected that Congress MPs had intervened, but this author learned that it was the then MEA Secretaries who had rebelled against the idea. The extent of interaction between the two communities was restricted to the occasional informal seminar or the even less frequent sabbatical at Jawaharlal Nehru University. For a variety of reasons, there was no direct academic input.

Policy planners and MEA diplomatists are privately scathing in their contempt for intellectuals. Academicians, the bureaucrats argue, were inadequately informed about contemporary problems, and had no idea of empirical reality or the mechanics of policy implementation; their involvement in policy-making would only introduce impracticalities and impair stability and continuity. Devoid of an independent socio-economic base, unable (unlike journalists) to express their views in influential publications on a regular basis, and often anxious to please the government of the day, India's intellectuals are not seen by policy-makers as a respectable community of minds but as irrelevances not worth treating seriously. The occasional conscientious MEA official reads scholarly journals and attends seminars at the Indian Council of World Affairs, subject to the limitations of time and his convenience. But the techniques by which the MEA keeps abreast of non-official opinion are few and far from searching, and the foreign policy bureaucracy remains insulated from most advances in thought outside the ministry.

To a great extent, however, the failure of the Indian intellectual goes beyond the imperviousness of officialdom. Standards, rarely high, have been further diluted under populist pressures for the expansion of higher education. In the upper reaches of academe, style rather than substance tends to prevail—when the Indian intellectual is not seduced by plausible theories, since ideology in Indian academia proves too often a facile substitute for original thought. There is a congenital lack of empiricism in most academic critiques; the tyranny of hypothesis and the absence of a discipline of facts abound in most intellectuals' views of government policies. These traits particularly manifested themselves in foreign policy critiques. 'With a very few exceptions,' one commentator noted, 'the Indian intellectual has been incompetent when he has not been unctuous, and afraid of embarking on a rational inquiry when he has not been afraid of the establishment.' Since independence 'there has not appeared a single significant work by an Indian writer discussing these fundamentals [national interests, options, means] with any depth or originality . . . To expect a good essay on the theoretical aspects of foreign policy is to expect the impossible.' Accordingly, an 'air of unreality' prevailed in most analysis of foreign affairs, which suffered from what former US secretary of state Dean Acheson had termed 'the clichés, the moralism, the emotionalism, the bad history, faulty analysis and just plain ignorance' of much American foreign policy criticism in the post–Second World War years.

The Indian intellectual's lack of interest in developing specialized knowledge in foreign policy led to an undue focus on marginalia, rather than on the conceptual basis of foreign policy. Foreign policy seminars tend, as one analyst put it, 'to make major comments on external political issues, rather than to come to grips with India's policies towards these issues'. The study of international affairs also lacks a solid academic infrastructure in the universities. Frequently conformism emerges, possibly because it was natural for the intelligentsia of a newly emergent nation to identify itself with that nation's posture in world affairs, though this is fortunately waning six and a half decades after independence. This attitude extended even to attempts to acquire specialization. Till the 1990s, the Soviet studies programmes at Jawaharlal Nehru University and similar institutions were more concerned with promoting Indo-Soviet friendship than with disinterested academics. It was, therefore, not very surprising that officialdom preferred to disregard intellectuals as lacking in critical integrity. Their anxiety not to offend the government only invited the scorn of those they wished to please.

These inherent weaknesses—lack of social approbation, resistance from the entrenched foreign policy bureaucracy, low standards of achievement and willingness to conform—were exacerbated by the guilt that Edward Shils had traced long ago: 'The Indian intellectual charges himself, and even more bitterly and frequently his fellow-intellectuals, with being "out of touch with the people".' While Shils saw this largely as an imaginary problem, it was a very real one for the intellectual elite. By their very acquisition of the attributes of intellectualism, they lost the direct mass contact that alone would have enabled them to influence either rulers or ruled. For many, their status as intellectuals symbolized privilege, and made them acutely conscious of (as well as vulnerable to attack because of) their distance from the concerns of the masses. In some cases, reflexive guilt drove them to mortgage themselves to the most visible self-proclaimed representatives of the masses—the political leaders. As a result the 'elite public opinion' represented by Indian intellectuals was neither well informed nor effective. Opinion bore little relation to analyses of reality, and even less to prospects for action. While opinion was expressed, it was usually without expectation that policy change would result from it. Ambassadors learned quickly that urgent and passionate discussions of policy were commonplace while action to change policy was rare. Discussion is an 'art form' in India, an egocentric ritual of simulated conviction or, at best, a second-hand expression of conscience. Its vitality is attenuated by its own irrelevance.

The only departure from this norm is when intellectuals turned to the daily newspapers, the proliferation of media outlets offering them multiple avenues for the expression of opinion. But despite exceptions, these had at best a limited impact on both the public and the MEA. Outside the academic community and some sections of the press, there is little interest or competence in foreign policy analysis. This is not true of the final category of intellectual who writes on foreign policy, the retired diplomat, though too many evade responsibility for conceptual soul-searching by devoting themselves to repetitive reminiscences, such as K.P.S. Menon's syndicated variations in the 1960s and 1970s on the theme of Indo-Soviet friendship. In more recent times, former foreign secretary Kanwal Sibal has become a prolific commentator on foreign policy issues from a distinctly hard-nosed realpolitik perspective. But with honourable exceptions like Salman Haidar and T.P. Sreenivasan, there has been little attempt to put practical experience in the field, so lacking in other intellectuals, at the service of institutional re-examination.

There are also limitations on the Indian intellectual that run deep in the political ethos. There are few Indian equivalents of the contextual documents and white papers issued by the British or Australian Parliaments (and earlier by Nehru). As for the annual report of the MEA, an inscrutable collection of banalities and itineraries, one critic bitingly observed that 'the only explanation for this consistently dull, drab and un-illuminating document is the assumption at the political level that the conduct of foreign policy is an esoteric subject best known to its practitioners'.

The problem of insufficient quality in public discourse about foreign policy is further augmented by an increasing resort to direct censorship of such material as is available. Publications from Taiwan, for instance, 'which contain statements on political issues relating to international affairs which are likely to prejudicially affect friendly relations [with China!]' were once forbidden, though mercifully no longer so; while, paradoxically, the Indian Council of World Affairs was once obliged to withdraw a book from the press because it contained banned Chinese editorials. As an editorialist in the *Statesman* protested at the time:

Censorship action under the Sea Customs Act is merely frustrating to the occasional scholar, who wants to know what attitudes others are taking, without affording any significant protection to the public.

Many foreign books on Indo-Pakistan relations, for instance, now have the maps removed before export. . . . This helps nobody here while foreigners continue to see erroneous matter which Indians cannot prevent them from reading and are, by deprivation, less well-equipped to refute.

Such restrictions on unpopular foreign opinions also impinge on the Indian citizens' right to hold the same views. But even that right has been abridged by far-reaching legislation. Freedom of expression under Article 19 of the Indian Constitution, already modified to include 'reasonable restrictions' to protect national security, was amended further by Mrs Indira Gandhi's government to proscribe material that impinged on 'national sovereignty'. In 1967, an Unlawful Activities (Prevention) Act was passed to penalize any action by an individual or association '(i) which is intended, or supports any claim, to bring about on any ground whatsoever, the cession of a part of the territory of India from the Union or which incites any individual or group of individuals to bring about such cession or secession; (ii) which disclaims, questions, disrupts or is intended to disrupt the sovereignty and territorial integrity of India'. As the then home minster explained to Parliament, 'If someone says that Government should settle the dispute with China or Pakistan peacefully, it would be a legitimate thing. But if it is said that India should give away territory to China or Pakistan to purchase peace it would certainly become unlawful.' Apart from rendering one part of the Swatantra Party's foreign policy platform illegal and depriving Indian intellectuals, policy advocates and columnists of a legitimate option for discussion, the act in effect denied the public the right to advocate what has since become India's de facto position, freezing the status quo on the northern borders.

Finally, Western scholars have found it increasingly difficult to obtain entry visas for India, the establishment apparently believing that India can be victimized by sloppy foreign scholarship. Intellectual quests for objective inquiry, it appears, are not valued at the expense of the national 'image'. This hardly accords with the requirement for serious and wide-ranging debate on foreign policy issues in a democracy aspiring to global status.

With the non-governmental intellectual unable to make any substantive impact on foreign policy, it becomes necessary to look beyond the power of reason and argument to that of numbers, to the broader majority of India's 'public'. No scholar can definitively pronounce judgement on whether a foreign policy should, by definition, reflect a 'national will', a set of popular preferences or only the calculated judgements of the ruling elite. But as the embodiment of a nation's collective personality and interests on the international stage, a foreign policy is bound to partake of the first two elements—in whatever measure—as certainly as it is bound to reflect the final stamp of the third. It is probably true that the impact of public opinion on foreign policy is everywhere limited, though there are considerable differences of degree among nations. But where the public is cited as constituting the justification for a foreign policy—which is most often the case with external affairs, and certainly has to be so in democratic India—the incorporation of the public's beliefs in that policy (to echo Falk's list of desiderata in our opening chapter) is essential.

There are obvious limits to the general public's interest in foreign policy: most people's preoccupation with sheer survival and related concerns leaves them with little time to spare for any understanding of the country's foreign policy. On the other hand, their very ignorance could be exploited by an opportunistic few for domestic political ends, especially since the Indian masses possess the ultimate power over their government, that of the ballot box. Indeed, they use this power somewhat more frequently than the intellectuals of the 'elite public': beyond a certain point, any increase in the characteristics of 'modernization'—rise in the level of education, exposure to mass media and other modernizing influences, and geographical mobility—actually produces not an increase but a decline in voter turnout. The government's dependence on the votes of the broader public provides the clue to the power of the masses—and therefore of public opinion in the broadest sense—on foreign policy. Concerns about the 'Muslim vote', for instance, have dominated Indian policies towards Israel, and the reluctance to display overt friendship to that country—by, for instance, extending invitations to prominent Israelis to visit India—can be traced directly to a desire to avoid provoking a domestic political reaction. India's frequent electoral contests—there is an election every six months, it sometimes seems, for one of India's twenty-eight state assemblies if not for the national Parliament itself—have contributed to a reluctance to take any foreign policy initiatives that could be exploited by other political parties at the hustings. Thus if Shimon Peres never gets to see the Taj Mahal as president—for fear of a Muslim backlash that would count in votes against the ruling party—he only has Indian electoral democracy to blame.

This may sound as if domestic politics has a major impact on foreign policy making, but in fact such impact is superficial: to pursue the same example, sensitivity to Muslim voters' views would not impinge on the substance of India's defence purchases from or security exchanges with Israel, even while it might prevent overly visible gestures putting the relationship on display. For in reality, the general public is crippled by its own lack of interest in national, let alone world, affairs. In a country where many are barely conscious of political issues beyond their own village or neighbourhood, let alone national questions, foreign policy is, at bottom, a remote concern.

And yet the world impinges more and more on the daily lives of Indians, especially urban Indians. What does it mean to be a young person in Delhi today? It can mean waking up to an alarm clock made in China, downing a cup of tea from leaves first planted by the British, donning jeans designed in America and taking a Japanese scooter or a Korean car to get to an Indian college, where the textbooks might be printed with German-invented technology on paper first pulped in Sweden. The young Indian student might call his friends on a Finnish mobile phone to invite them to an Italian pizza or even what they think of as an Indian meal, featuring naan that came here from Persia, tandoori chicken taught to us by rulers from Uzbekistan and aloo and hari mirch that first came to India only 400 years ago from Latin America. (And the most desi thing of all, of course, is suspicion of anything foreign.)

The fact is that, as I argued in Chapter One, today's young Indians are facing an ever more globalizing world in which international developments are likely to impact their daily lives more than ever before. As minister, I would say to my young audiences: 'You should want your government to seize the opportunities that the twenty-first-century world provides, while managing the risks and protecting you from the threats that this world has also opened you up to.' This is why they should care more about the substance of India's engagement with the world and less about the marginalia that currently dominates what little discourse there is about foreign policy among the general public.

We seek to redefine our place in a world that has changed from the one into which we emerged in 1947, just as we ourselves have changed a great deal in the intervening six and a half decades. We are today one of the world's largest economies, a proud player on the global stage with a long record of responsible conduct on international matters. But is our foreign policy apparatus commensurate with the challenge? Is our society as a whole imbued with a consciousness of the strategic opportunity that engagement with the globe offers? Can we be taken seriously as a potential world leader in the twenty-first century if we do not develop the institutions, the practices, the personnel and the mindset required to lead in the global arena?

Our foreign policy debates in Parliament and the media seem obsessed with Pakistan or with ephemera, or worse, ephemera about Pakistan. There is little appetite for in-depth discussion about, say, the merits of participating in the Non-Aligned Movement or the Conference of Democracies, or the importance we should give to such bodies as SAARC or the IOR-ARC. When I was minister of state for external affairs I suppose I should have been grateful, even relieved, at being allowed to get on with foreign policy formulation without the interference of the general public. But I was not; I was deeply frustrated by the indifference of educated Indians, because in my view foreign policy is too important an issue to be left to the MEA alone. Our society as a whole, and particularly its educated young people, must care enough about India's place in the world to participate actively in shaping our international posture.

And yet the picture around us is a pretty dismal one. International relations is a neglected subject on our campuses; my own alma mater, the prestigious St Stephen's College which has produced a legion of IFS officers and a slew of foreign secretaries, does not offer a course of study in international relations. The few colleges that do offer the subject do so in a formalistic and formulaic fashion that ill-equip the student to understand the realities of our contemporary world. JNU apart, few can hold a candle to the universities in China, Russia or the West that teach international relations to young people of a similar age. We do have a handful of thinkers about international issues and a fistful of think tanks, but in size, quality of expertise and range of output they all have a long way to go before they match the role played by, for example, their equivalents in the United States.

And what about the young people who must shape the future orientation of India to the world? A young scholar, Raja Karthikeya Gundu, recently wrote:

> Few Indian students go beyond the West for study, and even if they wanted to, there are barely any scholarships or resources from government or private sector to do so. The average Indian has barely any understanding of foreign cultures, norms and worldviews, and satellite TV and Internet have not managed to change this. Hence, in the absence of global exposure, Indians continue to be an inward-looking nation burdened by prejudice. Thus, it is no surprise that when Indians travel abroad for the first time in their mature years, they are often culturally inadaptable and even mildly xenophobic.

This strikes me as somewhat overstated, and yet there is a kernel of truth in it.

The situation will not improve unless we can improve the study of international affairs at our colleges and universities. In 2008 I was invited by my Singaporean friend Kishore Mahbubani to join a gathering, organized by his Lee Kuan Yew School of Public Policy, of some of the most eminent scholars of international relations (or 'IR', as it is known to the cognoscenti) to brainstorm on improving the current state of the discipline in India. I couldn't join his effort, but one scholar who did, Amitabh Mattoo, observed that 'There are few other disciplines in India . . . where the gulf between the potential and the reality is as wide as it is in the teaching and research of IR at Indian universities. Interest in India and India's interest in the world are arguably at their highest in modern times, and yet Indian scholarship on global issues is showing few signs of responding to this challenge.'

Today, IR is taught in more than a hundred universities in India, but in Mattoo's words, 'most of the IR departments have a shortage of qualified faculty, poor infrastructure, outdated curriculum and few research opportunities'. More than half the departments do not even have access to the Internet, and are so deprived of the rich wealth of online resources that students elsewhere in the world can command. Books and journals are in short supply. Little expertise has been developed in specific areas or countries of concern to India; to take one example, despite all the fuss about the reference to Balochistan in the joint Indo-Pakistani statement at Sharm el Sheikh in 2009, there is no major scholar of Baloch studies in India to whom either the MEA or its critics can turn. Foreign languages are poorly taught, resources for study trips abroad are scarce, research is of varying quality and opportunities for cross-fertilization at academic conferences practically non-existent. Whereas China, a latecomer to the field, has already developed, in the last three decades, a critical mass of students and scholars of IR, we are behind where we were in the heady days of the Nehruvian 1950s when we established bodies like Sapru House and the Indian Council of World Affairs, which we have allowed to atrophy.

The scholar Kanti Bajpai has argued that 'Rising powers seem to get the IR they need.' But it won't just happen. We need to change the way we all think about international relations—my younger readers, the future leaders of this country, and we, its present ones. The MEA has to be willing to play its part, in collaboration with those responsible for educational policy, to bring about the change I have been calling for, but there is no institutional proposal yet in place to make that happen.

To return to Amitabh Mattoo, he warns that 'India's inability to develop a sophisticated and comprehensive understanding of the world outside will have more serious consequences than just the dwarfing of a discipline. It could well stunt India's ability to influence the international system.' That is an outcome that, for all the reasons I have described, we can ill afford.

———

So much for the MEA, think tanks, public and intellectual opinion; but what about the formal structures in India's domestic politics that constitutionally could impact foreign policy making: the formal

Opposition in and out of Parliament, and the state governments in India's federal system? A vital element of India's governmental consensus, going back to the days of the independence movement, has been the parliamentary system of government, with its structure of an elected majority being confronted daily by an organized Opposition. Former British Prime Minister Lord Attlee testified to this on the basis of his experience as a member of a British constitutional commission. Indians, he noted, 'believed that the Westminster model is the only real one for democracies'; when he suggested the US presidential system to Indian leaders, 'they rejected it with great emphasis. I had the feeling that they thought I was offering them margarine instead of butter.' Indian politicians, including the communists, turned to the system with great delight, revelling in adherence to parliamentary convention, down to the desk-thumping form of applause, and complimenting themselves on their authenticity. (The CPI leader Hiren Mukherjee proudly asserted once that British Prime Minister Anthony Eden had felt more at home during question hour in the Indian Parliament than in the Australian.) Faith in the parliamentary system was reaffirmed in the open jubilation of the Indian political class when the post-war regimes of Pakistan and Bangladesh both opted to discard the presidential form of government; in the wide regret when the latter nation reverted to it; and in the public outrage that Mrs Gandhi should, during the Emergency, have contemplated abandoning the parliamentary system for a modified form of Gaullism.

In India, the Opposition members of Parliament enjoy a wide range of formal powers and responsibilities in the field of foreign policy— at least theoretically. Under Article 246 of the Indian Constitution, Parliament is empowered to legislate on 'all matters which bring the Union [of India] into relation with any foreign country'. Article 253 gives Parliament the exclusive legislative authority to implement treaties and international agreements, and Article 51 urges it to promote peace as a governmental endeavour. Parliament is also the ultimate authority in regard to the budget, its financial control over the appropriations of each individual ministry affording it a means of influencing the ministry's actions. The Lok Sabha meets normally for three or four sessions a year, for a total of seven to eight months, and at each session debates a statement by the foreign minister on the international situation. Once a year it also discusses the annual report of the MEA and the ministry's demands for grants (I was entrusted in 2011 with the responsibility of leading the Treasury bench's response to the Opposition's assault on the government's foreign policy in the Lok Sabha). Other opportunities for the expression of views on foreign policy come in parliamentary resolutions, moved by individual members, on such aspects of world situation as move them, from Chinese border incursions to the perennially popular issue of US arms to Pakistan.

The routine proceedings of Parliament include several devices for Opposition pressure on the government in the foreign policy field. Each house begins its day with Question Hour five days a week, followed by a 'zero hour' at which further issues could be raised. Most questions, 'starred' (requiring a verbal response), 'unstarred' (requiring a written reply) and 'short notice' (which usually meet with a verbal response), are submitted at least two weeks in advance, in order to enable the ministry concerned to formulate a reply. The Speaker, who admits relevant questions under the Lok Sabha's rules of procedure (Rules 38–58), also permits up to about six supplementary questions. None of these are particularly well informed, so they are not difficult for a well-briefed minister to handle.

Another possible technique is the use of the proviso for 'half-hour discussions' to seek clarifications of answers provided by the government during question hour. Under Rule 55, these relate only to matters of 'sufficient public importance' to warrant the extra time, and require three days' notice by at least three MPs. Rule 193 also provides for a short-duration discussion without notice, usually to draw the government's attention to a problem it has ignored, but it has not widely been resorted to. This is probably because the Opposition has access to a more potent device, the calling-attention motion, proposed by a member for precisely that purpose. Once such a motion is admitted by the Speaker, the government is obliged to answer it immediately or to seek time to make a statement. Such motions tend mostly to be on domestic issues, but can also provide the first clue to parliamentary interest in an international issue as well—as was the case with the Sharm el Sheikh joint statement with Pakistan in 2009—and generally oblige the government to take a stand on the question (which, in the case of Sharm el Sheikh, involved some serious back-pedalling).

Of even more serious import are adjournment and no-confidence motions. Under Rule 56 of the Lok Sabha, a motion could be raised to adjourn the house on an issue of urgent public importance; such motions have often been raised on foreign policy questions. No-confidence motions, or resolutions censuring the government, are relatively infrequently resorted to on foreign policy questions, the most significant exception being that relating to India's nuclear deal with the United States, which nearly brought down the UPA government in 2008. The Opposition can also seek to amend the President's annual address to Parliament, setting forth the government's general policy for the year at the start of the budget session in February or early March. In all these instances, the Opposition has opportunities to make its presence felt; it is consulted on the arrangement of business, the allocation of time (usually distributed among the various opposition groups in proportion to their strength in the legislature) and granted numerous opportunities to speak.

In addition to debates on the floor of the House, the Opposition is represented on parliamentary committees with responsibilities in the external affairs arena. Of these the most important is the Joint Consultative Committee on Foreign Affairs, created in 1953 at the suggestion of an independent member. The committee is an informal body, broadly representative of the composition of Parliament, which 'consults' with the minister for external affairs, who chairs its sessions, as opposed to the Standing Committee on External Affairs, which is chaired by an Opposition MP and can summon MEA staff to brief it, though it loses a lot of time on receiving visiting parliamentary delegations and inspecting passport offices. Other useful bodies are the Estimates Committee of the Lok Sabha, which examines the MEA's estimates of expenditure and in one instance (in 1960–61) was responsible for the reorganization of the ministry and its posts abroad; the Public Accounts Committee, which reviews government spending; and the Committee on Governmental Assurances, established in 1953, to check on the speedy implementation of 'assurances, promises, undertakings, etc. given by the Ministers from time to time on the floor of the House'. These committees help ensure the government's accountability to elected representatives for its foreign policy, but are rarely able to question the fundamentals or to have a direct impact on specific issues of India's external affairs.

Formally, therefore, the Indian Parliament enjoys considerable opportunities to influence the creation and conduct of foreign policy. Though it does not possess the rights of some other legislatures to ratify treaties, confirm ambassadors or dictate the composition of diplomatic and trade delegations, its legitimate role in foreign policy goes back to Nehru's very first speech on the subject, wherein he sought Parliament's approval for the course he charted for India in world affairs. Constitutionally, the executive initiates policy and Parliament scrutinizes and (thanks to its financial power over the ministry's grants) controls it.

The complicating factor, however, involves the limits ingrained in India's political culture on Parliament's involvement in foreign policy. Formally, Indian policy-makers pay great respect to the theory of parliamentary involvement—one former foreign minister, Y.B. Chavan, on one memorable occasion, seeking 'some mandate, some direction, some instructions, some suggestions from this honourable House'— but in reality the government seeks no real mandate from Parliament, considers no new directions, accepts no substantive instructions and responds to few suggestions. This may have devolved from a conception of the legitimate distinction in a parliamentary system between a law and a policy; the former emerges from open parliamentary discussion, the latter does not. 'It is, of course, essential,' declared one former Indian diplomat, 'for Government to *keep Parliament in touch* with the broad lines of its foreign policy, but for the government to conduct its foreign policy through Parliament is to invite confusion and deny itself any room for manoeuvring.' Prime Minister Indira Gandhi, for instance, was blunter than Prime Minister Manmohan Singh would ever be in firmly restricting the right of policy creation to the government: 'We have the responsibility,' she noted, 'whereas those who are not in power have the freedom and the right to advocate courses which may not necessarily be responsible.'

The prevalence of this assumption in Indian governmental philosophy may be illustrated by a statement from another end of the chronological spectrum, which encapsulates thinking before and since. Prime Minister Lal Bahadur Shastri asserted in the Lok Sabha in 1965, 'I want to make it absolutely clear that to run the Government is our responsibility and we are going to discharge it. We do take broad guidance from this Honourable House on matters of policy. But we cannot be given executive directions every day. It would be an impossible situation and I cannot accept it.' This was, of course, a reasonable view. But where does it leave Parliament in general, and the Opposition in particular, on foreign policy? It would seem that their only role is to raise issues that may be discussed but would have no tangible impact on policy.

It is true that even Jawaharlal Nehru, the great nurturer of Indian democracy and its institutions, insulated foreign policy from parliamentary influences. His government did not seek parliamentary advice on or consent to a single treaty or international agreement, including the Panchsheel declaration with China, and the agreements with Pakistan, Nepal, Bhutan and Sikkim. Nor did Nehru's administration tell Parliament of Chinese encroachments on India territory till 1959, after they had begun. At the same time, foreign emissaries, especially from China and the Soviet Union in the late 1950s, were given information not publicly available to the Indian people or their representatives in Parliament. The military and psychological disaster of 1962 exposed the bankruptcy of this policy. One key lesson from Nehru's China debacle must be that taking Parliament into confidence in advance offers a vital insurance to the government in the event of a foreign policy disaster, whereas a Parliament that discovers issues from the media after the event—as happened with the Sharm el Sheikh episode involving Pakistan in 2009—can express enough outrage as to constitute a constraint on the government's foreign policy options thereafter.

The various legislative devices outlined above make little difference. Despite Article 246, the field for parliamentary legislation in foreign policy is a limited one. Parliament's finance power has literally never been exercised, primarily because of the sheer weight of numbers disposed of by any government with a parliamentary majority, which is always able to push through the MEA's demands for grants without emendation. Private members' resolutions very rarely get passed, and never against the direct concerted opposition of the government. The foreign policy resolutions that have in fact been passed in Parliament over the years have been on such issues as the Soviet invasion of Czechoslovakia and the US invasion of Iraq, India's relations with specific countries, foreign aid, the repression of minorities in Pakistan, the execution of freedom fighters in the white-ruled Rhodesia and Chinese encroachments on the Indian frontier, issues on which either both government and Parliament were demonstrably helpless, or on which the passage of a resolution would appease critics without seriously affecting policy.

Question hour could have afforded better opportunities, but it has been ill-used on global issues. For one thing, it focuses on foreign policy only infrequently: one estimate is that questions dealing with the MEA only account for 4.5 per cent to 5.5 per cent of the total number of questions asked. Most questions raised in Parliament are of purely national or even local importance, since the MEA only comes up on one of the five days of the work-week in each House, and in any case not all questions are admitted to the floor of the House and the luck of the draw may leave the foreign minister with no question to answer on his allotted day. The Speaker, officially neutral but always a nominee of the ruling party, can and does disallow questions and adjournment motions, terminate debates, reprimand members and rule on disputes, and this authority can be and has been misused to disallow inconvenient questions and to shield ministers by preventing embarrassing supplementaries. Even when questions of import get through, the government devises ingenious ways of evading them, because of the ignorance of the MPs or sometimes through loopholes left by a careless Opposition.

This leaves only the committees and the debates themselves. The parliamentary committees in India dealing with foreign policy are bodies of very little impact, with the Consultative Committee on Foreign Affairs being more akin, as Krishna Menon noted, to a conference than a committee. Though composed of all the parties in relation to their strength in the House, the committees are not bound by the MPs' party stands, and their meetings are designed as a frank exchange of views, but often descend into ritual exercises and empty exchanges designed for no greater purpose than to justify the MPs' presence and allowances. The committees meet sporadically, and indulge in little more than a question and answer session. Under official guidelines, their discussions are strictly off the record, and no reference can be made to them in Parliament, which considerably diminishes their utility. As a non-statutory body, the consultative committee cannot summon witnesses, demand files or examine records, and the government is not bound to accept any of its recommendations, even unanimous ones. There is no record of any policy initiative emerging from the committee's consultations. The Standing Committee on External Affairs is not much better off, spending much of its time receiving delegations from an assortment of foreign countries for exchanges that are often mind-numbing in their formality. It does, however, review draft legislation relating to the MEA, and the minister is obliged to respond to its reports and comments on the MEA's work.

Similarly, parliamentary debates are unable to make a tangible impact, because they usually follow rather than precede governmental policy actions and because, when it comes to a vote, the Opposition is usually hopelessly outnumbered. From the government's point of view, debates on foreign policy have three time-honoured uses: they provide the outside world with evidence of Indian democracy at work, they have an educative impact on MPs and those members of the media and public who pay attention to foreign policy, and they help (*if* the government defends itself ably) to make policy acceptable. As Krishna Menon put it years ago, 'it's always the same; there are speeches, but all ends well'. In political development terms, they conferred legitimacy to the foreign policy making process, while doing little to augment its responsiveness to Opposition opinion. The government claims actively to encourage parliamentary participation and understanding, by such expedients as appointing MPs to parliamentary UN and goodwill delegations going abroad. In practice, such appointments operate as rewards for quiescence or support, and frequently compromise, rather than enhance, parliamentary independence. In any case, the tradition both in the committees and on delegations abroad to treat foreign policy as consensual meant that Opposition MPs were easily co-opted. Party differences, an Opposition MP explained to me when I carelessly mentioned political affiliation in one of my first meetings of the Standing Committee on External Affairs, ended when we met foreigners; before them we were Indians first, not political partisans.

It was significant that it was in fact an Opposition member who made this point to me, since both leading parties have tended to treat foreign policy as largely an emanation of self-evident national interest. Thus the policy platforms of the various political parties (with the exception of the communists, who still wax indignant about American imperialism) are largely devoid of disagreements on foreign policy, and even differences expressed are rarely pursued with much conviction. This is particularly the case when political parties in Opposition take positions not out of conviction but expediency—the belief that it is the basic duty of the Opposition to oppose. Thus the BJP opposed the Indo-US nuclear deal in 2007–08, even though it was the direct result of efforts begun under BJP rule, and constituted an outcome that the BJP would undoubtedly have presented with pride to the country had they negotiated it. As Wikileaks has since revealed, BJP leaders were privately assuring American diplomatic interlocutors that they were in fact supportive of the agreement, even while expressing vociferous opposition to it in Parliament and in the streets. The BJP's vote in Parliament against the Indo-US nuclear deal had far less to do with the substance of the agreement than with the opportunity it afforded to split the Left away from the ruling coalition and move a no-confidence motion that might have toppled the government. In other words, foreign policy considerations were subordinated to domestic politics once again.

It may perhaps be argued that no legislature can or should be expected to provide effective inputs to foreign policy. Yet that is precisely what the US Congress and the Israeli Knesset have frequently done, and the British Parliament has—with varying degrees of success—strived to do. Admittedly the limitations of Opposition performance I have traced are far from uniquely Indian, and would find parallels in several other democratic polities. Some of the problems are common to all parliamentary systems, where voting across party lines is rare on issues of national importance and the majority party is therefore not seriously threatened in foreign policy debate. Yet the ability of an articulate Opposition to propound the views of an important segment of the ruling elite—that 'effective public' that dominates discussion of policy in the media and thus indirectly in the coffee shops—and thereby to influence the government, is central to all conceptions of democracy. That it has failed to function as such in India is, at the very least, a pity.

The rise of regional parties in Indian politics has only underscored this phenomenon. Such parties, for the most part, see themselves as custodians of narrowly defined regional, caste or ethnic interests; national and international issues are far removed from their preoccupations. They are thus inclined to formulate their foreign policy positions with purely domestic politic considerations in mind—except when the issue has no impact on the government. Thus the leader of the Samajwadi Party, which bailed the government out in the no-confidence vote on the nuclear agreement, occasionally vents his spleen in Parliament on China's dark designs on India, but has never sought to ensure that his prejudices actually shape Indian policy. Nor, to my knowledge, has he ever made China an issue in any of his stump speeches on the electoral trail in Uttar Pradesh, the state that constitutes his political base.

So in India, the Opposition is generally only able to use Parliament for limited ends, such as the 'agenda-creating' function of raising an issue for debate. Effective parliamentary action in any democracy requires a united and focused Opposition, with some strong resonance for its views among the general public outside Parliament and particularly in the media, and the ability to threaten the ruling party's majority in Parliament. These conditions have almost never obtained on a purely foreign policy issue. The exception may be on foreign economic policy, such as FTAs and FDI, which have obvious and direct domestic political consequences. But India approaches such external initiatives in a strategic manner, evaluating their impact both internationally and domestically (for example, the FTA with ASEAN was not merely a foreign trade initiative, but an opportunity to reform the agricultural and plantation sectors of our economy). India has tended to take on such foreign obligations with a positive rather than a defensive approach, while being fully aware that any FTA has a domestic political impact and could be portrayed as causing short-term losses for important domestic constituencies. While the ASEAN–India FTA was judged to be a crucial element in India's engagement with Southeast Asia and persisted with despite the opposition of the coconut-oil producers of Kerala, the initiative to permit 49 per cent FDI in the retail sector was withdrawn the moment significant opposition emerged, not only from the formal Opposition parties but from members of the ruling coalition like the Trinamool Congress in West Bengal.

The FDI experience points to a larger reality in an era of coalition politics, where a ruling party often feels far more vulnerable to its own supporters than to the Opposition. While parties without a majority in Parliament can at best be humoured and at worst be ignored, parties that actually help constitute the ruling majority must be appeased if they feel strongly enough about an issue of policy—including foreign policy. The ever-present threat of a withdrawal of support by a coalition ally, which could even bring a government down, is far more potent than the most eloquent arguments of the official Opposition. Thus Mamata Banerjee, the Trinamool chief minister of West Bengal (Paschimbanga), single-handedly stymied a major agreement with Bangladesh on the sharing of waters from the Teesta River, which flows from West Bengal to Bangladesh. The Dravida Munnetra Kazhagam (DMK) in Tamil Nadu had similarly attempted to influence New Delhi's positions on the Sri Lanka civil war, but had proved less effective—not so much because of the intractability of Indian foreign policy, but because it was rightly believed that the DMK would not genuinely threaten the survival of the government by withdrawing support, something that it was not possible to say about Trinamool. In an earlier era, the DMK had similarly made strong noises about New Delhi's intention to cede the disputed island of Kachchativu, a favoured watering-hole of Tamil fishermen, to Sri Lanka, but the Government of India did so anyway.

The Indian vote in favour of a US-backed resolution critical of Sri Lanka at the UN Human Rights Council (UNHRC) in 2012 was an interesting departure from this norm, because it appeared to be prompted directly by the clamour from both the Treasury and the Opposition benches (both the DMK, a member of the coalition, and the All India Anna Dravida Munnetra Kazhagam, ruling in Tamil Nadu, demanded that India not oppose the resolution). While domestic politics undoubtedly played a crucial part in the government's decision—which was made, by all accounts, in the PMO and not in the MEA—it could well be argued that this was not the sole motivation, since the vote gave India the opportunity to send Sri Lanka a strong signal at very little cost to either the sender or the recipient. The resolution itself was rather mildly worded, calling upon Sri Lanka to do little more than implement the recommendations of its own Lessons Learned and Reconciliation

Commission. But it enabled New Delhi to be on the side of the angels internationally; to break free of its stifling self-imposed constraint of never voting in favour of any country-specific UNHRC resolution; and to convey to Colombo that its progress in fulfilling commitments to devolve genuine political autonomy to its Tamil minority was unsatisfactory. At the same time, pointing to domestic pressures gave it a certain plausible deniability with those in the Sri Lankan government who might otherwise accuse it of letting down a neighbour and friend.

Apart from a handful of issues, therefore, of which Bangladesh and Sri Lanka remain the most striking examples, it remains difficult to see domestic politics, whether in Parliament or outside it, as a major constraint on Indian foreign policy making. There is no doubt that demands in the political space have an impact on the foreign policy agenda, forcing the government to respond, but the extent of such impact is in most cases limited, except when the government finds it expedient to react to them.

Nor is the press a very useful contributor to an enlightened understanding of foreign policy, given its increasing penchant for sensationalism and its resultant overemphasis on trivia. The media has a specific role in forcing issues on to the political space, but it is more likely to do so on headline-grabbing marginalia like the Indian children in Norway than on issues of geopolitical complexity like the Teesta waters (it is estimated that the former issue occupied 200 times more television time than the latter). The dramatic rise of cable television as a purveyor of what is called 'infotainment' has been characterized by an emphasis on rating points or TRPs, which are best gained when controversies are whipped up, not when serious issues are explored in depth. Thus Indian television was almost single-handedly responsible for creating a crisis in Indian–Australian relations in 2009 by remorselessly focusing on the alleged victimization of Indians in violent attacks by racist Australian hooligans. Attempts on both sides to cool the temperature on the issue came up against the implacable commercial imperative of channels whipping up mass hysteria to drive up their viewership. On one occasion, during a lengthy interview at the MEA with a particularly egregious TV anchor—famed for his hectoring rants on assorted peeves, mostly unsupported by either fact or reason—the cameras stopped to change their tapes, and in the ensuing break I asked him whether he was really serious about the kinds of things he was alleging on air. 'How does it matter?' he asked perfectly reasonably. 'I'm playing the story this way, and I'm getting 45 per cent in the TRPs. My two principal rivals are trying to be calm and moderate, and they're at 13 per cent and 11 per cent.' The cameras were switched on again, and he immediately resumed his belligerent tone.

Yet such coverage can at best help set the agenda; it cannot drive policy. It can ensure that the government pays attention, but it cannot get the government to alter its position. It is, in other words, little more than a distraction, until the TV channel moves on to the next 'breaking news' it can milk for more TRPs. Unfortunately, however, the TRP approach has also affected the print media, which, in craven imitation, has itself descended into purveying scandal and sensation. With very few honourable exceptions, the Indian print media has relegated serious international affairs coverage to short articles on the inside pages. The result is that it is that much harder these days for Indians to find opportunities for balanced, informative and wide-ranging news and insight into world affairs in the popular Indian media.

The sustainability and success of India's international policy depends both on leadership by the Government of India and the active involvement of the Indian public and political opinion, particularly that of young Indians. The government is committed to protecting and advancing India's global citizenship, but that cannot be done without Indians becoming global citizens, and very few of them currently have the information, the education or the opportunity to evolve in that direction.

We are blessed with a new, globalized, impatient generation of Indians who rightly refused to be confined to the limited worldviews of older generations. The horizons of their world are ever widening. The prospects for international engagement, for more widespread prosperity, for more borderless success, have never been brighter. But to fulfil those prospects and to help them carve out a place for their India in the twenty-first-century world, India needs a radical overhaul of the domestic underpinnings of its international posture. The time to begin that overhaul is now.

Chapter Ten

India, the UN and the 'Global Commons': The Multilateral Imperative

Even though it has been five years since I left the service of the United Nations, the one question people have still not stopped asking me in India is when India is going to become a permanent member of the Security Council. The question goes to the heart of the new set of aspirations that prevails across the Indian middle class and its elite for a meaningful role on the global stage. The short answer I have been giving them for more than a decade is, 'not this year, and probably not the next', but there are so many misconceptions around the country (and the world) about this issue that a longer answer is clearly necessary.

The problem of reforming the Security Council is rather akin to a malady in which a number of doctors gather around a patient; they all agree on the diagnosis, but they cannot agree on the prescription. The diagnosis is clear—the Security Council reflects the geopolitical realities of 1945 and not of today. This situation can be analysed mathematically, geographically and politically, as well as in terms of equity.

Mathematically: When the UN was founded in 1945, the Council consisted of eleven members out of a total UN membership of fifty-one countries; in other words, some 22 per cent of the member states were on the Security Council. Today, there are 192 members of the UN, and only fifteen members of the Council—fewer than 8 per cent. So many more countries, both in absolute numbers and as a proportion of the membership, do not feel adequately represented on the body.

Geographically: The composition of the Council also gives undue weightage to the balance of power of those days. Europe, for instance, which accounts for barely 5 per cent of the world's population, still controls 33 per cent of the seats in any given year (and that doesn't count Russia, another European power).

And *politically*: The five permanent members (the United States, Britain, France, Russia and China) enjoy their position, and the privilege of a veto over any Council resolution or decision, by virtue of having won a war sixty-six years ago. (In the case of China, the word 'won' needs to be placed within inverted commas.)

In terms of simple considerations of equity, this situation is unjust to those countries whose financial contributions to the United Nations outweigh those of four of the five permanent members—Japan and Germany have for decades been the second and third largest contributors to the UN budget, at 19 per cent and 12 per cent, respectively, while still being referred to as 'enemy states' in the United Nations Charter (since the UN was set up by the victorious Allies of the Second World War). And it denies opportunities to other states who have contributed in kind (through participation in peacekeeping operations, for example) or by size, or both, to the evolution of world affairs in the six decades since the organization was born. India and Brazil are notable examples of the latter case.

So the Security Council is clearly ripe for reform to bring it into the second decade of the twenty-first century. The UN recognized the need for action as early as 1992, when the Open-Ended Working Group of the General Assembly was established to look into the issue, in the hope—or so then secretary-general Boutros Boutros-Ghali declared—of having a solution in time for the fiftieth anniversary of the world organization in 1995. But the Open-Ended Working Group soon began to be known, in the UN corridors, as the Never-Ending Shirking Group. Instead of identifying a solution or moving towards compromise, the group remains in existence, having missed not only the fiftieth anniversary of the UN, but even the sixtieth and now the sixty-fifth. Left to their own devices, they will be arguing the merits of the case well past the UN's centenary.

For a decade now, the 'Group of Four'—Brazil, Germany, India and Japan, or 'G4'—have been in the forefront of an attempt to win the passage of Security Council reform, fully expecting to be the beneficiaries of any expansion in the category of permanent members. They have been repeatedly thwarted.

The problem is quite simple: for every state that feels it deserves a place on the Security Council, and especially the handful of countries that believe their status in the world ought to be recognized as being in no way inferior to at least three if not four of the existing permanent members, there are several that know they will not benefit from any reform. The small countries that make up more than half the UN's membership accept that reality and are content to compete occasionally for a two-year non-permanent seat on the Council. But the medium-sized and large countries which are the rivals of the prospective beneficiaries deeply resent the prospect of a select few breaking free of their current second-rank status in the world body. Some of the objectors, like Canada and Spain, are genuinely motivated by principle: they consider the existence of permanent membership to be wrong to begin with, and they have no desire to compound the original sin by adding more members to a category they dislike. But many of the others are openly animated by a spirit of competition, historical grievance or simple envy. Together they have banded together into an effective coalition—first called the 'coffee club', and now, more cynically, 'Uniting for Consensus'—to thwart reform of the permanent membership of the Security Council.

Let us remember that the bar to amending the UN Charter has been set rather high. Any amendment requires a two-thirds majority of the overall membership, in other words 129 of the 193 states in the General Assembly. An amendment would further have to be ratified by two-thirds of the member states (and ratification is usually a parliamentary procedure, so in most countries this means it's not enough for the government of the day to be in favour of a reform; its Parliament also has to go along with a change). In other words, the only 'prescription' that has any chance of passing is one that will both (a) persuade two-thirds of the UN member states to support it and (b) not attract the opposition of any of the existing permanent five (or even that of a powerful US senator who could block ratification in Washington). That has proved to be a tall order indeed.

After all, who would countries want to see on an expanded Security Council? Obviously, states that displace some weight in the world and have a record of making major contributions to the UN system. But when Japan and Germany began pressing their claims to permanent seats, the then foreign minister of Italy, Susanna Agnelli, wisecracked, 'What's all this talk about Japan and Germany? We lost the war too.' (Other historical factors intrude: neither China nor South Korea is keen on Japan, with its record of atrocities seven decades ago, being rewarded today.) Even assuming such objections (notably from Italy, Spain, Canada and Korea among OECD countries) could be overcome, adding these two to the Council would, of course, further skew the existing North–South imbalance. So they would have to be balanced by new permanent members from the developing world. But who would these be? In Asia, India, as the world's largest democracy, its third largest economy and a long-standing contributor to UN peacekeeping operations, seems an obvious contender. But Pakistan, which fancies itself India's strategic rival on the subcontinent, is unalterably opposed, and to some extent Indonesia seems to feel diminished by the prospect of an Indian seat. In Latin America, Brazil occupies a place analogous to India's in Asia, but Argentina and Mexico have other ideas, pointing to Portuguese-speaking Brazil's inferior credentials in representing largely Hispanic Latin America. And in Africa, how is one to adjudicate the rival credentials of the continent's largest democracy, Nigeria, its largest economy, South Africa, and its oldest civilization, Egypt?

No wonder the search for a reform prescription—a formula that is simultaneously acceptable to a two-thirds majority and not unacceptable to the permanent five—has proved so elusive. Composition is the central challenge, but not the only one. There is also the question of the eventual size of a reformed Council: once additional permanent members are joined by additional non-permanent ones (to give more representation to regions like Latin America and Eastern Europe, which would otherwise be marginalized in the new body), would it become too large to function effectively? Is there a danger it would become more of a conference than a council, more of a debating chamber than a decision-making body? What about the veto? Permanent membership currently comes with the privilege of a veto, but there is less support across the UN membership for new veto-wielders than there might be for the abolition of the veto altogether. The G4, sensing the mood, announced they would voluntarily forgo the privilege of a veto for ten years. It did not noticeably add momentum to their cause.

But I do still believe the Security Council has to change sooner or later. The best argument for reform is that the absence of reform could discredit the United Nations itself. Britain and France have become converts to this point of view. I remember the late British foreign secretary Robin Cook saying in 1997 (on his first visit to the UN in that capacity) that if the Council was not reformed without delay, his own voters would not understand why. Cook, a fine statesman and a man of principle, did not realize that he was not destined to see any Council reform in his lifetime, let alone during his term of office. And yet he understood that reform was essential, because what merely looks anomalous today will seem absurd tomorrow. Imagine in 2020 a British or French veto of a resolution affecting South Asia with India absent from the table, or of one affecting southern Africa with South Africa not voting: who would take the Council seriously then?

There is perhaps another reason why the British and the French are genuinely keen on seeing the Council reformed right now. Currently, everyone is only speaking of expanding the permanent membership of the Council, not replacing the existing permanent members. If reform is delayed by another decade, there is a real risk that the position of London and Paris will not be so secure then; the clamour for replacing them with one permanent European Union seat would mount, and could prove irresistible.

So far, the other three permanent members have been somewhat more lukewarm about reform. Russia is officially pledged to support it, and has explicitly backed the claims of Germany, Japan and India to new permanent seats, but it is a matter for debate as to how enthusiastic Moscow really is. Its permanent seat on the Council was the one asset that, even during the shambolic years of the 1990s, allowed Russia to 'punch above its weight' in international affairs. Few Russians really want to see that position of privilege diluted by having to be shared with several new countries.

The United States and China are even more sceptical. China shares Moscow's reluctance to see its stature diminished, but this is all the more true since it now sees itself, quite justifiably, as having no peer in the world other than the United States, whose economy it is on course to overtake within the next two decades. As for the United States, it is still the sole superpower, and its isolation in recent years on various issues, notably relating to the Middle East, makes the American administration profoundly wary of giving new powers to countries that may stand in its way. It was striking that Washington's support of a seat for Germany faded away in the wake of Germany's vocal opposition to the 2003 Iraq war, and it took years to formally endorse India's bid, because it was conscious that New Delhi votes more often against Washington in UN forums than with it. (It finally did so in November 2010 during a visit to New Delhi by President Obama that was aimed at sealing a strategic partnership whose credibility would have been undermined by continued reticence on a Security Council seat for New Delhi. But there has been no indication whatsoever of the United States proceeding to 'action' its commitment by instructing its ambassadors, for instance, to lobby for a permanent seat for India or even for a swift resolution of the impasse over Council expansion.) In addition, the United States likes a Council it can dominate; Washington is conscious that a larger body would be more unwieldy, and a bigger collection of permanent members more difficult to manage, than the present Council. 'If it ain't broke, don't fix it,' American diplomats like to say.

But for much of the rest of the world, the Security Council is indeed 'broke', and the more decisions it is called upon to take that affect many countries—authorizing wars, declaring sanctions, launching peacekeeping interventions—the greater is the risk that its decisions will be seen as made by an unrepresentative body and therefore rejected as illegitimate. The United Nations is the one universal body we all have, the one organization to which every country in the world belongs; if it is discredited, the world as a whole will lose an institution that is truly irreplaceable.

But that could happen. And my worry, as an old UN hand, is that if Security Council reform drags on indefinitely and inconclusively key countries could begin to look for an alternative. Five years ago, as a candidate for Secretary-General, I asked in a speech: 'What if the G8, which is not bound by any Charter and writes its own rules, decided one day to expand its membership to embrace, say, China, India, Brazil and South Africa?' That is precisely what has happened since, with the establishment of the G20, albeit as the premier global macroeconomic forum, rather than the peace and security institution that the Security Council is. Nonetheless, China aside, the other countries could well say, 'Well, we're now on the high table at last—why not focus our energies on this body and ignore the one which refuses to seat us?' The result could be a UN dramatically diminished by the decision of some of its most important members to ignore or neglect it, while the G20 could well arrogate political responsibilities to itself, unrestricted by any constraint other than its own self-restraint. If that were to occur, the loss will be that of the rest of the world, which at least today has a universal organization to hold it together under the rules of international law—which is vastly preferable to a '*directoire*' of self-appointed oligarchs that a politically empowered G20 could become. So those small and medium-sized countries that are throwing up petty obstacles to reform are being rather short-sighted, not only because they fail to address the fundamental problem that I described as the 'diagnosis', but because their opposition, if it succeeds, could potentially undermine the very institution that many of these countries, now in the forefront of opposition to reform, have long seen as a bulwark for their own security and safety in an unequal world.

Of course, some answer that the UN is increasingly irrelevant as a world organization, and that it therefore makes little sense to clamour for a role of prominence in the Security Council. Such things have been heard in the West for a while, but the critics are wrong. Those of us who used to toil every day at the headquarters of the United Nations—and even more our colleagues on the front lines in the field—had become a little exasperated at seeing our institutional obituaries in the press. The UN's problems over Iraq had led some to evoke a parallel to the League of Nations, a body created with great hopes at the end of the First World War, which was reduced to debating the standardization of European railway gauges the day the Germans marched into Poland. But Iraq proved conclusively that even where the UN was rendered irrelevant to the launching of a war, it became indispensable to the ensuing peace, and the rebuilding that followed. As Mark Twain put it when he saw his own obituary in the newspaper, reports of the UN's demise are therefore exaggerated.

Since the best crystal ball is often the rear-view mirror, I hope I may be permitted a personal reminiscence into the question of change at the United Nations. For the UN has not just changed enormously in those first sixty years, it has been transformed in the career span of this one former UN official. If I had even suggested to my seniors when I joined the organization in 1978 that the UN would one day observe and even run elections in sovereign states, conduct intrusive inspections for weapons of mass destruction, impose comprehensive sanctions on the entire import–export trade of a member state, create a counterterrorism committee to monitor national actions against terrorists, or set up international criminal tribunals and coerce governments into handing over their citizens (even sometimes their former presidents) to be tried by foreigners under international law, I am sure they would have told me that I simply did not understand what the United Nations was all about. (And indeed, since that was in the late 1970s, they might well have asked me—'Young man, what have you been smoking?')

And yet the UN has done every one of those things during the last two decades, and more. The United Nations, in short, has been a highly adaptable institution that has evolved in response to changing times.

My firm view therefore remains that despite the heated criticism the organization has faced from some quarters in recent years—much of it ill-founded—the UN is as necessary today as it was in 1945, and it will be even more necessary tomorrow. Our search has been, and must continue to be, for a renewed, not a retired, UN. And it is in this context that the question of Security Council reform must be examined.

So what's the answer for India? In 2010, the G4 took the debate away from the feckless Open-Ended Working Group into the General Assembly plenary, and persuaded the facilitator of the process, the ambassador of Afghanistan, to come up with a text for discussion. Though his efforts have been hailed by enthusiasts as heralding a genuine breakthrough in the process, his text is still replete with square brackets, revealing entrenched and irreconcilable positions. Continued tinkering with a reform resolution will continue, but no resolution can attract enough votes unless the fifty-four-member African Union (AU) is persuaded to step off the fence it has been straddling for years. African opponents of Council reform have adroitly manoeuvred the AU into an impossible position under the label 'the Ezulweni Consensus' (named for the Swazi town at which the formula was agreed). The Ezulweni

Consensus demands two veto-wielding permanent seats for Africa in a reformed Council, a demand couched in terms of African self-respect but pushed precisely by those countries which know it is unlikely ever to be granted. The AU's rules mean that African positions are adopted by consensus, thus taking fifty-four potential votes out of the equation in favour of a political compromise.

As an Indian minister of state lobbying in Addis Ababa for Security Council reform, I pointed out somewhat mischievously that 'Ezulweni' meant 'Paradise', but that, after years of insisting upon, and failing to obtain, Paradise, it was necessary for African countries to settle for what could be achieved on earth. Africa's naysayers also know that insisting on a consensus decision makes it difficult for the majority favouring reform to move the process forward. After years of accepting this approach, countries like South Africa appear to be challenging the time-honoured emphasis on consensus. If the AU were to agree to a free vote in the General Assembly, the prospects of a reform resolution attracting the necessary 129 votes would brighten immeasurably.

As with most global issues, the key to breaking the logjam lies in Washington. Most of the naysayers are US allies who have been given a free hand by Washington's own lack of enthusiasm for reform. If a new (or re-elected) US administration could be persuaded that it is in America's self-interest to maintain a revitalized United Nations, credible enough for its support to be valuable to the United States and legitimate enough to be a bulwark of world order in the imminent future when the United States is no longer the world's only superpower, Washington could bring enough countries in its wake to transform the debate.

That is a task that the Security Council 'aspirants'—and notably the government of a transforming India now entering into a strategic partnership with Washington—are well positioned to perform.

As someone who has devoted three decades of his life to multilateral cooperation at the United Nations, my big fear remains that if reform does not come, many countries will despair and lose interest in the working of the world body. Alternative structures of world governance could emerge that would in the end undermine the one truly effective universal organization the world has built up since 1945—the United Nations.

'Reform or die' is a cliché that has been inflicted on many institutions. For the UN, at this time and on this issue, the hoary phrase has the additional merit of being true.

———

But the questions of world peace and security debated and decided at the Security Council do not constitute the whole story of the UN. As global governance has evolved, the UN system has become the port of call for innumerable 'problems without passports'—problems that cross all frontiers uninvited, problems of the proliferation of weapons of mass destruction, of the degradation of our common environment, of contagious disease and chronic starvation, of human rights and human wrongs, of mass illiteracy and massive displacement, and the governance of the 'global commons' (on which more later). Such problems also require solutions that cross all frontiers, since no one country or group of countries can solve them alone.

Global governance is not exactly the most precise concept dreamed up by political scientists today. It is used to describe the processes and institutions by which the world is governed, and it was always intended to be an amorphous idea, since there is no such thing as a global government to provide such governance. 'Global governance' is a term that tries to impose a sense of order, real or imagined, on a world without an organized system of government. It has four essential aspects.

The first is history. The principal institutions of global governance today are those that emerged after the disasters of the first half of the twentieth century. In the first half of the twentieth century, the world saw two world wars, countless civil wars, mass expulsions of populations and the horrors of the Holocaust and Hiroshima. Then things changed. In and after 1945, a group of far-sighted leaders were determined to make the second half of the twentieth century different from the first. So they drew up rules to govern international behaviour, and they founded institutions in which different nations could cooperate for the common good. That was the idea of 'global governance'—to foster international cooperation, to elaborate consensual global norms and to establish predictable, universally applicable rules, to the benefit of all.

The keystone of the arch was the United Nations—the institution seen by world leaders like former US president Franklin Delano Roosevelt and his successor Harry Truman as the only possible alternative to the disastrous experiences of the first half of the century. As Roosevelt stated in his historic speech to the two US Houses of Congress after the Yalta conference, the UN would be the alternative to the military alliances, balance-of-power politics and all the arrangements that had led to war so often in the past. The UN stood for a world in which people of different nations and cultures looked on each other not as subjects of fear and suspicion, but as potential partners, able to exchange goods and ideas to their mutual benefit.

Not that Paradise descended on earth in 1945. We all know that tyranny and warfare continued, and that billions of people still live in extreme and degrading poverty. But the overall record of the second half of the twentieth century is one of amazing advances. A third world war did not occur. The world economy expanded as never before. There was astonishing technological progress. Many in the industrialized world now enjoy a level of prosperity, and have access to a range of experiences, that their grandparents could scarcely have dreamed of; and even in the developing world, there has been spectacular economic growth. Child mortality has been reduced. Literacy has spread. The peoples of the developing world threw off the yoke of colonialism, and those of the Soviet bloc won political freedom. Democracy and human rights are not yet universal, but they are now much more the norm than the exception. The existence of the global system devised in 1945 helped make all of this possible.

These developments result at least partly from the second important feature of global governance—the emergence in the last six and a half decades of institutions, principles and processes that reflect this new reality. Global institutions benefit from the legitimacy that comes from their universality. Since all countries belong to it, the UN enjoys a standing in the eyes of the world that gives its collective actions and decisions a legitimacy that no individual government enjoys beyond its own borders. But the institutions of global governance have been expanding beyond the UN itself. There are selective intergovernmental mechanisms like the G8, military alliances like NATO, subregional groupings like the Economic Community of West African States, one-issue alliances like the Nuclear Suppliers' Group. Writers connect under International PEN, soccer players in FIFA, athletes under the International Olympic Committee, mayors in the World Organization of United Cities and Local Governments. Bankers listen to the Bank of International Settlements and businessmen to the International Accounting Standards Board. The process of regulating human activity above and beyond national boundaries has never been more widespread.

In parallel is emerging the third aspect of global governance today, the idea that there are universally applicable norms that underpin our notion of world order and therefore of global governance. Sovereignty is one, especially in a world where the majority of states have won their sovereignty after long years of colonial rule. Emerging from the principle of sovereignty is the principle of non-interference in other countries' internal affairs, equality and mutual benefit, non-aggression and coexistence across different political systems—the very principles first articulated by India's Jawaharlal Nehru in his famous Panchsheel doctrine with the People's Republic of China in 1954. At the same time, there has evolved a new set of global norms of governance that complement and expand (and, in some cases, affect) these principles, including respect for human rights, transparency and accountability, rule of law, equitable development based on economic freedom and, at least to most nations, political democracy. These are seen as desirable for all countries to aspire to, and while no one suggests that they can or should be imposed on any nation, fulfilling them is seen as admirable by most of the world and broadly accepted as evidence of successful governance.

The fourth feature is the global nature of the determining forces of today's world. As I have mentioned earlier, there are broadly two contending and even contradictory forces in the world in which we live today: on the one hand are the forces of convergence, the increasing knitting-together of the world through globalization, modern communications and trade, and on the other are the opposite forces of disruption, of religious polarization, of the talk of the clash of civilizations, and of terrorism. The two forces, one pulling us together, the other pulling us apart, are concurrent phenomena of our times, and the use by one set of forces of the instruments of the other (the terrorists of

9/11 and 26/11 using the instruments of globalization and convergence) is emblematic of the phenomenon. We have to recognize both the positive and negative forces of the world today, and, from it, a consciousness of the increasing mutual interdependence that characterizes our age.

People everywhere therefore have a growing stake in international developments. To put it another way, the food we grow and we eat, the air we breathe, and our health, security, prosperity and quality of life are increasingly affected by what happens beyond our borders. And that means we can simply no longer afford to be indifferent about the rest of the world, however distant other countries may appear.

Now these four broad aspects are descriptive of global governance, rather than prescriptive. But from such a description, it is clear that global governance rests on the realization that security is not indeed just about threats from enemy states or hostile powers, but that there are common phenomena that cut across borders and affect us all. Nor can they be solved by any one country or any one group of countries, which make them unavoidably the shared responsibility of humankind.

This idea has gained strong ground through the 1990s and through the first part of this century. There is an obvious list of such problems: terrorism itself, the proliferation of weapons of mass destruction, of the degradation of our common environment, of climate change (quite obviously because we cannot put up a fence in the sky to sequester our own climate), of persistent poverty and haunting hunger, of human rights and human wrongs, of mass illiteracy and massive displacement. There are financial and economic crises (because the financial contagion becomes a virus that spreads from one country to others), the risk of trade protectionism, refugee movements, drug trafficking. And we must not overlook epidemic disease. Take the SARS epidemic in China: initially there was an attempt to keep it quiet, but it was very easy for the virus to hop on a plane and show up in Toronto, and suddenly it became a global phenomenon, no longer something that could be contained in any one country. The same is true of AIDS, which travelled from the Congo to California and on to the world's consciousness, just as it is true of swine flu (H1N1) today.

The growing list of global 'problems without passports' also calls for solutions that cross frontiers. Individual countries may prefer not to deal with such problems directly or alone, but they are impossible to ignore. So handling them together internationally is the obvious way of ensuring they are tackled; it is also the only way. Some scholars of international affairs have begun to speak of an idea they call 'responsible sovereignty', the notion that nations must cooperate across borders to safeguard resources and to tackle common threats.

This kind of thinking is also reflective of the change in the way the world thinks about security. After 1945 and throughout the Cold War, the concept of security was taken as relating to nation states seeking to protect their territorial sovereignty and national interests from the threat or use of force by foreign powers. The security debate was framed in terms of defence, arms build-ups and military alliances. With the end of the Cold War and the receding prospect of superpower conflict, security theorists began to focus on threats to security based upon internal conflicts and internecine wars—civil wars, ethnic conflict, secessionist struggles and terrorist attacks—as well as the continuing dangers of the nuclearization of 'rogue states', those assumed to be more predisposed to using nuclear weapons than those who had developed them decades earlier.

These threats, however, are still seen in terms of the security of sovereign states. In the context of global governance, however, a new concept has emerged: the concept of 'human security', a notion that focuses more on the protection of the individual than on the sovereignty of the state. In the words of the 2003 report of the Commission on Human Security, security involves the need 'to protect the vital core of all human lives in ways that enhance human freedoms and human fulfillment'. The commission argues that 'the security of one person, one community, one nation rests on the decisions of many others—sometimes fortuitously, sometimes precariously', and that 'policies and institutions must find new ways to protect individuals and communities'.

How can such security be ensured? Clearly, there is an ineluctable link to the emerging concept of global governance. Human security cannot be the pursuit of any one nation, however rich or powerful it might be. It manifestly requires international cooperation within global bodies, as well as action by international and interstate organizations such as the United Nations itself (including through the operations of specialized agencies working on health, children, labour standards, etc., and the negotiation, conclusion and application of international treaties and conventions). What about the old-fashioned idea of security in the military sense? That is no exception: the UN conducts peacekeeping missions, and so do regional organizations like ECOWAS in West Africa and NATO in Europe, almost always acting under a mandate from the world body. These are all examples of collective military action in a global governance context, and they involve nation states ceding some degree of control over the deployment of their national defence and security forces to supranational institutions. Even a non-UN-authorized mission like that of ISAF, the International Security Assistance Force, in Afghanistan involves contributions from several countries, all in the name of a higher global good.

So the world has evolved significantly towards greater global governance since the end of the Second World War. And yet the global governance structures of today still reflect the realities of 1945 and not of 2012. As we look around the world of 2012, we cannot fail to note the increase in the number of major powers across the world since the structures of the international system were put in place in 1945. It is an undeniable fact that the emerging powers have moved very much from the periphery to the centre of global discourse and global responsibility, and they have now a legitimate and an increasingly voluble desire to share power and responsibility in the global system. So, too, do the so-called social forces—NGOs, civil society movements—which have become impossible to ignore in any discussion of global governance, but which lie outside the scope of the present analysis.

India feels very strongly that there is a clear need for an expansion of the Security Council in both categories—permanent and non-permanent. But it also sees the Security Council as part of a broader process of renewing the United Nations. Like many developing countries, India would like to see the General Assembly strengthened as the primary intergovernmental legislative body, which it is not yet; it has become too often a rhetorical forum, prone to declaratory effulgences without effect, rather than one which acts as a legislative body driving the action of the UN organization. The UN's Economic and Social Council too should become a more meaningful development-oriented body, and a serious instrument of development governance. A greater sharpening is also required in the focus and the operational efficiency of the UN funds, agencies and programmes, whose effectiveness is so important for so many of the world's vulnerable and developing people.

India is conscious, too, that the international financial institutions set up at Bretton Woods in 1944 are also in need of reform, since they too reflect the realities of a vanished era: Belgium, for instance, disposes of the same weighted vote as China in these institutions. The G20 summit in Pittsburgh in September 2009 set in motion a process for global redesign of the international financial and economic architecture, and is thus emerging as the premier forum for international economic cooperation. The G20 has become a meaningful platform for North–South dialogue precisely because the South is not completely outweighed by the North in the composition of the G20. India will use its position in this grouping to pursue a long-term objective of broad parity between the developed countries and the developing and transition economies in the international financial institutions.

This is reflected in the Pittsburgh summit decision to reform the Bretton Woods institutions, the creation of a mechanism for G20 experts to address regulatory reform, and plans to shift decision-making power (5 per cent of the IMF quota share and 3 per cent of the World Bank's voting power) from the developed world to the developing and transition economies. Nations like India, Brazil, Russia and China have called for higher figures—7 per cent of the IMF quota share and 6 per cent of the World Bank's voting powers—to be transferred. India has already established itself as a key player in the G20, where Prime Minister Manmohan Singh is a notably influential voice, and this institution—or a variant of it, such as a smaller 'G13' being touted in some circles as an alternative to both the G8 and the G20—could well prove a more valuable mechanism for international impact in the long term than the United Nations.

It certainly seems incontestable that the recent global financial crisis showed that the surveillance of risk by international institutions and early warning mechanisms are needed for all countries. In other words, it is important that, in the context of global governance, the developing countries should have a voice in overseeing the global financial performance of all nations, rather than it simply being a case of the rich supervising the economic delinquency of the poor.

India also has an evident interest in continued economic liberalization worldwide, which it needs to support overtly and actively, given its stake in freer global trade across the board in goods and services. This means that India would need to start taking more explicit positions in bilateral and multilateral forums in favour of keeping the world economic order open, and play an active role in ensuring such an outcome. New Delhi should, out of self-interest as well as principle, play to its own strengths by advocating liberalization in transnational labour flows, not just capital flows. It has been suggested that India should also take a lead in proposing innovative totalization agreements and tax treaties that would permit the movement of labour and human capital. Under the UPA government, India has energetically pursued global cooperation on issues of bank transparency, money laundering and the oversight of tax havens. This has obvious domestic benefits as well as international ones. Another area of domestic importance with international implications is that of FDI into India, which is currently lower than outward investments by Indian companies abroad. It is essential for India to undertake the domestic reforms necessary to attract and retain FDI; this implies vigorously pursuing the domestic economic reform agenda that many observers currently see as stagnating. All of these initiatives will make New Delhi a more credible and effective player in the Bretton Woods institutions and the WTO. India's interest in the idea of a 'BRICS Bank', floated at that grouping's New Delhi summit in 2012, is an indication of its willingness to challenge global economic assumptions, all of which are currently West-centric.

A reform package that incorporates both Security Council and Bretton Woods reforms could transform global governance, whereas failure to reform could doom it. The international system—as constructed following the Second World War—will be almost unrecognizable by 2030 owing to the rise of emerging powers, a transformed global economy, a real transfer of relative wealth and economic power from the West, or the North, to other countries in the global South, and the growing influence of non-state actors, including terrorists, multinational corporations and criminal networks. In the next two decades, this new international system will be coping with the issues of ageing populations in the developed world; increasing energy, food and water constraints; and worries about climate change and migration. Global changes, including India's own transformation, will mean that resource issues—including energy, food and water, on all of which demand is projected to outstrip easily available supplies over the next decade or so—will gain prominence on the international agenda.

The need for increased, more democratic and more equitable global governance will therefore be even greater. Let us look even further than the next two decades. Growth projections for Brazil, Russia, India and China indicate they will collectively match the original G7's share of global GDP by 2040–50. All four, probably, will continue to enjoy relatively rapid economic growth and will strive for a multipolar world in which their capitals are among the poles.

The experts tell us that, historically, emerging multipolar systems have been more unstable than bipolar or unipolar ones. The recent, indeed ongoing, global financial crisis underlines that the next twenty years of transition to a new system are fraught with risks. Global policy-makers will have to cope with a growing demand for multilateral cooperation when the international system will be stressed by the incomplete transition from the old to the new order. And the new players will not want to cooperate under the old rules.

The multiplicity of actors on the international scene could, if properly accommodated, add strength to our ageing post–Second World War institutions, or they could fragment the international system and reduce international cooperation. Countries like India have no desire to challenge the international system, as did other rising powers like Germany and Japan in the nineteenth and twentieth centuries. But they certainly wish to be given a place at the global high table. Without that, they would be unlikely to volunteer to share the primary burden for dealing with such issues as terrorism, climate change, proliferation and energy security, which concern the entire globe.

The dominance of a handful of small industrialized Western countries, especially in the international financial institutions (the so-called Bretton Woods organizations), looks increasingly anomalous in a world where economic dynamism has shifted irresistibly from the West to the East. With all of this, and the emergence of new powers and forces which, unlike China, were omitted from the high table in 1945, we have clearly reached a point where there is need for a system redesign of global governance to ensure that all countries can participate in a manner commensurate with their capacity.

Clearly, what we in India are looking for is a more inclusive multilateralism, and not, as some American and Chinese observers have suggested, a G2 condominium. There is a consensus in our country that India should seek to continue to contribute to international security and prosperity, to a well-ordered and equitable world, and to democratic, sustainable development for all. This we will continue to do, and we will do so in an environment in which our standing has clearly grown. 'India's voice carries more weight today in multilateral forums,' writes an astute observer, David Malone, 'largely due to its enhanced economic performance, political stability and nuclear capability . . . [O]n the international stage India now exerts real if still tentative geostrategic and economic influence.' This it does both in broader multilateral forums like those associated with the UN, and in smaller groups of selected countries with specific influence on an issue. It nominated an Indian, the able Kamalesh Sharma, to head the (formerly British) Commonwealth in 2008, but despite his convincing election to the position of its Secretary-General, there is little indication of that institution moving to markedly higher priority in Indian policy-making circles.

The need for increased, more democratic and more equitable global governance cannot be denied. Jobs anywhere in the world today depend not only on local firms and factories, but on faraway markets for the goods they buy and produce, on licences and access from foreign governments, on international financial trade rules that ensure the free movement of goods and persons, and on international financial institutions that ensure stability—in short, on the international system constructed in 1945. We just have to bring this system into the world of 2012.

Our globalizing world clearly needs institutions and standards. Not 'global government', for which there is little political support anywhere. But 'global governance', built on laws and norms that countries negotiate together, and agree to uphold as the common 'rules of the road'. Human security requires a world in which sovereign states can come together to share burdens, address common problems and seize common opportunities. If we are determined to live in a world governed by global rules and shared values, we must strengthen and reform the multilateral institutions that the enlightened leaders of the last century have bequeathed to us. Only then can we fulfil the continuing adventure of making this century better than the last.

———

From the foregoing emerges the idea that India can and must play an increasing—and increasingly prominent—role in the stewardship of what is called 'the global commons', the collection of national resources and institutions that are part of the often intangible patrimony of humankind. These include (but are not limited to) our environment; outer space and cyberspace; the waters of the oceans; and unexplored continents like Antarctica and the Arctic which may well, with global warming, become both exploitable and habitable. Because the global commons is, by definition, beyond the national jurisdiction of any specific country, the United Nations remains the most logical instrument for safeguarding the global commons and promoting the collective interest of humanity in protecting and developing it.

Yes, the United Nations is an often flawed institution. But at its best and its worst, it is a mirror of the world: it reflects not just our divisions and disagreements but also our hopes and aspirations. As the UN's great second Secretary-General, Dag Hammarskjöld, put it, the United Nations was not created to take mankind to heaven, but to save humanity from hell.

And that it has. We must not forget that the UN has achieved an enormous amount in its sixty-seven years. Most important of all, it prevented the Cold War from turning hot—first, by providing a roof under which the two superpower adversaries could meet and engage, and, second, by mounting peacekeeping operations that ensured that local and regional conflicts were contained and did not ignite a superpower clash that could have sparked off a global conflagration. Over the years, nearly 200 UN-assisted peace settlements have ended regional conflicts. And in the past two decades, more civil wars have ended through mediation than in the previous two centuries combined, in large part because the UN provided leadership, opportunities for negotiation, strategic coordination and the resources to implement peace agreements. More than 350 international treaties have been negotiated at the UN, setting an international framework that reduces the prospect for conflict among sovereign states. The UN has built global norms that are universally accepted in areas as diverse as decolonization and disarmament, development and democratization. And the UN remains second to none in its unquestioned experience, leadership and authority in coordinating humanitarian action, from tsunamis to human waves of refugees. When the blue flag flies over a disaster zone, all know that humanity is taking responsibility—not any one government—and that when the UN succeeds, the whole world wins.

This is what gives India, as a responsible global power, a stake in the success of the United Nations. In all of this, the Security Council remains the key instrument to determine policy, to bring about a convergence of world opinion on burning questions of peace and security, and to guide and supervise the organization's action. It is only natural that India, which has come a long way since it first joined the UN's founding members as a British colony in 1945, should expect a place at the high table while these questions are being discussed. But a key role in the other major multilateral institutions at (or emerging from) the UN is also indispensable in this effort.

It is said that the divisions at the UN over such issues as the Iraq and Libyan wars and the crises over Syria and Iran have led to a worldwide crisis of confidence in the international system. But as my Chinese friends at the UN used to tell me, in their language, the Chinese character for 'crisis' is made up of two other characters—the character for 'danger' and the character for 'opportunity'. There is a real danger that the organization will again be seen as increasingly irrelevant to the real world over which it presides. And yet there is an opportunity to reform it so that it is not only relevant, but an essential reflection of what our world has become in the second decade of the twenty-first century. I believe strongly that the UN needs reform, not because it has failed, but because it has succeeded enough to be worth investing in. And that India should help lead the effort for reform as well as play a visible and leading role in the revived UN emerging from its efforts.

Why does all this matter at all? Today, whether you are a resident of

Delhi or Dar-es-Salaam, whether you are from Thiruvananthapuram or Toronto, it is simply not realistic to think only in terms of your own country. What happens in South America or Southern Africa—from democratic advances to deforestation to the fight against AIDS—can affect our lives wherever we live, even where my voters are in southern India. And your choices here—what you buy, how you vote—can resound far away. We all graze on the global commons.

Of course, we cannot meaningfully speak of security today in purely military terms. Indeed, informed knowledge about external threats to a nation, the fight against terrorism, a country's strategic outreach, its geopolitically derived sense of its national interest and the way in which it articulates and projects its presence on the international stage are all intertwined, and are also conjoined with a country's internal dynamics. There can no longer be a foolproof separation of intelligence from policy-making, of external intelligence and internal reality, of foreign policy and domestic society. Indeed even the very image of our intelligence apparatus contributes to the perception of a country, especially in its own neighbourhood.

But can there be national security without a sense of 'global security'? National security is easily understood—keeping a country and its people safe behind defensible borders. What is global security?

As a former United Nations official, it is clear to me that, in an era of rapid technological advances, increasing economic interdependence, globalization and dramatic geopolitical change, there is no choice but to see security in all-encompassing terms across our globe. The assault on the World Trade Center in New York on 9/11 has already created global consciousness of one kind of danger that spans the globe, but there is more to it than terrorism. Some 2600 people died in the World Trade Center on 11 September 2001. But some 26,000 people also died on that same day around the world—from starvation, unclean water and preventable disease. We cannot afford to exclude them from our idea of global security.

While poverty and human insecurity may not be said to 'cause' civil war, terrorism or organized crime, they all greatly increase the risk of instability and violence. Catastrophic terrorism against the rich countries can affect the development prospects of millions in poor countries by causing a major economic downturn or forcing developed nations to focus on their own concerns. So global security can be said to rest in the creation of a kind of global order that responds to both hard and soft threats, and that does so through a network of states sharing common values and compatible approaches to governance. In this sense I would argue that India has a stake in such a world order, and that it also seeks to be the kind of society that ensures the safety and well-being of its citizens with full respect for their human rights, their basic needs and their physical security.

Across the globe, the threats to peace and security in the twenty-first century include not just international war and conflict but also civil war and internal violence, the insidious depredations of organized crime, the virulent menace of terrorism and the risks posed by weapons of mass destruction. And the threats facing the globe also include the scourges of poverty, of famine, of illiteracy, of deadly disease, of the lack of clean drinking water, of environmental degradation, of injustice, and of human insecurity. All of these threats make human beings less secure; they also undermine states and make them less secure.

Both within countries and across our globalized world, the threats we face are interconnected. The rich are vulnerable to the threats that attack the poor and, paradoxical as it may sound, the strong are vulnerable to the sufferings of the weak. Former UN Secretary-General Kofi Annan famously called for a new global security consensus based on the interconnectedness of such threats. 'A nuclear terrorist attack on the United States or Europe would have devastating effects on the whole world,' he wrote. 'But so would the appearance of a new virulent pandemic disease in a poor country with no effective health-care system. We must respond to HIV/AIDS as robustly as we do to terrorism,' he added, 'and to poverty as effectively as we do to proliferation.' In India as well, we need to tackle the same range of threats if we are to keep our people secure.

The world has clearly evolved since the era when the Cold War seemed frozen in place, borders seemed immutable, and the Soviet Union looked as if it would last forever. In the same vein, the new threats we have to deal with require new responses from the international system, for which new ways of cooperation may need to be devised.

Human security requires a world in which sovereign states can come together to share burdens, address common problems and seize common opportunities. If we are determined to live in a world governed by global rules and shared values, we must strengthen and reform the multilateral institutions that the enlightened leaders of the last century have bequeathed to us. In this interconnected world, we need an effective and representative United Nations, in all our interests. And as one who was once the Indian candidate for the secretary-generalship, I trust I will be forgiven for quoting Mahatma Gandhi, who famously said, 'You must *be* the change you wish to see in the world.' The UN is no exception. To change the world, the UN must change too.

I am convinced there is much that can be accomplished with the UN as the lynchpin of our system of global governance. I am not advocating world government; we all know that such an idea would be deeply unwelcome in many places, and is neither practical nor desirable in today's world. India is not alone in being proud of its sovereignty and unwilling to dilute it. But India has every interest in helping devise laws and norms in collaboration with other countries, and agreeing to uphold them as the 'rules of the road' for the global commons. And it is in India's interests to help maintain a forum where sovereign states can come together to do this.

So much for the architecture. But, as the old saying goes, a house is not a home. Something more—something extremely important, although not quite so tangible—is needed: the new UN must encapsulate the twenty-first century's equivalent of the spirit that informed its founding. It must amplify the voices of those who would otherwise not be heard, and serve as a canopy beneath which all can feel secure. The UN is, and must continue to be, a forum where the rich and powerful can commit their strength and their wealth to the cause of a better world. And it must continue to provide the stage where great and proud nations, big and small, rich and poor, can meet as equals to iron out their differences and find common cause in their shared humanity. The India of Mahatma Gandhi and Jawaharlal Nehru can certainly strive to ensure that the UN of the twenty-first century never forgets that it is both a child and a source of hopes for a better world—hopes that all human beings share. This is the only UN we have to help surmount the challenges posed by our shared space in the twenty-first century, and we need to do our best in India to ensure our rightful place in it—to ensure that it does the right thing and that it does the thing right.

———

What sort of role does India need and expect to play on global issues in the second decade of the twenty-first century, and beyond?

When India was elected (by record margin) to a non-permanent seat on the Security Council for the term 2011–12, it joined an unusually heavyweight set of countries. Germany and South Africa were elected at the same time, while Brazil and Nigeria were halfway through their two-year terms as non-permanent members. This also meant that, unusually, four international groupings were found on the Council in 2011: RIC, the Russia–India–China triumvirate that meets twice a year at foreign minister level; BRIC, which adds Brazil to the list and which became BRICS with the later incorporation of South Africa; IBSA, the India–Brazil–South African alliance of the three largest southern hemisphere powers; and BASIC, which brought Brazil, South Africa, India and China together during the climate change negotiations in Copenhagen in 2009. Interestingly enough, the only country that belongs to all four is India—a pointer to the extent to which India has become a fulcrum in global politics.

It also hinted at a larger and more important change in global politics. Half the members of the G20, the grouping that is now the world's premier forum on international economic questions, were serving on the Council, dealing with issues of peace and security. The 'permanent five' (P5) countries—the United States, Britain, France, China and Russia—that had become accustomed, in recent years, to arriving at deals among themselves and more or less imposing them on the ten non-permanent members, suddenly discovered that this was not possible with the five big ones, that expected to be consulted and whose acquiescence on key questions could not be assumed (as several of them showed by dissenting, for instance, over Libya, Syria and Iran). At the same time, the performance of the aspirant countries on the Council was described in Washington as if it were a job interview for the possible permanent seat, their 'responsible behaviour' (or lack thereof) as a harbinger of what is to come if and when they receive permanent status.

Whether this cramped India's style or not, it took itself seriously on the Council, surprised some observers by signing up to the West's key resolutions on Libya and Syria while opposing others, and responsibly chaired the Council's Counter-Terrorism Committee. India did not hesitate, in its first year on the Security Council, to argue the classic outsider's case for its transformation. As Foreign Minister S.M. Krishna declared, 'The international structure for maintaining peace and security and peacebuilding needs to be reformed. Global power and the capacities to address problems are much more dispersed than they were six decades ago. The current framework must address these realities.' But in almost the same breath he went on to assure the big powers that India would not challenge their major interests: 'We understand the expectations that accompany our Council membership. We are acutely conscious of the need for effective coordination between the P5 and the elected members, especially those whose credentials for permanent membership stand acknowledged. On issues concerning international peace and security, all of us are on the same page.'

One of the immediate implications of serving on the Council was the need to take positions on matters that in recent years some Indian mandarins have preferred to duck. These all proved to be matters that called for creative and courageous thinking, going beyond entrenched positions or reflexive allegiance to non-aligned solidarity. As one Indian critic trenchantly observed, 'It's no use saying India deserves a permanent seat at the UNSC because it represents one-sixth of humanity, if that one-sixth of humanity seldom expresses an opinion.' It is difficult to argue that India consistently passed the test; some of the bureaucratic and political contortions preceding its policy statements in certain areas led to contradictory and sometimes confused positions, not always rendered clearer by the official 'explanation of votes' that followed.

But the experience undoubtedly helped India come to terms with the new expectations of it in the changed global environment. One example was the difference between being an 'outsider' in the perennial jurisdictional quarrels between the Security Council and the General Assembly, to being a privileged insider. For instance, India had to reconsider its traditional opposition to the Council's tendency to broaden its own mandate by taking on issues New Delhi generally feels belong properly to the General Assembly. The Council has tended to stretch into areas like the prevalence of HIV/AIDS, climate change and the empowerment of women, which go beyond any strict construction of the term 'peace and security'. And yet, as a member both of the G20 and the Security Council, India may well see an interest in bringing up issues of food security or energy security, which touch on the core concerns of both groups and which afford an intriguing opportunity to take advantage of the interconnections between them.

On the whole, its performance served as an effective dress rehearsal for a more enduring role on the world body's premier decision-making organ. All in all, India's place on the Council offered an extraordinary opportunity, after two decades of absence from the global high table, to demonstrate to the world what twenty-first-century India is capable of. It used that opportunity to project itself as a responsible global power, one with its own independent views on major issues, and as a key voice on issues such as peacekeeping, human rights and counterterrorism, on which its own experience and perspective were of inestimable value to the international community. Though there are still several months of India's second year to go as I write these words, India should emerge from the experience with its reputation and credibility as a major global player enhanced. In any case, the world has been watching.

India has a long record of tangible contributions to the United Nations, for example as an outstanding champion of the principle and practice of technical cooperation for development—I believe it has provided more technical experts to the UN than any other country. It has also long been an effective voice on issues like the management of outer space, where its possession of a credible capacity in rocket and satellite development gives its views added heft. Similarly, its global status in the information technology arena makes it a natural to play a leading role in the governance of the Internet and in the emerging field of cyber security. On environmental issues, it has steered a careful course between accepting the common responsibility of humankind to protect the ozone layer through ecologically sound policies and defending the rights of developing countries to pull their people out of poverty despite some negative environmental consequences. (Given the unequal distribution of costs and benefits of mitigation measures required to promote a more sustainable use of the world's ecological resources while promoting the urgent task of human development, the environment is an archetypal issue for the management of the global commons, and India's role could be indispensable in helping craft the right policy framework, including, for instance, the transfer of 'green technologies' at affordable cost to the developing world.) India has even sent expeditions to the Antarctic Ocean in order not to miss out on staking a legitimate claim to being heard and respected on the issue of how that last unexplored territory is to be handled. Its navy has participated in international humanitarian and anti-piracy missions, both within and outside the aegis of the United Nations. All these are harbingers of the greater exercise of global responsibility across the wide range of domains in which the only possible effective action is the multilateral. (And more could soon follow, on such issues as the acidification of oceans, improved mechanisms to handle disputes in international waters and conflicts over maritime jurisdiction.)

All these challenges and opportunities could bring the best out of India, but they will also tax India's capacity to organize its own governmental and diplomatic performance well enough to cope. The development of a serious maritime capacity, for instance, will involve the creation and deployment of a blue-water navy able to exercise influence far from Indian shores; this in turn will require national resources to be generated and deployed for the task. Such an India will also need the bedrock of a solid, growing economy, dispensing a strengthened currency that (in keeping with its recent launch of its own international symbol, ₹) would be credible enough to support a new 'rupee diplomacy' in its own regional hinterland. The spillover effect of taking global duties seriously will imply the transformation and repurposing of entire swathes of India's governmental system. It cannot be taken for granted that this will be done, or done well, but the effort is worth making—and it will merit the kind of recognition and reward that India is already seeking on the Security Council.

Of course, there are issues where the multilateral negotiating forums present India a stark choice between standing up for its national interests more narrowly defined and the global responsibility to forge an accord. One such arena is the world trade talks, where the collapse of negotiations on the Doha Round in early 2008 was largely ascribed to India's intransigence in refusing a compromise on the key question of agriculture. (The talks have resumed and India is consciously making more conciliatory noises, but no substantive change in policy appears imminent.) Another is the climate change arena, where India's role at the Copenhagen Conference in December 2009 as a key component of the BASIC alliance with Brazil, China and South Africa managed, in the prime minister's words, to make it part of the solution rather than part of the problem. India's negotiating posture remains that it supports some reduction in the intensity of growth of its emissions and some measures in mitigation of global warming (both in evident self-interest, since the degradation of India's environment is India's own problem first and foremost); but that it will not agree to legally binding emissions cuts, since it believes these betray the Kyoto principle of 'common but differentiated responsibility' for global warming on the part of the developed countries and the developing. The challenge remains of reconciling two Indian interests, that of striving on the one hand for the global public good of a healthier environment across the planet, while defending on the other the right of Indians to develop themselves and emerge from poverty (a task that evidently requires energy, which in turn will produce emissions). But on both issues—trade and climate change—India has emerged as a key player, one of a handful of countries crucial to a negotiated outcome.

As India proceeds along the path of carving out a role for itself in the global multilateral space, there are some tasks from which it must not shrink. India's is a culture which values modesty in conduct and speech, but one boast we have not been shy of making is that we are proud of being the world's largest democracy. It is India's conviction, from its experience in maintaining this distinction, that democracy is the only form of governance that gives each citizen of a country a strong sense that her destiny and that of her nation is determined only with full respect for her own wishes. India should therefore be proud of being able to demonstrate, in a world riven by ethnic conflict and notions of clashing civilizations, that democracy is not only compatible with diversity, but preserves and protects it, even while serving as a tool to manage the processes of political change and economic transformation so necessary for development.

This is an obvious repudiation of the argument that democracy is incompatible with development, but India has nonetheless been reticent on advertising its own experience and quite unwilling to use it as a calling card in its international relations. For many years India was a reluctant and rather minor participant in the work of the US-inspired Community of Democracies, not wanting to promote an affinity with the West at the expense of its traditional image as the leading trade unionist of Third Worldism. I changed that when I led the Indian delegation to the community's conference in Lisbon in 2009, proclaiming India's commitment to the democratic principle while at the same time using the same forum to push for greater democracy in global governance ('We hope that our common ideals of democratic inclusiveness and a level playing field will guide members of this community in supporting reform of the international governance system,' I suggested somewhat self-servingly) and to seek the support of the world's democracies in India's fight against terrorism. I could not forget India's bureaucratic preference to keep a discreet distance from Bush-era democratic proselytization around the world, but I believed it was necessary for India to help square the circle. 'Let us cherish and value what we have in common as democracies,' I suggested, 'but let us also respect what makes us different from each other, and appreciate that it is in the nature of democracies to be responsive to the very different preoccupations of their own internal constituencies.'

Democracy is, of course, a process and not just an event; it is the product of the exchange of hopes and promises, commitments and compromises which underpins the sacred compact between governments and the governed. But it makes no sense for India to abjure, on grounds of non-aligned principle or developing-country solidarity, its own democracy on the international stage. The Non-Aligned Movement, in any case, is, in the words of the Indian analyst C. Raja Mohan, 'politically divided, economically differentiated and ideologically exhausted'. It cannot be the be-all and end-all of India's international posture. The last century has, despite many horrors along the way, given us, in the famous phrase, a 'world safe for democracy'. India has every reason to work, in the twenty-first century, to establish a world safe for diversity.

This raises broader questions about India's positions on international issues of democracy and human rights, where for a variety of reasons (mainly to do with the inadmissibility of external interference in a newly independent country's internal affairs) India has more often found itself on the side of developing-country violators of human rights than of First World democracies. Hard-headed calculations also often come in: as our discussion in Chapter Three on Myanmar reveals, India accepted the capacity of the junta in Naypyidaw to stifle dissent, jettisoning its own sympathies of Aung San Suu Kyi and her party in favour of an amoral realpolitik that enhanced India's security in its 'soft underbelly' and opened up access to Myanmar's natural resources. India's temporizing responses to repression in Myanmar and elsewhere have raised an uncomfortable question we all need to face: can India afford an ethical foreign policy?

For many years after independence, the answer to that question seemed an obvious one: we couldn't afford a foreign policy that was anything else. Having fought for our freedom against colonial oppression, Pandit Nehru and his colleagues saw themselves as voices for democracy, justice and fairness in the world, and they did not hesitate to express an Indian view of world affairs steeped in these values. Nehru and Krishna Menon, in particular, relished doing so: on issues like Indo-China, South African apartheid and the Suez, they saw themselves as giving a voice to the voiceless and the marginalized of the developing world, often against the great-power hegemons of the day. Indian foreign policy pronouncements were regularly couched in the language of transcendent moral principle. Nehruvian New Delhi spoke often, and our government, for decades, seemed to take greater satisfaction in being right than in being diplomatic.

Few challenged India's right to do so: the land of Ashoka, Akbar and Mahatma Gandhi seemed, to many, to have earned the authority to speak from an elevated ethical podium. But even in those early years there were those who wondered whether it was wise to transform the conduct of international relations into a kind of moralistic running commentary on world affairs. Our moral superiority began to grate on many otherwise well-disposed foreigners even when our positions were unexceptionable; but when we strayed from our own professions of virtue at home, such as over Kashmir or Goa, our critics found it easy to dismiss our foreign policy as posturing humbug.

As time began to tarnish the glow of our independence struggle and the hard realities of national interest became the principal yardstick for both the conduct and the expression of our foreign policy, we quietly abandoned many of our ethical formulations. The gap between profession and practice was in any case becoming more and more glaring. Silence, or at least discretion, was clearly preferable to moralizing—at least in a world in which the inventors of non-alignment had signed a treaty with the Soviet Union, the advocates of democracy had suspended it in a state of Emergency, the vocal opponents of international capitalism had gained the most from globalization, and the leading advocate of disarmament had become a nuclear power. We were now less ethical in our pronouncements, but we were also less hypocritical.

But it has always been difficult for a pluralist democracy to entirely overcome its own instincts in favour of democratic pluralism. So in Nepal we worked to democratize the monarchy, and facilitated the country's transition from a state of rebellion to one of constitutionalism under UN auspices. In Bangladesh we spoke up for democratically elected civilian rulers, even when they pursued policies that were inimical to us (and we have done so again when they were in jail). In Myanmar, when the generals suppressed the popular uprising of 1988, our government initially reacted as most Indians would have wanted it to: India gave asylum to fleeing students, allowed them to operate their resistance movement on our side of the border (with some financial help from New Delhi), and supported a newspaper and a radio station that propagated the democratic voice. For many years, we were on the side of democracy, freedom and human rights in Myanmar—until reality intruded. On Sri Lanka, we danced a complicated dance between supporting the legitimate government in a murderous civil war and standing up for the political rights of the beleaguered Tamil minority. Our vote in the UN Human Rights Council urging Sri Lanka to do more in that respect broke free of our self-imposed prohibitions on supporting country-specific resolutions (which had aligned us in the past on the side of several unsavoury regimes resisting censure by the international community for their abuses of human rights). It was, in a sense, a blow in favour of a more ethical foreign policy, but it remains to be seen whether a new pattern will evolve—one more in keeping with Nehru's glorious invocations of India's soul.

The argument for India to be true to its soul in the multilateral arena ought not to be a controversial one, but New Delhi has been notoriously reluctant to preach to others. Centuries of having foreigners telling you what to do and speaking for you abroad, all the while justifying their enslavement of you as part of a 'civilizing mission', have created in India a chronic unwillingness to allow the former imperial powers ever to dictate terms to the rest of the world again. This deep-rooted streak (which sometimes comes across as bloody-mindedness to newer generations of Westerners untainted by first-hand experience of colonial domination) will never be entirely overcome until India arrives at a new default stance in favour of liberal democracy through its own internal processes. This may take a generation to occur, as the West needs to understand, but India is undoubtedly heading in that direction.

There are also postmodern questions about nationhood and world order that may need to be confronted in the twenty-first century. The Treaty of Westphalia gave birth to the modern conception of the state, first adopted in Europe and more or less followed by the rest of the world in the post-colonial era. Yet in our increasingly interconnected world we are becoming more and more conscious of how our own ground realities seem to defy the hermetically sealed boundaries of the Westphalian nation state. We live in a region in which Pashtuns straddle Af-Pak, Punjabis and Kashmiris are found on both sides of the India–Pakistan divide, Bengalis across Bangladesh and India, and Tamils in both India and Sri Lanka, to take just a few examples. The time has come for us to think harder about how to deal with the interstices of modern states and pre-modern identities. India can help the world think more wisely about such matters, given that our whole country is a lattice work of interstices. Twentieth-century India was anchored in a dour defence of sovereignty; it is not inconceivable that twenty-first-century India might be better placed to think of connections transcending nation states. It will take imagination and creative diplomacy, two qualities which have not always gone together in New Delhi's governmental circles. But the future is a different country, and Indians require no visa to go there . . .

———

India has, in recent years, witnessed a sea change in the way it treats its diaspora. For some decades after independence, the Government of India kept its distance from the far-flung children of the motherland, making it clear that their obligations lay with their countries of adoption. Even when things went wrong for Indians settled in foreign countries, senior Indians were not averse to delivering lectures to the effect that these no-longer-Indians had made their beds abroad and should learn to lie in them. In the 1980s, however, as a serious cash crunch prompted the government to try and bring home some of the resources of Indians abroad, a new attitude dawned. The hands-off approach gave way to an all-enveloping embrace.

India is now the only country that has an official acronym for its expatriates—NRIs, for 'Non-Resident Indians'. In my book *India: From Midnight to the Millennium,* I jokingly suggested that the real debate was whether NRI stood for 'Not Really Indian' or 'Never Relinquished India'. The nearly 25 million people of Indian descent who live abroad fall, of course, into both categories. But the 1600 to 2000 delegates who flock to India from some seventy different countries every year for the Pravasi Bharatiya Divas (Overseas Indian Day) celebrations are firmly in the latter camp. They come to India to affirm their claim to it.

And they come in larger numbers than ever, their enthusiasm undampened by the grim news that litters the Indian newspapers they find upon arrival. Many are not, strictly speaking, NRIs, but PIOs—people of Indian origin now carrying other countries' passports (both together are subsumed under the label Pravasis). Two presidents of Guyana, vice-presidents of Suriname and Mauritius, prime ministers of Fiji and Trinidad and Tobago, and a former governor-general of New Zealand, are all people of Indian origin who have attended the Pravasi gatherings; so have Malaysian politicians and Gulf-based entrepreneurs, tycoons from Hong Kong and titans from the United States, all united by the simple fact of shared heritage—the undeniable reality that even exiles cannot escape when they look into the mirror. They are united, too, in the words of a typically thoughtful and inspiring inaugural address by Prime Minister Manmohan Singh one year, by an 'idea of Indianness'. It is an idea that enshrines the diversity and pluralism both of our country and of its diaspora. In a land that is home to Indians of every conceivable caste and creed, the Pravasi Bharatiya Divas celebration affords to Indians—including former Indians—of every conceivable caste and creed the welcome assurance that they are indeed at home.

The Pravasi Bharatiya weekends usually fall on the anniversary of the return to India of the most famous NRI of them all, Mahatma Gandhi, who alighted from his South African ship at Mumbai's Apollo Bunder port on 9 January 1915. It is curiously appropriate that the event, organized by the newly created Ministry for Overseas Indian Affairs, usually in cooperation with the Federation of Indian Chambers of Commerce and Industry, takes place in different cities each year, as if to embrace the whole country geographically the way in which India seeks to embrace the world with this jamboree.

In his speech to the gathering in 2005, the prime minister traced what he characterized as four waves of Indian emigration: the first, in pre-colonial times, featured Indians leaving our shores as travellers, teachers and traders; the second involved the enforced migration of Indian labour as indentured servants of the British Empire; the third, the tragic displacement of millions by the horrors of Partition; and the fourth, the contemporary phenomenon of skilled Indians seeking opportunity and challenge in our globalized world.

I would probably divide the fourth wave further into two distinct categories: one of highly educated Indians, often staying on after studies abroad in places like the United States, and the other of more modestly qualified but even harder-working migrants, from taxi drivers to shop assistants, who for the most part see their migration as temporary and who remit a larger proportion of their funds home to India than their higher-earning counterparts. But in today's world both sets of 'fourth wave' migrants remain closely connected to the matrbhumi: the ease of communications and travel makes it possible for expatriates to be engaged with the country they left behind in a way that was simply not available to the plantation worker in Mauritius or Guyana a century ago. To tap into this sense of allegiance and loyalty through an organized public gathering was an inspired idea of the previous NDA government, one which the UPA government has built upon through its creation of a 'one-stop shop' in the form of a dedicated ministry.

So I have been mildly surprised by the cynicism of the many desi journalists who thrust microphones into my face during these weekends and ask me if it isn't all a waste of time. 'What does a conference like this actually achieve?' they want to know. 'How is it useful?' This is a remarkably utilitarian approach to the occasion, and I suppose I could have responded by pointing to the many parallel seminars being run by state governments to attract NRI investment, or the session on disaster management that was added one year in the wake of the tsunami. But I preferred to make a larger point: that sometimes the real value of a conference lies in the conferring. Perhaps it is time we realize that instead of counting how many new millions were raised for tourism in Rajasthan or pledged for reconstruction in Port Blair, we should appreciate how much it means to allow NRIs from sixty-one different lands the chance to share their experiences, celebrate their commonalities, offer their ideas and swap visiting cards. Because when India allows its pravasis to feel at home, it is India itself that is strengthened.

This is why I strongly and publicly opposed a move some years ago to reduce the frequency of the annual Pravasi Bharatiya gatherings to one every other year. My argument was clear: this would be a mistake, since the occasion has clearly acquired a momentum that it would be a shame to disrupt. When a locomotive has been gathering steam, why apply the brakes? The dialogue between India and its diaspora has only just begun, I argued: let us not interrupt it.

But it is fair to ask why NRIs matter to India and what would be gained by continuing what one critic called 'a pointless jamboree'. 'These NRIs have left the motherland and gone off to make their fortunes elsewhere,' one Mr A. Mukesh wrote to me. 'They have abandoned India. India does not owe them anything. Indeed, it is they who owe the country that has educated them and given them the opportunity to better their lives abroad.' To Mukesh and others like him, the money spent on celebrating the Pravasi Bharatiya Divas would be better spent in the villages of India.

But I am not suggesting that India 'owes' its NRIs anything, other than an occasion to affirm their Indianness. And of course, while it is a fact that many, perhaps most, of the recent wave of Indian emigrants have benefited from a subsidized education in India before going off to make their living elsewhere, that is not true of many of the pravasis in attendance, who are descended from earlier waves of (often forced) emigration to the far-flung outposts of the British Raj a century or more ago, and who return unburdened by any reason for guilt. Finally, the needs of India's villages are great but the choice is a false one: the NRIs are as committed as any resident Indian to India's development, and have raised and remitted a great deal of money home for the purpose. (Non-resident Gujaratis, for instance, are prominent bulwarks of the 'Vibrant Gujarat' business summits that have helped steer investments to that state.) The expenditure on the Pravasi Bharatiya Divas is not diverted from more worthwhile national causes, but is rather raised specifically for this purpose from sponsors, notably FICCI, which bears the organizational burden entirely.

To turn to the core question, then: why do NRIs matter to India?

Simple: as a source of pride, as a source of support, and as a source of investments. It is entirely natural for Indians to take pride in the successes of their erstwhile compatriots abroad. I once remarked rather cruelly to an interviewer that the only country where Indians as a whole did not succeed was India. That is fortunately no longer the case, as signs of Indians' increasing prosperity are evident everywhere one travels in India, but Indians abroad have certainly given us all a great deal to be proud of. One recent statistic from the United States shows that the Indian-American family's median income is nearly $75,000 a year, slightly more than Japanese-Americans', but some $20,000 higher than the figure for all American families. That kind of success is not merely at the elite end of the scale: in England today, Indian curry houses employ more people than the iron and steel, coal and shipbuilding industries combined.

So we can be proud of the impact Indians have made on foreign societies. But pride is not merely an intangible asset. Living in the United States, I have been struck by the extent to which the success of our NRIs has transformed the public perception of India in the United States. A generation ago, when I first travelled to the United States as a graduate student in 1975, India was widely seen as a land of snake-charmers and begging bowls—poverty marginally leavened by exotica. Today, if there is a stereotypical view of India, it is that of a country of fast-talking high-achievers who are wizards at maths and who are capable of doing most Americans' jobs better, faster and more cheaply in Bangalore. Today IIT is a brand name as respected in certain American circles as MIT or

Caltech. If Indians are treated with more respect as a result, so is India, as the land which produces them. Let us not underestimate its importance in our globalizing world.

The presence of successful and influential NRIs in so many countries also becomes a source of direct support for India, as they influence not just popular attitudes, but governmental policies, to the benefit of the mother country. That two right-wing Governors of US states (Piyush 'Bobby' Jindal of Louisiana and Namrata 'Nikki' Randhawa Haley of South Carolina) are of Indian descent ought not really to make many liberal-minded Indians proud, but it does, because it adds to Indians' sense of self-worth when they see 'people like us' in positions of international prominence. A Canadian provincial premier, Ujjal Dosanjh, several British Lords and lower-house parliamentarians, and even some members of the European Parliament hail from India and are no longer embarrassed to admit to their origins. One feisty former Canadian MP, Ruby Dhalla, is particularly popular in Indian political circles, which she frequents at least as often as her former 'riding'.* They are welcomed in India as people who have achieved power abroad, which makes them all the more worthy of adulation here. And the role of Indians in their adopted countries' politics goes beyond the handful who have achieved election to the many who stuff envelopes, run campaigns and especially raise funds for non-Indian politicians, which makes their views impossible to ignore. The contribution of well-heeled and politically active Indian-Americans to the shift in US policy from indifference to pro-Indianness in recent years simply cannot be overestimated.

But the idea of NRIs as a resource for India goes beyond whatever influence the elected leaders among them can exercise. I haven't even mentioned NRI investments in India—from the remittances of working-class Indians in West Asia that have transformed the Kerala countryside to the millions poured into cutting-edge high-tech businesses in Bangalore or Gurgaon by investors from Silicon Valley. The remittances have been lifesavers for India during the global recession, because they kept increasing even as FDI nosedived. While FDI plummeted to just $19 billion in 2011, NRI remittances went steadily up from $25 billion

---

*'Riding' is Canadian for 'constituency'.

in 2006 to over \$46 billion in 2008–09, the first year of the recession, to \$55 billion in 2009–10 and \$57 billion in 2010–11. The faith of Indian expatriates in India has kept their money flowing homeward; the NRIs have become, in effect, the National Reserve of India.

But we shouldn't get carried away—overseas Indians still invest a lower proportion of their resources in India than overseas Chinese do in China, and they complain vociferously about the non-tariff barriers occluding their entry into the Indian market. Encouraging them to do more—and giving them reasons and opportunities to do more—is certainly a worthwhile task for the Ministry for Overseas Indian Affairs in New Delhi. No doubt this will mean, in turn, putting up with new and repeated demands from NRIs. Expatriate extremism, a phenomenon I had anatomized in my book *India: From Midnight to the Millennium*, is now mercifully a rarity, especially with the eclipse of the Khalistan movement that had been financed by wealthy if misguided Sikhs in North America. But expatriate agitation for several worthwhile causes is entirely legitimate and surfaces quite audibly at the Pravasi gatherings. One issue is that of voting rights: India, shamefully, is one of the few democracies that denies absentee ballots to its own expatriate citizens, though they are now allowed the vote if they are willing to come home to cast it. Another is the perennial call for genuine dual citizenship, which the cynically misnamed Overseas Citizenship of India (OCI, essentially nothing more than a lifetime visa) most certainly is not. But so what? A government that seeks the allegiance, support and money of its diaspora should also be willing to be accountable to it. Hosting a forum once a year where the pravasis can make their views known seems to me a very small price to pay indeed.

A larger question is one of the extent of India's responsibility, if any, to the well-being of its diaspora in their new homelands. While the government has indeed stood up (somewhat ineffectually) for the rights of oppressed Indians in Fiji and acted (with somewhat better results) on the media outcry over violence directed against Indians in Australia, it has not consistently been able to defend the rights of its citizens or PIOs abroad. New Delhi's chronic reluctance to interfere in the internal affairs of sovereign states is an inhibiting factor; so also is the tension, for instance, between needing to maintain good political and economic relations with a country and seeking to protect the welfare of Indian workers in it, which has hamstrung India's ability to protect pravasis in places as far apart as Uganda, Saudi Arabia, Malaysia and Fiji. This leaves New Delhi in the somewhat paradoxical position of not making the problems of NRIs a foreign policy priority, while treating their successes as a national achievement and seeking to benefit from their resources and remittances.

———

As this broad overview of what Germans might call India's Weltanschauung suggests, India already bestrides the world in important ways, engages with it at several levels and has developed a stake in safeguarding and promoting interests that go beyond the strictly national. As it contemplates enhanced responsibilities across the globe in the twenty-first century, it fulfils one essential requirement: India is at home in the world.

Chapter Eleven

'Multi-Alignment': Towards a 'Grand Strategy' for India in the Twenty-first Century

When researching in 1977 the doctoral dissertation that became my first book, *Reasons of State*, I was told by a (then already retired) Indian diplomat that 'Indian diplomacy is like the love-making of an elephant: it is conducted at a very high level, accompanied by much bellowing, and the results are not known for two years.' Indian diplomacy has become somewhat sprightlier since those days, but the gentle indictment of a style of foreign policy-making that was widely considered to be long on rhetoric and short of hard-headed substance still echoes through the corridors of New Delhi's South Block.

At the time, I lamented the low correlation between foreign policy as conceived and articulated by decision-makers and national interests in security and geopolitical terms. This point was obviously a rather contentious one. It was presumptuous of me, in my early twenties, to decry the lack, as I saw it, of a strategic vision on the part of India's policy-makers beyond the bromides of non-alignment. I wrote passionately about the failure to define a conception of the Indian national interest in other than universalist-ideological terms—itself a manifestation, no doubt, of my academic over-reliance on public declarations and official statements, albeit supplemented by several astonishingly candid interviews (Mrs Gandhi's government had just fallen in the elections of 1977 after her disastrous experiment with Emergency rule, and every one of her key advisers and foreign ministers was available and willing to talk freely, never expecting her to come back to power). India's declaratory effulgences about non-alignment featured rather too many references to 'peace' and 'friendship' as cardinal motivations and attributes of foreign policy, which I argued were scarcely adequate substitutes for a clear conception of the nation's specific goals in foreign policy, their realizability and the tasks to be performed in order to attain them. In Nehru's time, I averred, the Sino-Indian war was the most dramatic, but not the only, demonstration of this failure; and yet just nine years later, India's masterly handling of its foreign policy objectives in the 1971 Bangladesh crisis offered a convincing counternarrative.

My argument was all the more sustainable because of the widely prevalent view of Nehru's foreign policy as a value in itself, as (in one Indian scholar's formulation) an 'imperative' not to be judged by the 'mundane criteria of success'. Indeed, after 1962, success was an inappropriate criterion to apply to Nehru's foreign policy. As a global stratagem, non-alignment might initially have gained India some freedom of manoeuvre between the superpowers and brought it a prestige and influence out of proportion to India's true strength, but it did not serve Nehru well in his hour of crisis. No wonder non-aligned scruples were quietly jettisoned by his own daughter in 1971, when realpolitik, rather than woolly declarations of non-aligned solidarity, was needed and pursued, and India rushed willingly into the Soviet embrace as a shield against a possible Pakistani–Chinese alliance. Though New Delhi proceeded gently to distance itself from Moscow thereafter (including concluding defence deals with France, the United States and the United Kingdom in the 1980s), the lingering effects of that embrace remained apparent in Indian policies on Cambodia and Afghanistan, and it was only with the end of the Cold War in 1991 that India once again became truly non-aligned—at a time when there no longer were two powers to be non-aligned between.

It should go without saying that every country needs a foreign policy that is linked to national interests concretely defined. To meet this test, the Indian government should have been able to develop and possess a view of the national interest in regional and international affairs, and to apply it in practice; the 'national interest', in this formulation, should be a concept transcending the mere enunciation of foreign policy principles. It is worthwhile to advocate peace and good neighbourliness as a *national principle*, for instance, but such advocacy becomes irrelevant if there is a belligerent army marching across one's borders; *national interests* then demand capable military self-defence. This may seem self-evident, but the distinction has been blurred in less clear-cut situations over the years by the makers and articulators of India's foreign policy. Indian diplomacy has often been seen by close observers as more concerned with principles than interests—a tendency that infects Indian negotiating strategies as well, making New Delhi less likely to compromise since principles are usually immutable while interests can be negotiable.

Even India's diplomatic style, it has been suggested, often privileges intellect over interest and process over outcome. Our diplomats combine brilliance, hard work and flair with a talent for winning debates that can sometimes be counterproductive. David Malone has noted that Indian diplomats' 'perceived need to outflank all potential or actual rivals and impress all comers sometimes leads Indian practitioners to monopolize attention through rhetorical brilliance and to spend as much time on impressing the gallery as on tending effectively to Indian interests. The cleverest person in the room may win many arguments, but still not win the game.' The tendency to get carried away by the sheer momentum of diplomatic argument, he suggests, leads 'Indian officials, when in international forums . . . to pursue outcomes or adopt positions that are contrary to the objectives of Indian foreign policy set at the political level.' This has led a sympathetic observer, Edward Luce, to suggest that 'India is rising in spite of its diplomacy.' Such a view may be harsher than justified, but it does suggest that a gentler and more accommodative tone should be developed that accords better with the demands of the multilateral high table at which India expects to be seated.

In defining the Indian national interest, there are fundamental domestic verities that foreign policy must either promote or at least not undermine: India's liberal democracy; its religious, ethnic and cultural pluralism (a term I prefer to the more traditional Nehruvian 'secularism'); and its overriding priority of pulling its people out of poverty and ensuring their economic well-being. These are as fundamental to our national interest as preserving an effective, well-trained and non-political military that will secure and protect our borders, as well as security forces that will deal with domestic sources of conflict, from misguided Maoists to secessionist insurgencies. If all of these elements and objectives constitute India's core national interests, New Delhi must maintain the domestic structures and capacities to pursue them, as well as strive to ensure the shaping of a world order that permits, and ideally facilitates, their fulfilment.

This requires, as Jawaharlal Nehru presciently noted half a century ago, that priority be given to success on the domestic front: 'I do not pretend to say that India, as she is, can make a vital difference to world affairs,' he said. 'So long as we have not solved most of our own problems, our voice cannot carry the weight that it normally will and should.' His words remain true fifty years later, though India's recent economic successes have already given its voice more weight than it has possessed for some time, and this process should continue unless India slips backward drastically at home.

India's basic approach in international affairs goes back to the days of the Constituent Assembly: as the doyen of Indian strategic studies, the late K. Subrahmanyam, put it, India's grand strategy during the second half of the twentieth century 'involved a policy of non-alignment to deal with external security problems, the adoption of the Indian Constitution to address governance challenges, and a partly centrally planned development strategy to accelerate growth'. This was fine in the initial years, but was clearly inadequate as a grand strategy by 1991 and seems very much in need of updating in the second decade of the twenty-first century.

It was against this background that India's National Security Annual Review in 2010 unnecessarily averred that India was now the world's fifth most powerful country, outranking traditional powers such as the United Kingdom, France and Germany. Citing the country's population, military capabilities and economic growth, the Review, issued by the MEA, placed India behind only the United States, China, Japan and Russia in a ranking of global power. For a country still excessively focused on problems in its own neighbourhood, distracted (if not obsessed) with Pakistan and kept off balance by China, this seemed a somewhat far-fetched claim.

The three elements mentioned—population, military capabilities and economic growth—are worth examining in turn. Certainly, India's huge population could be a huge asset. India is a remarkably young country, with an average age of twenty-eight, and 65 per cent of its population under thirty-five. We could have a great demographic advantage in 540 million young people under twenty-five, which means we should have a dynamic, youthful and productive workforce for the next forty years when the rest of the world, including China, is ageing. But we also have 60 million child labourers, and 72 per cent of the children in our government schools drop out by the eighth standard. We have trained the world's second largest pool of scientists and engineers, but 400 million of our compatriots are illiterate, and we also have more children who have not seen the inside of a school than any other country in the world does. We celebrate India's IT triumphs, but information technology has employed a grand total of 5 million people in the last twenty years, while 10 million are entering the workforce each year and we don't have jobs for all of them. Many of our urban youth rightly say with confidence that their future will be better than their parents' past, but this will only happen across the board if we are able to grow our economy to be able to provide employment opportunities for them, and if we can educate and train them to take advantage of these opportunities. The alternative is already starkly visible: there are Maoist insurgencies violently disturbing the peace in 165 of India's 602 districts, and these are largely made up of unemployed young men. In other words, if we don't get it right (and we still have a long way to go both in education and in vocational training), our demographic dividend could even become a demographic disaster.

India's military capabilities are real and their quality has been demonstrated time and again both on the battlefield and in a large number of challenging United Nations peacekeeping operations. But whether in terms of structure, equipment and training the Indian military establishment could yet measure up to the European powers the Review says it has supplanted remains to be proven.

Security in the conventional sense is one area where success or failure at defining and applying national interests becomes most apparent. India has never been a belligerent or expansionist power, and its rise is largely seen by the world as non-threatening; the flip side of that is that it is also seen in some quarters as congenitally pacific and non-assertive. Domestic arrangements reflect some of this passivity. In Chapter Nine, we examined the extent to which the MEA is prepared and resourced to guide a credible role for India on the world stage. But the Ministry of Defence (MoD) is no better equipped to engage other countries on international security issues. As Ashley Tellis has pointed out, 90 per cent of the MoD's personnel is focused on acquisition and there is only one joint secretary entrusted with the task of handling global security cooperation. The resultant lack of capacity has been embarrassing: as Tellis tells it, a number of training exercises scheduled in recent years between the Indian and foreign militaries have had to be called off at the last moment since India simply could not get its act together. This has, inevitably, led to a serious loss of credibility for the country.

As K. Subrahmanyam observed, 'India has lacked an ability to formulate future-oriented defence policies, managing only because of short-term measures, blunders by its adversaries, and force superiority in its favour.' The structure of the armed forces and the nature of defence policy making, planning and training leave much to be desired; there is little coordination among the three services, and proposals to create either a chief of defence staff or a US-style position of chairman of a joint chiefs of staff committee have never been implemented. (It has been suggested that this is because the political class is wary of giving the military too much power, but if true, the country's long record of military subordination to civilian authority makes that concern seem somewhat far-fetched.) There are both a national security council and national security advisory board, but neither can point to a stellar record in promoting policy coherence and strengthening strategic planning. The services lack serious intelligence capacity and world-class area studies expertise; even issues of nuclear policy and strategy do not bear a significant military stamp, partly a reflection of the strong civilian desire to keep the armed forces out of the nuclear area.

It does not help that India's defence bureaucracy is largely unprofessional, a result of the generalist culture that pervades the IAS. In most other countries, the civilian officials of the ministries of defence are security professionals with training and experience in strategic thinking and defence policy. In India, however, they are mostly IAS or Central Civil Services officers who have been assigned to the MoD after running districts or family planning programmes; as one bureaucrat sardonically told me, 'They have been doing other things that have no relevance to defence, and then one day they are put in a place where they are supposed to be strategic thinkers and have to deal with officers of Indian armed forces, who are thorough professionals. How can you not expect a disconnect?'

Few countries face quite the range and variety of security threats that India does —from the ever-present risk, however far-fetched, of nuclear war with Pakistan or China, with both of whom we have unresolved territorial disputes, to Maoist movements in 165 of our 602 districts, secessionist insurgency in the North-East, and terrorist bombs set off by Islamist militants in metropolitan markets. And yet we have not yet evolved a comprehensive national security strategy to cover this entire spectrum of threats. As a democracy, India needs to undertake a strategic defence review that brings in all elements of the security services, the public at large and elected representatives in Parliament, to produce a national security strategy. But such an exercise has not even been attempted.

With the government not yet having formally approved the long-term integrated perspective plan (LTIPP 2007–22) formulated by the military's headquarters integrated defence staff, there is little effort to align India's defence expenditure and purchases with any systematic strategy to modernize and enhance India's combat capacity. Instead, defence procurement—when it is not delayed by a political reluctance to make potentially controversial decisions involving large sums of money—is being undertaken through ad hoc annual procurement plans, in the absence of long-term policy. Whereas China spends 3.5 per cent of its GDP on defence and Pakistan officially spends 4.5 per cent (an estimate that omits counting US military aid and the vast sums allotted to intelligence and counterterrorism operations, which would take the figure well above 6 per cent of GDP), India's defence budget clocks in at the very modest level of below 2 per cent of GDP. At these levels, any meaningful modernization that will substantially enhance India's combat capabilities remains a chimera, and the money at the disposal of the military remains inadequate to upgrade and replace the ageing and obsolete weapons systems with which the Indian defence services, armed police and paramilitary forces are replete.

The absence of a chief of defence staff or a permanent chairman of the joint chiefs—which means there is no single point of military advice to the government on defence strategy—is compounded by the lack of any tri-service integrated theatre commands in such vital emerging areas as the management of aerospace and cyber warfare. The same is true in the maritime arena, where there is a crying need to integrate Indian Ocean policy, naval development and deployment, coastal infrastructure and security, the coast guard and civilian shipping, all of which currently report to different masters and do little to coordinate with each other. Serious morale issues have also arisen over such issues as the welfare of ex-servicemen, whose campaign for 'one rank-one pension' has not met with a satisfactory response; the embarrassing continuing absence (finally to be rectified following a decision in 2012) of a national war memorial to honour the many sacrifices of India's military men and women; and the needless controversy over the date of birth of the army chief, who in 2012 even went to the Supreme Court against his own government and showed up the bureaucratic incompetence that afflicts even such basic military record-keeping.

Among India's most important strategic challenges is that relating to nuclear strategy. India has had to acquire its nuclear literacy the hard way: it is confronted on two of its borders by nuclear-armed states, China and Pakistan, with which it has fought several wars; both still maintain claims against Indian territory and both have a history of nuclear cooperation with each other. At the same time, India has been described by K. Subrahmanyam as 'a reluctant nuclear power'. Mahatma Gandhi and Jawaharlal Nehru were horrified by Hiroshima; both wanted India to strive for a world free of nuclear weaponry. But despite several Indian initiatives for nuclear disarmament, that goal proved a chimera, and India gradually came to the conclusion that as long as some states possessed nuclear weapons, India could not afford not to, especially once it became clear in the late 1970s that Pakistan was well on the way to acquiring nuclear weapons. India's doctrine of no-first-use, and its principled opposition to nuclear proliferation, is consistent with its view that nuclear weapons are an abomination and their possession is intended only to deter. However, Pakistan's refusal to sign on to a similar pledge means that the threat remains of Islamabad resorting to the use of nuclear weapons if it found itself emerging second best in a conventional conflict. This has undoubtedly inhibited India's possible responses to terrorist acts emanating from Pakistan, for instance. The need to develop an assured second-strike capability is immense and vital. This should be allied to a significant maritime nuclear capacity and the possession of an effective missile defence system. It is by no means clear that all these are in place; instead it is widely believed that India has fallen seriously behind Pakistan in the race for nuclear credibility.

The role of the Indian armed forces is principally to constitute a credible deterrent in itself; in K. Subrahmanyam's words, 'preventing wars from breaking out through appropriate weapons acquisitions, force deployment patterns, the development of infrastructure, military exercises, and defence diplomacy'. This is a far more demanding task than conducting routine peacetime operations would normally have been, because with unsettled borders on two sides, the security of the country lies in a credible conventional military capacity that can serve as a deterrent against any adventurism from a possible adversary across the borders. We can be proud of our armed forces, which have distinguished themselves in a number of conflict situations, but we still have a long way to go before we can boast of the kind of integrated and well-resourced defence structure that warrants the National Security Review's claim of great-power status for India.

As for economic growth, it is real and impressive. As the IMF predicted, India overtook Japan in 2012 in PPP terms to become the world's third largest economy. (Japan's GDP of $4.3 trillion did not grow in 2011 after its trifecta of earthquake, tsunami and nuclear disaster, whereas India's $1.3 trillion GDP, which converts to $4.06 trillion in PPP, went up by at least 6.2 per cent.) In addition, India's GDP growth in its Twelfth Five Year Plan (2012–17) is projected at 9 per cent, up from 8.2 per cent in the Eleventh Plan (2007–12). But these figures mask a number of genuine problems, from falling FDI inflows ($19 billion in the 2010–11 fiscal year, one-third the size of inward remittances), widespread corruption which exacts high social and political costs in addition to the obvious economic ones, and high inflation, especially as a result of rampaging fuel and food prices. India's political environment has not proved conducive to fast-tracking the next generation of much-needed reforms, such as opening FDI in retail (floated and then 'suspended' by the government in the face of vociferous opposition, including from within its coalition's own ranks) or reforming labour laws (which currently do more to protect the jobs of those who have them rather than encourage investment to create new jobs). For India to assert itself credibly as a global, and not merely an emerging, power will still require a longer track record of savvy international and domestic policy making, effective economic management and solid progress on the ground in infrastructure, especially roads, ports and power generation.

Nonetheless, there is little doubt that India's leadership since 1991, and particularly under Prime Minister Manmohan Singh since 2004, has shrewdly played its international cards well in the midst of the changing global environment. A foreign policy that ensures friendly relations with countries that are sources of investment, of technology, of energy or (potentially) of food security has been put in place, and a number of previously problematic relationships, from the United States to Israel, have been improved dramatically. Problems on India's borders have been dealt with reasonably effectively and sources of serious trouble adroitly kept at bay.

The question remains, however, of whether all this is taking place within the framework of a credible 'grand strategy' to replace the be-all and end-all carapace of non-alignment that had previously dominated India's strategic approach to the world. To conceive of a grand strategy one needs a vision of the kind of world that could best secure and promote India's national interests. Should India work, for instance, for a multipolar world order, as repeatedly advocated by Russia and China? The Indian-American scholar Sumit Ganguly is sceptical: 'Would a multipolar world order, with a number of powerful states which are either indifferent to or implacably hostile toward India's key national security interests,' he asks, 'be necessarily preferable to American dominance?' The answer perhaps seems more obvious in a New Delhi allergic to any kind of foreign dominance than it does in Professor Ganguly's Washington, but the question is a pertinent one.

So is my earlier focus on the definition of the Indian national interest. This would require grappling, for instance, with the question of whether India sees itself firmly in the camp of liberal democracies besieged by Islamist terrorism and critical of Chinese authoritarianism, and led, for all intents and purposes, by the United States. In a posthumously published essay, K. Subrahmanyam argued:

The real question about the future world order is whether it is to be democratic and pluralistic, or dominated by one-party oligarchies that prioritise social harmony over individual rights. If the US remains the world's predominant power, and China is second, India will be the swing power. It will therefore have three options: partnering with the US and other pluralistic, secular and democratic countries; joining hands with China at the risk of betraying the values of its Constitution and freedom struggle; and remaining both politically and ideologically non-aligned, even if against its own ideals.

He left no doubt about which choice he would make: 'The emerging Indo-US partnership,' he argued, 'is not about containing China. It is about defending Indian values from the challenges of both one-party rule and jehadism, and realising a future in which poverty and illiteracy are alleviated.'

This is by no means a unanimously held view in New Delhi: if anything, the Indian strategic community tends to the almost consensual position that, despite common social and political systems with other democracies, and the fact that it has usually been more secure when surrounded by elected democracies in its own region, India should not actively promote democracy around the world. The Indian aversion to preaching our own virtues to the world is a reasonable one, but India has in fact been actively engaged in democracy promotion, having been for many years the largest single donor to the United Nations' Democracy Fund. But as always, India does not want to see itself pre-committed to any bloc, even one of democracies, for that would infringe upon its freedom of decision-making; New Delhi would prefer, as always, to judge each issue for itself, on a case-by-case basis. The old obsession with strategic autonomy remains. The question is how to make that autonomy a springboard rather than a straitjacket.

A similar question now arises: how should New Delhi balance its energy needs and its political values in its dealings with, say, Myanmar or Iran, where one set of interests (the need for energy security) contends with another (the upholding of democratic values in the former case and the maintenance of partnerships with major countries like the United States, in the latter)? Should the essential internal priority of doing whatever it takes to eliminate acute poverty at home prevail over all other considerations?

A sweeping 'yes' is in fact not enough to cover all possible situations, because a nation, by definition, has more than one way of placing itself in the world and more than one point of interface with other major powers. Even if it were to take a hard-headed realpolitik position on national self-interests as China does, and refuse to be swayed by democratic scruple when direct and tangible economic benefits are at stake, it still has to weigh the consequences of the choices it makes on other relationships—for example, deciding whether it is willing to antagonize the United States as the price to pay for maintaining energy supplies from Iran.

At the same time, much of what we are in the process of accomplishing at home—to pull our people out of poverty and to develop our nation—enables us to contribute to a better world. This is of value in itself, and it is also in our fundamental national interest. A world that is peaceful and prosperous, where trade is freer and universally agreed principles are observed, and in which democracy, the coexistence of civilizations and respect for human rights flourish, is a world of opportunity for India and for Indians to thrive.

If this century has, in the famous phrase, made the world safe for democracy, the next challenge is to make a world safe for diversity. It is in India's interest to ensure that the world as a whole must reflect the idea that is already familiar to all Indians—that it shouldn't matter what the colour of your skin is, the kind of food you eat, the sounds you make when you speak, the God you choose to worship (or not), so long as you want to play by the same rules as everybody else, and dream the same dreams. It is not essential in a democratic world to agree all the time, as long as we agree on the ground rules of how we will disagree. These are the global principles we must strive to uphold if we are to be able to continue to uphold them securely at home.

Because, as I have argued, the distinction between domestic and international is less and less meaningful in today's world, when we think of foreign policy we must also think of its domestic implications. The ultimate purpose of any country's foreign policy is to promote the security and well-being of its own citizens. We want a world that gives us the conditions of peace and security that will permit us to grow and flourish, safe from foreign depredations but open to external opportunities.

Whether global institutions adapt and revive will be determined by whether those in charge are capable of showing the necessary leadership. Right now many of us would suggest that there is a global governance deficit. Reversing it would require strong leadership in the international community by a number of powers, including the emerging ones. India is an obvious contender to provide some of that leadership.

In March 2012, the authors of a report entitled 'Nonalignment 2.0' put it well when they argued that 'India must remain true to its aspiration of creating a new and alternative universality. . . . India already has enormous legitimacy because of the ideological legacies its nationalist movement bequeathed to it. But this legitimacy, once frittered away, cannot be easily recovered. India should aim not just at being powerful: it should set new standards for what the powerful must do.'

This is a huge challenge, and one to which India must rise. An analogy from another field is not encouraging; many would argue that India has not acquitted itself well when given the chance to have a global impact in one domain—that of the sport of cricket, where India accounts for more than 80 per cent of the game's revenues and perhaps 90 per cent of its viewership, giving it an impact on the sport that no country can rival. According to Lawrence Booth, the editor of the 'cricketers' bible', the *Wisden Cricket Almanack*, writing in its 2012 edition:

India have ended up with a special gift: the clout to shape an entire sport. . . . But too often their game appears driven by the self-interest of the few. . . . Other countries run the game along self-serving lines too; cricket's boardrooms are not awash with altruism. But none wields [India's] power, nor shares their responsibility. The disintegration of India's feted batting line-up has coincided with the rise of a Twenty20-based nationalism, the growth of private marketeers and high-level conflicts of interest. It is a perfect storm. And the global game sits unsteadily in the eye. India, your sport needs you.

Clearly, international opinion does not believe that, in its domination of world cricket, India has set new standards for what the powerful must do. Broadening the analogy to global geopolitics, one could well say: India, your world needs you.

So India must play its due part in the stewardship of the global commons (including everything from the management of the Internet to the rules governing the exploitation of outer space). We can do it. India is turning increasingly outward as a result of our new economic profile on the global stage, our more dispersed interests around the world, and the reality that other countries, in our neighbourhood as well as in Africa, are looking to us for support and security. The 'problems without passports' that I have referred to need blueprints without borders—blueprints that require rules which India can contribute to making. The creation of global public goods is a new challenge, and it is one that a transforming India can rise to.

India has the ability and the vision to promote global partnerships across the broad range of its interests; it only needs to act. In a 2012 speech, National Security Adviser Shivshankar Menon stated that 'As a nation state India has consistently shown tactical caution and strategic initiative, sometimes simultaneously. But equally, initiative and risk taking must be strategic, not tactical, if we are to avoid the fate of becoming a rentier state.' He provided an instructive example of what this would mean in practice:

> It means, for instance, that faced with piracy from Somalia, which threatens sea-lanes vital to our energy security, we would seek to build an international coalition to deal with the problem at its roots, working with others and dividing labour. Today the African Union has peacekeeping troops on the ground in Somalia. We could work with others to blockade the coast while the AU troops act against pirate sanctuaries on land, and the world through the Security Council would cut their financial lifelines, build the legal framework to punish pirates and their sponsors and develop Somalia to the point where piracy would not be the preferred career choice of young Somali males.

This is an intriguing idea, one which so far remains in the realm of ideas rather than of implementable policy. But it is an encouraging indication that responsible Indians are already thinking beyond the established prisms of conventional policy-making to a broader and more effective Indian internationalism in the twenty-first century.

While global institutions are adapting to the new world, regional ones could emerge. The world economic crisis should give us an opportunity to promote economic integration with our neighbours in the subcontinent who look to the growing Indian market to sell their goods and maintain their own growth. But as long as South Asia remains divided by futile rivalries, and some continue to believe that terrorism can be a useful instrument of their strategic doctrines, that is bound to remain a distant prospect. We in South Asia need to look to the future, to an interrelated future on our subcontinent, where geography becomes an instrument of opportunity in a mutual growth story, where history binds rather than divides, where trade and cross-border links flourish and bring prosperity to all our peoples. Some will say these are merely dreams; but dreams can turn into reality if all of us—India and its neighbours—take action to accomplish this brighter future together.

At the same time there is a consensus in our country that India should seek to continue to contribute to international security and prosperity, to a well-ordered, peaceful and equitable world, and to democratic, sustainable development for all. These objectives now need to be pursued while taking into account twenty-first-century realities: the end of the Cold War, the dawning of the information era, the ease of worldwide travel and widespread migration, the blurring of national boundaries by movements, networks and forces transcending state frontiers, the advent of Islamist terrorism as a pan-global force, the irresistible rise of China as an incipient superpower while retaining its political authoritarianism, the global consciousness of 'soft power', and the end to the prospect of military conflict between any two of the major nation states. All these elements—discussed in the course of the preceding chapters—must be considered in formulating the grand strategy for India in the twenty-first century.

India too has changed. Its economic growth and entrepreneurial dynamism, both allowed to flourish only in the last couple of decades, have created a different India, which therefore relates to the world differently. 'Material well-being is supreme,' wrote Kautilya in the fourth-century BCE *Arthasastra*. Twenty-five centuries later, we may have returned to his timeless wisdom. India's economic growth has significantly added credibility to the country's international profile. After decades of being portrayed as a poor and backward nation, India's transformation into a global force on the back of its economic triumphs and its technological prowess is a new fact of life. There has been a profound reassessment across the globe of India's international importance and future potential. New Delhi's success in handling its internal problems, including secessionist movements, has also confirmed the perception of India as a serious power, in Malone's words 'the cohesive anchor of its subcontinent and wider region'.

India's generous aid programmes, its extensive international peacekeeping commitments, the personal stature of its prime minister (described in a leading international poll as the world's most respected governmental leader) and its indispensable role in the making of G20 policy, all testify to a nation that has, in President Obama's words, 'emerged' and is making a significant impact on international affairs. The path to taking on more ambitious responsibilities on the global stage lies ahead. Instinctive approaches formulated at a time when India was a major recipient of foreign aid, and saw itself as a developing country needing to assert itself in the face of the hegemony of the former imperial powers, are no longer entirely relevant when India gives as much aid as its receives, makes more foreign direct investments than it gets and is seen by other countries as a source of assistance, guidance and even security. The time has come for India to move beyond issues of status and entitlement to a diplomacy of pragmatism and performance in helping guide a world that it is now unchallengeably qualified, together with others, to lead.

At the same time, it is important not to be carried away by hubris. Shiv Shankar Menon put it well in a recent speech:

We must always be conscious of the difference between weight, influence and power. Power is the ability to create and sustain outcomes. Weight we have, our influence is growing, but our power remains to grow and should first be used for our domestic transformation. History is replete with examples of rising powers who prematurely thought that their time had come, who mistook influence and weight for real power. Their rise, as that of Wilhelmine Germany or militarist Japan, was cut short prematurely.

Real power may not yet be India's, but its weight is incontestable and its international influence is already being exercised in creative new ways. One example of India's constructively deployed influence that is worth examining in detail is India's aid policy.

India's aid programmes in its neighbourhood and in Africa have been characterized by a willingness to let the recipient set the terms, respect for the priorities and the culture of the recipients, and a focus on projects that promote self-reliance, economic growth and political democracy (including women's empowerment). Though some 75 per cent of India's aid is tied to the provision of goods and services from Indian suppliers—an excusable condition for aid coming from a developing country—it has by and large been welcomed as helpful, less intrusive and less disruptive than other countries' (the traditional donors') aid programmes have tended to be. As such it now forms an essential part of India's projection to the world.

This too echoes ancient Indian wisdom. A millennium and a half ago, the great king Harsha declared: 'Before, while amassing all this wealth, I lived in constant fear of never finding a storeroom solid enough to keep it in. But now that I have spread it in alms upon the field of happiness I regard it as forever preserved!' The 2011 Africa-India summit in Addis Ababa, Ethiopia, at which the Indian government pledged $5 billion in aid to African countries, drew attention to a largely overlooked phenomenon—India's emergence as a source, rather than a recipient, of foreign aid. For decades after independence—when Britain left the subcontinent one of the poorest and most ravaged regions on earth, with an effective growth rate of 0 per cent over the preceding two centuries—India was seen as an impoverished land of destitute people, desperately in need of international handouts. Many developed countries showcased their aid to India; Norway, for example, established in 1959 its first-ever aid programme there. But, with the liberalization of the Indian economy in 1991, the country embarked upon a period of dizzying growth, averaging nearly 8 per cent a year since then. During this time,

India weaned itself from dependence on aid, preferring to borrow from multilateral lenders and, increasingly, from commercial banks.

Today, the proverbial shoe is on the other foot. India has begun putting its money where its mouth used to be. It has now emerged as a significant donor to developing countries in Africa and Asia, second only to China in the range and quantity of development assistance given by countries of the global South. The Indian Technical and Economic Cooperation Programme as established in 1964, but now has real money to offer, in addition to training facilities and technological know-how. Nationals from 156 countries have benefited from ITEC grants, which have brought developing-country students to Indian universities for courses in everything from software development to animal husbandry.

In addition, India has built factories, hospitals and parliaments in various countries, and sent doctors, teachers and IT professionals to treat and train the nationals of recipient countries. Concessional loans at trifling interest rates are also extended as lines of credit, tied mainly to the purchase of Indian goods and services, and countries in Africa have been clamouring for them.

In Asia, India remains by far the single largest donor to its neighbour Bhutan, as well as a generous aid donor to Nepal, the Maldives, Bangladesh, and Sri Lanka as it recovers from civil war. Its humanitarian assistance to Indonesia and Myanmar in the wake of the 2004 tsunami and the 2008 Cyclone Nargis, respectively, was swift and effective, and its rapid provision of aid after humanitarian disasters in Pakistan and Tajikistan was exemplary. Given Afghanistan's vital importance for the security of the subcontinent, India's assistance programme there already amounts to more than $1.2 billion—modest from the standpoint of Afghan needs, but large for a non-traditional donor—and is set to rise further. As described in Chapter Three, India's efforts in Afghanistan have focused on humanitarian infrastructure, social projects and the development of skills and capacity. Futher west, its long record of aid to the Palestinian refugees has now been augmented by a significant assistance programme to the Palestinian National Authority.

In Africa, India's strength as an aid provider is that it is not an over-developed power, but rather one whose own experience of development challenges is both recent and familiar. African countries, as I mentioned earlier, look at China and the United States with a certain awe, but do not, for a moment, believe that they can become like either of them; India is a far more accessible benefactor. Moreover, unlike China, India does not descend on other countries with a heavy governmental footprint. India's private sector is a far more important player, and the government often confines itself to opening doors and letting African countries work with the most efficient Indian provider that they can find.

Similarly, unlike the Chinese, Indian employers do not come into a foreign country with an overwhelming labour force. Whereas China's omnipresence has provoked hostility in several African countries, Indian businesses have faced no such reaction in the last two decades. Indeed, Uganda, where Idi Amin expelled Indian settlers in 1972, has been actively wooing them back under President Yoweri Museveni.

Finally, India accommodates itself to aid recipients' desires, advancing funds to African regional banks or the New Economic Partnership for Africa's Development. Its focus on capacity development, its accessibility and its long record of support for developing countries have made India an increasingly welcome donor. Its creation of a Pan African e-Network, described in Chapter Seven, is an impressive example of its ability to showcase its strengths while providing an indispensable service with no tangible direct benefit to itself. It is, of course, a far bigger bilateral donor than it is a multilateral one: it gives some aid to and through the UN and AU bodies where its own identity as a giver is blurred, but this is dwarfed by its bilateral offerings. Nonetheless, it is increasingly seen as an aid giver, not least by a large collection of recipients.

This could not have been imagined even twenty years ago, and it is one of the best consequences of India's emergence as a global economic power.

At the same time India is not the incipient 'superpower' that over-enthusiastic supporters have described it as being. I earned some notoriety in 2010 when I suggested at a public event that we could not be a 'superpower' when we were still 'super-poor'. I did not go quite as far as the historian Ramachandra Guha, who wrote in the *Financial Times* in July 2011 that 'India is in no position to become a superpower. It is not a rising power, nor even an emerging power. It is merely a fascinating, complex, and perhaps unique experiment in nationhood and democracy, whose leaders need still to attend to the fault lines within, rather than presume to take on the world without.' Discounting the overstatement, it is true that there are still a number of essential unfinished agendas to be attended to at home, and foreign policy must be seen as an instrument to help us fulfil them.

Indeed India is coming of international prominence at a time when the world is moving, slowly but inexorably, into a post-superpower age. The days of the Cold War, when two hegemonic behemoths developed the capacity to destroy the world several times over, and flexed their muscles against each other by changing regimes in client states and fighting wars half a world away from their own borders, are now truly behind us. Instead we are witnessing a world of many rising (and some risen) powers, of various sizes and strengths but each with some significant capacity in its own region, each strong enough not to be pushed around by a hegemon, but not strong enough to become a hegemon itself. They coexist and cooperate with each other in a series of networked relationships, including bilateral and plurilateral strategic partnerships that often overlap with each other, rather than in fixed alliances or binary either/or antagonisms. The same is true of the great economic divide between developed and developing countries, a divide which is gradually dissolving; on many issues, India has more in common with countries of the North than of the global South for which it has so long been a spokesman. Neither in geopolitics nor in economics is the world locked into the kinds of permanent and immutable coalitions of interest that characterized the Cold War.

The new networked world welcomes every nation; it has little room for the domination of any superpower. (Mohamed Nasheed, the deposed president of the Maldives, said in a wonderful documentary about global warming and his efforts to save his country's shorelines: 'You cannot bully us. We are too small; you *will* be seen as a bully'!) We live in a more equal era. Relationships are contingent and overlap with others; friends and allies in one cause might be irrelevant to another (or even on opposite sides). The networked world is a more fluid place. Countries use such networks to promote common interests, to manage common issues rather than impose outcomes, and provide a common response to the challenges and opportunities they face. Some networks would be principally economic in their orientation, some geopolitical, some issue specific. Contemporary examples of such networks range from the IOR-ARC to the Nuclear Suppliers' Group and from the BASIC negotiating alliance on climate change to the membership of the G20. Many more such networked alliances are clearly on the anvil (or, more appropriately, in the diplomatic Petri dish) of global cooperation.

In such a world, I once suggested, India would move beyond non-alignment to what I dubbed 'multi-alignment'. This would be a world in which India would belong to, and play a prominent role in, both the United Nations and the G20; both the Non-Aligned Movement (reflecting its 200 years of colonial oppression) and the Community of Democracies (reflecting its sixty-five years of democratic development); both the G77 (the massive gathering of over 120 developing countries) and smaller organizations like IOR-ARC (as argued in Chapter Four); both SAARC and the Commonwealth; both RIC (Russia–India–China) and BRICS (adding Brazil and South Africa); as well as both IBSA (the South–South alliance of India, Brazil and South Africa) and BASIC (the partnership of Brazil, South Africa, India and China on climate change issues which emerged during the Copenhagen talks). India is the one country that is a member of them all, and not merely because its name begins with that indispensable element for all acronyms, a vowel!

'Multi-alignment', it is true, is at one level an amoral strategy: it would see India making common cause with liberal democracies when it suited India to do so, and dissenting from them when (as on Myanmar, Iran and on certain aspects of the Arab Spring) it was expedient for India to preserve relationships that the other democracies could afford to jettison. It is also a promiscuous strategy, since it exempts no country from its embrace; China, a potential adversary with which we have a long-standing frontier dispute that occasionally erupts into rhetorical unpleasantness, nonetheless is a crucial partner in several of these configurations. It is a strategy of making and running shifting coalitions of interests, which will require some skilful management of complicated relationships and opportunities—in policy environments that may themselves be unpredictable. That should not be excessively difficult for governments in New Delhi which, for more than two decades, have had to spend their time and energy on managing coalitions in Indian domestic politics.

Multi-alignment also constitutes an effective response to the new transnational challenges of the twenty-first century, to which neither autonomy nor alliance offer adequate answers in themselves. An obvious example is dealing with terrorism, which requires diplomatic and intelligence cooperation from a variety of countries facing comparable threats; but also shoring up failing states, combating piracy, controlling nuclear proliferation and battling organized crime. In addition to such issues there are the unconventional threats to the peace that also cross all borders (pandemics, for instance), and the need to preserve the global commons—keeping open the sea lanes of communication across international waters so that trade routes and energy supplies are safeguarded, ensuring maritime security from the Horn of Africa to the Straits of Malacca, protecting cyberspace from the depredations of hostile forces including non-governmental ones, and the management of outer space, which could increasingly become a new theatre for global competition.

Strategic autonomy is all very well, but it cannot be the be-all and end-all of India's attitude to the world. Our sovereignty is no longer under threat; there is no power on earth that can presume to dictate to India on any international issue. It is time for us to build on our much-vaunted independence of thought and action by treating our strategic autonomy as a platform from which to soar, not a ball and chain around our ankles. As a major power we can and must play a role in helping shape the global order. The international system of the twenty-first century, with its networked partnerships, will need to renegotiate its rules of the road; India is well qualified, along with others, to help write those rules and define the norms that will guide tomorrow's world. Rather than confining itself to being a subject of others' rule-making, or even a resister of others' attempts, it is in India's interests (and within India's current and future capacity) to take the initiative to shape the evolution of these norms as well as to have a voice in the situations within which they are applied. That is what I have called Pax Indica: not global or regional domination along the lines of a Pax Romana or a Pax Britannica (in which military victory by the Romans and the Britons, respectively, ensured that peace prevailed because potential adversaries were too exhausted to resist), but a 'Pax' for the twenty-first century, a peace system which will help promote and maintain a period of cooperative coexistence in its region and across the world.

This 'Pax Indica' must be built and sustained on the principles and norms that India holds dear at home and abroad. It would see a democratic and pluralist India working for a world order that sustains and defends democracy and pluralism; a 'multi-aligned' India serving as one of the principal fulcrums of a networked globe, in which countries pursue different interests in different configurations; an India free of poverty, growing and engaging in trade and investment in and with the rest of the world, and upholding arrangements that make such trade and investment relationships possible; an increasingly prosperous India, prepared to share the benefits of its prosperity with other nations on its periphery and its extended (land and maritime) neighbourhood; and a technologically savvy India, setting its sights on, and lending its expertise to, the management of outer space and cyberspace in the common interests of humanity.

The title of this chapter suggests that it offers thoughts 'towards' a grand strategy for India. My friend Keerthik Sasidharan asked me, 'When the state is weak, or at best a wobbly or "jelly" state, can it project a "grand" strategy?' I believe the Indian state is not as weak as its critics imply, and that the outlines of a grand strategy have been implicit in its approach to the world in recent years. The present volume has attempted to pull some of these strands together into a credible tapestry, but it is still a work in progress, with many weaves yet to emerge from the loom. Perhaps one of the readers of this book will take the argument further—if not today, then in twenty years, when many of the trends discerned in this book will have fructified, or withered on the vine.

In keeping with Nehru's original vision, the 'Pax Indica' I have outlined would not even principally be about India at all, but about India's sense of responsibility to the world of which it is such a crucial part—and whose destiny it has earned the right to help shape.

Acknowledgements

This book is a work of reflection, not scholarship, though it draws upon a variety of published and unpublished sources. As a harried member of Parliament attending to his own research and writing amid a number of other preoccupations, I consciously cast this work as an extended analytical essay, devoid of footnotes or reference material. However, most of the attributed quotations in this volume can be found in one or another of the handful of books and other sources cited in the Bibliography.

Though a number of friends inside and outside the diplomatic profession have contributed (sometimes unknowingly) to my appreciation of the issues analysed in this book, I would like to single out for gratitude my former MEA colleague Sandeep Chakravorty and my occasional op-ed collaborator Keerthik Sasidharan, who ploughed through the entire manuscript, for their invaluable comments and insights. To them, to my son Kanishk Tharoor and to my friends Virat Bhatia and Arun Kumar, who offered comments on specific portions of the book, as well as to my editors Jaishree Ram Mohan and Udayan Mitra of Penguin, I am most grateful. Nonetheless I remain solely responsible for the contents, arguments and conclusions of *Pax Indica*, and responsibility for any sins of omission or commission is mine alone.

Portions of the book have appeared, in different form, as articles or columns in the *Asian Age/Deccan Chronicle, Times of India, Guardian, The Hindu, Mail Today, Fortune India*, the journal *Ethics and International Affairs* and in my internationally syndicated column (issued through Project Syndicate), all of which publications are gratefully acknowledged.

It also bears stressing that though I am a member of the Indian National Congress party and a Member of Parliament, the opinions expressed in this book are strictly personal and engage neither the

Government of India, nor the political party of which I am a member, nor any other institution with which I may happen to be associated.

My wife Sunanda rightly forced me to devote the time necessary to complete the book when its writing, beset by too many other distractions, had been dragging on for far too long. For her determination, tenacity and love, I have no words that are adequate. I promised her that the book would be in her hands in time for her birthday, and I present it to her with gratitude as a humble offering—and a promise fulfilled.

New Delhi, March 2012   SHASHI THAROOR

Selected Bibliography

Cohen, Stephen P. *India: Emerging Power*. Washington, DC: Brookings Institution Press, 2001.

Damodaran, A.K. *Beyond Autonomy: Roots of India's Foreign Policy*. New Delhi: Somaiya Publications, 2000.

Datta-Ray, Sunanda K. *Looking East to Look West: Lee Kuan Yew's Mission India*. New Delhi: Penguin Books India, 2009.

Dixit, J.N. *Across Borders: Fifty Years of India's Foreign Policy*. New Delhi: Picus Books, 1998.

——. *India's Foreign Policy 1947–2003*. New Delhi: Picus Books, 2003.

——. *Indian Foreign Service: History and Challenge*. Delhi: Konark Publishers, 2005.

Emmott, Bill. *Rivals: How the Power Struggle Between China, India and Japan Will Shape Our Next Decade*. London: Allen Lane, 2008.

Jha, Prem Shankar. *Crouching Dragon, Hidden Tiger: Can China and India Dominate the West?* New York: Soft Skull Press, 2010.

Khilnani, Sunil, et al. 'Nonalignment 2.0: A Foreign and Strategic Policy for India in the Twenty First Century'. New Delhi: Centre for Policy Research, 2012.

Malone, David. *Does the Elephant Dance? Contemporary Indian Foreign Policy*. New Delhi: Oxford University Press, 2011.

Markey, Daniel. 'Developing India's Foreign Policy "Software"', *Asian Policy* 8(2009): 73–96.

Menon, Adm. Raja, and Rajiv Kumar. *The Long View From Delhi: Indian Grand Strategy*. New Delhi: Academic Foundation, 2010.

Meredith, Robyn. *The Elephant and the Dragon: The Rise of India and China and What It Means for All of Us*. New York: W.W. Norton, 2007.

Mohan, C. Raja. *Crossing the Rubicon: The Shaping of India's New Foreign Policy*. New York: Palgrave Macmillan, 2004.

——. *Impossible Allies: Nuclear India, United States, and the Global Order*. New Delhi: India Research Press, 2007.

Muni, S.D. *India's Foreign Policy: The Democracy Dimension*. New Delhi: Foundation Books, 2009.

—— (ed.). *The Emerging Dimensions of SAARC*. New Delhi: Cambridge University Press India, 2010.

Nawaz, Shuja. *Crossed Swords: Pakistan, Its Army and the War Within*. New York: Oxford University Press, 2008.

Nehru, Jawaharlal. *The Discovery of India*. New Delhi: Penguin Books, 1946 text, reprinted 2011.

——. *Selected Speeches*, Vols I–III. New Delhi: Government of India, 1963.

Siddiqa, Ayesha. *Military Inc.: Inside Pakistani Military Economy*. London: Pluto Press, 2007.

Talbott, Strobe. *Engaging India: Diplomacy, Democracy and the Bomb*. Washington, DC: Brookings Institution Press, 2004.

Tharoor, Shashi. *Reasons of State: Political Development and India's Foreign Policy under Indira Gandhi, 1966–1977*. New Delhi: Vikas, 1982.

——. *India: From Midnight to the Millennium*. New Delhi: Penguin Books India, 1997.

Internet research: Numerous articles, blogs and essays by Brahma Chellaney, Sumit Ganguly, Salman Haider, Amitabh Mattoo, A.G. Noorani, Nitin Pai, Kanwal Sibal, T.P. Sreenivasan, K. Subrahmanyam and Ashley Tellis. Statements and speeches by Indian foreign policy makers, from www.mea.gov.in. Transcripts of speeches by Shivshankar Menon and Shyam Saran, circulated by email.

Index